MEANWHILE
there are
LETTERS

MEANWHILE

there are

LETTERS

THE
Correspondence
OF EUDORA WELTY AND
ROSS MACDONALD

Edited and with an introduction by
SUZANNE MARRS
&
TOM NOLAN

Arcade Publishing • New York

First Edition

Arcade Publishing books may be purchased in bulk at special discounts for sales promotion, corporate gifts, fund-raising, or educational purposes. Special editions can also be created to specifications. For details, contact the Special Sales Department, Arcade Publishing, 307 West 36th Street, 11th Floor, New York, NY 10018 or arcade@skyhorsepublishing.com.

Arcade Publishing® is a registered trademark of Skyhorse Publishing, Inc.®, a Delaware corporation.

Visit our website at www.arcadepub.com.

10 9 8 7 6 5 4 3 2 1

Library of Congress Cataloging-in-Publication Data

Meanwhile there are letters : the correspondence of Eudora Welty and Ross Macdonald / edited and with an introduction by Suzanne Marrs and Tom Nolan.—First edition.
     pages cm
   Includes bibliographical references and index.
  ISBN 978-1-62872-527-8 (hardback); ISBN 978-1-62872-548-3 (ebook)
  1. Welty, Eudora, 1909-2001—Correspondence. 2. Macdonald, Ross, 1915–1983—Correspondence. 3. Authors, American—20th century—Correspondence. I. Marrs, Suzanne, editor. II. Nolan, Tom, editor.
  PS3545.E6Z48 2015
  813'.52—dc23
  [B]   2015005957

Cover design by Georgia Morrissey
Cover photograph of Eudora Welty © by Charles Nicholas, courtesy The Commercial Appeal-Candow Media; cover photograph of Ross Macdonald © by Hal Boucher

Printed in the United States of America

To
Rowan Taylor – SM
and
Loretta Weingel-Fidel – TN

CONTENTS

Introduction

---※---

"You are in my thoughts every day and dear to my heart."

—Eudora Welty to Kenneth Millar, October 30, 1981

"Pathos, gentleness, courage, feminine fluorescence and iron discipline, the blessed light at the windows."

—Kenneth Millar, describing Eudora Welty, June 11, 1974[1]

ON the afternoon of Monday, May 17, 1971, mystery writer Ross Macdonald—alias Kenneth Millar, of Santa Barbara, California—was engaged in a bit of real-life detection in the lobby of New York City's legendary Algonquin Hotel. Alerted by savvy Manhattan colleagues, he was on a stakeout, hoping to encounter Eudora Welty, the world-famous, award-winning, bestselling author from Jackson, Mississippi, with whom he had been corresponding for a year and who had recently given his novel *The Underground Man* a rave on the front page of the *New York Times Book Review.* His stakeout paid off. As Welty approached the hotel elevator, Millar/Macdonald went up to her and introduced himself. Abandoning whatever plans she had had, Welty was thrilled to sit and talk with the man whose written words meant so much to her.

Millar had begun their correspondence with a 1970 letter praising Welty's novel *Losing Battles,* and they had in the past year exchanged messages ranging from the very personal—Millar's grief at the death of his daughter—to the literary—Welty's review of Ford Madox Ford's biography. They had come to believe that, through their separate links to Ford, their lives were powerfully connected. "When I got your letter today," Millar had written to Welty on April 20, "something went through me like a vibration of light, as if I had had a responsive echo from a distant star." And she had responded, "Thank you for telling me this, which has made me a part of some perfect occurrence. Nothing ever gave me that feeling before, and I doubt if anything ever will again."[2] Then the "Algonquin magic" of meeting face to face convinced both Eudora and Ken that the perfect occurrence had not ended.

When Ken set out two days later for his native Canada, he sent a note to Eudora: "I never thought I'd hate to leave New York, but I do. I feel an unaccustomed sorrow not to be able to continue our friendship *viva voce*, and in the flesh, but these are the chances of life. But there is a deeper and happier chance which will keep us friends till death, don't you believe? And we'll walk and talk again. Till then, Ken." A postscript immediately followed: "Meanwhile there are letters."

Indeed there were—enough to prompt an extravagant rhetorical question: Was there an epistolary romance of literary masters in the twentieth century more discreet, intense, heartfelt, and moving than the one between Eudora Welty and Kenneth Millar, who exchanged hundreds of letters between 1970 and 1982? Though a small fraction of their correspondence seems to have been lost, there remain some 345 pieces—more of them by Welty than by Macdonald, whose Alzheimer's disease stopped him from writing after May 1980, while Welty continued to send him messages until she was convinced, eight months or so before his death in 1983, that he could no longer comprehend them.[3] Those letters reveal the loving friendship of two writers, a single woman in Mississippi and a married man in California, whose unique bond at once observed the proprieties and expanded the boundaries of how close two kindred, creative people might become through thought, will, and the written word.

These two authors command devoted followings both in halls of academe and the territory beyond. Welty, called the "finest fiction writer of our time" by critic Cleanth Brooks and the "greatest short story writer of our time" by novelist Ann Patchett, received awards ranging from the Presidential Medal of Freedom to the French Legion of Honor and continues to inspire much scholarly inquiry.[4] Many a critic has attempted to explain the mysteries in her stories while others have recognized that unresolved mystery is the essence of both their genius and their widespread appeal. Macdonald has received more popular but less scholarly attention. Nevertheless, John Leonard, writing in the *New York Times Book Review*, called Macdonald a "major American novelist," and Michael Kreyling more recently asserted that Macdonald grafted "the detective novel successfully to the main branches of the American novel." Welty, the serious writer who deals in mystery and who became a cultural icon, and Macdonald, the detective novelist whose impact transcends generic limitations, made quite a pair—both aesthetically and personally.[5]

Early experiences did little to portend the confluences that would envelop the lives of Eudora Welty and Ross Macdonald.

Born in 1909 in Jackson, Mississippi, Eudora grew up in a sheltered and stable environment. She and her two younger brothers were cherished by doting parents. Christian Welty provided well for his family as he moved up through the ranks of the Lamar Life Insurance Company in Jackson, and Chestina Welty, a former teacher, managed the household. The family was a close-knit one, and rectitude was a given for each family member. The children obtained a good education at the grade school across the street from their home and at the high school a half mile away. Eudora, after graduating from Central High at age sixteen, attended the Mississippi State College for Women for two years, because her parents felt she was too young to venture further afield. Only then did she continue her education at the University of Wisconsin and later at Columbia University's Graduate School of Business, compiling as stellar a record at these institutions as she had at ones closer to home.

For Ken Millar there was no shelter. Born in 1915 in Los Gatos, California, he would not know a stable home life for many years. His Canadian parents almost immediately moved their family to Vancouver, where his father, John Macdonald Millar, became the pilot of a harbor boat and where his parents quarreled often with each other. Then in 1920 Annie Millar, left by her husband, took her son back to Kitchener, Ontario, where she had grown up. For the next nine years, Kennie would be shuffled from one relative to another, from one rooming house to another, from Kitchener to Wiarton to Winnipeg to Medicine Hat, and back to Kitchener. His sexual initiations, both heterosexual and homosexual, came early, as did his forays into theft and his acquaintance with pimps, prostitutes, and con artists. He was a bright student who did well in class until the fall semester of his senior year in high school, when he lost the will to excel and saw his scholastic standing plummet. Ultimately, he resolved to stop this downward slide and with the help of teachers managed to right his life and his grades. Henceforth, he would adhere to rigid standards of morality and an almost Puritan work ethic. His hopes for a college education were thwarted, though, until his father died, leaving a sum that paid for four years of study at University of Western Ontario. Ultimately, Kenneth would enter the University of Michigan and earn a PhD with a dissertation on Coleridge.

Though shelter marked Eudora's early life and its absence marked Ken's, such divergence did not last nor negate the powerful forces that would unite them. Their careers began within three years of each other—Eudora published her first story in 1936, Ken in 1939; both had their writing delayed by World War II, Ken more than Eudora because he served in the US Navy during these years. Each moved soon afterward into an established career and eventual critical acclaim, Eudora first and more fully. Her many awards, besides the Presidential Medal of Freedom and French Legion of Honor, would include the Gold Medal for Fiction from the National Institute of Arts and Letters, a National Book Award, a Pulitzer Prize, and thirty-eight honorary degrees; her fiction would be taught at colleges and universities around the globe; and she'd be the first living writer published by the Library of America. Ken's writing career developed more slowly—he received Gold and Silver Dagger Awards from the British Crime Writers Association, a

Grand Master Award from the Mystery Writers of America, the first Award of Merit bestowed by the Popular Culture Association, and the *Los Angeles Times*'s Robert Kirsch Award for his distinguished body of work about the West. Thirty-two years after his death, and seventeen years after publishing Welty, the Library of America at last brought out Macdonald's work, including him in the grand pantheon of American writers.

Eudora and Ken were both true to their talents, committed to the writing life—Eudora to serious fiction, though she saw such fiction as having mystery at its core; Ken to the writing of mysteries, though he defined complex possibilities for the genre. Each saw writing not as a way of focusing upon self but as a way of expanding experience and understanding of the world beyond. Each loved language, the rhythms, the images, the idioms that constitute an individual sentence. Each saw reading, reading widely, as complementing and enriching the writing life. And each longed to share life with a partner who felt the same way.

Eudora had thought fellow Mississippian John Robinson might be that partner. She had known him from their high school days together and had traveled with him, his brother, and his sister to Mexico in 1937. When he returned from service in World War II, she helped him type and revise stories, sent his stories to magazines, asked her agent to represent him, and praised his work. In 1947, she made extended stays in San Francisco, where he had moved. Then, in 1950, he followed her to Europe, where she was enjoying a Guggenheim Fellowship. But John ultimately lacked the drive, the commitment to writing that was Eudora's. And John eventually realized that his strongest commitment would be to a man, not to any woman, not even to Eudora, whom he loved as a friend.

Ken had met his future wife, Margaret Sturm, while they were both high school students in Kitchener, Ontario, had begun a relationship with her late in his college career, and had married her the day after graduating. A year later their daughter, Linda, was born. Like Ken, Maggie wanted to be a writer, and she became a published mystery author before her husband did. But sharing the writing life did not make for happy family relationships. The Millars early on fought with each other and subjected their child to the conflict. Their marriage, though much more companionable in time, came to be one of almost separate lives beneath one roof. Still, Ken honored the vow "till death do us part" and expected others to do likewise.

But by 1977 Ken knew Eudora well and surely sensed that they could have managed a truer union of writing lives than he and Margaret had achieved. When a Santa Barbara couple he counted as friends decided to separate, Ken told Eudora that this decision "convinced me of what I didn't use to believe, that divorce could be a suitable end to a marriage."[6] Yet a divorce of his own was not forthcoming. Margaret was in poor health and needed him, and Ken was already caught in the early stages of Alzheimer's disease. He had relished Eudora's living presence for a few days in New York in 1971 and in Jackson in 1973; the two had shared weeklong summer visits at the Santa Barbara Writers Conference in 1975, 1976, and 1977, with Margaret also in attendance. But they would not meet again until 1982. If Ken briefly nursed a change of heart, it had come too late.

It was not, however, and had never been, too late for a different order of intimacy to prosper between them. In letters Welty and Macdonald brought their stylistic powers to bear on a wide range of topics. They expressed their admiration for and reliance on each other. They discussed the writing process, the translation of life into fiction, and the nature of the writer's block each encountered. They looked back at literary history: Eudora reported on reading *Middlemarch* for the first time while she was in New York, of rushing back to the Algonquin at day's end with the "delicious" prospect of reading more; Ken praised Henry James's *The Wings of the Dove* as "marvellously wrought" but "overcharged with electricity." And they commented on many other writers that they loved: Ford Madox Ford, Anton Chekhov, Virginia Woolf, Jane Austen, F. Scott Fitzgerald, Flannery O'Connor, Henry Green, Katherine Anne Porter, Elizabeth Bowen, Wilkie Collins, John Buchan, Ring Lardner, Dashiell Hammett, and Margaret Millar among them.

Their shared interests, of course, extended beyond the world of fiction. They often discussed political leaders and public issues. Eudora described a National Council on the Arts meeting with President Nixon in the Oval Office:"I felt a bad hypocrite to touch him. (I who had never missed a session of Watergate.)"; she and Ken both deplored the Christmas 1972 bombing of Hanoi; and he passionately declared "the really great threat of the future" to be "the mishandling of oil tankers in the world ocean."[7]

Letters about their separate and common friends further marked the confluence of their lives. Ken told Eudora about Herb Harker: his attempts to become a writer, the death of his wife, his devotion to his young sons, and the eventual publication of his novel *Goldenrod*. He told her about Fred Zackel, a young cab driver and aspiring novelist whom they both had met in Santa Barbara, whom Ken had encouraged to pursue a writing career, and who finally became both a published writer and a professor of writing. Eudora told Ken about the disappearance of Duncan Aswell, the son of her friend Mary Lou, about Duncan's decision to reestablish contact with his mother, and about the understanding she felt Ken had extended in his novels to unhappy and unsettled young people like Duncan. She told him about Diarmuid Russell, who was her devoted agent and friend, and about Russell's father Æ, whom Ken and Eudora each acknowledged as an inspiration. And she told him about Reynolds Price, the younger writer she had encouraged. Reynolds and Diarmuid, she reported, were fans of Ross Macdonald.

Eudora and Ken also shared a love of travel and of visiting new and old places. Though his wife wanted only to remain at home, Ken managed to take trips both with her and alone, and he told Eudora of them: of revisiting the Ontario of his youth, of walking the streets of London, of venturing solo to Venice. And Eudora reported on her travels to New York City, to London to meet V. S. Pritchett, to France on a driving tour with old friends, and across Canada by rail.

Above all, each valued the unique friendship, consciousness, talent, and existence of the other. They discussed the wonder of the Apollo 14 moon landing, sent each other limericks, cheered the arrival of the two-volume, reduced-type edition of the complete *Oxford English Dictionary*, and reported on movies like *Chinatown*, *Young Franken-stein*, and Woody Allen's *Manhattan*. They worried over, celebrated, and consoled one another—dreamt about each other, dreamt of dreaming about each other, sent one another messages in their dreams.

Of particular significance is the impact each writer had on the other's work. Eudora credits Ken with suggesting the key scene in her Pulitzer Prize–winning novel, *The Optimist's Daughter* (1972), and with encouraging her to publish *The Eye of the Story* (1978), a collection of critical essays. In fact, she dedicated *The Eye of the Story* to Kenneth Millar. For his part, Ken felt that his friendship with Eudora had been a key to the development of his novel *Sleeping Beauty* (1973). As he told her, "Being in touch with you this past year or so has been an inspiration to me. I hope you will take the risk of letting me put your name on the dedication page."[8] She was delighted.

As Ken encouraged Eudora's autobiographical impulse, which would come to a full flowering in her memoir *One Writer's Beginnings* (1984), so she urged him to commit childhood memories to paper, which he did—in several essays and prefaces written in the 1970s, and in his last chapters of attempted fiction.

The letters concerning Ken's battle with Alzheimer's disease are perhaps the most emotionally charged in this collection, and Eudora's fragmentary manuscript "Henry" addresses this ordeal. We are honored to include excerpts from "Henry" at the close of this book.

In 1952, long before she met Kenneth Millar, Eudora Welty had written a story that in some ways seems to prefigure their relationship. In "No Place for You, My Love," she describes a married man from New York and a single woman from Toledo who meet by chance in Galatoire's Restaurant in New Orleans. They then spend the day together, traveling south of South, all the way to the Gulf of Mexico. Alone together, far from home, they are nevertheless reticent. The suffering that love has brought to both these individuals leaves them in quest of "imperviousness"; they want to avoid exposing their situations to each other. The man will not discuss his wife with the woman from Toledo, and the woman resents his intuitive recognition of her plight: "How did it leave us—the old, safe, slow way people used to know of learning how one another feels," she wonders. But as much as they may desire to shield themselves, a relationship springs up between them. When they finally reach land's end, they go into a local bar and dance to music from a jukebox. At that moment, they know that "even those immune from the world, for the time being, need the touch of one another, or all is lost."[9]

Both Eudora and Ken did need the touch of one another; Margaret Millar was essentially a loner; she often seemed to value separateness over connection except when her own health failed and she depended on her husband's reassurance and assistance. That was not true for Ken and Eudora; they cherished relationships, shared acts of imagination, whether they engaged others in the pages of books, in their hometowns, in far-flung locales, or in intimate personal encounters. Barred from fulfillment in marriage, they found connections of the imagination and spirit by sending letters to each other, with Eudora continuing to write even when Ken was no longer able to put pen to paper. "Your spirit lives in my mind, and watches my life," Ken told Eudora in 1978, and later that same year, she assured him that, despite the distance between Mississippi and California, "our spirits have traveled very near to each other and I believe sustained each other—This will go on, dear Ken."[10]

The letters Eudora and Ken exchanged might well have been lost. Ken hid Eudora's to him, perhaps fearful that his wife would resent his treasuring of them. Happily, his friend Ralph Sipper, a rare-book dealer, who purchased Ken's library and papers from his widow, found the letters in the pool house of the Millar home and returned them to a grateful Eudora. Now in possession of both sides of this extensive correspondence, Eudora considered destroying it. She consulted Reynolds Price, who helped convince her to save the letters and leave them in her will to the Mississippi Department of Archives and History.[11] That decision has made this book possible.

Meanwhile There Are Letters is organized chronologically and can be read as a narrative, with each chapter receiving a brief introduction and with commentary appearing as needed for context and clarity. The headings for each letter identify the letter writer, the recipient, and the date of composition, but typically do not identify the location from which the letter was sent. Both Eudora Welty and Kenneth Millar wrote most of their letters at home (1119 Pinehurst Street, Jackson, Mississippi, for Eudora and 4420 Via Esperanza, Santa Barbara, California, for Ken). When either wrote from different locales, those places are identified in the letter heading. Endnotes provide information about the people, places, books, and historical events mentioned in the letters.

Neither Eudora nor Ken gave letters the meticulous revising and proofing that their writing for publication entailed and that computers now facilitate. Instead, they wrote by hand, or in Eudora's case, often at the typewriter, with a sense of urgency, of eagerness to put letters in the post, to be in touch. We have transcribed the letters as written, complete with inconsistencies and oddities of punctuation and spelling, though we have silently corrected obviously unintentional typographical errors and have replaced underlining with italics for the sake of readability. We have not supplied italics when underlining was omitted—in Eudora's typed letters (nearly a fourth of those she sent), underlining would have been a laborious process, one she frequently chose not to undertake. When Eudora and Ken added marginal comments to their letters, we have inserted them into the text as postscripts or at indicated points. Ellipses, clarifying information, or dates we have supplied are in square brackets. We hope our editorial decisions help to create a reading experience akin to the one Eudora and Ken found so crucial to their lives.

Our separate biographies of Eudora Welty and Kenneth Millar led us to work together editing their letters, and doing so has been an enriching and rewarding experience. We (Suzanne in Jackson, Mississippi, and Tom, in Glendale, California) have discovered the many virtues of editing correspondence via correspondence, even if our own letters were sent electronically as emails. We have also come to appreciate how much more intensely Eudora and Ken responded to the very personal, eloquent, and often ardent letters sent to each other via the sometimes frustratingly slow and sometimes incredibly prompt US Mail. Their letters, it seems to us, constitute a triumph over time and distance. "Meanwhile there are letters," as Ken wrote when he and Eudora parted after their first meeting, is not only a statement regretting separation; it is also one celebrating the written word and the enduring connection it would provide.

MEANWHILE

there are

LETTERS

CHAPTER ONE

"I love and need and learn from my friends, they are the continuity of my life."

————— ❧ —————

1970–1971

IN 1970 Eudora Welty finally published a long novel she had been working on since 1955. The story of a family reunion in 1930s hill country Mississippi, Losing Battles was a cause for celebration at home—Welty's friends threw a party featuring all the food mentioned in the novel, including fried chicken necks—and a cause for celebration nationally. The New York Times Book Review dispatched Walter Clemons to interview Welty, and the two got on famously, talking not only about her new novel but also about her love of mysteries, especially those by Ross Macdonald: "Oh yes! I've read all his books, I think. I once wrote Ross Macdonald a fan letter, but I never mailed it. I was afraid he'd think it—icky."[1] The newspaper account of that never-mailed fan letter called forth one from Kenneth Millar, a.k.a. Ross Macdonald, one that would be both mailed and received.

Kenneth Millar to Eudora Welty, May 3, 1970

Dear Miss Welty:

This is my first fan letter. If you write another book like *Losing Battles*, it will not be my last. I read that wonderful secular comedy with enjoyment and delight, and in the course of reading it discovered a fact about language that had never been quite clear to me before: There is a recognizable North American language which speaks to all of us in the accents of home; and you have invested and preserved it at its truest. (My uncles and aunts in Canada used essentially the same language—words, imagery, jokes—as your Banner people.) This will of course come as no surprise to you.

I have other reasons to be grateful to you. You spoke of me most generously to the *NY Times* reviewer. No compliment has ever pleased me more. You may live to regret it, for I'm getting off to you a large heavy collection of my novels called "Archer at Large," just out.

Yours faithfully,

Kenneth Millar

(Ross Macdonald)

Eudora Welty to Kenneth Millar, May 10, 1970[2]

Dear Mr. Millar,

That was a fine surprise you gave me, and what pleasure—Thank you for your letter. It was bread coming back before it had been cast upon the waters, after I hadn't sent you mine.

I'm so pleased you liked my book! What you say about a recognizable *North American* language that speaks to us all is a new thought to me—I had no way of learning about it, and if you think I've got at some of that essence, I'm more pleased than I can tell you. It also takes some of the load off my mind about the impertinence of thrusting so *much* Southern dialogue at readers from far away—But I believe in the risk too, because it seems to me only the local and only the particular do speak, that only what is true at home makes the sticks to build the fire with whatever imagination. It is lovely to know that an unknown Canada and an always known Mississippi have no trouble talking to each other.

Your book hasn't come yet so I am still looking forward. Thank you for such generosity. I've been reading your books as they came out since away back when you were John Ross Macdonald, and it's not only the first reading but returning to them that gives me a great deal of pleasure. Isn't *The Chill* in the new collection? I love that one in particular. What fascinates me is reading with the sense of the one who has invented the characters and the one, himself a character, who is in progress of finding out their secrets down to the last, identifying them for good, moving them one by one into their right places & locking them into the whole to make the pattern—these two making one, the same "I" telling the story. It's so right. It must be what happens with all fiction writers in their own ways. It's in the writing that I learn what is the real case with my characters—People come first, then knowing about them, listening back. But in the form you use, the method is pure, the scrupulous search or strategy is the same thing as the truth it's uncovering—And this is not only compelling but moving. It's the real beauty of the novels' construction, to me. But all the details as you go are so fine too—I really enjoy your work sentence by sentence, so it's a treat to be getting *Archer at Large*—Thank you again. And please give my regards to your wife, who also has my admiration.

Yours sincerely,
Eudora Welty

Millar was as familiar with Welty's work as she was with his, having followed it since her stories had appeared in the 1930s in the Southern Review. *He told his publisher, Alfred Knopf, that receiving this letter from Welty seemed the nicest thing that had happened to him since Knopf had taken him on as an author in 1947.[3] Other happy letters would follow in 1970, but the next extant one reported a tragedy.*

Kenneth Millar to Eudora Welty, December 14, 1970

Dear Miss Welty:

I haven't been able to answer your beautiful letter, which filled me with joy and made me cry, but will let the quotation opposite allude to it. I must also thank you for the gift of your book, *mutatis mutandis*.

I'll reciprocate soon. You didn't know my daughter Linda but you have suffered grievous losses in recent years and would perhaps wish to be told that Linda died last month, very suddenly, aged 31, of a stroke in her sleep. She left her husband Joe and their son, who have become central in our lives. But I am willing now to grow old and die, after a while. Our very best wishes, seasonal and personal,

Kenneth Millar

[*Millar's moving letter is written on a card reprinting the Navajo "Prayer, Mountaintop Way"*:

Restore all for me in beauty,
Make beautiful all that is before me,
Make beautiful all that is behind me,
Make beautiful my words.
It is done in beauty.
It is done in beauty.
It is done in beauty.
It is done in beauty.]

The brief life of Linda Jane Millar had been marked by emotional pain, mental illness, and public trauma. A bright teen but a social misfit in her Santa Barbara high school, Linda drank alcohol in secret and was involved in a 1956 hit-and-run accident in which a thirteen-year-old boy was killed. Three years later, still on probation from that disastrous event, while at college in Davis, California, Linda disappeared for eight days, during which Ken Millar took part in a much-publicized, three-city search for "the mystery writer's missing daughter"—who was found, with the help of private detectives, in Reno, Nevada. Linda married a computer engineer in 1961 and had a son in 1963. The three were living in Inglewood, California, in November 1970, and had just spent a fine afternoon with Linda's parents in Santa Barbara. "Life is so very good on certain days," Millar wrote his Knopf editor in its immediate afterglow, "that one almost lives in fear of having to pay for it in full."[4] Four nights later, Linda died in her sleep.

Welty too had, as Millar noted in his letter, "suffered grievous losses in recent years." In 1959, her brother Walter had died as the result of complications from a crippling form of arthritis, and then in 1966, her mother and her brother Edward died within days of each other, her mother from a stroke, Edward from a brain infection that struck while he was hospitalized for a broken neck. Twenty-five years earlier, Welty had witnessed her father's death during a blood transfusion. She well understood the pain Ken Millar and his wife were enduring.

Eudora Welty to Kenneth Millar, December 19, 1970

Dear Mr. Millar,

Thank you for writing to me—I've only just got home after two weeks away and found your card—the grief of what has happened to you, its beautiful prayer. I am sorry—I believe you feel as I do. I don't think myself that numbness is really merciful—not for long. Do you remember what Forster said in *The Longest Journey*—"They'll come saying, 'Bear up—trust to time. No, no, they're wrong. Mind it. In God's name, mind such a thing.'" It's good that the little boy is seven—that gives him a good strong memory, and the memory will be the right one, unharmed—It will be like the Prayer, Mountaintop Way somehow, maybe. You saw this—I hope it will be for you.

There was also a telegram under my door from the *NY Times* asking if I could review your new book—which I'd so much like the chance to do—but the telegram was days old, & I'm afraid they couldn't have waited on my late reply. I'm glad to know about the book.

This is a frivolous little Christmas card, but I'm sending it anyway because it's about a bit of wildlife—The man who wanted to do it, a young NYC book dealer, had never seen a guinea and neither had his artist—I guess they don't streak across 5th Avenue very often—So these were copied out of the dictionary—Anyway, it might amuse you.[5] Many wishes to you both,

Eudora Welty

Eudora Welty to Kenneth Millar, January 15, 197[1]

Dear Mr. Millar,

The Underground Man is extraordinary, and I did get to review it after all for the Times. If you'd feel like looking it over, I made you a carbon, and if I did you wrong somewhere there'd be time to cut, at least—they'll be cutting, themselves, most likely, because although I know better than send more than they ask for, that's just what I did. It's a beautiful book. You can see I thought so.

Many good wishes to you and I hope things go a little easier these days.

Sincerely yours,
Eudora Welty

It had seemed before to Ken Millar that he often experienced the extremes of bad and good fortune at the same time. Now, in the wake of Linda's death, came the remarkable news that his latest novel would be reviewed—celebrated—by perhaps the most admired writer in America, in the country's most influential book-paper.

Kenneth Millar to Eudora Welty, January 19, 1971. Telegram.

MY DEEPEST THANKS FOR YOUR MAGNIFICENT REVIEW BLUSHING I FIND NOTHING I WISH CHANGED REGARDS KENNETH MILLAR.

Kenneth Millar to Eudora Welty, January 19, 1971

Dear Miss Welty:

How generous you are, and how fortunate I am that the *Times* sent you my book after all, and that you were willing to review it. As you know a writer and his work don't really exist until they've been read.

You have given me the fullest and most explicit reading I've ever had, or that I ever expected. I exist as a writer more completely thanks to you.

It's particularly gratifying that you should like my boy. Ronny is a fairly exact portrait of my dear grandson Jimmie, now seven going on eight (and the line about "Calling Space Control" is Jimmie's own). By the kind of irony and recompense that Archer and you are familiar with, Jimmie has come more into our care in recent months. He and his daddy spend their weekends with us, which is a lucky thing for Margaret and me. We're doing all right, except sometimes when one wakes up at three o'clock in the morning when, to revise Fitzgerald's line, it's always the dark night of the soul. But that overstates the case and may give you the impression that we are in trouble. Perhaps we are but not greatly more so than most people manage to endure and survive.

Your review filled me with joy, as your earlier letter did. I have been able to encourage other writers, but never until now have the tables been turned so blessedly on me. To you I can confess that I left the academic world to write popular fiction in the hope of coming back by underground tunnels and devious ways into the light again, dripping with darkness. You encourage me to think that there was some strange merit in this romantic plan.

Margaret sends her love with mine. If you haven't seen her excellent last year's book, *Beyond This Point Are Monsters*, we'd like to send you a copy.

Sincerely yours,
Kenneth Millar

P.S.—It was particularly thoughtful of you to send me a carbon of your review. I assume you received the wire I sent you last night but, service being what it is, perhaps I should reiterate, blushingly, that there is nothing in it I'd like to cut. I did make one change in the proofs of the book which should probably be put into your quote on the last line of the final page, 11: "and jailbirded him" becomes "jailbirding him," preceded by a comma.

K.M.

Eudora Welty to Kenneth Millar, January 24, 1971

Dear Mr. Millar,

   Your telegram came early next morning, while I was having my coffee, and made me feel happy all day. Then your letter—relief in full, and I am so pleased you found the review did convey what I meant it to and didn't wrong the book along the way. The easy part was saying what I thought, but you know it was that part about the fairy and romance where you might have wished I hadn't felt called on to say so much. And the hard part was trying to give a good notion of the nature and power of that plot without doing any harm to its secrets. It was a great pleasure to write it but I had to watch out the whole way not to indulge in the piece I would really like to do, where it would be all right to follow all those things through and say what you'd really done in the light of the whole. You could tell how I'd had to cut at it with the scissors, and where, in what I did get down. So thank you for your understanding. I counted on it, on its being all right to ask you (though in general I suppose it would be a nutty thing—a fairly good thing, too—for reviewers to consult the authors), feeling we would have wanted the same kind of rightness in the review. What you said made me proud.

   As you know, they think the world of you at *The Times*, and it was such a plum for them to give me this—the galleys were just about worn out before they ever quit passing them around among the staff. Walter Clemons said they'd try not to cut much of the too-long review (he says they like it), he would be the one and he loves the book—when he sends a proof I'll fix it about the jailbirding. Those Snows!—One of the things I hated most to leave out in my piece was that interview—chillier than *The Chill*, the end of *The Chill*, that last line—but sustained the whole way, absolutely hair-raising and at the same time so hair-raisingly funny, with the mother following every line of the son's "confession" with a correction of his grammar.

I'm glad that's your little boy. I sort of felt the "Calling Space Control" line was real—nobody could have made up that seat-belt buckle. He was lovely all the way.

Yes indeed I've read *Beyond This Point Are Monsters* and like it enormously. It's so nice of her and you to offer to send me a copy—I did own one, but someone I lent it to has run off with it and I would delight in having it back on my shelves. I've read you both since the beginning, which means I read Margaret Millar first, the books as they came out—so that goes back a good long time. So many years of pleasure to thank you for—and being able to say it to two writers in the same house—it's fine, I can say it twice—thank you. I wish I had something new to send—I haven't, but I might send something old—it's in the same spirit.

The clipping's from the local paper the other day—how these little tatters and remnants of those things go drifting about the world. And I doubt if the man has any idea of who he's named after—his mother just thought the sound was right, somehow. I must stop. I can't tell you how pleased I was to hear from you, so quickly. As for coming up into the light, I see you do it in every book, and "dripping with darkness" you make it a pretty splendid way to show something forth. Whatever it is you may ever wish to do, my best wishes to it—as we all must wish for one another.

Yours sincerely,
Eudora Welty

Welty's review of The Underground Man, *which would appear in the February 14, 1971,* New York Times Book Review, *treated Millar's novel as a work of serious fiction deserving the close attention of* Times *readers: "*The Underground Man *is written so close to the nerve of today as to expose most of the apprehensions we live with," Welty declared, as she expressed admiration for Macdonald's craftsmanship. "It is the character of Archer," she noted, "whose first-person narrative forms all Mr. Macdonald's novels that makes it matter to* *us. [. . .] As a detective and as a man he takes the human situation with full seriousness. He cares. And good and evil both are real to him." This character, she further contended, comes to us in a prose style of "delicacy and tension, very tightly made, with a spring in it. It doesn't allow a static sentence or one without pertinence."* [6]

Before this review appeared, *Welty wrote to Ken's wife. Margaret Millar had sent her most recent book to Eudora, and now Eudora responded, sending thanks along with a copy of an out-of-print Welty story collection. Then worry about the Millars' safety displaced Welty's focus on fiction: an earthquake had rocked southern California. Ken immediately sent reassurance and told her that, in the midst of the earthquake turmoil, he'd been interviewed by* Newsweek *for a cover story. By separate mail, he sent an inscribed copy of his new book: "For Eudora Welty, whose sympathetic imagination has enhanced the life of this book and the life of its author." Welty told him she had "never read an inscription as beautiful as this."* [7]

The Underground Man *would not be the first Ross Macdonald title to enter the* New York Times Book Review*'s bestseller list; it was preceded onto that chart, in 1969, by* The Goodbye Look—*which had also been reviewed on the* Book Review*'s front page by William Goldman. But Welty's memorable appreciation of* The Underground Man, *so well-expressed and by such a significant author, helped Lew Archer's sixteenth novel become an enormous national hit: "the first runaway mystery in many years," according to the* New York Post. [8]

Eudora Welty to Kenneth Millar, April 3, 1971

Dear Mr. Millar,

The Underground Man's up where he belongs, riding high, and it does make me rejoice to see him go and watch the excitement your book is causing—and just now in the library I saw they'd snatched it for a movie. The Newsweek piece [March 22, 1971] seemed careful and serious and good—did you think—?—and it was nice to see the magazine reward itself with a salute like that for seeing the light. I wish your issue of Newsweek were still in effect so that in the post office and the library and the supermarket and everywhere there's a newsstand from here to yonder, everybody would still be walking around with the gaze of Archer's eye on them. That was enjoyable. I mean, for all your readers. It was good to see the Saturday Review's comment and especially Walter Clemons's review in the Daily Times—as I know, he longed to say much more, and next time will get to, I hope.[9]—Anyway, what this book is bringing about must give a lot of people high spirits—I just wanted to add my note of joy.

Love and wishes to you both,
Eudora Welty

I am trying to review Arthur Mizener's biography of Ford Madox Ford—I'm not sure I can stand Arthur Mizener on Ford, anyway. (I found you like Fitzgerald (so do I), and wonder if M. really could have done well by him.) I've been reading all the Ford I can, to get a little balance.[10]

Kenneth Millar to Eudora Welty, April 6, 1971

Dear Miss Welty:

Your letters *always* bring a note of joy. I must admit that I got an enormous kick out of the *Newsweek* cover, particularly since it came three weeks delayed, and never guaranteed. When I walked into the Thrifty drug store and saw my own face peering at me a la Holmes, it was a strange moment but one I'm glad I lived to experience. Don Freeman saw the Face on a Paris newsstand and sketched the scene for me, with only the *Newsweek* cover in color.[11] And I had a card from a friend in Capetown, S.A. At the moment I'm working my way back into my private self. I think for once that having a pseudonym can be an advantage: let *him* (or Archer) stand out there in the unaccustomed glare while I get on with the always fragile privacies.

I've been doing a couple of unaccustomed reviews, too. You make it look so easy; but it isn't. It's interesting to me that you should be reviewing Mizener on Ford, and you are right in supposing that Fitzgerald, whom I have venerated since my college days, was not done right Arthur, in my opinion. Mizener's book on Fitz was the first of that sort, which accounts for its success, as well as its failure. Mizener is not a very good writer, and would naturally have little real feeling for either Fitz or Ford.

I've seen a part of Mizener's Ford biography and was struck by what seemed to me its rather dull antipathy toward its subject. It's not as dead and ugly as Mark Schorer's life of Lewis, but it veers in that direction. Biographers should write about figures they love, or at least warmly hate. Perhaps I'm saying too much on the basis of what I've seen of Mizener's Ford, and I have to admit that Ford is another writer to whose defense I automatically spring. One would have thought that his services to literature, not to mention his direct contributions, would have earned the tolerance of other writers for his foibles. But he's the most maligned good writer I can think of, and I'm afraid that Mizener has gone pussy-footing along with it.

Another friend of mine, Richard W. Lid, has been reviewing this same book, which is how I happen to have seen a part of it. (Through Dick, I also met Ford's daughter Julie, a good and nice person somewhat lost in the world, in Pasadena). Dick wrote his own book on Ford—an analysis of the major novels which I think is the best thing done on him so far. Could be I'm prejudiced: I worked on it with Dick—*this in confidence*—and in fact he dedicated it to me. So when you told me you were involved with Ford, it closed another circle, dear Miss Welty, with a tinkle. But it's no coincidence, is it? All writers admire *Parade's End* and love *The Good Soldier*, and hate to see them fall into fumbling hands, unimaginative hands.

Would you like me to try and get hold of a copy of Dick's book (R.W. Lid, *Ford Madox Ford: The Essence of His Art*, U. of Calif. Press, 1964) and/or his review of Mizener, and send it on? Neither would tell you anything you don't know, but they might please you.

It was delightful to get your note, and Margaret concurs, with love,

As always,

Kenneth Millar

Eudora Welty to Kenneth Millar, April 10, 1971

Dear Mr. Millar,

That you helped work on a book on Ford was a glad surprise that at the same time seems only the most natural thing in the world. I can see how congenial that would be—and your copy of Mr. Lid's book came safely in the same mail with your letter. It was so wholly generous of you to let me read your own copy, and dedicated to you as it is, and at this very point, when Mizener in his jovial disparagement was about to get me down. It's what I needed. I'm glad you found him lacking too. (I'd started off with something like your remark about *who* should write a biography.) That's restoring.

It seems to me I can see your mark on the chapters I read at the first moment—having turned at once to "The Good Soldier"—in the awareness of what Ford is doing in that marvelous book plus the (your) working writer's special knowledge of pure technique and the deep-lying reasons for all its steps. It's completely absorbing and I want to go right on, but I wanted to thank you for such thoughtfulness and to let you know the book's safe and a real help and certain standby. I don't need to tell you I undertook the review not for love of Mizener but for love of Ford.

I wouldn't wish this Mizener on you for review—at the same time I'd like to read what you'd say. Are the reviews you're doing for the Times where I can look for them?

More later. I heard the tinkle all right, and how could it be coincidence?

A nice Easter to you both, and love,

Eudora Welty

Kenneth Millar to Eudora Welty, April 12, 1971

Dear Miss Welty:

I now have a copy of Dick Lid's review of Arthur Mizener's book, and send it herewith. You needn't return it. I think it's quite good, don't you, though Dick himself feels that he was (for professional reasons no doubt, Dick being chairman of the English Dept. at San Fernando Valley State College in Northridge) over-kind.

In haste, as always,

Ken Millar

P.S.—I still don't know who he wrote this review for—one of the academic journals, though.

K.

Eudora Welty to Kenneth Millar, [April 18, 1971]

Dear Mr. Millar,

With many thanks I'll be sending your book back to you in the morning, and I hope it gets there all right. You helped me more than you knew, and I needed it more than I knew. Well, the more I read of Mizener the more insensitive and wrong-headed he appeared to me. There was never any question about what I felt about Ford—his power, and the greatness of him—but there were such big holes in my knowledge (when I read him I would always gravitate back to "The Good Soldier," and lately I'd seen the selected autobiographies and impressions about to come out, edited by Michael Killigrew, sent along by the Times) that I needed all I could learn—I had to be as fair as I could, or what I wrote wouldn't count. You went to so much trouble for me. The Lid book is fascinating and the writing so good—precise and meaningful and calling up so much—you must know how coming in the wake of the Mizener prose it refreshed my mind. (This isn't to ask, but I do think you must have done more than a little for that book.) It was good to know from his review—but I confess I didn't dare read it till after I'd written mine—that a Ford scholar spoke for the unfairness of method and inferiority of vision that I felt so strongly myself in Mizener's book. I can't agree, though, with that "sympathetic" in his opening sentence—which may just speak for my failing in getting too mad.

There was a personal complication. Ford, who helped all those other young writers, helped me too—he tried to interest a publisher in my stories. He couldn't—it must have been one of the last things he busied himself on, it was the last year of his life—but I have about four little notes he sent to me, out of the clear sky, in that handwriting Mizener found so hard to read.

So you see—and I wish I could have done a better piece. All of a sudden I learned (they called me) the deadline was that very day (Thursday), two weeks earlier than I'd understood over the phone, so I had to write it overnight and wire it to them. They'll have to cut it, but you can see it the way I wrote it, if you'd like to. (I'll put it in with your book) Best wishes to you both. Gratefully, with love,

Eudora

Kenneth Millar to Eudora Welty, April 20, 1971

Dear Miss Welty:

That was no tinkle, that was a gong. You need have no concern about not having written an adequate review. Your piece recurs like the sea—that same sea which you glimpsed between the tunnels, that [Frank] and [Fordie] see[12]—and breaks on Mizener's miserable head in waves of *salve indignatis*. If, to come back to my original image, if you had hardened your prose any longer in the smithies of your wrath, you might have destroyed him completely with its vibration. As it is I'd say that you have succeeded in destroying the effect of his lousy book, and that that is what needed doing. It may be possible now for another life of Ford to be written eventually. (It should fall into the hands of someone like Peter Green who did so well, I thought, with a much smaller subject, Kenneth Grahame.) Given Mizener's standing in the academic world, where style and moral discernment are at best grace-notes, and where the good doctors hesitate to mention the sponges and towels that their fellow surgeons have lost, the job you have done almost had to be accomplished by an independent imaginative writer. You did it nobly, and that adverb is exactly the one I want.

It was a privilege to give you an assist—more of a privilege than you realize unless I tell you more. Which of course I am going to do. I live in literary history, as I once told Alfred Knopf when he began to fail and I volunteered to help him with his memoirs. (He proudly refused.) I live in literary history, held close and wide in its recurring circles. For much of my youth I had nowhere else to live, and I fell into the habit, which persists, of relating my only moderately interesting self to writers everywhere. I gather that this is generally true of writers, as we make our fantasies real, build them into the sloping side of the culture, digging down through the layers of the past and up through the present into the light again.

When I got your letter today, something went through me like a vibration of light, as if I had had a responsive echo from a distant star. As if a half-imagined relationship to the great past had come real in my life before my life ended. It came down to me through you, through your defense of the tradition of humane letters, but I think above all through the fact that Ford had done you a service, or tried to, and you had done me one—that *personal* connection with history is what tripped the gong—and I had done Ford a service, though not a personal one, by helping Dick with his book. I sometimes think, don't you, that these musical and moral recurrences are almost the whole meaning of life and art, or at least the grounds of their meaning.

Dick will be delighted when I tell him that you found his book useful, and something more than useful. There is a fact about it and Mizener's book which explains the sullen acquiescence which spoils the beginning of Dick's review. Mizener used Dick's book and neglected to acknowledge his rather considerable debt, even to name Dick's book. But Dick is not in a position professionally to challenge Mizener openly, or thought he wasn't. Let me explain further that Dick was let go by the University of California on the stated grounds that his Ford book was not acceptable as proof of critical or scholastic competence. I know that sounds incredible, but it is literally true. The book was being published by the press of that same university, and was formally reviewed by TLS. Wrenched loose and "demoted" to the state college system, Dick rose in seven years to the headship of his department. I suppose my point is that there is a human story behind every book, or even every review. I wonder what Mizener's is.

But your review is more than a placing of Mizener. It's a praise of Ford—your turning prism is perfect—and a statement of gratitude and fealty to the great past. I'm so glad that someone, and particularly you, had the heart and eloquence to write it. Margaret was crazy about it, too.

I'm sending on your generous gift of the picture, to Julie via Dick, who keeps in touch with her and her husband and their son, who is in his early twenties.[13]

As always,

Ken

Eudora Welty to Kenneth Millar, April 23, 1971

Dear Mr. Millar,

With it all told it is a perfect thing. When your earlier letter came, and I saw the pattern begin to come out, I knew it would matter to you, as it did to me, but when your letter this morning told me in what way—all I can say after reading it is that I took it to my heart and that I feel glad that I ever happened along when I did, and the way I did, to be part of it—glad for my own sake, my own beliefs too—I believe it was bound to happen for you somehow. But thank you for telling me this, which has made me a part of some perfect occurrence. Nothing ever gave me that feeling before, and I doubt if anything ever will again. And it takes recognizing, all around. The perfection of such a thing itself, I believe in, just as if it were familiar, not rare, and the extraordinary is really the least surprising by the nature of it—I believe in it, and I trust it too and treasure it above everything, the personal, the personal, the personal! I put my faith in it not only as the source, the grounds of meaning in art, in life, but as the meaning itself.

It is good to know you found the review to do what I hoped it might do. I see better why John Leonard asked me to do it, with my scholarly lacks—I had to do it anyway, for the reason of my own. That's an appalling story about Mr. Lid's career and the book—I don't comprehend anything very much about the academic world, I guess—the only way I've ever seen it (since I got out of college) was from the outside, as a visiting writer or something. What villains it must have. I think Mizener is even dangerous to have around. He's evil, to me.

Yours ever,

Eudora

Kenneth Millar to Eudora Welty, April 27, 1971

Dear Miss Welty:

I'm so grateful that we understand each other and feel alike. General truths aren't worth much until they're applied, and ill-intentioned intelligence is worth less. University people sometimes forget that, and judge themselves not by what they do but by what they say, or what they think about what other people do.

It was thoughtful of you to send on that good picture of Ford and it has gone to the right place now, to Julie, who has only a few sparse mementoes of her father. But she is a cheerful woman, decently married (to a man who is writing a novel about FMF!) and working in the office at Claremont College, I believe. She will value that picture, and even more your Defense of Ford.

A footnote to the progression in which we were carried forward into clearer understanding: the day after your last letter came, a young man who was in my house for the first time, a hopeful writer, out of a blue sky said: "Did you ever hear of Professor Lid? He was the best teacher I ever had!" So the succession goes on, not apostolic but real and breathtaking, and breath-giving.

Love,

Ken

Though still addressing her as "Miss Welty," Millar—acknowledging the closeness and deep emotion he felt—for the first time signed off with love. Welty, in response, also sent tactful love to "Dear Ken"—after which she to him would be "Dear Eudora."

Eudora Welty to Kenneth Millar, May 3, 1971

Dear Ken,

Your letters are like tokens of goodness and kindness coming to me out of a terrible world. Not "like"—they *are*. Thank you for the book too—I got it from Dr. Lid, with his inscription, and I'll be thanking him. It will be good to read it straight through now out from under pressure, and I am so glad to have it.

Do you know about the thesis being written on you at the University of Chicago—I can tell you because I heard it in Jackson from the Chairman of the English Department there, Gwin Kolb, who was here on a visit—this is [his] home town. (I went to a little party for him and he told me because he'd read the review in the Times.) So there you are.

I looked up this off-print (Texas Quarterly, of about ten years back) hoping you might like it—and to read it for a part of my letter—of my thanks.

Love to you both. Take care.

Eudora

A week after sending Ken an offprint of her essay about English novelist Henry Green (1905–1973),[14] Eudora sent him a pamphlet Doubleday, Doran had used in 1941 to publicize her first book, A Curtain of Green. *It featured a cover picture of the author in the dappled light of a camellia shed made of lath and included her story "The Key" and the introduction Katherine Anne Porter had written for the new book. On the pamphlet, Eudora wrote: "A very early example of jailbirding/For Kenneth Millar (and Archer)/from Eudora Welty/ Found April 12, 1971." ("Jailbirding" referred to a visual image from* The Underground Man *with which Eudora had ended her discussion of that book in the* New York Times Book Review.*)*

Eudora Welty to Kenneth Millar, May 11, 1971[15]

Dear Ken,

This goes back to when I was working on the Ford review—and then it goes back 30 years beyond that. I was trying to find something in my mother's desk and found this, which I hadn't seen since its own day and I'd forgotten it existed. It came together with other things—I wrote on it to send you, and then our letters outdated it. I'd felt a little reluctant before—the gushy way I wrote to K.A.P.

about Ford, and one or two things K.A.P. sort of made up about my life, out of benevolence and out of having too little to go on, and you wouldn't know this. But the thing is it's one more little piece, it belongs nevertheless.

My mother took the snapshot, in a local camellia shed.

That was the day (finding this) that the memory of Cairo came back to me—Cairo, Illinois. It was once when I was going north on the train and it was running away off schedule so that we went through Cairo by daylight, the one time for me, and I could see from the bridge. It's the high railroad bridge and long trestle over a wide reach where the Ohio and the Mississippi and (I believe) a little local river too all come together. It took a long time to cross it and the train went slowly, and while we were still on it I saw high up in the light a long ragged V of birds flying south with the river. I kept hearing in my head all the way that beautiful word "confluence"—"the confluence of the waters"— everything the eyes could see was like the word happening. I don't remember that there were any houses or roads or people anywhere, just treetops and water and distance and sky and birds and confluence. It may not be so rare but I thought so then and I do now—it's all so rarely the blessing falls.

Love,

Eudora

Kenneth Millar to Eudora Welty, May 12, 1971

Dear Eudora:

I greatly enjoyed your essay on Henry Green, don't know the passage about Mr. Rock and the starlings, and would like very much to be introduced to it at your hands. It's many years since I've read any Henry Green at all, and then only two or three (*Blindness*, *Living*, I remember.) You make him sound like just the novelist I need for my mature years.

I don't think I ever told you, my writing friend from Alberta, Herb Harker, and I performed an experiment with some pages of

Losing Battles, our purpose being to test the hypothesis that there is a continental popular language. The experiment consisted of his listening to me read dialogue aloud and stopping me when I came to a word that wouldn't have been used in Cardston, Alberta. The only word he stopped me on was "choicy": *he* would say choosy. Herb's own novel, by the way, about a brokendown rodeo rider and his two boys, has been going the rounds and looks as if it has found a home, with Putnam. If so, it will be his first published fiction, after 25 years of writing, at age 45.

I'm off to New York this Sunday to receive an award! The award is of no great moment—a "Lively Arts" award from the Advertising Women of New York—but the occasion is lent a special glow by the fact that Will Durant will present it, and he was a great figure in my young life. In fact, his book "The Story of Philosophy" introduced me to the subject and made a great difference: Berkeley! Hume! Schopenhauer! Perhaps I'll have a chance to tell him about it.

You mentioned the four letters, or notes, you had from FMF. Did you ever see the para he wrote in 1938 to Stanley Unwin about you? (*Letters of FMF*, ed. Richard M. Ludwig, Princeton, 1965): [In the paragraph that Ken inserted into his letter at this point, Ford recommended Eudora's stories for English book publication, asserting that short stories of "such beauty and so beautifully written" might overcome the "usual objection" to this genre.]

Congratulations again, now that I've seen it in print (with only one word changed?) on your Ford defense. It badly needed doing, since the disrespectful book has spawned a batch of disrespectful reviews from writers who have no independent sources of information.

The *Gatsby* galleys are being auctioned next Tuesday in New York. I'm going to try to get to the sale, just for fun—I'm not a collector.—I plan to stay at the Algonquin and permit myself to feel like a writer.

Love,

Ken

Before Eudora received Ken's letter about his upcoming trip to New York City and the Algonquin Hotel, she left Jackson headed for that very location herself. She arrived on Saturday, May 15, for a two-week sojourn. By Monday, Newsweek writer Ray Sokolov (who had done that magazine's cover story about Ken), along with Walter Clemons and John Leonard of the New York Times Book Review, tracked Ken down and told him Eudora was at the Algonquin. There on Monday afternoon he waited until she returned to the hotel, introduced himself, and a long, animated conversation ensued. As they parted, Ken invited Eudora to dinner the following night. She had a previously arranged engagement with her Random House editor, Albert Erskine, but promised that she would try to reschedule it.[16]

Eudora Welty, Algonquin Hotel, New York City, to Kenneth Millar, Algonquin Hotel, New York City, Monday [May 17, 1971]

Dear Ken,

Albert said coming out Wednesday would be just as good, so we could have dinner tomorrow night if that's still easy for you—Someone at Knopf just invited me to a party for you beforehand, and I'll be so pleased to come to that too—

I hope your award and all will be fine this evening. I'm still finding this so amazing and still trying to take it in—

See you tomorrow—

Eudora

Kenneth Millar, Algonquin Hotel, New York City, to Eudora Welty, Algonquin Hotel, New York City, [May 18, 1971]

Dear Eudora:

I'm so delighted you can come to dinner and to Alfred's party beforehand. I'll see you there, or perhaps you would like to go over to his apartment in a cab with me, leaving the hotel lobby about 4:45.

I think one of us must be fey, and possibly both.

May Sarton, who read a poem tonight, sends her best to you.[17]

Ken

On the evening of May 18, Ken escorted Eudora to an elegant cocktail party at the home of Alfred and Helen Knopf on 55th Street just off of Fifth Avenue. There Ray Sokolov and Walter Clemons were also present and could see that their efforts to bring the two writers together had been a success. Later Ken wrote to Alfred Knopf, saying, "Your party was and will remain one of the high points of my life" and calling Eudora "my good angel." After the party, Ken and Eudora went out for dinner and then walked around Manhattan, not getting back to the Algonquin, where their rooms were now side by side, till after midnight. "I took him down Broadway," she remembered, "and he just came to life. He said, 'Now this is where it is.' The side streets had been sort of genteel, but here everything was going on. There was a cop chasing a man, shooting; the fire department was whizzing by. In fact I was kind of scared, with people running through the streets. But Ken just said, 'Oh, my.' He knew what all that was about. I said, 'I've never seen a man chase another man in public with a gun before.' He said that was an old story to him. And all this time he was so calm, and rather formal and everything; but he was all eyes and ears. He had a great inner calm, supposedly, but I think actually he was pretty emotional. But he had such control: the most controlled person I ever saw. [. . .] He respected other people, in a very grave way, and he would wait for them to speak."[18] Millar's eyes were an amazing color, she thought: an almost violet-blue; and, when expressing enjoyment, he had a full and wonderful laugh. The two of them had spoken about books and authors, about their own family histories, about themselves and each other. They had had a magical evening, but that evening would be their last time together for two years. The next day, Ken would travel on to Kitchener, Ontario.

Kenneth Millar, Algonquin Hotel, New York City, to Eudora Welty, Algonquin Hotel, New York City, [May 1971]

Dear Eudora:

I never thought I'd hate to leave New York, but I do. I feel an unaccustomed sorrow not to be able to continue our friendship *viva voce*, and in the flesh, but these are the chances of life. But there is a deeper and happier chance which will keep us friends till death, don't you believe? And we'll walk and talk again.

Till then, Ken

Meanwhile there are letters.

From Kitchener, Ontario, where Margaret met Ken and both attended a celebration of their careers at the dedication of their old hometown's new library, Ken sent Eudora an evocative scenic postcard.

Kenneth Millar to Eudora Welty, May 23, 1971. Postcard of "THE KISSING BRIDGE West Montrose, Ontario—Near Kitchener—The only remaining covered bridge in Ontario, built in 1881."

Dear Eudora:

This bridge was built to last. Much of the country around here is essentially untouched, and riotously beautiful at this spring season. The people—German and Pennsylvania Dutch—are very much themselves, like a little nation. Altogether most pleasant to this quasi native son—I'm even talking the language. And treasuring fond memories of New York and you.

Love, Ken

Eudora Welty, Lexington, Kentucky, to Kenneth Millar, June 3, 1971

Dear Ken,

It was such happiness to spend that time together. I feel that there wouldn't ever have been a time when we wouldn't have been friends, not when sympathy can work both backwards and forwards, and go anywhere—it would have made itself known at some point, as it did. But the way it happened that we came to meet was wonderful and right and exactly timed.

I was so glad that the occasion that brought you was a celebration, and that I could be a part—Thank you for seeing to it that I was there at the gathering at Alfred Knopf's—John Leonard and Raymond Sokolov and Walter Clemons and the movie man and all, together in one room, and Mr. Knopf rendered so benign and so gratified and filled with pleasure, he could hardly let the party end. Then we had that lovely evening, which is now part of my life.

I hope Canada was all you hoped and all good, and that now you're both safe back in the cool clean quiet of Santa Barbara and at work again—I won't be home myself till next week, and this is coming to you from Lexington, Kentucky. My task has been to get from New York to Granville, Ohio, to Sewanee, Tennessee *slowly*. (I think I told you I was being given two honorary degrees—too close together to go home in between.) But it's very hard to get anywhere slowly. I took a bus from NY to Columbus, Ohio, called a Luxury Special—reserved seats. But I could hardly believe my eyes when they spread a red carpet over the asphalt at the Port Authority Bus Terminal on 8th Avenue for us to walk over, and when we were welcomed aboard by a hostess wearing a red cape and a little red pillbox hat with a crown insignia—she looked like some little Roxy usherette summoned back from movieland—"Folks, we want you all to be comfor'ble." She served us every mile, it seemed, with food on little trays—ham sandwiches, peppermints, pea soup, apples, coke, cookies, in no particular order, just constantly, and all free. There was inexorable Muzak. I believe this bus went all the way to Los Angeles. But looking out the window was peaceful—while it was rural Pennsylvania & Ohio, the Mennonite and Amish country. I spent the night in Columbus, Ohio, & thought of Thurber. Another bus ride, and another Holiday Inn in Lexington. But you can't be confused which Holiday Inn is which, because there's a picture of Man o' War hanging over the bed here. Tomorrow I get on to Chattanooga, not too early for them to be ready for me. And after Sewanee, home—*It'll* be ready for me. I need to work.

Thank you for the note you left for me. I do feel the same. When I think of our meeting now I believe there was never the slightest danger of its not happening—everything was pointing and headed the other way.

Love and wishes to you both,
Eudora

Kenneth Millar to Eudora Welty, June 8, 1971

Dear Eudora:

Your letter from Lexington came yesterday, with the description of your journey between doctorates. I think the bus companies must be competing with the airlines, but at least you were spared the in-flight movie: on my latest trip it was Elvis Presley's latest. Your mention of passing through the Mennonite country of Pennsylvania touched a chord, as perhaps you knew it would. My maternal ancestors farmed there since 1700 and about the middle of the last century walked up to Canada and settled in Southern Ontario. My grandmother was a Mennonite, and her church was my first church, or rather Sunday School, rather grim and frightening, I think. The area around Kitchener, where Margaret and I visited the other week, is heavily populated with Pennsylvania Dutch and German people and while I turned my back on that place and its life long ago, I feel strangely and wonderfully at home there. Driving around Kitchener was like reading an old poem in which the words were street signs that I remembered as I read them. I hadn't been back there in eleven years, and this was my first time as a free stranger. One of the first things that happened was a visit I made to the farm where I worked for a year and several summers in my teens. It's called Oxbow Farm, because it's enclosed in the deep bend of a river, the Grand River, and I found that it had been bought by the Conservation Authority and would be preserved as a public park. The man I worked for, or rather his son, Ray Snyder, has himself retired and bought a house directly across the river from which he can look out over his farm.—It was a wonderful month to get out into the Canadian country. The woods are still there, green overhead and wet underfoot, with ponds and small lakes scattered at random everywhere, and millions of trilliums. M. and I went birding with Ray Dickinson, a retired high school science teacher who taught us both in the thirties and later became the area's leading conservationist. All three of us took great pleasure in visiting a recently designated wilderness area known as the F. W. R. Dickinson wilderness, after him. Ray must be the most rational man I ever met, gentle and calm. He wasn't always, when he was a teacher, but he was so good at teaching you didn't know he was good. He showed us a rose-breasted grosbeak, and fifteen buffalo in a fenced field, but no pileated woodpecker, though one has been seen in the area.—It was strange to see near-wilderness and near-metropolis cheek by jowl. Kitchener has quadrupled in my time, to a current population of 180,000, and is starting to build what I consider skyscrapers, buildings ten or twelve stories high. But it's only now beginning to gain assurance in its own German culture—I attended a ceremony two Sundays ago which sort of signalized this. It was the reburial, in Kitchener, of all the German war dead (prisoners, internees) who had died in Canada during the last war; 119 Germans came over from Germany to attend the ceremony; and the place was thus recognized as the "capital" of German Canada. Half Deutsch and half Scots as I am, I felt very much at home in that company.

But the best ceremony I participated in, and the one I will remember longer and in greatest detail, was our conversation as we dawdled across town the other night, and in the morning. Yesterday, an hour or two after I got your letter, I got a really good idea for a book. Hope to send it to you in a couple of years. Travel safely home. Love, Ken

P.S.—Don't miss last Sunday's Times Book Review. There are complimentary words about you both in Wilfred Sheed's opening column and Walter Clemons' closing one. Clemons did a smashing job on the Pulitzer Prize. You're going to have to subscribe to his weekly!

K.

Eudora Welty to Kenneth Millar, June 16, 1971

Dear Ken,

I was so glad to get your letter, which came the morning after I got back home. What you tell me about the new book delights me—I look forward to the day when I see it, and all in between is the pleasure of knowing you're writing. When I got my mail being held at the postoffice, I found the covered bridge from Ontario, and the book had come safely too. So thank you for all. I've started Mr. Bruccoli—liked his approach and design immediately, and will be writing you later when I've finished it. So good to have the chance to read it.

Just last night I managed to get hold of that Book Review you alerted me to, only without telling me what was on the inside pages, and there we both were, in some shadowy sort of way or other, you three times and me twice, like shadows of our visit left behind. I wonder what you thought of the parody. I didn't think it was too worthy—it didn't seem in very accurate tune to me, but I may not be a good parody judge.[19] Parody's the highest salute to eminence, and my feeling is it ought to be perfect or nothing. That's hard. He did touch on some key points. I think Walter Clemons might have done a good one—he's a student of the form, I believe. Yes, that was a grand whack he took at the Pulitzer—that line-up was really awful, wasn't it, and followed by Walter's nice orderly conclusions. I *am* subscribing—to the Book Review alone—the Sunday Times in the bulk sometimes takes 10 days to pull in to Jackson, and who wants it?

The visit back to Kitchener sounds filled with fine things. The old friends, the country still beautiful, still wild, and the springtime. And at the other end of it, they must have felt very much rewarded too, to have you there—the teacher must have been so deeply pleased.

The Weltys came over about the same time as your German ancestors, from the German part of Switzerland, and went to Pennsylvania and on to Southern Ohio. Farmers, teachers, and preachers—some of them were Amish (I *think*—anyway they were pacifists) and the tale is that my father's ancestor decided to join up in the Revolution and jumped on his horse and rode away to fight the Red-Coats, and was thrown out of the church for it. They were turned into Methodists. In my case, it's my mother with the Scots and Irish ancestors, by way of the Carolinas and Va.

My trip was nice at the end too. At both places, friends I hadn't seen in a long time. The occasions were so different—at Denison, they had graduation in the stadium, the speaker was the Commissioner of Education from HEW, making a direct and, it seemed to me, thoughtful effort to reach from one generation to the other (his daughter was a student), and a dog came along to the platform in the line when they got their diplomas—a nice dog—came more than once, I think he got four degrees, one in music. At Sewanee, we had it in the chapel—rose window, banners hanging, organ music, vivid procession, and medieval to the point where the valedictorian delivered his address in Latin. I had to kneel at the Bishop's throne and place my folded hands in his lap, and he held them while he and the Vice-Chancellor spoke back and forth over my head, all in Latin—I don't know *what* they really made me. I stayed with the Vice-Chancellor and his wife (she's Canadian) (he's Mississippian) and there were a lot of doings up there on the mountain, but I especially enjoyed a long morning's talk with Allen Tate—he's built a house up there, where he lives with his young wife and two radiant little boys, just toddlers. Allen said, "It's foolish, I'll never see those boys grow up." But they will have had him for a father.[20]

When I got home I sent you that book about the seals—maybe a seal is waiting to give it to you in the water. This is my convergence story—not three roads—one road, but the strands I was bringing together are not wholly unfamiliar ones to you. One of my earliest stories, and in the romantic pessimism of my youth—and, I guess, to finish the story—I thought the bird would have to be killed. But of course it doesn't.

Love,

Eudora

Kenneth Millar to Eudora Welty, June 22, 1971

Dear Eudora:

It was thoughtful of you to send me the seal book, and in a way peculiarly fitting. I love seals and swim with them and play tag, sometimes close enough to reach out and touch, but I don't touch. Seals— I'm actually talking about sea lions here—have terribly powerful jaws, have to to eat raw fish. But I've never heard of one attacking a human being in the water. In fact it appears, doesn't it, that most of the tales we hear of ravening beasts like wolves and mountain lions have been invented by us to excuse our own bloodthirstiness.

Your beautifully imagined story, "A Still Moment," deserves a better response than I am able to give it. The death of the heron is superfluous, as you say, but then, given Audubon and his habits, the death would have occurred. Birds are still being killed by their closest students, and at the moment the California Condor is in danger of being studied to death, its nests invaded by the men who are paid to protect it. So there is an unexpected angry truth in your story which continues to carry a long way.

Your name has magical effects. When I mentioned to Matt Bruccoli that I'd sent his book to you, he immediately offered to send me another, so that you can keep that one.[21] I hope you like it well enough to want to keep it. He misses things but there is nothing made up in his account. Matt just phoned from Los Angeles today, announcing that he would be here later in the week for a Mexican lunch. He is in process of publishing under his own imprint (with Gale Research of Detroit) a checklist of my printed writings, including the most embarrassing of juvenilia. I feel somewhat asinine being made the subject of such a study, complete with pictures, but nevertheless I cast no insurmountable obstacles in the path of my friend who wanted to do it, indeed gave him all the help I could, and feel quite good (though asinine) about the whole thing. The truth is I'm enjoying the attention that is being given my work, while secretly doubting that it's worth that much attention. But I'm impressed by some of the people who find it interesting.—I thought the parody in the *Times* was funny but not entirely accurate. Prose parody requires at least as much skill as its subject.

I'm glad you came through your doctorates unscathed, though it was a near thing at Sewanee where you might have been beatified, in Latin, unbeknownst; but fittingly. A tendency to saintliness is your only fault. Your story "A Still Moment" is so beautiful and wise that it utterly baffles me.

Love,

Ken

Eudora Welty to Kenneth Millar, July 1, 1971

Dear Ken,

What a fine thing, to have Mr. Bruccoli's book to keep. I'd just finished it, and was about to write you how much I liked it. That was nice of him, but especially generous of you to let me keep your own copy that he'd inscribed to you and to Archer—no wonder! I value it very much. It must have been the most fascinating thing to do—even the *amount* of it was fascinating, I should guess, as long as it didn't kill him. He sorted out and interpreted and tracked down and assembled into order all that mass of evidence in a very strict way and to its full conclusion, in very much the way an author works with his own novel, I think. He gives things their true weight and clear light and identity, he sets the chronology faultlessly in line, and he cares for every word, as Fitzgerald cared. Mr. B. knows the seriousness of the word. (I was sorry to read that about Malcolm Cowley—all those silent emendations.) I trust Mr. Bruccoli. He goes to the heart of the novel, in a steadfast and undeflected way. And to the man too, my feeling was. He's so good about the magazine writing, for instance, making clear how it came out of F's lack of knowing how to manage money and not a lack of dedication. And about the whole relation between the work and the life of the man—the strange way the novel seemed to be running ahead and life coming a stage behind, to catch up and show him [by] trag-edy what it was he'd been writing about, teaching himself, and now enabling him to recognize and know. He—Mr. B—so carefully keeps in clear, in his reconstructions, what is central to the novel and was permanently so from the first—how the novel was only deepening and accumulating its strength through all the changes, and finally cohering. It's thrilling to watch the novel move into focus through this other way too—though a different experience from reading it, following all those lists and graphs. It seems almost incredible that anyone else should ever be able to find his way in another man's working papers—I felt strange following *him*, into that strange but oddly familiar country where most of us have wandered by ourselves—all those name changes, like the answering calls of birds, those transpositions and peregrinations, those recurring but indelible little pictures on the mind, those private ways to number pages and scenes. But when he'd finished, the feeling it left me with was a sense of victory more than heartbreak—it was such a beautiful novel, and it got written. And published, in spite of the poor printing it had and the bad treatment it got, in spite of everything. The fact that a scrupulously-edited edition is still needed does point a finger at Mr. Bruccoli himself, and his list of the emendations he would make is right there—but it's true, he's *done* the main thing, and what a job it must have been. I can't think of any writer who deserved it more. It was needed, and it was a real way of paying respects. All the way through the study you couldn't miss knowing the passionate love he has for Tender is the Night itself. Oh, and one of the best things he did, I thought, was showing over and over again what a good critic F. was of his own work, come hell or high water. I'm so glad that through you I got acquainted with this study. Thank you for it. I wish Mr. B. could have won at that auction—who did, something like the U. of Texas? Did he get to set eyes on the galley?

I'm glad to know about the check list—a very good thing, with plenty of space left under "Forthcoming."[22] I'm glad for his sake you're clearing his path for him this time. You *could* make it twice as *hard* for somebody, probably, in other circumstances. I do share your feeling about juvenilia. Does it have to be in? A poem I wrote to the twilight in the St. Nicholas League was published in an anthology of the magazine and I wanted to kill myself.

I'm so glad you liked the seal book. I thought you must have been close to seals, because of a character you had with sea-lion eyes, but I didn't know it was that close—to swim with them and play tag, but another thing, I liked all the oral tradition in it, the stories told in those little rooms, the company listening and helping, or hindering, and the sense of the life of another element so near as that, sometimes tragic, sometimes funny, sometimes comforting.

That little story I popped in my letter you read with kindness and I feel contrite because I didn't think to tell you what it was all to do with—you wouldn't normally know all about the Natchez Trace in the early 1800's and who was on it, to start with? The Trace was alive then with every kind of traveller there was—running as it did as the only path through the unrelieved wilderness, 300 miles from Natchez up to the Tennessee River. There were merchants going home with their gold (no way to get back up-river) and robbers and murderers and Indians and soul savers and fugitives and conspirators with world-wide schemes—and Audubon—all the seekers and bringers and takers and learners and believers—passionate times. I read their journals and records—everybody wrote things down, not only Audubon. So far as I know, Audubon and Lorenzo Dow and the outlaw never did meet, but they were visionaries all. I forgot to tell you that the outlaw was haunted by a vision that he saw of a white horse standing across his path that he believed to be Christ (he says in his diary). So I supposed what if they did meet, and their separate and conflicting visions of the world (and eternity) could converge in the given moment there in the heart of the wilderness, might they not all see the same thing? Just a bird coming down—it was too frail a thing, no dramatic force. But to me it had potency because of the rest of what I felt—that some kind of wonder or divinity is really *there* at such a moment—clear outside the figuring of our minds or the demands of our emotions or any greed to carry it off—is innocently nourishing itself, following its own course, is living and beautiful, like the heron. The story of course failed but it's oddly close to me still. You must have sensed there was a lot of my feeling in it, which made you forbearing. I still feel it. I've tried to teach myself better ways to write, to guide my characters so they talk it out and act it out, but I think they may be still saying and acting out the same thing. There are revealing moments possible in any sort of circumstances—maybe fleeting, but indelible—and they have an integrity of their own, a life. Some original wonder is still there, buried however deep under whatever human destructiveness. Don't you think?

Well, I have to get on to my latest story now, which is supposed to come out as a book by itself next spring and I want to revise it.

The title of it is (or was) "The Optimist's Daughter." —And I was looking in Ring Lardner, in *What Of It?*—the Wilmerding rooters' song is in "Taxidea Americana," I noted—and the wonderful Cinderella story told in the vernacular has this, which I'd forgotten if I ever caught on at all: "Her name was Zelda, but they called her Cinderella on account of how the ashes and clinkers clang to her when she got up noons," and "'Listen, Scott,' they says, for that was the Prince's name: 'we have found the gal!'"[23]

Bless all their memories.

Love, and I hope the attention goes on and on growing and that you feel good and happy about it. This is the way it ought to be—*don't* feel guilty at praise! Dear Ken, you have been good for a long time now. Let other people have the guilty feelings, for not having paid the right heed. Just you feel proud.

Love,

Eudora

Kenneth Millar to Eudora Welty, July 2, 1971

Dear Eudora:

I had some wonderful news the other night. Herb Harker phoned from Calgary to tell me—But let me sketch out a setting for this news: Fifteen or sixteen years ago a young Canadian Mormon, about thirty, turned up in my Adult Education writing class here and wrote a series of wildly farcical stories about American hillbillies—people with whom he had nothing to do, really. Over the years Herb and I became friends and I learned that he was a high school graduate from Cardston, Alberta, who had served in the Canadian army, studied painting briefly, then got married and made a living for his wife and four sons by working as an oil-company draftsman here and in Calgary. As a former Albertan, I tried to turn him back [toward] his roots—and he went back to Canada for a while, then reappeared here. About five years ago, under the influence of a new intellectual movement in the Mormon Church, he began to write serious fiction about the life of Mormons and, writing in the morning before work, produced a longish novel about the Saints which I thought should be published, but wasn't. Last year he finished another novel, *Goldenrod*, about a brokendown rodeo rider and his two sons. This is the book that's been looking for a home, and last week as Herb phoned to tell me, it was taken by Random House, I *think* he said by Charlotte Meyerson. Herb has been writing unpublished for twenty years; and now he'll be part of the Canadian Renascence.

Not in the same category of important events, but important to me nevertheless, is the fact that I've sort of started a book, sooner than I expected to. It's pure self-indulgence: I feel so much more natural when I'm working. Coincidentally I've decided to go to England for the publication of *Underground Man* in October. The publisher is urging me, and I really need no urging. I love England, and haven't seen it since the Fall of 1936. Margaret is thinking seriously of going along. We're not getting any younger, as they say, and M. has never been off this continent. A friend of ours at Antioch College, Nolan Miller, is opening a "European branch" in England this Fall, and he will provide another landing point. I used to thrive on loneliness but now I depend on friends.

Matt Bruccoli was here for a couple of hours the other day, and we had lunch. He said he drank champagne with you and Robert Penn Warren on the occasion of the latter's wedding. (I now have the other copy of *Composition of Tender*.)

Your "convergence" story keeps haunting me. It baffles me, as I said, perhaps because though the three men are influenced and go their ways, essentially the death of the heron leads only out of this world, in two senses. I don't believe the story of the Cairo convergence that you wrote to me about has been written yet. Could you write it from now about this? Or are the involutions of your thought beyond the reach of such a simple suggestion?

I hope you weren't offended by my joke about your beatification and your saintliness. It's no joke, really. I adore your virtue.

Ken

By July Eudora had finished proofing the introduction and captions for a book
*of her photographs (*One Time, One Place*), and she was able to work on*
expanding her New Yorker *story "The Optimist's Daughter" for book publica-*
tion. Ken's suggestion that she write about her response to seeing the convergence
of the Ohio and Mississippi Rivers at Cairo, Illinois, she would eventually take
as part of this expansion. But some time would pass before she informed Ken
that she had done so.

Eudora Welty to Kenneth Millar, July 8, 1971

Dear Ken,

We'll never have a chance to catch up, because our letters cross
every time—but that's all right.

I'm excited about your book going strong—I don't ask you about it
because I don't like to be asked about something not finished, myself—
Superstitious, I guess. But I cross my fingers—(This doesn't mean I
don't know it will be a good book.) I too feel absolutely the best
when I'm working. Glad you are. And that's wonderful about the visit
to England up ahead—I hope everything works out for you both to
go—Might you even be going on a boat? Let me know about it—

No, you made me laugh, of course, at what you said about whatever
it was the Bishop of Middle Tennessee did to me at Sewanee—The rest
of what you said came out of a sweetness and charity that has to be yours,
not mine—Ken—I thank you for it—Only I feel better to think of you
seeing me as I am, no better, (and no worse, I hope!) always—As I'll try
to do by you. I think we'd agree that if both of us were fine saints, we'd
reliably intercede for each other, wouldn't we? (Is that what saints do?)

"Zelda" came the Saturday before the 4th of July and I was so
pleased to see it—[24] Thanks for your thoughtfulness in lending it to
me—I've only looked at the index & the pictures (heartbreaking)
so far—and read the Santa Barbara paper, to see if maybe there was
something I was supposed to catch? I missed it. It (*Zelda*) is waiting
for the coming weekend to which I look forward greatly. I'm glad you

have your own copy again of *The Composition of Tender*. I won't let it shatter my faith in his work, but Mr. Bruccoli is mistaken about drinking champagne with me at Red Warren's wedding—I wasn't there.[25] Who could it have been, I wonder? I'll keep my eye out for your young Mormon, and what good news indeed. It must have made you feel terribly good—and rewarded. He's had a lot of fortitude. (People who don't really love to write don't understand how much fortitude a writer is willing to live with, and live by.) It's good he had the support you gave him, all through.

I think what your instinct is about my story is probably exactly right. I see—It would be the only real way to take hold of it. But I could do it better all new—and maybe some day I will.

This is just a little one, to atone for last time. I'm listening to my this year's best mocking-bird—new this year, and a virtuoso—he's more pearly in the breast, & plumper, than the usual, too—like an opera star. Sings on the wing—and half the night too.

Love,
Eudora

P.S. The young son of a friend I told you about that was missing is all right. He is living another life and is not ready yet to get in touch, but voluntarily called up a friend on the phone. The relief—! Though so much is still a question.[26]

Kenneth Millar to Eudora Welty, July 12, 1971

Dear Eudora:

For once our letters didn't cross, though I've been wanting to answer your fine letter about Bruccoli's book—what a pity that he should make a mistake in life after producing such a careful work of scholarship, but then surely all of us are better in the work than in the life—but I've been wholly used up this past week or so by my work and another project. I used to think of an idea over the weekend and start the book on Monday, but now it takes me endless time and trouble to get one underway. I'm not complaining, having no reason to. Like you, I'm superstitious about talking about a book in progress; also I wouldn't know what to say. Plot stories, like mine, are like a cake, useless until thoroughly baked and done. Or a page from a newspaper such as I sent you, without the essential clue to hang it on. (I wonder if the detective and thriller forms weren't strongly influenced by newspaper format, as McLuhan says Symbolist poetry was). But I included that newspaper with *Zelda* just because it was handy and thought you might like to see it, not read it.

The other project has been reading again the news of yet another friend who has placed a book. For over two years my closest friend Robert Easton has been writing a rather definitive history—technical, social, political—of the Santa Barbara oil spill. Last week Delacorte took it and proposes to put it out in both hard and soft covers, and push it. This is an important event not only for Bob Easton, whose *magnum opus* this is, but for Santa Barbara, which is still fighting the oil companies in the channel and gradually making progress. Bob wrote a beautiful book in his twenties—*The Happy Man* (Viking), about the California ranching west—but was set back hard by the war, and now after years of effort as a writer has come back rather strong. His isn't a wonderful fairy tale like Herb Harker's—Bob went to Stanford and Harvard, and married Max Brand's daughter—but it's a happy consummation all the same. Today, by way of celebration, Bob walked into the back country and caught some rainbow trout.

Our plans for Europe—you notice that England has now expanded into Europe—our plans progress, and we are now thinking seriously about going to Switzerland *before* London, and to Russia *after*. Does Russia sound far out? It isn't, really, since as I may have told you the Canadian Ambassador in Moscow is my oldest friend, and recently invited us to come and stay with him. All of a sudden it begins to seem possible. Bob Ford is a poet and very close to some contemporary Russian poets (whom he translates), and he is also close to the modern Russian painters.[27] But the main thing is that I haven't seen him for over fifteen years, and I begin to realize that I won't live forever. Russia has always fascinated me, most recently as I read Solzhenitsyn and now Nadezhda Mandelstam's *Hope Against Hope* (which I strongly recommend if you haven't seen it.) No, we shan't be going by boat—we can't stay away that long—and the transpolar planes go direct from Los Angeles to London in 12 hours. Margaret may not make it to Russia, but I expect I shall. Two days ago she bought a mink coat with Russian autumn in mind, but today she took it back, as being wrong for her: the weight of the skins of dead animals. She was right, of course, we're not too happy with possessions. Free-flying birds, yes! Our best to your mocker, and love to you, as always. Ken

P.S. I already knew about the Natchez Trace—I wonder how?—Glad your friend's son called in. There are thousands of him, aren't there?

Eudora Welty to Kenneth Millar, August 1, 1971

Dear Ken,

Did you hear them just say on the Moon: "Boy, that view is unearthly!"?[28] Isn't that wonderful? After all these centuries, the word turns into the plain literal. (Just looked it up—1611. 1. rising above what is characteristic of earth; . . . heavenly. 2. not belonging to the earth (1802).) And 1971, it's Boy, this view. (By the way, what do you think meaning 4 of Moon is: "an appearance in the sky resembling a moon"?—that's the OE meaning.)

I was so glad to get your letter, and what wonderful news about the trip. Having London in between will bring out everything strange and new in the other two. By now, of course you may have expanded to Paris and Peking. That was lovely about Margaret (may I call her?) and the mink coat. I think I understand her feeling, though I was never put to the test. (After I got home from the U. of Wisconsin, I remember, I gave my fur coat to the cook, but it was only possum! and I'd already worn it for two years, and don't believe I could have lived without it, either.) People may turn around and point at her on the streets of

Moscow, of course, for being furless. It will be the complement of that time when one of the Russian greats—Turgenev—?—got stared at, to his puzzlement, on the streets of Paris—he was wearing his tall fur hat.

Robert Easton's big book on the Santa Barbara oil spill being now about to happen and come out in a way respectful of its importance must fill you both with a great good feeling. If it will do what it should be expected to, it will reward a lot of hard work on your own parts, I imagine, and the whole community must be rejoicing about it.

And now this much lesser and only temporary nuisance of that rail strike, getting your lettuces and our chickens. And the sleeping sickness. I'm glad you're getting out of the country—into who knows what, but they will probably have lettuces and chickens and clean mosquitoes.

That was a splendid long time you had on the best seller lists, and if it's over for now here, it will just be beginning in England and so on, I hope. Wasn't it tiresome the way Time, after all those months, never did learn the way to spell Macdonald? Correcting themselves never was their long suit.

I hope the new book goes well. I agree, like a cake—like making jelly, I once wrote in a lecture on writing a short story. I'm working all day every day too, and at night at the moment reading 95 applications for grants in the humanities to be given by the U.S. Gov't. They aren't any of them alike so far. I don't mind anything but having to go to Washington to weed out the finalists. Not weed out—anyway. (Weed in?) It's interesting to know the Government can give out some of its money as well as take it in. Late, late, I read Zelda. Absorbing—I'm not certain I want her to do it, Miss Milford slowly pressing and pushing her way like an earth-mover into the old exhausted battlefields that might better be left quiet and grown over. And she writes like a witness, but she wasn't. Scott broke Zelda's vase. Zelda screamed at him. Scott hit her in the face. Scott's cousin was there for the weekend, so Miss Milford writes down the plays according to her, all fifty years old and maybe what they really meant was lost on the cousin in the first place. It may be wonderfully factual, but it may still not be true—I feel it's not. And it makes you want to warn people everywhere to burn their letters. The kind of thing Mr. Bruccoli wrote is entirely the opposite and altogether worth doing, and I so much prefer that. And of course for myself I am so much for Scott and so very partial that I expect I'm not reading it fair.

Mr. Bruccoli wrote a nice letter to me asking if I had something for his press—but I haven't just now—I would have been pleased—anything on hand that hasn't been printed already. And I had a letter from Julia Ford, also coming from the long way round through you. Mr. Lid gave her the picture, which she says she had never seen, "and I now have it stuck in the frame of a portrait of him painted by Ford Madox Brown when he was a young boy, where it makes a rather pleasant closing of the circle." So it made a message for you too.

When you wrote that the old friend you'll be visiting in Moscow is a poet and knows the poets there, I thought at once of a friend of my own who was there within the last few years, who is a poet too, and knows the poets, and has translated Vosnesensky [Voznesensky].[29] His name is William Jay Smith. We've known each other since 1950 (in Florence)—he dedicated a book of his poems to me once. They might have met in Moscow and walked down the Nevsky Prospect together, talking away about everything—wouldn't it have been easy?[30]

Take care—I hope all the plans go wonderfully well—book plans, trip plans, and all.

Love,
Eudora

(didn't know this was going to be so long—)

Kenneth Millar to Eudora Welty, August 14, 1971

Dear Eudora:

I loved what Ford's daughter Julie said about the picture you sent her, and the fact of it stuck in the corner of his grandfather's portrait of him. These chiming recurrences are really what Ford's best novels rest on and reenact, and they confirm his novels. Again, what you say about your friend William Jay Smith whom you knew in Florence sets up a new set. Bob Easton spent a year in Florence around 1950, but that isn't the coincidence I'm most struck by. For my other Bob, Bob Ford, the friend in Moscow, is a close friend of Voznesensky's and has translated a number of his poems. V. even consults him about his work in progress! All this I know by hearsay at a distance, and from the evidence of Bob's poems, which include a number of translations from the Russian. For seven years Bob and I didn't correspond. Then our letters crossed, as I told you. I heard from him once more, and answered accepting his invitation, but then for about six weeks—these last weeks—I've been living in suspense, imagining that in some way my letter had struck the wrong note, or gone astray. I wrote several more times, without response, and had just about given up—not without attempting to phone Moscow, but when my call went through it was 4 a.m. Moscow time, and I had to cancel it—when the day before yesterday I got the long-awaited letter from Bob explaining that he had been on leave for five weeks in Paris, and urging me to get started on a visa, which I have now got started on. But the suspense is only partly over. Because I'm to be the private guest of a non-Russian official in Moscow, my request for a visa will have to go all the way to Moscow and be supported by Bob there. Well, it's an interesting kind of suspense, and better than the kind which just ended, when I sometimes imagined—as I am prone to do; this is one of the scars of childhood poverty—that my old friend had snubbed me.

He never has, in all the years of our friendship going back to 1935 when we were sophomores in English and History at the University of Western Ontario. His father was the editor of the local paper (and later became chancellor of the University) and my father was dead. What equalized Bob and me was a common interest in literature, and history, which transcended everything else—in our senior year we were joint editors of the literary annual, and wrote most of it—and we were equalized further by a physical illness he had which was more devastating than anything that had happened to me. Bob was a basketball player until his sixteenth year, when some form of muscular dystrophy crippled him. He can walk, but he has difficulty getting out of a chair. When he falls down, as he once did in Trafalgar Square, he can't get up again. The worst of it was the doctors' prognosis that he would surely die before he was thirty. Well, he's 56, and going strong. The effect of his illness was to make him extraordinarily adventurous, both intellectually and physically. He went down to Cornell to study history under Carl Becker, took a course in Russian for the fun of it, and shortly became the only Russian-speaking member of the Canadian Department of Foreign Affairs. He has been to Samarkand, and the headwaters of the Amazon. In December he plans to take a trip to China.

Our youthful friendship was very close. I used to support him on the icy Canadian streets, and he always treated *me* well. He was my daughter's godfather. Our friendship persisted without words after we gave up writing to each other. When I visited him in Ottawa fifteen years ago—after not seeing him for a dozen years before that—he said we continued our youthful conversation as if we had just stepped from one room into another. Or did I say that? No matter. So you can see that my trip to Russia, if it comes off, will be one of the large closing movements of my life; closing the circles, I mean, not closing my life, though I suppose that shadow-moving is also deeply involved here. Bob of course has his eye on further horizons. He and his wife Thereza (onetime Brazilian delegate to the United Nations) are planning their trip to China in December, with Lillian Hellman!

I trust I don't bore you with tales of my friends. They are what interest me and are, I suppose, my means of writing about my life, to you. Matt Bruccoli isn't an old friend but let me say a word about him. He wrote me a detailed account of a situation which didn't occur at R.P. Warren's wedding—Matt wasn't there—but involved a kind of jollification in a classroom, with champagne-drinking—and Matt believes you were there. If you weren't, I'm not going to tell him, he's simply mistaken. I know *your* memory couldn't be mistaken.

Good luck with your writing, and your other work. You work yourself hard, Eudora, but you seem to thrive on it. What could be happier than a working writer? My hardworking minkless wife Maggie would say the same, and join me in sending you our love, as always,

Ken

Eudora Welty to Kenneth Millar, September 1, 1971

Dear Ken,

As I always am, I was glad to get your letter. By now I hope the suspense of the visa is over, that Moscow answered Yes, with your friend's help, and everything now is set. That's a wonderful thing in store—the reunion—everything coming round, and coming right.

I do like reading what you tell me about your friends, and do get a feeling of what they have meant and do mean. My own play the same large part in my life. I take it as a compliment when you write of them to me. I love and need and learn from my friends, they are the continuity of my life.

Thank you so much for letting me read *Zelda*, and I hope my keeping it so long didn't keep somebody else waiting. I'm glad I read it, had never dreamed there was all that *to* Zelda. How can she be both so monstrous and so touching[?] Those naked letters, and every line of them you had to read with her writing them and with Scott reading them. Miss M. [biographer Nancy Milford] did a thorough job, Lord knows, painstaking and exhaustive. I never did get over my basic mistrust of the whole job, though. She could have used less stuff and discriminated more. The thing she did leave out was Scott's mind— to me. The creative mind. His intelligence comes out here in his letters, and his tragic awareness, his enormous and honorable courage and killing work. But what turned his life into his fiction is not just an equals sign, is it—I think she equates them, in her biographical way, because of resemblance. A small thing—she should have known about the salamander. It was something we used to do here, look for the salamander in the fire, just as we looked for faces in the clouds. Did you? It was one of the most moving and terrible and prophetic things Zelda said—that she'd thought she was the salamander, but she wasn't.[31] I'm glad Scott died first. The deliberate acts of strength it took him to live and to give—that was made clear as a document.

Your friend Dr. Lid sent me a good Fitzgerald paper, which he said you suggested he do. It was a good thing to read right then, at the end of Zelda, as I expect you thought it would be. I liked it fine. That was so thoughtful of you—and I'll write Dr. Lid and thank him soon. I just read The Last Tycoon again the other night.—By the way, the book I sent along with Z. is one Walter Clemons had passed to me, he's reviewing it for the Times on Sept. 14 (?). I thought you might be interested in it. [*A Sort of Life* by Graham Greene, reviewed in the September 12, 1971, *New York Times Book Review*.] Did you know that Walter is going to leave the Times and go to Newsweek? I think it was hard for him to decide—I hope it will work out well for him. He'll get to review a lot, and as he likes, and work a lot at home. And those clippings I put in for cushion duty you might like to look at—and of course throw away. I love trials, and the naïve reporting thereof—the crazy verbatim remarks that find their own way into print that way in small town papers. (I apologize for the bad boy's being named Kenny.)

Speaking of Moscow, I slept in a house in Washington, since I wrote you last, that used to belong to Donald Maclean.[32] A nice house on a quiet street near the embassies. When the present family moved in, they found 12 telephone *lines* (not extensions) to the house, phone jacks in every room, and there was a pretty big switch board in the basement. One phone jack in the closet, in the room I slept in. It belonged to my friend's mother—the very room for a lady who would name her daughter Guinevere[.] Philby had undoubtedly been in that closet—or phoned in. (Nothing rang while I was there in the house—I listened.)

Thanks for your good wishes for my work. It is going pretty well— at least I have that feeling of hoping I won't get run over before I finish it. I think that's a good sign, don't you? I send everything going on in your house my best too.

A young Englishman I knew from my summer in Cambridge— he was the young student who did all the dirty work when they entertained our Conference—called me from New Orleans the other night and said he'd like to come up and spend the day. He brought a young American friend—lives in St. Louis now. They had just come down the Mississippi on a barge line from St. Louis to New Orleans—a pilot ship pushing 14 barges. They told me everything—and I love a world-in-itself of any kind, don't you? They had of course been in the confluence of the waters at Cairo. They went under the bridge by daylight, around the point and up into the Ohio, where they *held*, for two hours—taking on cargo. Then, when it was done, they just let the current carry them around and down into the Mississippi—they said it was the most graceful thing you could imagine. Of course I knew there is steady traffic in that place all the time, but these were the first people I'd ever seen who had ever, or just come out of being in it, in the confluence arrived at my house with the story to tell. I hadn't seen Michael for 6 years, and this was what he came for.

Good luck with all. Love to you both,

Eudora

Eudora Welty to Kenneth Millar, September 12, 1971

Dear Ken,

I just saw that piece of Wilfred Sheed's—in the Sept. 5th Times. I must say I think that was pretty bad of him. It wasn't a good piece anyway, it was condescending and illogical, even a little perverse. But do you think his saying all your good reviews could be a blight could *make* them a blight? I don't think so, do you? Who is he trying to scare off? But it's troubling, the fact that he wrote that.[33]

I don't understand the motive of it—I don't see how it could be critical. If it does appear to him that good writers outside the fields he accepts as interesting are infringing on others' exclusive rights by their very virtues, he's lost in the woods. Instead of being glad to find out about these good writers, he is sorry. He wishes we hadn't told him. His whole vocabulary and his whole tone struck me as intended to offend. I don't see at first sight how anything in it could really touch you or do you harm, but I don't know enough about it not to be troubled. I would so badly hate to think that rightful praise being dubbed over-praise could turn it into that frost and blight he tried to predict. I wanted to reply to him, but of course the one who could not do that, among others, is me. He also appeared to me to have a lot of nerve to say what he did on the basis of reading two of your novels, wide-apart ones, and not the new one at all, the one whose review provoked him to his remarks. That's just unprofessional, to start with. And he went so out of his way to sound knowledgable—he couldn't be, and he didn't apprehend the lovely form and working out of "The Zebra-Striped Hearse" a bit, from what he said. That he suddenly discovered you knew what you were doing he thought was *your* new discovery. He'd like you to stop right there!

Your own work is the living answer to anything he could say,—I just hate his having said it. I was interested mildly in Sheed, read two of his novels and some of his criticism, and I know he's bright, but his dark side rather scared me in the novels, and he's cruel somehow. But this little exercise, that turns into a sort of little threat, does make me unhappy. I wonder what John Leonard thought as the editor when that came in. He scrupulously had to let him say it, I guess.

Love,
Eudora

Kenneth Millar to Eudora Welty, September 13, 1971

Dear Eudora:

It's good of you to have thought about me, with such delicacy of feeling, as always, when you read the article by Wilfred Sheed. I didn't like it much, but I think I'm safe in saying that I'm not really upset by it, nor do I expect it to damage me. If he had wanted to damage me, he would have had to do a much cleverer and better informed piece (which indeed he is capable of). You can't really attack a writer intelligently without reading him, and Sheed's enormous contempt for the detective story shielded me: he didn't really think it was worth his while.—There is an irony here. I've been following Sheed ever since he was drama critic for *Commonweal* (which I subscribed to for years because my daughter married a Roman Catholic, our dear son-in-law Joe) and have read a great deal of his criticism and I think all of his novels. His most recent novel, about a critic like himself, disturbed and disappointed me, but I won't go further into that. The point is that he has been one of the brilliant comers in my book. But he has forced me to choose between my good opinion of him and my good opinion of myself. Don't *you* be upset, Eudora. We're really not. I think I'd rather be mentioned controversially than not mentioned at all; and there may be an interesting letter or two come out of it. But *I* can't write one of them, any more than you can.

We had good news today. Margaret's *Birds and the Beasts Were There* is finally back in print after several years out. It's her favorite book, and I forget whether you've ever seen it. All about our early days breaking into the birdwatching business at the same time, by the way, that I was writing *Zebra*. If you don't have it I'll send you a copy. I haven't thanked you for Graham Greene's autobiography, which I have read with interest and passed on to Henri Coulette, my friend from Pasadena who teaches at Cal State L.A. and spends the summers here. Henri, in case I haven't told you before, is a poet, and his second volume has just been published by Scribners. I read it through last night for the third or fourth time and it seemed awfully good to me. *The Goldschmitt Family*. I'd send it to you but at the moment mine is the only copy in Santa Barbara (Henri having returned to Pasadena yesterday.)

Which brings me back to Bob Ford (I don't feel safe unless I'm in touch with a poet) who unfortunately for me has been recalled to Ottawa for the Kosygin visit to Canada and will be absent from Moscow throughout the period that I was to visit him there.[34] I'm not terribly disappointed—since I'll see Bob one way or another in the next year or two—but it deprives my trip of the air of high adventure that it had, and prevents me from closing a kind of personal circle: the last time I went to Europe I spent two months in Nazi Germany. In response to my question and yours, Bob answers that he does indeed know William Jay Smith and greatly admires his poetry. Of his translations from the Russian of Voznesensky, though, Bob points out with a certain Canadian rigor that they are based on renderings into English by Russian scholars, not on the Russian originals. (This won't make your day, any more than it did mine.)

Having ruled out Russia, alas, we've got our trip squeezed down into a fairly manageable 3 ½ weeks—four days in Paris, where *L'homme clandestin* is being published October 5, the day of our arrival; three in Geneva; three in Edinburgh, where some of both our ancestors came from, roughly; three in Yorkshire, on account of the Brontes, living friends, and York Minster; and ten in London beginning October 18, publication date. I'm particularly keen about the London part, having stayed there for a month in a youth hostel when I was twenty, and so is M., who has never been off this continent before. We've both shied away from European adventures, partly on account of the Fitzgeralds' example: they're the most important couple in our lives that we've never known: and our very strong feeling that North American lives have to be lived out in North American terms. Properly, Dr. Diver's life was just beginning when he started to practice in Upper New York State. No confluences in Europe![35]

It was wonderful to hear from you today. The year is changing. I can hardly wait now to really get into my book come November. Love, Ken

P.S.—I'm sorry your generosity to me should have involved you in any way in this Sheed business. He really struck out quite carelessly at several people.

Another subject. Concerning M's *Birds and Beasts*, I have a feeling that I've written to you before. It's been much on my mind—a pleasant burden—as we've been trying to get it back into print this past year. M's editor, Lee Wright, is the one who really swung it.

K.

Eudora Welty to Kenneth Millar, September 30, 1971

Dear Ken,

I'm thinking you're about to take off—and what a really fine trip it sounds, every phase you've mentioned—I hope you're both going to have a wonderful time.

Thank you for writing me right back about old Wilfred Sheed. I was certain you would have what he wrote sized up for what it was and what it could and could not do—and I felt convinced you were accurate and also pretty wonderful about it. Most readers of the *Times* are bound to be of the same opinion about a critic who would write good *or* bad words about a writer without ever reading him. I'm looking for some letters about it. Yes, there's an irony there—and one here, of a less personal kind—I'm on a reading committee for grants, and I voted Sheed a couple thousand dollars to write his criticism, saw him get it last May. I *do* think he has talent and I was strong for him. Though "Max Jamison" [title character in a novel by Sheed] did something to me that lowered my best hopes in a rather sinister way—all that castigation in him may *all* be self-castigation? Well, he may get a dose he deserves to get now from the readers. No, I *couldn't* mislike him more—

That's good news about *The Birds and the Beasts Were There* being back in print. You did tell me a little about the writing of it. I'd like ever so much to see it, and I'd love you to send me a copy when you think about it—I'll send you something of mine in return, that ought to be in print by the time you get back [*One Time, One Place*]. I don't know if it would interest you—some of it's pictures. There are a few pages in front about a little period of my life—I think the only time I ever wrote about myself directly. What about all those French, English, Scots, and Swiss birds? Did anything ever sing to Emily and Charlotte on the moors above Haworth? You will hear—

(In Italy I once took a horse & cab and told the driver to take me where I could hear a nightingale—now I forget the Italian, which I learned for the occasion—and he most enthusiastically did. And the nightingale did.) La rossignole! Or is that the French nightingale?

How lovely to know all the time you're seeing everything you have a book to come back to. Have a wonderful time—My wishes & love to you both and to *The Underground Man* on its day in London and to *L'homme clandestine* (I love that!) in Paris on October 5—

Bon voyage and come safe home.

Eudora

I'm working so hard now. This may sound scatterbrained.

Kenneth Millar to Eudora Welty, October 1, 1971

Dear Eudora:

I was so delighted to get your letter—you may be scatterbrained with work, and more power to your writing arm, but your brains when scattered are better than other people's in full focus, and are decidedly not with their internal lightnings blind. I won't attempt to answer you properly except to assure you that the *affaire* Sheed (as we soon-to-be Parisians call it) has blown over as far as I'm concerned, and didn't really hurt much at the time. After all he merely used up a good part of the second page to question my right to be on the first page (oddly enough, I did the first page Cain review that he mentioned, too.) Yes, I'd vote him a grant.

I enclose a note from Robert Ford in Moscow (please return eventually) because I think you might be interested, in him and the situation. Certainly I'm bound to get to Russia one way or another, and have promised to go in two years. If the currently planned trip works out maybe M. will come to Russia, too.—M sent you today, via the local ARK book store, a copy of the new printing of her bird book. We look forward to the book of yours you promised, with its rare personal remarks. I find myself moved toward autobiography of late, but will postpone it indefinitely, perhaps forever. Good luck with your work, with everything. We're off Monday. Love,

Ken

P.S.—I slept in the fields one night in England and was wakened in the morning by a skylark, but never had a nightingale. Mockingbirds, yes! K.

Kenneth Millar to Eudora Welty, October 31, 1971

Dear Eudora:

Your volume of photos came, and we really loved them. Whatever you may think about the printing process—I didn't notice anything that got in the way—it must give you great satisfaction to have these tangible mementoes, so much clearer and more permanent than mere memory. I know the satisfaction we have in them, and they aren't even our memories, but as we look at the pictures we seem to see the people through your eyes—respectful, even loving, but quite illusionless. And I felt a certain envy of you for having had the wit and skill to record all that, and wished I'd been able to do the same for the Canadian countryside of my youth. Margaret's bird book, which she traded you for your book, arouses some of the same envy in me, and of course much deeper emotions in me as well, because it was about that happy middle period of our lives, between the pains of youth and the partings of age, when experience came rushing like a river in spate, and Margaret caught it. Her book has become so poignant for me I can hardly bear to read it, but of course I do. I hope some of this personal quality in it carries over to you. My favorite pages are quite near the end, about the small creatures in Rattlesnake Canyon threatened by the fire.

London was quite a pleasant place to be, but three weeks away from home were enough. Before we even got there, in Switzerland Margaret and I took a cable car to the 12,000-foot level of Mont Blanc and M. caught cold, which somewhat damped her feelings about England. But the cold got better instead of worse, and we were able to see quite a bit of London, and the countryside one day as far as Oxford. My publisher Collins gave a party for booksellers and the press, which ought to help my book if books are helpable by that sort of thing. I gave a number of interviews, trying not to repeat myself but gradually running down. Well, it had to be done, that once, to fill out my idea of my life, but I'm glad to be home with my revivified wife and my dogs who hardly seem to have missed us at all; and with grandson Jimmie, who did, and who grew an inch.

I hope we can restore hope in the world. A great deal has to do with the United States' finding itself again. This idea isn't out of place in a letter which began with thanking you for your pictures. We'll treasure them, Eudora, as we do all of your manifestations and traces, which are all of a piece.

Love,

Ken

P.S.—Your introduction seems to reveal an autobiographical urge which you should give its head at much greater length, may I say?

K.

Eudora's introduction to One Time, One Place *was in part an autobi-ographical account of her 1930s work as a photographer. The* Optimist's Daughter, *an expanded* New Yorker *story on which she had been hard at work for some time, was also autobiographical in nature, but it drew, often obliquely, upon personal and family history, both recent and distant, rather than her professional life. This translation of life into fiction, now in its sec-ond incarnation, had proved difficult. Earlier in the fall, when Eudora sent the manuscript to her Random House editor, Albert Erskine, his evaluation was very positive. But when she sent it to Reynolds Price, he expressed some reser-vations, and she undertook another set of revisions based on his reaction. Still, by November 6, the revision process had largely ended. The book that would win the Pulitzer Prize had almost reached its final form, as Eudora reported to Ken.*

Eudora Welty to Kenneth Millar, November 7, 1971

Dear Ken,

It was good to get both your letters, the one before you left for Europe and the one after you got back—and I was glad to know how it all went off and that you were home and happy to be there. It sounded as if the trip had its pleasures, though it's too bad about Margaret's catching a cold going up Mt. Blanc (she needed that fur coat after all) and about your not getting to Moscow this time—but you can do that later. Maybe when Far Side of the Dollar and Black Money are going around in Russian, you could be going around there too. Anyway, how lovely to be in London, turned loose in the streets, and when evening's coming on. I've seen few capitals, but it's the one I love best. If the Observer prints one of their good interviews about you, do please let me know—I don't see it any more. Meanwhile, I hope you're back into your new book and that every bit goes well and all to please you.

Of course I read Margaret's book with the deepest pleasure. Not only because of all it said about the birds, and so beautifully, but because of what it conveyed about your lives there and your house, all of that, for which I cherish it too. (To have put that fire into the fiction of The Underground Man—that was a deed, just like pouring water on the roof.)[36] I want to write her a long letter which is in my head. It is really a radiant book.

You were generous about my picture book—I hoped of course you would look at it as you did. I don't have much wish or ability to write anything autobiographical for its own sake though—it was only in this book as a due explanation. In fact, I can't deal directly with my own life. I've just finished revising a long story—or short novel, I believe they wish to call it—which is nearer the nerve than anything else I ever tried. It will be out in the spring. "The Optimist's Daughter" is the name of it—I will send. All Sept. & Oct. on this job I got so impatient with myself because something was wrong with my right hand—seems I've just worn it out writing, isn't that the limit—dr. says two bones scrape together. Don't worry, this doesn't hurt, because I can type left-handed and with the other forefinger—and every day I practice writing left-handed—I suppose if we had to, we could all write with our noses or with a pencil in our teeth.

Thank you for letting me see Robert Ford's letter—highly interesting. So glad he and my friend Bill Smith really did meet—it seemed they would have just had to. Bill was poetry consultant at Library of Congress that year—and when Vosneshensky [Voznesensky] came over here to read, Bill traveled some with him and introduced him on the platform and such like, and I think that's the origin of his translations, which weren't as you know actually translations from the Russian language but approximations made with help—which he could read to audiences in parallel to V's readings.

I have to go to New York in a week, to work on a committee again, and I'll remember how lovely it was the other time, when we got to meet. The days have just gotten cool here, no rain at all though—I see a number of warblers in the trees—some tufted titmice, kinglets, Carolina chickadees. For the last 2 years, some evening grossbeaks have been coming to Jackson—not supposed to ever go s. of Virginia, the book says—I went to look today, but they aren't here yet—such a lovely poetic name they have, and what manners!

Love to you, and to Margaret, and your birds and beasts. Good luck in all, Eudora

A week after writing to Ken, Eudora was indeed in New York, where she filled her days visiting friends, seeing Follies *with Jackson arts reporter Frank Hains, attending a National Institute of Arts and Letters dinner, celebrating her agent Diarmuid Russell's birthday, and working on* The Optimist's Daughter *with Albert Erskine. Then she headed to Washington, DC, where old chums John and Catherine Prince were her hosts for Thanksgiving dinner.*

Back in Jackson, Eudora began to answer letters that had accumulated and to send notes of gratitude. First she wanted to thank Margaret more fully for The Birds and the Beasts Were There *than she had in a letter of October 28, 1971.*

Eudora Welty to Margaret Millar, December 5, 1971

Dear Margaret,

I've never stopped wanting to write to you again about "The Birds and the Beasts Were There"—the special quality the book has in abundance for me has stayed with me, and I've thought about it many times. The feeling of life alive—the burst of knowledge and finding out—not only that, which is the radiance of the book and goes all through it, but the other half of the matter, the seeing it precisely and in full response, the *pleasure* of it—But the words of Keats you end with really contain all I was fumbling to say,—the gift of being a part of what you see, that's what I loved in your book. I felt this was where all the exuberance and the spirit came from, as well as the exactness, like what the bushtit knew—under which leaf the white fly had laid her eggs and where the spider had hidden his dinner fly and all of that—being nothing compared to where the doughnuts were—this example just at random. And of course the feeling in it comes through everything, and the Coyote fire made me cry not only because of the fire but because of the telling of it. And Lord, the many, many funny things—Melanie—the note to Ken to go very slowly past this window or crawl so you won't disturb them—the mourning-dove in the bird feeder—I was with you everywhere but with the rats. Not with Richard—in addition to everything else, not even sober. I loved the story of the baby spotted owls—well, I could make a list of favorite parts of the book, but I believe most of all I liked the way it came to you—the onset of that whole world, out there alive and to be learned whole, just waiting. That was beautiful. Also it makes a measure of how happy you must have been when you had written this book. Which is nice to think of.

Although before I read your book I was pretty ignorant about birds, I ought to have had a little background—if I'd had the wits, but I hadn't—because the one and only state authority on them lived in our house for 25 years, Miss Fannye Cook of Crystal Springs. In the Depression, my mother rented her a little apartment in our house. She was a lot like Miss Beals. When I read "Beals," I thought "Cook," like a password exchanged. She'd put herself through study at the Smithsonian and educated herself to the one single purpose of bird study. Never married—next to birds, she liked turtles. She began and ran the Wildlife Museum, just about on her own. She used to keep an annual appointment in the Gulf of Mexico with the birds returning from South America—she'd go out in a boat past the farthest bit of island, so she herself—an old maid sitting up in a row boat not missing a thing—would be the first landing spot the birds would see, and they'd light all over her and be too tired to know her from a post—she gave them water and banded many, and had them come back again and again to her hands. Her surroundings were *nothing* to her except for bird connotations. One Sunday morning she invited me to go with her to see some birds, and we went "across the river"—the bootleg part of Jackson (Miss. being dry)—then a nice, tree-hung river, now a drainage ditch, the Pearl—and pulled up in the yard of a night-spot called, appropriately, First Place, and parked. Miss Cook said we were likely to see both red-eyed and white-eyed vireos. Well, sitting on that bench outside First Place were what I would call red-eyed and white-eyed vireos, left-overs from Saturday night, but Miss Cook didn't waste any time noticing them. She was stopped once by a road-block on the Natchez Trace where they were chasing an outlaw in the swamps, just where she was headed, and she told the fellows she had no intention of interfering with either them or the outlaws, and she would thank them not to interfere with her, she was looking for some birds, and she went right on (She called all men "fellows.") I used to find baby hawks in the bathtub and once an owl in the refrigerator. I helped her hunt for a baby bat in the window curtains, and found it. She asked for a little warm milk, fed the baby bat from a medicine dropper, and then I saw a baby bat belch. It was not quite as long as her thumb, and looked like something out of Hell—I'm glad it's not a bird. Miss Cook herself was very elegant and stern, strict, matter-of-fact, rather impatient with human beings, and once, in the West, she was climbing a mountain and as she got level with the top she saw a rattlesnake looking right into her eyes. She just looked right back. She knew all about him.

I read a lot of "The Life of Birds" after I got onto him in your book—partly because his name is Welty—and was fascinated, though isn't his scientific language sometimes hilarious—"The magnetism of a suitable nesting site was attested by the construction by a Rufous Ovenbird of its globular mud nest on the axle of a wind-mill." And the marvelous photographs—I love best the Long-tailed Tit photographed beside his nest (His mate may have made it?), of cobwebs, moss, and hair, covered with lichens, and warmly lined inside with as many as 2,000 feathers, it's just such a wonderful picture and a wonderful creature and wonderful achievement. I love the nest of the Fairy Tern subsp. candida, that lays its egg in the angle between 2 leaflets of a frond of the coconut palm, and the natives betting on whether the young will hatch before the leaf falls. I like Cousin J. C. (I'm going to claim him) better than most other writers in the 598 D shelf of the library I've been looking into, even if he is a bit humorless and sees nothing funny in painting mustaches on female flickers—in a man named Noble painting mustaches on female flickers. But those extraordinary facts, when recounted perfectly plainly, sound like allegories, don't they, sometimes—I thought so often in the chapter about the nests.

I've got off on other people's birds when it was your birds I loved reading about. And the book brought something back to me I'd lost the feel of, in a way—the family feeling of the rush to learn, the immediate looking it up in a book, the whole-hearted plunge into the new experience—my house was like that, too, and it was lovely to be taken back into that world, a while, through the world of your book. Thank you again for sending it to me.

Please give my love to Ken too and I hope all goes well with you both. Will you be going out on the Christmas Count this year?

Love,

Eudora

Eudora Welty to Kenneth Millar, [December 5, 1971]

Dear Ken,

Just a little line in with my letter to Margaret to say I hope all goes well with you and that you're getting good work done. In New York I heard your name spoken, by John Leonard in the Times office and by Walter Clemons in the Algonquin where we were having coffee. In Westport when I brought [a] copy of my photo book out to Albert Erskine's, he remarked that a copy had been in the house but Matthew Bruccoli had been over for an evening and had taken it away with him he thought. I said good, I owed it to him. I had the feeling we might have just missed.

It's a quiet Sunday evening, a gentle rain has stopped, a camellia named Bernice Bodey has opened a flower, and a white-throated sparrow is singing, just now and then. I haven't been working because of a bad right hand—over-use and arthritis, it seems—but it's being helped and I hope to begin some stories—would love to write right through Christmas. More next time.

Love,

Eudora

Sensing a breach of decorum when Eudora's second thank-you letter arrived before his wife had answered the first, Ken responded on Margaret's behalf. For the only time in a letter to Eudora, he expressed reservations about the state of his marriage.

Kenneth Millar to Eudora Welty, December 6, 1971

Dear Eudora:

You'll doubtless be hearing from Margaret eventually—she's a much worse correspondent than I am, and that makes her poor indeed—but I do want to thank you right away for your wonderful letter in response to her book. It isn't my book, of course, but it's about the life we shared, and your letter imaginatively recreated it for me. Those were our best years, on Chelham Way. The present is good enough, with more of the same, but we've lost a good deal of our unconscious glee. Of course the book is about loss, too—the valuing of what is inevitably lost. I don't mean to sound sad—it has to be lost or losable before you can value it right, and there *is* more of the same. Yesterday, about 200 yds. out at sea—Miss Cook without a rowboat—I saw two parasitic jaegers chasing a tern and stealing the fish he had caught. They were swifter than swifts, and I never saw one for sure before, though they appear from time to time on our coast. I yelled to Margaret, who was close to shore: "Jaegers!" She thought I said *danger*, but saw none, so paid no attention. Yes, we'll be taking part in the annual Bird Count on December 19, covering the area around our house (about 2,000 acres, and 500 houses, with a mile of ocean front). I'll be doing the beach and the water, which are easy compared with the island birds—I'm far from an expert, as M's book makes clear. But I learn a little, from other people not books, every year. And I have the joy of feeding our birds every day. I guess the quail are my favorites.

I'm sorry about your hand, and I hope your letter to us didn't cost you too much pain. Arthritis and allied ailments can be a dreadful nuisance, but may I urge you not to give up on it but continue to seek expert advice. Nearly twenty years ago, in 1952, I was so badly crippled by gout that I was housebound in a wheelchair for months; wrote a whole book, a not very good book (*Meet Me at the Morgue*) with a not very good title, when all I could move was my fingers. Then pharmacology caught up with gout, and now I'm virtually free of symptoms, haven't been on crutches this year! My point is simply that you shouldn't give up on your hand, though I realize arthritis hasn't been mastered as gout has.

It was good to have word, through you, of John Leonard and Walter Clemons, whom I'm following now in *Newsweek*. I noticed there that Walter Clemons picked "Revelation" as his favorite Flannery O'Connor story. I have preferred "Everything That Rises . . ." but will settle for "Revelation." Would you?—Speaking of John Leonard and Walter Clemons reminds me that my French clippings have come in, and my favorite sentences among them are from *magazine littéraire* (Nov 71): "On voit ce qui, dans cette histoire de crime [répercutée?] sur plusieurs générations, a pu séduire une romancière sudiste telle qu' Eudora Welty. *The underground man* s'est en effet vu accorder le privilège, sans précédent pour un rom[a]n policier, d'un article en première page du *New York Times Book Review*, signé de Miss Welty, dont les interventions publique[s] sont pourtant fort rares." (!)[37]

Both our loves, Ken

And happy writing Christmas, dear Eudora. Am reading PERMANENT ERRORS—fine![38]

P.S.—Herb Harker's first novel *Goldenrod* has now been optioned for a movie. But he's still working as a draftsman in a Calgary oil office. K.

Eudora Welty to Kenneth Millar, December 17, 1971

Dear Ken,

That was the nicest thing, to get a letter back from you—thank you for it. And don't let Margaret think for a minute I expected any reply at all to my letter—I was the thanker—and after all, I know from her book how busy she keeps. The fact is, I'm the worst correspondent I know, if you go by the cartons standing around in my room full of unanswered mail—some letters 2 years old—and my conscience won't let me throw them away, though by now the writers have certainly given me up. Now & then I dust them a little, with a Kleenex, like Archer.

How fine to be getting in reviews from the French edition—and to be able to read them. It delighted me to read what that one said, what I thought he said, making you *une romancier sudiste*—and there's truth in it, don't you agree? The same things matter, the same problems absorb and enchant us all—and that is the real kinship, isn't it? But I did not comprehend that word "interventions"—which my little dictionary says means just "interventions."

We must talk about Flannery O'Connor some time. Isn't she wonderful? She can strike like a bolt of lightning (thunder?). I would settle for "Revelation" too, I think, though there are all those rivals— for the boldness and power and hair-raising wonder of the revelation itself that she makes happen before our eyes. I loved it on another count for the way she made Mrs. Turpin not only outraged that this assault [. . .] had been made upon her, but disappointed and hurt that it *hadn't* been made on those others, the white-trash, right there and ready-made for it, deserving it.

No, it doesn't hurt to type, as I ought to have told you, I just unlearned the touch system and went back to hunt-&-peck—found where the keys are again. What got me, I think, was just *where* it hit me—my right hand—where I really live, my psyche or something, but learning about anything with the other hand is a way of talking back to it. And I'm lucky—it's not the bad kind. It saddened me to know about the gout. I admire what you did and I even know what you did, in a close at hand way and dating from that same year, and the courage it took, because of my brother Walter. He had a virulent strain of rheumatoid arthritis—of which he died, in 1959, at 43—he never stopped trying, either. The wife and two little girls he left are my family now—the little girls now grown, one just had her first baby this year, the other just got married last month. I know I am blessed, Ken. We'll all have Christmas dinner together—and I hope you will have a lovely one too—your little grandson must be a wonderful age for Christmas. And I hope never the crutches again. Fine swims in the ocean every day instead, and a new bird every day—or an old bird friend.

Reynolds would be so pleased to know you are reading his book with sympathy—I'd like to tell him. It's good about "Goldenrod"—I hope the movie happens.

Good luck on the bird count this Sunday, on land and on sea— good luck on everything, and Christmas wishes to you both, and hopes and love,

Eudora

CHAPTER TWO

"We haven't known each other terribly long, but we know each other well."

———— ❧ ————

1972

IN 1972 Eudora and Ken were not able to continue their friendship "viva voce and in the flesh," but, as Ken had hoped when they parted in 1971, there were letters. There were also books: On the heels of One Time, One Place *came an Archer mystery in manuscript, then typescript form and a new Welty novel published to rave notices by distinguished reviewers. Paul Theroux, writing in the* Washington Post, *found* The Optimist's Daughter *to be "a superb affirmation of life and of healing." And Howard Moss in a front-page* New York Times Book Review *called Eudora's novel "a miracle of compression, the kind of book, small in scope but profound in its implications, that rewards a lifetime of work."*[1]

Kenneth Millar to Eudora Welty, January 1, 197[2]

Dear Eudora:

We were so delighted to see the reception of your book of photographs in the *New Yorker*. It's a permanent record of everything including you, though you are no more visible than the sun which also made the pictures possible. Now *all* of us are your fans, even grandson Jimmie who of course can't read your books—*Willy Wonka and the*

Chocolate Factory is more his speed (and, you know, it's a pretty good book)—but he can read your pictures, and did last night. The dear boy seems to be full of beans, is doing well in school and everything and has well survived a bad year.

I'm rather glad that 1971 is over. Alternations of good and bad fortune are always wrenching even when [illegible word]. May I say that your friendship and understanding both spoken and unspoken lightened the year as nothing else did. We speak of you often, and think of you oftener.

We started the new year by taking our bikes out to the University and wheeling around the campus, still empty for the holidays, until we'd clocked eight or nine miles. It was clear and bright. Those adjectives apply to Reynolds Price whose book [*Permanent Errors*] dedicated to you I finished the other week, with some of the excitement I read Joyce with when I was twenty. The same ruthless courage, moral and linguistic, yet highly original. I imagine you take just pleasure in that dedication. You know, I opened the book expecting to find your name there, and am reminded now that Reynolds Price was involved, by long-distance telephone, in the Algonquin magic. If I remember more such pleasant things, I'll have to revise my judgment on 1971. Even our Christmas bird count was the best ever in Santa Barbara: 201 species if the black-chinned hummingbird is allowed. Our important, *i.e.* unique, contribution was a pair of white throated sparrows who feed here every day, and did that day.

My agent Dorothy Olding is in town—M.'s agent, too, in fact she was M's agent before she was mine—after an unusual trip from New York via Nassau, [. . .], the Panama Canal, and San Francisco, in company with Ngaio Marsh who is on her way home to New Zealand.[2] We have lunch with Dorothy tomorrow, but before that I hope to get a stint done on my book. I'm off to a reasonably good start but the holidays have wreaked havoc on my schedule, which I suppose is what holidays are for.

We're looking forward to *The Optimist's Daughter*, keenly.

Our love, as always,

Ken

Eudora Welty to Kenneth Millar, January 14, 1972

Dear Ken,

I value so much what you told me—if my friendship helped, I am glad. You were speaking out of the deep kindness and perception of your own when you told me. 1972 will be a *good* year, I hope—everything in it, and evenly so, all the way through. Thank you for the lovely account of New Year's Day, when it was clear & bright and you and Margaret had been wheeling all around the University (making circles around the University) and the well-started novel was waiting for you up ahead. (I hope that makes circles around it too, and goes everywhere you like.)

I was delighted about the Christmas bird count, to see the unique contribution was the pair of white-throated sparrows, the ones you didn't have to go a step to see but came to you, the same as every day. A couple of their cousins live in my yard—six inches worth of Assyrian Kings, with those beards—

Jimmie looked at my pictured book? —I'm pleased. Also that you think of it as you do. —And thanks for sharing in my pleasure at what Brendan Gill said in the *New Yorker*—I was unprepared for the magazine to notice it at all, and then so generously and imaginatively.[3]

I thought, I'll send Jimmie my children's book [*The Shoe Bird*]. But I read it again, just to see (it's 1964) and it wasn't good enough. It was the best I could do at the time, and parts are all right, but it's not good enough for Jimmie. Not to mention that one of you would have to read it to him, and most of the characters are birds. I'm sending him a book of Bill Smith's poems that he wrote for his own little boys—they were younger than Jimmie is now, but I don't think poems have anything to do with age, do you? I like them.

It's good to know you think so well and highly of Reynolds Price. It will please him so to know it—and I feel he's at an important point in his life just now. He is both good and smart as a person, and as a writer he has, to me, a remarkable amount of control over a strong force of feeling, and though the control can be icy, the feeling is human &

warm. And I feel he has a lot of substance—and a lot of work yet to come. He read "The Galton Case" at my house & then everything of yours he could find—he felt some affinity there about family feeling, family mystery—he could tell you better for himself—maybe will. I was terribly pleased & proud at that dedication. Yes, he *was* part of it—he called up & was reading "The Far Side of the Dollar," open beside him. I'd timed my trip so as to see him get a prize. And all the time you were headed there to get a prize, and that's how I was there to meet you.

I will indeed send you and Margaret "The Optimist's Daughter"— there are supposed to be copies in the spring. It will be valuable to me to know your opinion, even more than it would be ordinarily, because you never saw it in its earlier version and would come to it cold & clear. I changed it some—then I changed it back some—It is so close to me that I have held onto it for two years, uncertain about publishing it alone as a book. It's about sad things—about a few of those things one can't ever change but must try through fiction to make something with. The question is, did I make it? And without doing hurt to lives I cared about? I worked & hoped—There is one paragraph in it, key, that never existed in the first version at all, and it wouldn't be there now if it hadn't been for our writing each other some letters. You will know. It came nearly at the end, where and when it came to me—came back to me.

Good luck in everything and love to you both, to you all,

Eudora

Despite the fear that her children's book was not good enough for Ken's grandson, Eudora put it in the post anyway.

Kenneth Millar to Eudora Welty, February 3, 1972

Dear Eudora:

It was so thoughtful of you to send Jimmie your *Shoe Bird* after all, as well as William Jay Smith's *Boy Blue*. He was here over last weekend, and enjoyed them both. So did I. We both love wacky humor, which is the very essence of your *Shoe Bird*, though it has its strange beauty, too.

I've not yet finished with Smith's adult poems, but will return them soon. I heard from Bob Ford the other day, by the way: for setting up the Kosygin trip to Ottawa and shepherding him around Canada (the most Bob has seen of his native land in many years) he's been given the Order of Canada, he writes, and is now, by virtue of seniority, the chief of the foreign diplomatic corps in Moscow.—Yet it seems less likely to me as time goes on that I'll ever go to Russia, or perhaps even back to Europe. Perhaps to Italy, which I've never seen. Yet the Old World is weary and wearying to me. I love the New World and value every minute here, even of pain, where I never know what is going to happen next. I don't mean this to be a Know-Nothing reaction. Bob and I "started" in the same place, with the same education. He will end his days in Paris, where he has bought an apartment, I in California on my hill, or in some adjacent valley. God knows this continent is difficult enough, but at least it is our own. Yet perhaps it could be said that Bob and I are almost equally remote from our starting place—which for the sake of the argument I take to be Ontario, though I was born here and didn't reach Ontario until I was nearly four—and that California and Moscow are both capitals of the *new* New World, they with Solzhenitzyen, we with the Shuttle? (You know, precisely because California has a foot in the future, it's taken a lead in saving the physical past, though.)

I suppose Jimmie is a boy of the future. His father is a computer engineer who helped to design equipment for Apollo (not the god) and he and his son seem to live in natural ease in Los Angeles. J. watches much television and patterns much of his behavior on what he sees (while aware that he is "acting" or, much of the time, joking); indeed, he may become an actor, a fate I once thought worse than death, having done some college acting myself; but for Jimmie it might be an interesting way to live. Really, I have no conception of what he may become. He's a fine boy with a great regard for other people, notably for his father. What more could you ask of a boy?

I'm working hard at my book and making some progress. Margaret has turned away from writing, at least for the present, and is concentrating on getting herself in shape. Last month she rode 250 miles on her bike. This month (Feb. 5) she is 57. She will meet age head-on, and refuse to grow old without a struggle. I am likely to grow old without knowing it. How well you keep the girl alive in yourself, dear Eudora, which is one of the reasons I loved your book about the Shoe Bird.

Love,

Ken

P.S. The New World: true speech, unfiltered light, few monuments; nostalgic, perhaps, but not for Europe.

K.

Eudora Welty to Kenneth Millar, February 26, 1972

Dear Ken,

Thank you for the good letter you wrote me, especially when you were—are—carrying around that novel in your head. (I like thinking of something of order and coherence and without one blessed fault being made there, some each day.) I was *so* pleased to know you and Jimmie both got some laughs out of "The Shoe Bird." It was good to know the nonsense travelled—sometimes it does, sometimes it doesn't—and to be let off for trespassing in bird country. It delighted me to be told a little more about Jimmie, who sounds one to be proud of and to watch out for, to wait and see things happen for. Think of growing up taking the Apollo connection for granted—right in the family. Like a pony.

I've had a nice piece of news I wanted to tell you—the Institute of Arts & Letters is giving me their gold medal for fiction this year. It was decided by ballot among the members, so I was pleased about that. You are always glad for the good luck of your friends, so I wanted you to know.

I've just been out west!—well, from here it was. From there, it would be just a little bit less east—San Antonio. Two friends who live in Santa Fe came there for a week—one's a painter and she was opening a new wing in a museum with an exhibition, a big moment, and I went out to be in on it.[4] Do you know San Antonio? I'd never been there—I must say I'd never expected to shed tears in the Alamo, but the sense of history and real human beings is very strong in there. Positive, and personal. The living Texans we met were 40-to-sit-down-to-dinner kind (i.e. the museum benefactors), dining room tables on two floors, and Monets on the wall—there was a little line of beautiful Mary Cassatts going up the staircase wall, that you couldn't really look at, for being too close and for having to go on upstairs—the only way you could have seen them any less well would be by sliding down the banisters. Anyway, I had a week to observe Texans in, surrounded by Texas. Had to spend the night in New Orleans coming home (I go by train) and there in Doubleday's I saw the Bantam edition of *The Underground Man*, and got me one and read it again that night. It seemed to me I saw still other new things in it this time, it yields so very much. It pleases me to have the little paperback with the bits of Walter Clemons and me, among the rest, bound in with it. By the way, Reynolds Price says in a letter—you didn't mind if I told him what you said about *Permanent Errors*?—that your words "gave me a real shock of pleasure, coming from that head, from behind *those* eyes. I'll cherish them, and hope some day to be able to thank him in person and return my own great admiration. I want to read *The Galton Case* again—it's been in my mind ever since I began my novel to read it: the father-son theme, the search."

I had a lot of other things to tell you, it seems to me—I may write you again soon—just little things, but I don't expect you to answer while you're working.

Love,
Eudora

Kenneth Millar to Eudora Welty, February 29, 1972

Dear Eudora:

It's always wonderful to hear from you, and the news in your latest letter—that your fellow writers had voted you the gold medal for fiction—made it particularly wonderful. It must make you happy to have your work so valued, after the huge delicate rigorous labor of doing it. It makes your friends happy, too. If ever a woman cast her bread on the waters, it's you. It seems to me that you remember all the things that are worthy of being remembered and then, in the gaps of existence, you invent more worthy things. It is not only for you that your life has been fortunate.

We enjoyed your quick sketch of San Antonio. We don't really know the town but have changed planes there on our way to Corpus Christi for the birds. Now we really must stop over in S.A. We'd been thinking of going to Texas this year but it would interfere with my book to go there in March or April for the migrations, and we may decide on British Columbia, later. It was there I first came to consciousness (surrounded by Japanese children!) and that province still has some of the awe of the first place seen.

I'm glad you passed on my words of admiration to Reynolds Price—such a talent needs and deserves all the encouragement to be had—but I never expected such a response from him. It makes me wish I were younger, almost. Not really. It makes me glad that Reynolds Price is young, with great achievement behind him and greater ahead.

Some of Jimmie's manly and direct and interested quality seems to have filtered through my lines to you. He's one of those young people who are so good that you wish them never to change—as we used to say, a credit to his father and mother. There's only one thing Jimmie does that after a while we have to tell him to stop, and that's play the piano. He only knows one tune—"Silent Night"—and he massacres it loud night after loud night.

Margaret's in good shape, the more so that she just sold the ten-speed bike on which she's been wearing out her knees, but she still has left a less abrasive three-speed. Spring is coming on apace, with hardly any winter (and almost no rain) to justify it. I've taken a long weekend and really enjoyed it, swimming in the ocean for the first time in a month. Yellow acacia dust is everywhere. Your letter came as part of this general spring feeling. It gives me an occasion to tell you how much I loved *Losing Battles* and love its author. Margaret concurs.

As always,
Ken

Eudora Welty to Kenneth Millar, March 26, 1972

Dear Ken,

Your beautiful letter I didn't deserve—it made me wish I did, or could some way even this late. Thank you for it. I was pleased about the medal—and now Katherine Anne Porter has told me she's the one who's going to present it to me, my old friend—since 1938—and at age 84, "wearing a beautiful white pants suit of Italian silk, darling, I'm having it made." (I went by to see her, a week ago, to thank her—she lives outside Washington and I had to go to NY for a few days—she cooked lunch, we drank champagne, talked 6 hours—Carpe diem, I know it more every diem.)[5] It snowed and snowed in NY, and the wind just howled in off the East River—but now I'm home, I can write you from my spring to yours. The stage we're having now is when the pear trees are still half in blossom and at the same time coming out in small thin bronze colored leaves, each with a silky white line around it, and the size of little ears. Every shade of gold and green and amber and pale yellow in the trees along the streets—wisteria, dogwood, the last of the azaleas, and climbing roses in the yards. When the iris come out, that will be high spring. Does the ocean change with spring too—the color or the wind or the kinds of birds you see? I hope you have been fine—swimming closer by if not in the ocean for the month you missed. And writing. Your word about Margaret and her bicycle—bicycles—leaves me in awe. I'm glad she's in shape, but how many miles does it take, and on a ten-speed bicycle? (I didn't know there was one.) Anyway, let me say a selfish wish that she's ready now to write another book. —The other night, I was looking through my sister-in-law's books for something and came upon "The Iron Gates," which I remembered having sent my brother Walter when he was in the Pacific—I'd never known he'd brought it through the war and brought it home with him, and there was his name where he'd written it in.[6] (Saw a *Publishers Weekly* with a Random House ad over several pages including my book and your friend Herbert Harker's *Goldenrod*.)

It was nice to see John Leonard for a minute at the Times—we always speak of you—and to see Walter Clemons at dinner. (ditto) He's due to write a sort of wrap-up piece on the McGraw Hill-Irving-Red Fox ring-around-the-rosy, after an interview at McG.H.[7] I thought *Newsweek* on *Time* was the best reading in the whole thing, didn't you enjoy that?

I hope you will get to pay a return visit to British Columbia, when your book is all finished. It sounds as if you should, from what you said of it. Were you the teacher? (Of the Japanese children). Once I saw the shore of B.C. only, and once only, from the deck of a Seattle-Victoria ferry, and it looked like a silver country lying up there in the morning.

I wanted to ask you if you had the two-volume edition of the OED.[8] I got sent it, for a wonderful present, the other day, and it wouldn't have seemed possible the day before that such a thing could ever be owned or in the house, just by a person. (I felt the same way about a pencil sharpener, the kind you grind with a handle, a thing I supposed only schools and offices could have—then one day realized I could too.) Now I see the dictionary right here in front of my eyes on my own table—and I hope you'll tell me it's on yours too, and you knew you could have it & I can think of you and Margaret as looking up, reading, never stopping, to your hearts' content, like me. On looking up "gratitude," trying to see how to thank my friend, I found it once meant "an expression of thankfulness, now rare" with the example: "A thrush broke forth into a gratitude of song."

With love to you and to Margaret—Jimmie too,

Eudora

Kenneth Millar to Eudora Welty, April 16, 1972

Dear Eudora:

Thank you for your marvellous letter about spring in Mississippi—it's spring in California, too, and to the delight of the hummingbirds the bottlebrush in our garden is exploding in red blossoms, and, yes, you can see the spring on its way when you look out over the sea, literally on its way, with schools of whales and flights of scoters and Bonaparte gulls and other birds all heading north (toward the silver shores of British Columbia). That's a wonderful image of Katherine Anne Porter—she'll be wearing white pyjamas when she comes—and when you tell me you had lunch with her it's as if you had had lunch with Pallas Athene. I'll never forget the impact *Pale Horse* had on me when it came out, in my first year of teaching and of marriage, I think.—Yes, 1939—I looked it up.

Leaping from great things to smaller, Herb Harker, whose book you were kind enough to notice in the *PW* ad, has now had a rousing good review from Barbara Basson (and will be getting another from me in *NYTBR*) which makes me think the book *Goldenrod* should do quite well. (I've asked Herb, by the way, to send you a copy of it because you might rather enjoy it). I think it's since I last wrote you that early one evening as I was leaving the beach on a Sunday several weeks ago, I looked up and there was Herb with his two younger boys (he has four boys, two of them through college and employed in Calgary); they had just driven straight down here from Calgary and the dust of the journey was still on them. Since then Herb has taken a furnished apartment and got back to work on his second book, after a two-year interval of anguish and delay during his wife's fatal illness. I'm very fond of Herb and his boys and think it's rather a miracle that in his mid-forties he should bring forth a fresh and lively first novel. His youngest son, Brian, is the same age as Jimmie, by the way— nine—and within twenty minutes of this meeting they were exchanging confidences about their lost mothers. Jimmie has recovered from the trauma, for a reason that can be easily stated, and was, by him, today: "I don't want to go *away* to college because I wouldn't want to leave my dad"; but Brian, much more recently bereaved, is angry and sad, while his father still doesn't quite know what hit him. Margaret and I, let me add, appear to be over the worst of our daughter's death. We find ourselves becoming interested again in the external world and even responding to it, Jimmie being our representative there. He's a good boy, and gives every sign of staying that way.

My book such as it is is moving along towards the end of the first draft. I can't vouch for its quality but am simply grateful that I was able to get it written—rewriting is less impossible. Between drafts we'll head north with the Bonaparte gulls, for a week or two, perhaps as far as British Columbia which I woke from infancy into in 1918, but perhaps not that far.

Love,

Ken

(and from "Iron Gates" Millar)

P.S. I wasn't a *teacher* of the Japanese children, I was just another child. K.

P.P.S—Am enjoying, and will soon return, Wm. Jay Smith's poems. K.

Eudora Welty to Kenneth Millar, April 17, 1972

Dear Ken,

I'm sending you my new book [*The Optimist's Daughter*] today, and want you to be sure it's coming without any pressure to read it soon or write to me what you think about it—I just wanted to send it while it's new. In fact it's so new they haven't even sent me my copies—then darn it, I found them in a store—I had to bring home a few for my friends—they're the first, after all.

I hope your own book's going exactly as you want it, and that all's well with you both—Good luck on everything.

I'm all right—needing to get back to work—a story that had me licked for a while.[9] The spring's so beautiful. Yesterday my young niece & her new husband took me up the river (the Pearl) in their boat. This inland town now has a reservoir & you can get away up this feeding river, where you could never go before. It's all serpentine & brown.— Big cypresses & forest oaks—untracked sandbars—red-winged blackbirds, woodpeckers, & an owl & probably countless other birds you or

Margaret would have seen but I didn't—I love the sign that I guess is in all marinas? "Leave No Wake"—You can't imagine how odd a boat is in Jackson.

I think of you & send love with my book. When you do sometime write me about it I'll be so glad to know but think of me as patient meantime—

Love,
Eudora

Kenneth Millar to Eudora Welty, April 24, 1972

Dear Eudora:

The Optimist's Daughter came, and I read it over the weekend. It's a marvellous piece of writing, with so much in so little space—whole families of characters, whole ranges of experience. It seemed to me that towards the end particularly, you got into quite new territory, even for you. The whole business of the mother and the "other place," under the threat of the trapped bird, and then the *confluences* opening out, filled me with joy. I felt as though I had been allowed somehow to leave a fingerprint in your enduring clay. That's too static an image. To see you flying like an entrapped bird through a house of symbols * and a community of voices. You really do fly in this one.

* A symbol is always a part of that which it symbolizes.—S. T. Coleridge

My own book, the only similarity between which and yours is that the daughter figure is named Laurel, is getting close to the end of the first draft and at least I'm past the stage where I know I can't finish it. The white-crowned sparrows are leaving. The great horned owl, the large female, flew by just after dark, which we think is good luck. Margaret is in fine shape, working slowly and bicycling a good deal. We feel again lucky to be alive.

Love, Ken

Eudora Welty to Kenneth Millar, April 30, 1972

Dear Ken,

Your letter brought me joy—The Optimist's Daughter is closer to me by far than anything I ever before tried to write, and I expect it is different—All the part about West Virginia is true fact—That's my mother and her mother and father, brothers, the place, all, and Laurel in West Virginia is me, just coming to, at the age of you in British Columbia, perhaps. Baltimore is true. The dedication is to my mother. So I am glad that the story you came to put your touch on was this one—It was part of the confluence, wasn't it? And isn't it? You had called it up and so gave me the key image, the symbol that was a part of its own meaning. It was right—you know it was *right*, but the stronger thing was it was only after time had passed—three months, or four—that I recognized this as also a part of my story. The story already existed, had been printed a year ago (New Yorker) and I was revisiting it for the book, when I saw it belonged and saw where—It was like the gong, you know, giving another reverberation. So I've wanted so much for you to read it to know what you thought of the story—while knowing you were at work on a first draft and just bringing it to an end, which is hard at the best of times, and hesitating more because I didn't want the subject of it, coming now, to give you pain, or Margaret pain. But of course I know that comes out of life itself, not the story—Thank you for your understanding in reading it right away as you did, and for your letter, which I cherish. And for the Coleridge—The fingerprint is of course unlike that of anyone else—ever. As for the clay, who can say about what may last and what will be ephemeral in stories we write, but the feeling that made them, if it travels at all, has a life of its own for a while before it's gone, don't you think? Long or short doesn't matter so much as if it lives at all.

It didn't really surprise me to know about your Laurel—I hope the draft is finished now and you can feel good about it—I'm glad Margaret is feeling again like working too. The great horned owl comes in the right hour every evening, I hope, bringing good luck to the house—

Will you get your trip any time soon? My best to Margaret—I'm really so happy to know you think as you do about my book. No matter what happens to it now out in the world, I will feel it's all right and safe—

Love,
Eudora

The "key image, the symbol" credited to Ken had surfaced in Eudora's memory almost a year earlier when she wrote to him, and he had subsequently asked her to use this very memory in fiction. Now she had. As The Optimist's Daughter *draws toward its close, protagonist Laurel Hand dreams of the train journey she and her late husband, Philip, had shared from Chicago to Mississippi en route to their wedding. In this dream Laurel recalls the moment on a high railroad bridge when she and Phil "were looking down from a great elevation" and could see the Ohio and Mississippi Rivers "moving into one" even as the trees along the shore seemed to converge on the horizon and the birds above flew in a V-shape:*

> All they could see was sky, water, birds, light, and confluence. It was the whole morning world.
>
> And they themselves were a part of the confluence.[10]

For Laurel, this dream embodies the continuity wrought by love, the living nature of memory itself, and the confluence of lives that her husband's death has not ended, a confluence as powerful to her as that of two mighty rivers. For Eudora, creating this passage, as Ken had suggested she should, also marked the ongoing confluence of her life with his.

Kenneth Millar to Eudora Welty, May 31, 1972

Dear Eudora:

It's time I acknowledged your lovely letter, which I've had for nearly a month. The month has gone by like a dream while I got my ms ready for the typist and started feeding it to her, madly rewriting as we go. I haven't the faintest notion how it might look to someone else, but at least it's getting finished. In the evenings Margaret and I have taken up bicycling regularly, up and down the hills of Hope Ranch where we live; at least I've taken it up, she's been doing it for years. We seem to have turned a corner in our lives, away from the past to the future, or is it the present? The present is probably best—it's the time of the world of nature whose outskirts we live on. There are quail all over the place these days, vociferously organizing, hawks in the air, and vultures—five vultures at once yesterday, circling tipsily over the house—a good omen in my book.

Jim and his father have been coming every weekend, and they've taken great steps together in the past year. "My dad" is the phrase most often on Jim's lips; he is determined to be an all-round boy, and indeed it seems to come easily to him. Important as our friendships and other relationships are—perhaps I should except the relationship of love—these family comings-together seem to be the essential ones in life. As your new book says, I think. It's been interesting to watch the reactions of other minds to *The Optimist's Daughter*. Your book is being read with understanding. Of course it's done with exquisite clarity. But its subject—one of its subjects—the pain and the possibility of growth—is not too common in American letters. Pain is so much regarded as merely terminal. It was sweet of you to be afraid that your book might hurt us, as if anything originating with you could. We have learned to live with the fact of death. What other way is there to live? I'm so glad that the Other Place actually was your mother's, and can imagine the shivering delight you took in feeling your way back through time almost to the verge of consciousness, and then in a way beyond it into your mother's childhood world.

We didn't take our trip after all. I wanted to stay with the book—my motto is "if you stay with the work it will stay with you"—and the biking evenings have been a perfect substitute. Maybe later in the year. Meanwhile we travel a good deal in Hope Ranch. (Did you know that our Santa Barbara Christmas bird count was second in the country to Freeport, Texas?)

This is a year of great fulfillment for you—enjoy it, dear Eudora. (We enjoy it with you.)

Love,

Ken

Eudora Welty to Kenneth Millar, June 10, 1972

Dear Ken,

Your novel's with the typist—hooray! I've been gone three weeks and my mail came out in a sack, and when I untied it and reached in to pull out the first letter, it was yours, with this good news. I hope when you see it all typed out it will seem in every way good to your eyes, or just ready to be, while you've got your pencil. I don't see how it could be other than pure excellence. Of course I want to read it so soon as I ever get a chance. Walter Clemons and I were both outdone at that interviewer from Esquire who had the nerve to come to see you after having read only three of your books.[11] "And not even The Underground Man—can you imagine?" Walter said. "He ought to be consigned to Infamy where he belongs." It was nice to read things you'd said, nevertheless, even though it must have been like talking into a vacuum, with a man who couldn't follow up anything you'd said or go on to any connecting point. It was nice to see the picture—and to see that Jimmy looks so exactly what he sounded like from your letters, a beautiful and manly little boy, and if ever there was a picture of a boy growing tall while you're looking at him, this is it.—I know Walter was thinking how good an interview you and he could have had together. (I wish Newsweek could do it twice, then Walter would get his turn.) (He will manage it some day.)

Thank you for watching out for my reviews, and for being happy for me at the good ones. It always seems such a miracle to find your book has met with understanding after all, and well I know I am blessed, with reviewers who have the rare qualities of Walter and Howard Moss and—do you see The New Republic?—James Boatwright.[12] It makes me wish, not for the first time, that you could have had through all these years and books the same understanding. You haven't had at all, and still can be glad when it comes the way of others.

New York was lovely—a number of my old friends were there at the same time, and I felt in the middle of my favorite people the day I went to get my medal. I thought of you when the grey-eyed goddess appeared in her white silk pants suit—just as you said. It was gallant and wonderful of her to come, and she was having the time of her life then at the party. With that white pants suit she wears quite a good deal of emeralds. In glory, really.

June 14—This didn't get finished, and I'm glad because I get to add onto it after your second letter came today—with Jim Boatwright's review in it, the very one I wanted you to see! Thank you for such kind thoughts about my book—you are right, of course, and I feel how wonderfully they have each contributed some vital thing to what has been said about it—It's astonishing.

As it happened, I just met Jim Boatwright—who is just as nice a man as he could be—I came home by way of Virginia, and he & Reynolds Price and I had a weekend in the Blue Ridge around Lexington—A heavenly part of the world, but having just come out of *those* mountains I am staggered by your account of those bicycle rides up & down yours. One more feat you can do probably better than anybody else, except I hear Margaret's bell ringing merrily along beside yours. How does the typed job look? Tell me some day. How soon before we get to read it? Luck and love from Eudora

P.S. *Goldenrod* is here—I want to read it soon—

P.P.S. I'm so glad you like Henry G.! The *Concluding* passage I love most is about the starlings at evening (the night of the dance).

Kenneth Millar to Eudora Welty, July 22, 1972

Dear Eudora:

It was wonderfully generous and thoughtful of you to send me Reynolds Price's volume of essays [*Things Themselves* (1972)]—which I am enjoying—and a *double* stroke of friendship to send it to me via Price himself. He enclosed a moving letter which quite astonished me. All three of us seem to live very much in feeling—the only way to live. *The Optimist's Daughter* has sent me back again to your early stories. I love them all but this time was particularly struck by "Death of a Travelling Salesman." *Daughter* is not your first deeply dreamed meditation on death. The enclosed piece by Alan Pryce-Jones from *TLS*, by the way, doesn't say very much but what it does may be of interest to you.[13]

I seem to be approaching the end of the rewriting of my new book (Sleeping Beauty?), having never worked harder in my life, I'm happy to say. I think it has turned out okay, at least it's a little different; will be eager to know what you think of it. It's rather fun to come up out of a book and look around and see the world again. It looks pretty good. M. and I have taken to bicycling in the evenings between dinner and sundown, a fine way to end the day, and we know all the dogs and most of the birds within five miles of here. From the hills we climb, on a clear evening, we can see the channel islands twenty-five miles offshore gleaming in the late sunlight like a legendary country. For the first time in years I feel like visiting the islands again. I had a chance to go to Africa with a group next week, but turned it down. My typist is going, though ("And as for living, our servants will do that for us") which is one reason I've had to get the book rapidly under control: nobody else but Alice can read my writing, or so they tell me.

I should explain that Alice is not a "servant"—I just couldn't resist the quotation—but a friend of long standing who does this typing primarily because she wants to. And how can she afford to go to Africa? Well, one of her daughters inherited a small fortune from an aunt, Alice's sister, and later the daughter married a wealthy young man. She thereupon gave her mother $100,000! This will come in handy not only for trips to Africa, since Alice and her husband George are approaching the age of retirement.

I thought a year or two ago that I might be approaching that age myself, but things have changed—you being one of the powerful changers both by precept and example (your recent book was a notable action as well as a notable book, and has been widely recognized in that light); and now I think my life will go on in full spate until it stops.

I wish the same for you. I wish you renewal again, and am sure it will come.

Love,
Ken

P.S.—Got more Henry Green from England—*Party Going* and *Living*! Do you like Ivy Compton-Burnett? K

Eudora Welty to Kenneth Millar, August 6, 1972

Dear Ken,

Thank you for that letter—everything was such good news. It's so cheering to know you feel really fine again—for keeps, too, is the feeling I get from your letter. I'm admiring and glad and believe very much in all that lies ahead for you—as I'm sure you know. It's grand news about the book being really done and those few quiet things you've remarked about it, when put together, make me even more anxious to see it than I would have been anyway. Now I've been told the title—with a ?—so I've possibly read two words of it. "Sleeping Beauty" sounds full of good omen—Many wishes for it, clear through—

It did please me to know you had received Reynolds' new book and were reading it with such interest—You wrote him a wonderful letter—he told me how happy & excited it made him. There *are* certain ways of feeling that join us all, I think you're right, and certain themes, too. I don't always agree with Reynolds, which is immaterial, but I am so *for* him in this book as in all of his. But my understanding of a writer still comes to me best through the stories he writes—comes fullest.

The Xerox* I made you is out of an old Paris Review I tracked down—I thought you might be interested or amused by some things in it. And also I find I have two copies of *Caught* so I'm giving you one, in case you have a wish to read it—it's the war. So is *Back*, but *Caught* is the Fire Service one.

Did I tell you I know Henry a little? Back in the 50's in London, I met him at a party—well, it was a party for his book that was out that day—*Nothing*—so that would be the year. Then I saw him after that a little and like him so much. I'm telling you so I can explain how I know one more thing connects up: he loved more than anything, he told me at length, coming upon the person, the family conversation, the story, that is a link—that fills in the long connection with the past that's missing (personal past always, I believe I'm right)—He wanted really to touch the person who'd touched the person who'd touched—who'd spoken & listened & knew. "The only thing is," he said, "when you *find* that person, they don't remember the right thing, do they ever? The very thing you've waited panting to ask"—Well, that's the fate of life, often but not always, that books can improve on. Yours in particular.

Thank you for the TLS article, which I never would have seen—It was nice to have the notice in an English paper, and maybe it's the very thing that helped decide a publisher over there to take on *Optimist*—I used to be always published over there but nobody wanted *Losing Battles*.

"Death of a Travelling Salesman" was my first story—I'm pleased to know it stands up for you—I wrote it when I heard a travelling salesman tell about "borrowing fire"—it was what it took to make me see the whole thing, and when I think of the story now it's in those words.

—The loudest *whirr*—I wondered if some helicopter was trying to land in my yard—It was a cicada (? A "locust" is what we say here) caught by a cardinal, and making that noise non-stop, like a stuck car horn—The cardinal had him on the ground while his mate looked on from a branch right overhead. The locust as big as a mouse! But the cardinal got away with him, (solo—didn't give any away) though he must have finished up deaf, as well as fat.

Some other things I wanted to say but now they have to wait till next time—*I'm* deaf!

That was a lovely story about your typist.

Thank you for all in your letter and the wishes for me. Mine to you. My best to Margaret too, and love,

Eudora

I kept thinking how you hated that fire up north of you.
*Couldn't find an envelope—I'll mail tomorrow. It's an interview with Henry Green.

I got Bill Smith's books back safely—I meant to tell you—Thanks—

Kenneth Millar to Eudora Welty, August 8, 1972

Dear Eudora:

I can't think of anything I'd rather have than, at your hands, a copy of a Henry Green novel I haven't read. I haven't read *Caught*.—I've had the enclosed book here for several months waiting to be sent to you but I wanted Hank Coulette to write in it and he has been in Europe, in Paris where his father was born and graduated from the Conservatory before he (père) emigrated to the States, and in Warsaw and Krakow where he (Henri) read at the universities under the sponsorship of Zbigniew Herbert, who is quoted on the back of the jacket. Donald Justice, who is quoted on the inside flap, says there are three writers whose books he watches for in the bookshops—I'm not making this up!—Agatha Christie, Eudora Welty, and me. I'm naturally pleased that *The Optimist's Daughter* is being published in England, but rather shocked that *Losing Battles* wasn't, or hasn't yet been. I think it's a wonderful book, and so would a lot of Englishmen—a book I expect to reread and reread. I'm so glad you intend to go on writing—you *have* to as long as you keep improving. You give the impression of being able to glide effortlessly at this level until you're a hundred. Which I hope you do.

Two days ago a prof. of math named Paco Lagerstrom rushed up to me on the beach and announced that he had seen a condor circling high over the Biltmore Hotel, where he was staying (the man not the bird.) Well, it turned out to be a Magnificent Frigate Bird, actually rarer than a condor on this coast though common enough, as you know, on the Gulf. It was the second Frigate Bird seen here in recent years. I missed this one. But yesterday a Caspian tern went by.

Maggie and I are doing a lot of biking in the evenings, did I tell you?—close to a thousand miles in the last three months, between dinner and dark. We both feel good. The days float by very quickly now that I'm not working, just catching up with my friends. Tomorrow I have lunch with William Eastlake and W.H. Ferry, who have been active in the anti-war movement. Today Hank Coulette was in town, and I asked him if the poem on page 43 was not the origination poem of the Goldschmitt volume, and he said it was, with those that follow. I hope you like them. If you do, I'll send you his long poem about Paris during the war.

Thank you so much for your dear letter. Love, Ken

Eudora Welty to Kenneth Millar, September 15, 1972

Dear Ken,

I was delighted when the copy of *The Family Goldschmitt* arrived from you, and autographed too by Henri Coulette, and since then I've read the poems two or three times around—with increasing pleasure. They are new to me, though Mr. Coulette's name I've known through you and others, and I find them full of refreshment and funny a lot of the time, while certainly *giving pause*. Vigor & wit branching out all over. I may not understand them all rightly, or yet, but I am not through reading them yet. I feel very much pleased to have a chance at meeting a poet and friend whom you think so much of. The little incidental things that amuse me—one is the poem about the concierge at the Hotel des [Saints] Pères. In addition I admired it for a personal reason—I *know* it's the same Madame who was the galvanizing presence when I stayed there for a couple of months [in 1949] introducing myself to Paris, same way. —I felt a pretty sharp summons from her out of that poem. Her eyes *were* like ice cubes, real life came back, like her following glance clear out of the poem. It was a sense of the inscrutability & defiance in all taken-for granted things, like our own skins, our left hands, doors—that pleased me most. Thank you for sending it to me—I treasure it. Thank Henri Coulette for signing it, too.

I'm afraid this sounds inadequate because I'm writing in a house full of banging and footsteps on the ceiling & stairs, and in a sifting of plaster dust and just dust—getting the whole house sheetrocked. How do you best the cracks that must appear out of *earthquakes*? We live on shifting clay right on top of a salt dome, so I've read—anyway, we *slowly* crack—it takes about 3 years not 3 seconds. (I'm talking about houses, not people!) So finally I'm getting this done in the hope it'll stave off some of it—Anyway, I hole in, in this room or that, leading a very odd displaced life, & reading in the daytime, which to me seems dissolute. Have you read Julian Huxley's *From an Antique Land*?[14] I never had before—it's got wonderful things in it. When a strange bird comes out, I think of the Millars. For instance, in the Colonnade of Palmyra, out came a covey of sandgrouse. He describes how they adapt to the desert—"The adults gather each evening to drink at the nearest oasis maybe many miles from the nest; after satisfying their own thirst, they wet their breasts thoroughly and fly back to let their young suck the moisture from the damp feathers." He heard a Great Tit in Petra.

Are you still cycling every evening, & far & farther? *When* is the book? I feel so anxious to see it—& wish all the good things for it. Early in the fall?

Mr. Bruccoli's book finally got here—I ordered it a long time ago—it was your name that jumped out of the page (as did the lines from *The Galton Case* at the head of a chapter in *Hoax*), in the quote you gave it.[15] Shall read soon. And I *missed* your review of *Goldenrod*, I don't always receive my *Book Review*—which I'd like to find. I did enjoy the novel—from that belt-buckle the size of a postcard, I began to see his virtues. The children were the best things in it, to me. I sometimes wished his hero could *think* better—(I know I speak as an author pretty prone to nitwit heroes.) But strength and a feeling of & for the physical world were there, & unfailing. Central. Are they making the movie? And what of the movie of *The Underground Man*? Are you content about it?

(Big bang.)

The long dry spell we've had for two months just never lets up—I keep the sprinklers going and this is nice because of all the tiny birds

I might not see otherwise—I've seen—I *think*, but I just have a book to go by—parula warblers—& I know the kinglets & chickadees & gnatcatchers—In the magic early hours before the workmen get here, I sit by the window drinking my coffee & watch them play in the water.

About that condor you were hearing of—do you remember?

A condor who couldn't call quits
Was giving the bird-watchers fits—
Simply besotted
With being spotted,
He booked himself in at the Ritz.

(I had to change his reservation from the Biltmore, couldn't rhyme it.)

Forgive the poor letter that comes late to answer your fine ones. I'll write when all is straight in the house again. But it's nice to learn the terms of these sheet-rockers—"I've just got to float out a few little seams"—

Happy coming-out to your *Sleeping Beauty*, and love,

Eudora

Kenneth Millar to Eudora Welty, September 18, 1972

Dear Eudora:

A condor who started to tilt more
And more said: "I can't stand this guilt more.
(This weird existential guilt more.)
I'm retiring from soaring
And, though it is boring,
Shall live out my days at the Biltmore."

But as I think I may have mentioned, it turned out to be a Magnificent Frigate Bird. (We didn't see it, but once saw one on Padre Island—a *truly magnificent* bird said to be over seven feet in wingspread which is almost comparable with the wingspread of the condor. A condor *was* seen in town a few days later, soaring over the Old Mission, so we feel ever so slightly in touch with the primitive still. We're in the habit of calling him our canary in the mine.) We haven't really begun the season's birding, which comes to a climax in the Christmas Count in which last year S.B. placed second in the U.S.A. in the number of species sighted. I don't mean to boast—sometimes I think bird-watching is this city's major activity, and there are over 750 members in the local Audubon Society. And a lot more birds than that—I think some 340 or 350 species year-round.

Your response to Henri Coulette's book of poems was wonderfully generous, and Hank will be just as pleased with it as I am, and with the fact that you and he apparently had the same *concierge* in Paris. Hank has a difficult life preserving his sensibility and humor while teaching under the somewhat regimented conditions of a giant education factory which is, however, his own alma mater. After his father's death he went to work as a printer's devil in his early teens, missed high school entirely (claiming to be the only Ph.D. in the U.S.A. who never went to high school) but wangled his way into Cal State L.A. and took his doctorate at Iowa with a volume of poems. I'll send you his first volume, which contains one of the best longer poems written in this country since (and about) the war. Hank comes here for the summer, which is how I happen to know him well.

I'm glad you thought reasonably well of Herb Harker's book. Herb suffered the even greater deprivation of never getting to college. He turned up in his early thirties, some fifteen years ago, at my adult education writing class and while I can take small credit for his achievement—he's a natural—I'm very happy about it. His book is doing well enough to support him while he writes his next (he wrote *Goldenrod* while supporting himself as a draftsman) and there are movie offers, though none nailed down. After growing up in a society—Alberta, which I know—where literary arts are not valued, now his whole life has changed.

I've been meaning for some time to ask you a question, and your warm interest in *Sleeping Beauty* has encouraged me to come to the point. I'd like to dedicate the book to you. Would you object? We haven't known each other terribly long, but we know each other well, do we not, and if I have to wait to a later book my writing may fall off in the meantime. I hope it hasn't already. Being in touch with you this past year or so has been an inspiration to me. I hope you will take the risk of letting me put your name on the dedication page.

The book won't be out until April or May of next year. I just sent in my corrections last week or so. My editor, Ashbel Green, recently sent me your *Washington Post* interview which I thought was absolutely splendid, moving and true.[16] I hope you were pleased with it. I'm also very glad to learn that you are bringing out your Lectures. A man who lives down the road from me, former professor of U. of Minnesota who retired to write—his name is Ted Clymer—Ted Clymer told me he heard you lecture at the annual meeting one year of the National Council of Teachers of English, and you held the vast audience spellbound.

Caught is terribly good, so good that I'm saving it to read all at once like a poem. Love, Ken

P.S.—Liked *Hoax*, too. Have you seen *The Santa Claus Bank Robbery?* (1920's Texas)[17]

Eudora Welty to Kenneth Millar, October 2, 1972

Dear Ken,

Your letter has made me happy, proud, elated, and so moved by your generous act of friendship—I feel you must know it, but I was so late with telling you! You did get my wire, I hope—I'd had to go to Washington to a meeting, then I stole a few extra days in New York (I cast a careful look around the lobby & dining room of the Algonquin, thinking, then, it might be time for you to come in about your book) and had got back just at dark to my house torn up by the workmen who're doing a month's job on it—no lights in the front part, and wires and telephone cords and drop cloths in the hall, just a path between sheeted furniture—then back in the breakfast room there was a light that went on and under it on the table a little heap of mail with your letter, and after the excitement of reading it I saw it was *ten days* old—you must have wondered why in the world I hadn't answered. So I made my way out again & went downtown & sent the wire, though they wouldn't accept it for delivery that night. On the way home I remembered the other time I got in from N.Y. to find a days-old telegram under the door from John Leonard asking if I'd review *The Underground Man*, and how I'd gone out again that night too to send him a wire, and so afraid I'd be too late and he'd let somebody else have it. I wish I could tell you how much I value and cherish the dedication of your novel. You would have to already know and I trust my feeling that you do. And I am so anxious to get a look at the book. You will manage me a chance for that when you can, won't you? The one thing I know about it, aside from the name, is that it's good. You do know you can't write any other way. Never can.

I saw Walter Clemons in N.Y.—he's bought himself a nice old brownstone directly across the East River from his office, in Long Island City, and fixed it up with a vacant lot behind it transformed into a garden & patio, and is as happy as can be. The only thing still to come is his piano—did you know that Walter is a first rate jazz pianist and once made his living in a nightclub?

I loved your Biltmore lines—I'll write you again and answer the rest of yours before long—If this has sounded not too coherent, it was from my joy about *Sleeping Beauty*. But that will go on.

Love and gratitude,

Eudora

Kenneth Millar to Eudora Welty, October 2, 1972

Dear Eudora:

I was so happy to get your wire—it was good of you to wire—and am greatly looking forward to ornamenting my book, such as it is, with your name. Everything you do is done with such generosity of feeling, the value of occasions is doubled and redoubled. For me this is a great occasion. I wish I could provide a great book to go with it. But we do what we can.

It's just been raining lightly for an hour or so, the first real rain we've had in the last eight months, and though it's stopped now I hope it's an earnest of what's to come. Our drought has been the worst here in a hundred years, and we've had to overdraw on our water supplies. There's only one possible advantage in this, that it may slow down the influx of population which has been the ruination of so much of California. I hope I'm not anti-human but I'd rather look at a flock of birds than a flock of people. This has been a great season for terns, by the way, with five or six species fishing in the channel for the past month. And have I mentioned that the pelicans are reinstating themselves here after near-extinction—flying in from Baja California? I see them every day when I go down to the beach. They've hatched a few young here, too, since the DDT ban.—I've been reading Hawthorne chronologically, with respect bordering on awe; it's like watching the (or a) American soul being created before one's eyes, taking us from the frontiers to the brink of Henry James. Love, Ken

Kenneth Millar to Eudora Welty, October 10, 1972

Dear Eudora:

I dreamt of you last night and this morning on the wings of the dream I went down to the P.O. and got off to you a typescript of *Sleeping Beauty*. It's actually a Xerox of the original typescript before it was fully corrected and I included with it some carbons of later corrections which you can disregard or not as you choose. I don't know what you will think of the book but it has honest work in it, and some of the things that concern me. I've been creeping up for some time on that avgas spill, which actually occurred on the ship I was on off Okinawa, and I still don't know for sure how it happened or who was responsible.

My sleeping dream was happier than my waking dream. I dreamt that I was visiting you in your house which seemed to be undergoing renovative construction as indeed you told me it had been. A good deal of bicycling also went on. There was a social gathering, and you fed us with the help of a black mammy. (I'd been looking at your photographs recently.) The only dialogue I recall was from me to you. I said: "You make me happy." I say it waking, too. Love, Ken

Eudora Welty to Kenneth Millar, October 12, 1972

Dear Ken,

To let you know the manuscript came, safely, and it's just wonderful of you to have sent me this early look—an answer to a wish is what it is. I am so happy about it, and now with it, right here on my table. I'll be *in* it, happily and on the instant—I just wanted you to know it was here, and I'll take care of it and get it back to you—you really were doing an angelic thing when you did this, more than you know, with a timing that makes a great difference—I'll write you after I've had the joy of reading—Thank you—Love to Margaret and the Santa Barbara birds too. And thank you for your letter—Love,

Eudora

Eudora Welty to Kenneth Millar, October 15, 1972

Dear Ken,

You've made something unique, and all so quietly—I wish I could tell you how much I love and admire it—You said it was different, and it is, but it seems to me more of a continuation, in the natural logic of your writing, a pushing further of what you always knew how to do. This has been a wider fling of the net—you've caught together (& shown they belong together) not only families but powers—which are a family too—and that felt pattern—felt already on page 35—it's extraordinary work—is going to make all *one*, every component part, connected as only you know how to do, but this time the connections will bring together & relate not only human beings, but those stronger, older *giants*—greed & fire & waste & hurt & killing—all kin. And your story, with its delicate sure threads, holds the double thing together, holds idea & act & meaning in one—with mystery kept central, at the heart, where it belongs—the urgent meaning of a human life or a death, that needs to be found out—"It's what it's all about, isn't it?" Lampson says. You could say it's another part of the forest, but your same vision, so unmistakably your own, is turned on it wide & clear & full—That's what matters, what makes it. The novel has so much authority and force from your long thought and feeling—there isn't anything in it that doesn't speak its meaning. It's very beautiful. I felt constantly moved by it. I read it straight through, twice, on two days. The admiration I feel for the making of it is more, even, than I've felt for all the other novels you've done. I'm glad you sent it in the manuscript form, those pages brought what you were doing even closer to another worker. I have always thought so much of the carefulness, caringness, of your writing, its particularity and evocation (I can't think of a word now that ought to say it better) and this time it made new ways for work, I felt. The way the scenes are lit is just wonderful—the lonely scenes & the crowded ones—the shadows so *there* with those walking. There's the sense of the world *as* a world—a planet—and of the cliff-edge of the world—and the end of the world—and the campfires & caves & shelters & way-station along the edge of it—people only waiting—All the fires—each isolated seemingly at first, but all one, another family— and the violence breaking out in sparks like the fires again, only banked up in time. All black & white, the color going to ash. It's all this set against human vulnerability—in the helplessness and beauty of the girl Laurel. And not the least of the book's real daring is your keeping her from view, and always in the mind, in her danger, until the very last page—a page so moving, and so like magic—with the fall onto those black rocks at last, & the smoke coming swirling, and the kiss and the sleeping beauty found alive, beginning to stir—and all brought about through, not magic after all, but Archer's knowing—work & faith, in the end. Archer is the best he's ever been, in this one.

It seems to me that in writing directly of themes that engage you, have engaged you, so closely, you've found material of quite marvelous possibilities, in *your* hands—in which your story's particular realities and its images & symbols are all but identical—you made them so—the spills, the fires, the endless city, the lights—And the *birds*—The birds moving through it are very beautiful and not for decoration but to express what's important to you, to the novel—Just by being, they're the advocates of the other side. One source of the novel's fascination is the constant sense of opposites you keep up—the opposite of all the dreadful things happening in the living and fleeting presence of beauty—the birds. It makes us always aware of the vulnerable heart still alive in the world and in danger—which is what your book is about. They were marvelously entered into the shooting scene. And there's that sentence, "As if to preserve some kind of natural balance which required live things to be in the air at all times—" It brings tears to my eyes again just to repeat it. Nobody else at all could ever have written that. Sentence by sentence, all of it, the story's intertwining situations, seem to reflect the overarching truth of what we're doing to life in the world, & what we're failing to do for one another. The characters are shadow-casters, there at their fires—

It's a deeply moral book, and you've made every aspect of that visible, dramatic, and haunting. Sometimes I was put in mind of the passionate & mysterious lithographs of Goya, made out of *his* time. Handling these personally meaningful things could not have been easy. (So terrible about Okinawa—) But you've been able to make them parts, rightly related parts, of a piece of work that has goodness—a beautiful piece of work, unique, and signifying a great deal.

I was glad to hear about that dream. The dialogue turned things around a little—you're *giving* happiness, Ken. I was happy to have the book come on the strength of the dream. I think it was on the strength of knowledge, too—that I couldn't have waited till spring to read *Sleeping Beauty*. I am so filled with joy and pride to have my name on that page—

And how lovely to come on those names and things I knew—not only Laurel, which you'd told me about—*Permanent Errors!*—

If you and Margaret had headed this way when you started riding in the evenings, & just kept coming, you could have been here by now—I'd thought of that. When the house is fixed, come really.

Love and wishes, and all good things to you—& to your beautiful book—Eudora

I'll send back the ms. soon—it *was* so generous of you to send it.

Kenneth Millar to Eudora Welty, October 23, 1972

Dear Eudora:

What a wonderfully generous response you made to me and my book. I abandoned myself to indulgence and simply sat and read your letter over several times with tears in my eyes. It was one of the great moments of my life. Thank you particularly for mentioning Goya, whose work I so love—just to be mentioned with him, however undeservedly, is thrilling. But apart from matters of relative excellence—and of course I know I don't belong at Goya's end of the scale—it's so very satisfying to have a dear friend and good artist discover some validity in my attempt to make something striking and true out of the popular art and common tragedies of this time. And without ever mentioning Vietnam, the book is somewhat about it. Our destruction of Okinawa, while militarily necessary, I suppose, was the prelude and preparation for Vietnam. I must add, by the way, that while our carrier had a gasoline spill during that battle, the ship did *not* blow up, so I wasn't writing directly about personal suffering. The present suffering, by which I am physically unthreatened, is (morally) worse. And it had its roots in the loss of virtue which gradually occurred among our fighting men, and society, during the long last war—the transition from a tradition of service to one of bureaucratic careerism out of touch with humane standards, the application of a business ethic to matters of life and death. I hope some of these things cast a shadow across my book.

About the title, "Sleeping Beauty," I have a young reader currently in France—he's the son of the poet Donald Davie—who writes that it's "not your style" (Patrick Davie is only 13 or 14) but it was validated for me by Henry Green's use of the phrase on p. 198 of *Party Giving*: ". . . as though it was her part she had to play to evoke good times, alone, on top of this ivory tower with his dreaming world beneath, sleeping beauty, all of them folded so she imagined into their thoughts of him." I mean the use of the phrase as a generalized abstract noun. Well, the beauty is sleeping indeed but your sweet and penetrating thoughts, Eudora, awaken her continually, indeed become her.

This past week I made copy-editing corrections, and people keep coming from the east and/or the past, tomorrow the daughter of an old Ann Arbor friend, Allegra Branson, daughter of H.C. Branson whose John Bent detective stories you undoubtedly remember; Hank later did a Civil War novel, *Salisbury Plain*, which is impressive in its Stendhalian way, but I prefer his detective stories, especially *The Leaden Bubble*.[18] I hope to see the elder Bransons in a few weeks when I go to Ann Arbor to receive what they call a "distinguished achievement award" from the university—these are awards voted annually by the various faculties, did I tell you? I don't much look forward to the public occasion but can't duck it, either—I suppose we have to accept the circularity of our lives, when the spirit ascends and also when it descends. Hank Branson was well-known before I had written a book, and was, after Margaret, the first mystery writer I knew in the flesh. He came to our house one night, he and M. having simultaneously published books, and knocked on the door and announced himself. We were also friends for several years, but I haven't seen him at all in nearly twenty. There's a lot to be said for living in one place as you have.

Yes, I would like to visit you at home some day, as my dream undoubtedly said—I was probably envious of your *Washington Post* interview: what a lovely interview that was. It's very difficult for Margaret and me to make travel plans, since we don't travel easily, separately or together, but I'm sure some day I'll get within distance of Jackson. I've got to see that new sheeting on your home. May it protect you from all harm.

Love,

Ken

P.S.—Glad you liked the *Permanent Errors* mention.—The ms got back safely, very fast. Thank you.

K.

Clearly, Ken's novel Sleeping Beauty *was a tribute to Eudora that extended beyond its dedication. His character Laurel, so patently based upon his daughter Linda, had by coincidence or confluence the very name Eudora had given the title character in* The Optimist's Daughter. *In* Sleeping Beauty, *Lew Archer searches the room of Laurel, who has gone missing: "The only personal thing I found," he records, "was a letter folded into a book of stories entitled* Permanent Errors." Permanent Errors, *the book Reynolds Price had dedicated to Eudora, now appeared in the book Ken had dedicated to her.*

Eudora Welty to Kenneth Millar, November 19, 1972

Dear Ken,

I've been carrying your letter around in my purse, thinking I could answer it in my car, but it didn't do—but now the painters are out of my house after 6 weeks! And privacy is back, and I can get to my typewriter. As I've thought about your book, it's seemed to me the whole of it might rest on the one image—Archer's wish that he could throw the gun and send it cartwheeling over all their heads and over the edge of the world (forgive me if I don't say it right). And just as surely as the oil surges in on the tide and up onto the beaches, and just as surely as all the fires in the story are brought into relationship, the filth and the fires of all war are implied and say Vietnam, though you leave it unspoken. The intensity of the scenes has a moral source, and a moral strength. (This was what made me think of Goya.) I think all this time you've been taking a popular form and making it something entirely of your own, and in *Sleeping Beauty* to the highest degree yet. It's not new country for you because it's been there all the time (or so it seems to me) but is more openly revealed around us—and explored for us as Archer detects. I may be speaking clumsily of something that's been so delicately achieved. "The dangerous lair of the past" is there, as in the other novels, but this time the danger shows itself in its high blaze and its long shadows as never before, and you've given it its full implications. The title as looked back on after the story ends is responsive to all that too, and I think from the first we know it to be as you meant it, an abstract noun.—I was delighted to be told that one of the threads of your book led back to Henry Green—there are many threads in it leading back to things I cherish but most of all I cherish the book itself. My gratitude and pride in the dedication are things I think of every day.

I hope the unusual rains you spoke of haven't made threats on Santa Barbara the way they've done—carried out—on Big Sur. And I hope your trip to Ann Arbor to get honored didn't happen right in the middle of their bad weather. Good for them to vote you the distinguished achievement award—they ought to do it every year. Only I suppose you would have to make a speech every year then.

My brother Walter, by the way, was at the U. of Michigan getting his M.A. probably when you were there (he was born the same year as you, if your book jacket knows, 6 years younger than me), and he was at Okinawa when you were too—communications officer on a mine sweeper. I was glad to know the carrier you were on did not blow up—as it might have so easily.

You looked on the Washington Post piece very kindly, and I'm glad you thought I passed—to me it was like being given an exam, any interview is, but an exam in a nightmare when you have to answer true-and-false and multiple-choice questions on a subject you have forgotten to bone up on—sounds absurd, I won't try to say more. Henry Mitchell, though, is an engaging and congenial soul, comes from Memphis, where he used to work on the Commercial Appeal as TV critic on weekdays and garden page editor on Sundays, and I'd already met him once. He has a good wild streak, and we talked about everything in the world, and he didn't take any notes—I was glad—so I think maybe some of the things he put in *Henry* said. I talked about you but that wasn't in there. I mailed you a copy of the Southern Review the other day, which has an interview with me in it too—this was a sober schoolteacher with a tape recorder, and if I didn't flunk that one it was because I corrected the paper myself. I don't know what may have come through. Faulkner's thing in the Meriwether article is quite moving, don't you think?[19]

We're having our first cold days now, and it's frantic behavior out there at the bird feeder. The white-throated sparrow sings these days. The trees are still in leaf and this year we have some bright color (hickory sweet-gum dogwood maple oak)—often we don't have, it's more like a faded tapestry. I would eat lunch in my car near a beautiful ginko tree that was so bright even its shadow on a white wall looked radiant. By the way, did I tell you that Jackson has a zebra-striped Volkswagon camper? I see it every day on the way to the grocery—property of some young people who have moved into a house that was lived in for years by a Professor Pitard, old French violin teacher and leader of the 3-pc. Orchestra that played in silent movie days. (I can imagine how they would accompany the tearing about of that zebra.) They *must* have copied your book.[20]

The house will be steadier now, I hope, with the sheetrock in, and now if 7 maids with 7 mops sweep it for half a year (me), do you suppose—? But I rather like to clear away and clean up. When I come to "Party Going," somewhere in those stacks in the middle of the living room floor, I want to look up your page. I'd better start to work now.

Love,
Eudora

Have a fine Thanksgiving. If and when you do go on one of your birding excursions to Texas or the like as you've done in the past, I hope you'll let me know. I'd better give you my phone number now while I think to, not in the book—601-353-7762. I could meet you & Margaret in New Orleans or somewhere, in between, even if you couldn't get to Jackson. But of course I would love to see you here.

Kenneth Millar to Eudora Welty, December 4, 1972

Dear Eudora:

I've been on not *one* trip but *two* since my last letter, and yours, and I think your peripatetic habits must be catching—you make moving about the world sound so interesting. And indeed I found it to be, though I'm glad to be home again. The first trip, to Ann Arbor and Canada, took a week. Ann Arbor turned out to be more fun than I expected: my last time there was overshadowed by the old doctoral drive—I wrote *Ivory Grin* and finished my dissertation on Coleridge in the same seven-month period—but this time all I had to do was talk to people, mostly informally, though I met one class in American studies and made one speech about the intention of popular art, which is to express a society to itself in terms it can understand. Talk to people, and go to the Michigan-Purdue football game, the first Michigan game I ever attended (I used to write a newspaper column on Saturday afternoons.) I did have a chance to look up my dear old friends Henry Branson and his wife Anna, who were so close to us when we lived in Ann Arbor. Hank wrote some marvellous mystery novels, as you doubtless know—you perhaps remember *The Leaden Bubble* and if you don't please give it a try,—but then matriculated into the historical novel, to his present regret, and was lost to us. American writers have a hard time going on as they get older. Only a few, like you, keep on getting better. I'm glad you're planning more stories, an intelligence I owe to your *Southern Review* interview, which I thank you for sending me. It made a lot of sense and sounded exactly like you. *I* love Phoenix Jackson, too, and it sent me back to her story.[21]

From Ann Arbor I went on to Kitchener, Ontario, where I had a couple of good sessions with my father-in-law Henry Sturm. He is almost blind and almost deaf and almost 89, but he loves to talk and retains great mental incisiveness, remembering everything. His source of information is daylong radio. He is physically hale. Henry was a great hockey coach and sent more players into the National Hockey League than any other man. He was mayor of the city and 36 years on the council. He left school in the fourth grade and went to work aged eleven; he is partly responsible for the fact that Kitchener has the best small-city library I've ever seen: I almost lived there as a boy. But poor Kitchener has been bitten by the growth bug and is losing its fine beloved ethos. Its energy is frightening. Skyscrapers are sprouting like toadstools. The streets were jammed with traffic, foot and car, at 6:30 in the morning when I left for the Toronto airport, a day or two ahead of schedule. I was so glad to get home that I could even tolerate the sight of the oil platform as we flew in over the sea.

My second trip, taken with Margaret just this last weekend, was in a wholly different direction, into the interior (Calif.) valley which is the one place outside of Texas where sandhill cranes [may] be found in any number. We were lucky. When we arrived on the Carrizo Plain, traveling by chartered bus with 30 other local Audubon people, 3,000 cranes were standing in the water of Soda Lake. A thousand took to the air as we were watching, flew over us in long lines bending unbroken like lines of music, then burst into actual music, a gleeful melodious grumbling and celebration as they came down into the harvested fields to feed. I think it was the greatest natural sight I ever witnessed.

The word "celebration" reminds me of you and what you said about yourself, that it is in your nature to celebrate the things you write about. Fortunate are those your pen touches. I'm one of the fortunate ones, and am still warm from your goodwill toward this latest book. Perhaps now those glorious cranes will lead me around the corner, or the bend, toward another. As I saw them I remembered your remark about my remark about "live things in the air at all times," and both remarks gathered meaning. Perhaps I shall yet become a celebrant, too.

I'm glad you thought well of Herb Harker's book. His son Rand came through last week on his way to Mexico, with *his* first novel, and waited while I read it. It needs rewriting, as I told him, but he has a talent which, if it is allowed to grow, will perhaps surpass his father's who started so late.

Thank you for the word about your brother Walter.

Love,

Ken

P.S.—Had a first today: *Blue City* was published in Russia, serialized in two parts in what appears to be a literary magazine. K.

Kenneth Millar to Eudora Welty, December 25, 1972

Dear Eudora:

When your package arrived the day before yesterday, I couldn't imagine what was in it. But it was marked "Perishable," so I knew it couldn't be anything you'd written. It was a work of art in its own way, though, so beautifully ornamented with pecans (from your own tree?) and full of them, and utterly delicious. Margaret pronounced it "the best Christmas cake I've ever eaten," and I concur. It was so thoughtful of you to send it to us—the kind of loving gesture that you make so often and so well, and that the blessed recipients will never forget.

We had a pleasant Christmas, and tonight are enjoying the quiet aftermath of it, Jimmie having left this afternoon for his other grandfather's house fifty miles down the coast. Last night we went to an adult's-and-children's party at a neighbor's—Ted Clymer's house—and we all sang carols with Margaret at the piano. The children loved it, but for us older ones the carols didn't quite shut out the din of the world. I wish I could have heard you on television, but Channel 28 (NET) isn't available in our area. But I understand your interview will be repeated, and maybe I'll have a second chance.[22]

The sea was rough today, with two sets of waves contending from two directions, southeast (approximately) and northwest—our shoreline rings almost east and west—and the water offshore was white and foaming like a milkshake. I lasted almost ten minutes and finished off in the pool, swimming sedately back and forth with M. It was a warm sunny day, and even now at night it isn't cold. I'm a little chilly, though, a little scared, because I don't quite know what is happening to the country, or has already happened. A friend, formerly in the government, writes from Washington about "the coming constitutional crisis," as he calls it. I believe the country has gone through a moral crisis and failed to recognize it. We proceed cheerfully on our desperate way like a man with a bad doctor and a fatal illness.

But I don't mean to end on a note of despair. I believe we'll turn back from our own violence, and see what we have done as something that we can never do again. What other meaning could this present violence have?

Meanwhile I eat your Christmas cake and think that with the help of your books I can reconstruct from its sweet dense subtle mass (as Proust reconstructed France) the whole blessed unknown south.

Love,
Ken

CHAPTER THREE

"Love—& connections"

————— ❧ —————

1973

WITHOUT a doubt, Eudora and Ken were kindred souls. Yet much separated them—half a continent, to begin with. More to the point, there was his marriage: that thirty-five-year partnership, through thin and thick, health and sickness, with the mother of their deceased and only child.

From the day in 1938 that the Millars exchanged wedding vows, Ken and Margaret had often been at cross-purposes. They loved each other but found marriage stressful; yet they had worked hard over the years—Ken perhaps harder than Margaret—to keep their union intact, encouraging each other in common pursuits, from the writing of books to the playing of Scrabble, from swimming to bicycling to bird-watching. Thus they could take pride in what many might call the success of their marriage—though Margaret used instead the odd word "prolongation." But their daughter's sudden death in late 1970 had saddened and maybe somewhat separated Ken and Margaret. As Ken had written a year earlier to Eudora about himself and Maggie: "We have lost a good deal of our unconscious glee."

Maggie was often irritable with Ken in public. During these years she was unable to write (and even unwilling to read), while his career and reputation soared. Ken Millar nevertheless was firmly committed to a marriage that over the years had become more platonic than passionate.

For her part, Eudora Welty had many male friends who were married, and she thought of their wives as friends. She typically, for instance, sent letters to both William Maxwell, her New Yorker editor, and his wife, Emmy, not to just one of them; they seemed an inseparable pair to her. Eudora and Margaret Millar, on the other hand, did not yet know each other, and Eudora felt more than affection for Margaret's husband. Still Eudora's sense of honor and respect for the institution of marriage were a match for her new friend Ken's.

So there was a guarded quality to the letters they exchanged. Eudora was careful to inquire about Margaret, though at times as a seeming afterthought; Ken made a frequent point of mentioning Maggie, though often just near sign-off. And neither Millar nor Welty yet declared in open fashion the fonder feelings that seemed to flow beneath the surface of their prose.

Eudora Welty to Kenneth Millar, January 12, 1973

Dear Ken,

I've just been breaking the ice on the birdbath here too. But not going swimming here! Happy New Year, and Happy Birthday wishes back into December and Sagittarius, for many happy and happier returns of the day.

I had the same kind of Christmas as you, with my family, and, I think, the same feeling about the awful things we were perpetrating upon that midnight clear [in Vietnam]. I hope and hope, while knowing there's damage that can never be undone and something lost we can never get back. Just hope for the end of the killing—I think it has to come soon, don't you? And I believe it will happen as you said in your letter, that we will see what we have done as something we can never do again.

Tell me what happened this year about the Christmas Bird Count.[1] I hope Santa Barbara kept up its grand record, and that you saw the same pair of white-throated sparrows on the right day as last year. If you could have counted those thousands of sandhill cranes you saw—but then, they belong in a count of your own. I can't forget the picture you gave me of their long lines of flight that went over, bending unbroken, and going into song.

That's a fascinating thought that you're coming out in Russian now. Can you get somebody who can translate it back for you, just to see what they make of *Blue City*? And will they now go through the whole list of your books? (Am I right, in thinking *Blue City* was the first written or not? I now wait for it to appear along with your other early ones newly in paperback—have enjoyed reading *The Doomsters*, *The Dark Tunnel*, and *Trouble Follows Me*, all for the first time—seeing things from their beginnings. The pre-Archer ones seem to be *looking for* Archer, far-flung and extravagant (talent-to-burn) searches for Archer, though of course entirely themselves too. But I guess it could be impossible to read them without knowing now what's to come. So my feeling may have been that I was looking for Archer.

Your trip to Ann Arbor and Canada sounded like a pleasure, in spite of the work attached. I'd like to have heard your speech about the intention of popular art and wonder if you are going to publish it somewhere—don't you think you should? Or did you have it written down? Let me know if it's in print. (I see the NYT Book Review, where it might well should be.) Never have I come upon *The Leaden Bubble*, though I've heard of it for years, but I will one of these days.

You were kind to have gone to the trouble of watching that Buckley program—I hated to think of your doing so.[2] It was something I couldn't get out of doing, because of being grateful to the local ETV station which has been good to my work, but I am not at home in the Buckley element. I felt strung-up and not very smart. Halfway through, I realized that Mr. B. wasn't really too informed on the subjects he'd started—too late to go back and get first things straight. It was a strange experience—he entered a minute before the program was to start, and exited the minute it was over, brought his own director and staff, and wore make-up on the backs of his hands—all of this may be standard. I wish Walker Percy had been on with him alone—he could have accomplished a lot more.—How strange to think you watched the program in the house of a neighbor who had once long ago been in my house. She wrote me a letter—which I must ans. after I investigate what happened to her friend.

I've been reading too the Quentin Bell biography of Virginia Woolf. I hadn't somehow hoped for too much from it, but it is a good piece of work. It defines its limits, stays within them, and from there gives a clear-headed, deeply informed—rather, uniquely informed—calmly understanding picture—it's set in perspective and surrounded with the people and events and ideas that had the vital connections with Virginia. He tells it with restraint, and much of it is terrible—have you read it? Virginia Woolf was the first writer—modern—whose work burst upon my imagination like fireworks—when I read "To the Lighthouse" I felt I couldn't contain my joy and excitement. I'd read all the Bloomsbury memoirs, etc., of recent years, and yet almost quailed before this one because the reviews had put me off. I thought it was something quite different. For one thing, Q.B. writes so well.—What a hero Leonard [Woolf] was!

If you know anything to do about grackles, I wish you'd tell me. Against them, not for. Here the temp. is 23 this morning, and they've decided to occupy my bird feeder—the new one, the plexiglass tube supposed to "discourage" the big birds. Of course they can't get their beaks in the holes, but they swoop down on it and cover it and swing on it, and the little birds can't get to it all day. This morning—I've been flapping a dishcloth at them from the kitchen window—as they scattered, a blue jay came on signal and hung upside down on the feeder and tried to hammer a hole in the plexiglass with his beak. He must have a pretty good headache still. Life seemed to be easier when the only feeding stand was a free-for-all. Now I've got demonstrators and protesters.

It was sympathetic of you to say not long ago that you thought a book of my essays might be a good thing. It is a problem to me to know just what to do. The pieces were all written as needed for the lecturing and so on I was doing, '50's & '60's, and were the best I could do, and I think are respectable pieces of work—but what puzzles me is whether or not they will mean anything to readers now. To the young, what meaning would a paper on "Place in Fiction" have? That was the subject of the one I worked on the hardest. Nobody really cares about many of the things I feel most passionately about— and I am not for a minute saying that I consider the beliefs dated or the subjects, rather, dated or unimportant. They matter more than ever—to me. Another consideration that stops me is that a book of these pieces might seem to be saying I thought of myself as a critic, with some systematic theory about literature—of course none of that is so. I love books—that's about it. All the pieces were written about what I like, more than a little for my own pleasure. This would probably be my criterion when I chose what to include. Somehow I can't start in—I would risk my neck on a story without this kind of hesitation. I can be professional about stories, that's the reason, I suppose, and as any sort of essay writer I'm an amateur, and feel vulnerable altogether. So I mull it over.

I've gone on for too long, but it had been too long a time since I wrote—Is everything all right with you and Margaret, & Jimmie? I had a sort of flu but all right now, and hope all of you are well. Many wishes, and love,

Eudora

Ken was quick to respond to Eudora's letter, point by point. He certainly wanted to ease the dissatisfaction she felt about her national public television appearance with Walker Percy on William F. Buckley Jr.'s program, Firing Line. *Buckley, who had come to Jackson for the December 12, 1972, interview, which aired on December 24, sought to challenge the two southern writers about their decisions to remain in the South during the struggle for civil rights. He seemed not to recognize "the moral and political resource," to use historian David Chappell's words, that white southerners who were "sickened by segregation" yet remained at home, provided the civil rights movement.[3]*

Kenneth Millar to Eudora Welty, January 22, 1973

Dear Eudora:

You and we seem to have acquired one of the new tube feeders at the same time—I gave M. one for Christmas—and to be having the same kind of problems with them, if multiplicity of birds can be considered a problem. You have too many grackles and we have too many bandtailed pigeons, but I trust the larger birds will tend to get discouraged after a while. The beauty of the new feeder is that the pigeons can't deplete it so readily as ordinary feeders. Yesterday, by the way, an acorn woodpecker, a medium-sized bird, was hanging upside down from the bottom rung of ours, and reaching *up.*—We had a fairly successful Christmas count this year, 197 species as compared with 202 last year, but there was just enough slippage in our pelagic count to take us out of national contention. Some of our group staged a second count in condor country, sighting ten condors and ten golden eagles as well as a host of other birds. But the main thing, after all, was the *human* activity. The comings and goings of the birds don't really depend on us, and the true measure of a bird count is the number of people involved and the quality of their interest. Ten years ago a little local bird count with about thirty members became the S.B. Audubon Society. Now we are over 800, and we are a force!

The friend who once visited you in Mississippi, lucky woman, and who wrote you recently—Carnie Clark—is interested in birds, though not yet an ardent watcher. And *birds* are interested in Carnie: the other day a sharp-shinned hawk broke her study window and died of the collision on the floor. Carnie is a retired teacher and a very useful person in civic, mainly liberal, organizations. Several of her close relations have died (and lived) tragically—lives that I won't go into, but I take a certain somber amusement from being told by Carnie's bright and aged mother that my books are opening her eyes to the harsher side of life. She is, by the way, a Boston Brahmin who was a close friend of John P. Marquand and is very proud of the fact.

I agree with your feeling that the Buckley show didn't work too well, but you are wrong if you think there was any inadequacy in your performance. You simply weren't given a chance to speak freely about things that are important to you. I felt that Buckley was very much on the attack—a strategy of ignorance—and that both you and Percy were silenced by hospitality, B. being on your ground. Well, Buckley got his comeuppance very shortly when his show was cancelled. He was in Santa Barbara the other day, house guest of an old friend of mine, Hugh

Kenner—a friendship that began to lose its virtue about the time that Hugh became literary godfather of the *National Review*, and has now eroded—but a friendship that I regret. In the late forties and early fifties Hugh and I taught each other a good deal, he more than I.[4] Who is our most brilliant literary scholar? Alas, it is Hugh Kenner.—This summer he leaves Santa Barbara for Johns Hopkins.

ORDER OF PUBLn

DARK TUNNEL 1944

TROUBLE FOLLOWS ME 1946

BLUE CITY 1947

THREE ROADS 1948

MOVING TARGET 1949

It's kind of you to give those early books the credit of looking for Archer. Heaven knows they all needed a *person* at the center, and his absence may have been what they were about. I'd just made the shift from Canada to the U.S., in 1941, and sort of exploded outward into the vacuous freedom of American air (though my most influential teacher at Ann Arbor—on me, I mean—was the Englishman W.H. Auden who incidentally when *he* was a young man used to review mystery novels for the London papers, and whose example helped to teach me not to be ashamed of my trade; or Margaret of hers.)

The speech I gave in Ann Arbor this time around was just a short one, and extempore, so that I don't know what I said nor does it matter. But a good many years ago, in Ann Arbor then too, I gave a more formal address on detective fiction (at a Popular Arts festival where W.C. Handy played his trumpet!) and later published it as an essay in *Show Magazine*, which promptly, with that issue, expired.[5] But I should think that old essay is hardly worth raking up. *Your* essays, if I may judge by the wonderfully eloquent one on Green, matching the eloquence and supple suavity of that master himself, *your* essays are a different kettle of fish and I feel strongly should be collected. "Place in Fiction," as we lose it, is precisely the sort of thing that should be seized and held. Whatever is valid, you know, finds or even creates its own public. Also you have become, though you may not quite realize it, a national spokesman for everything to do with art and knowledge, and your record should be made complete. (Margaret considers you the leading creative woman in the United States; and she doesn't get any argument from me.)

I've finished the final corrections on *Sleeping Beauty* and committed it to the printers; hope to send you a copy in late March. I'll be interested in your reaction to the cover design. Now don't maltreat your grackles. Love, Ken

P.S.—I'll probably have to go to Russia, to my old(est) friend Bob Ford the Canadian Ambassador, to get my Russian translations translated back (though that sounds like rather thin fun.) The title of *Blue City*, Bob tells me, was translated into "In My Home Town." Which isn't bad. That book was dedicated to Bob, by the way, and I imagine he had something to do with getting it serialized in Russia. I've written to you about him before, and will again, especially if I do make that Moscow hegira.

Kenneth Millar to Eudora Welty, January 31, 1973

Dear Eudora:

Just a note to thank you for your "Three Papers on Fiction" and to report that I read them these last two evenings with delight.[6] I think they are beautiful, wonderfully poised on the knife-edge of pure truth. Perhaps what makes you uncertain about them is precisely their most valuable quality: they were written by an artist in your own figurative language, cut from the same piece of imaginative cloth as your stories. They are not written in the language of the schools, into which even most artists tend to shift when they write criticism. And partly for that reason they manage to get and stay closer to the meanings and workings of fiction than almost anything I can remember. You yourself are there in the prose, close up to and involved with the things you love, and I think it would be a mistake to hold these papers back from further publication. They are beautifully clear, succinct and to the point, done with great art;

and I loved all your examples. What you do with Faulkner, for instance, is astonishing and will send me back to him now for the dozenth time. Thank you very much for the book.

It may be, as you suggest, that some of your other essays and lectures are more uneven or of less central value. But I honestly can't conceive of you ever having written anything in this line that shouldn't be retained for the use of future readers. So though you haven't really asked my overall opinion, sight unseen, I'll give it anyway. I think you should collect your pieces fugitive and otherwise ("I was a fugitive from Eudora Welty") with a foreword saying what you choose about their origins, and turn the book loose into the stream of history. It won't sink, and it won't embarrass you. After all, you *are* a teacher and a lecturer and a critic; these pieces are a proud part of the record, and your main work will be better understood through them. Coming back to the "Papers on Fiction" which I have just read, they give what seems to me a uniquely clear account of the relationship between the writer and the techniques of his work.

Are you watching the ten-episode documentary being shown Thursday nights on Educational TV about "An American Family"? They're a Santa Barbara family, and the producer Craig Gilbert has publicly credited me with bringing him to Santa Barbara.[7] Indeed I spent some hours with him here, but had nothing to do with his ultimate choice of a family. Their story is beautifully done, painfully engrossing, and perhaps the best thing ever shown on television.

I am personally involved, or have agreed to become so, in another television venture. Canadian Broadcasting Corp. is going to do a ten- or twelve-part dramatization of *Edwin Drood*, and several mystery writers have been asked to invent possible endings, all of which will be given on TV.[8] So I'm about to reread the book and see what I can find there.

I gather from your mysterious and modest hints that Jackson is going to honor you, as it should, and that M. and I may be invited to attend the occasion. If the timing permits, we'd love to have a reason to visit you in your home town, and your suggestion of it is most pleasing and moving to both of us.

Love,

Ken

P.S.—My bird expert M. doesn't think the grackles will give up of their own accord, and says you may have to feed smaller birds in restricted spaces available only to them. K.

Eudora Welty, Washington, DC, to Kenneth Millar, February 8, 1973

Dear Ken,

Your letter was intuitive—you put your finger right on my causes of worry, and I'm heartened by what you say—not only because of your understanding and generous spirit about them, but because of your being able to give them a fresh as well as an experienced eye. (This sounds as if you have one fresh eye & one experienced eye.) It is true that I could have written them no other way, but when you report they won't sink (I was scared they'd sink right away) I do take heart and hope you're right. I'm getting them together, and the fugitive from E. W. at this writing is one called "How I Write"—I bet I never catch up with that one![9] Done on request, I remember, & given that impudent title, which the editor left in—

The date of that invitation is May 2. Can you & Margaret possibly make it? I didn't mean to make a mystery of what it was, but was trying to warn you about something I thought already on the way—The Miss. Arts Festival this year is going to have a (or an?) Eudora Welty day, and the invitations are for a party and a play and the rest I'm not sure of—I think I have to do a reading at some point. They wanted me to give them a list of friends from out-of-town they could invite ahead of time, and an alert now, "written by girls with pretty handwriting"— they may still be looking for *them*. What will be going on in the Arts Festival I haven't heard yet. Of course I was pleased about their dreaming this up, but I do live far away from many of my good friends, and farthest of all from you, probably—And I know what a sort of nerve it is to think people could pick up & take off for Jackson, to a welcome however warm. It would be just lovely if you could come. You both have so many fans here that want me to tell you *they* want you to come, too. Maybe I will have some different birds here by that time. Or you could plan a real bird trip that would let you come by to visit me (I'm a real bird)—Avery Island? This may exactly coincide with when you're going to Russia—on a real hegira—

That's delightful news about *Edwin Drood*—Or it sounds so to one who would like to see the dramatizations with their various endings. I think I'll read it again myself & get ready—though will we get to see it, eventually, in the U.S.? Our Miss. ETV isn't showing "An American Family"—but that doesn't mean it won't be scheduled later, and I do hope to get a look at it. I'd read about it and had learned it was a Santa Barbara family, but did not know you had brought its producer there and spent time helping him—It has a strange overtone of the story overtaking the real, from accounts. Do you remember that wonderful movie "Dead of Night" with Michael Redgrave about the ventriloquist whose dummy starts getting the upper *hand*? [10]

This *is* Thursday, and I'm in Washington D.C. where I see the program *will* be shown. But I won't be where I can watch it. I'm here on a Nat'l Council on the Arts meeting[11]—Of what use I can be I am still waiting to find out, but I've been to 3 meetings and don't think I've helped. Depressing atmosphere in a way—but I hope. It seems so much easier to help people in the other arts—you can give painters galleries and exhibition assistance, and composers and musicians concerts & audiences & tours, and play people & dancers all sorts of opportunities, but writers don't come in bunches or need anywhere to perform, just privacy and time. Difficult to fit in with all this grandiose machinery. To get a good lecturer such as W. H. Auden to some of our poor little (poor financially) colleges down here, now—in the South. I'm glad you got his message in that early day—Speaking of Mr. A. He was the first poet I ever heard—(and I couldn't always hear.)

I'm running up to N.Y. for a few days after this Washington week-end is over—just for a little refreshment. I'm reading all of Willa Cather again—Read "The Song of the Lark" on the train coming. I love trains, and my early memories of trains are so vivid, and the trains in "The Song of the Lark" are so wonderful, & so important. It was lovely to read this one riding in the night. Do you like her? What vitality—I think she's magnificent—True and ardent and wide-expanding, her view is—I like to read all of somebody chronologically as you did Hawthorne.

I'll promise (again) to write a better letter next time. Yours are always beautiful and do me so much good, Ken—I'm ashamed to be as poor as I am in reply. But with many wishes, & thanks, & love all the same,

Eudora

I do feel so good that you responded to those 3 pieces as you did. Thank you. It must be vanity, but I would feel desolated with them in print to think they no longer connected with life—It would just mean I didn't write them well enough—I want to do things *well*!

Eudora Welty to Kenneth Millar, February 24, 1973

Dear Ken,

Your swimming pool has splashed again, from what I read—I hope no harm came—are you all right?[12]

It's like spring here, but it's sure to be cold again before spring's here reliably (is it ever?). Mockingbirds dancing on the grass—they aren't reliable either—and birds singing but I'm not reliable on their names. In N.Y. the temperature was a round zero—up in the country, where I spent 2 days, it was snowing and besides the titmice & chickadees at my friends' feeder were some cross-bills, which I'd never seen before. This was at the home of my old and dear friend Diarmuid Russell—he is also my agent, and I was his first client 1941—He is ill and I had not been sure I'd get to see him, but he was well enough and it was a happy and good visit. He is one of your longtime readers, and he is the first person

I'm going to make a present of the new book to—He was so delighted to know about the dedication. He's asked me about you, saying "Obviously he knows Yeats and so on" which interested him in you long ago (he is AE's son), and so by now I know a little I could tell him—and none of it surprised him.[13] As a little boy in Dublin it used to be his duty to bring his father a new detective story every day—begged, borrowed, or somehow, and of course D. read them for himself—I think he began with Buchan[14]—your man. He (D) put me onto him (B) too, in time.

I have just lost a good friend in the death of Elizabeth Bowen[15]—I loved her, and such was her vitality and zest and tireless absorption in life—*care* for life, hers & others, deeply both—it never occurred to me that I might not be going to see her again—

She was one of your most devoted readers, and I remember years ago when she first came to my house, her telling me that wherever she went in the U.S. (She was on a long lecture tour) kind hosts put out some cosy English murder in a vicarage for her "when of course what I wanted was Ross Macdonald"—I'm not sure she didn't say "beloved Ross Macdonald"—(Henry Green was always "beloved" to her too.) In the last few years Elizabeth had got to be very good friends with Agatha Christie, by the way, in London, and told me how she'd come to revere her as "an older friend"—which sounded right because you didn't think of Elizabeth as being in any way old too,—though she herself thought of herself right along, accurately, as being "as old as the century"—we took lots of little excursions in each other's company, in her car in Ireland and in my car in Mississippi—She saw everything—felt places almost hypnotically—She said she never saw so huge a moon in her life as came up over St. Francisville, La., as we rode out the ferry—and in Natchez I think we both saw a ghost (a first for me)—I was showing her that wild octagonal house there, never finished, the hammer thrown down at the start of the Civil War—called "Nutt's Folly" (after its builder Dr. Nutt), and a man came out of the woods, presently, and showed us over the whole 3 empty floors, offered us a drink (at 10 in the morning) and took a dollar tip, but there wasn't any such person, so we learned later.[16]—I'd been waiting to see her again to tell her that I had come to know you—I wish *she* had! Yet she knew so many things intuitively about writers. I wish she could have read *Sleeping Beauty*. I'm hoping to see a copy, with jacket, before too long now. (Do you like the jacket?) I saw Walter Clemons in N.Y. and he was eagerly waiting to get hold of it.

Love—& connections—

Eudora

"Only connect"—so urged E. M. Forster, an author Welty and Millar both admired (and whom Welty had met in 1954 when invited to his rooms at King's College, Cambridge).

Eudora and Ken began with avidity to collect instances of their mutual professional and personal connections: threads, which drew them closer in a tapestry of shared acquaintances, mutual passions, common experience—a real-life enactment of their fiction-visions in which multiple individuals are joined by ties seen and unseen and in which the present is inextricably bound up with the past.

Kenneth Millar to Eudora Welty, February 26, 1973

Dear Eudora:

It's good to hear that you are safely home again from the cold east, and good to hear word of your friend and agent Diarmuid Russell of whom of course I have heard (being your agent must have made him famous.) Indeed his father was an important figure in my life when I was a boy in my teens. For some reason it was AE who carried first and furthest, of all the Irish Revival men, to the Canadian wilds, perhaps because he was the most assimilable by a provincial society which loved its poets to be bards (though its leading writer was Stephen Leacock), and I started out being a bard myself, a beardless bard. For deeper reasons—both were in some sense oppressed provinces of the empire, as the Canadian Hugh Kenner pointed out in his book on Joyce long ago—the Irish Revival and Rebellion were enormously interesting to Canadians, suggesting a way to feel if not to act—original feeling being the most difficult thing for provincials to come by. And by the time I was twenty Ireland was so much on my mind and in my conversation that Margaret, whom I was sort of courting then, was of the belief that I was an Irishman. I almost was. I got hold of a smuggled copy of *Ulysses* when I was twenty, sat up all night reading it, and within half a year I was in Dublin. I quickly found that Dublin was not what I wanted, and that what I wanted was portable. So I went back to Canada and married Margaret and together we conspired to escape to the United States, which was what we *both* wanted; but it took several years. Please tell Diarmuid Russell what a splendid and benign figure his father presented to our minds when he was young, and he remains so, really the height of Dublin civilization though it had greater depths than his, and he found himself surrounded by several of the greatest writers in English. Just thinking about the Irish Revival stirs me now. I escaped from Canada by way of Ireland.—Poor Ireland now.

I'm sorry you lost your friend Elizabeth Bowen. No wonder we grow more thoughtful as we grow older. I loved some of her stories— do you remember her wartime stories? was the title *Ivy Gripped the Steps?*—and think it remarkable that she enjoyed mine. These connections made through you however distantly are important to me. I've spent my life living by and for such connections, tuning in on relayed signals from the far side of the world, a pioneer of the McLuhan village in a way, but the connections are personal. (I seem to have been invaded by, or you bring out in me, an autobiographical demon. It's my response to your sympathetic interest, which certainly deserves a better response.)

These connections are so important because, for one thing, it seems to have become rather difficult for the two of us to travel. I've put off replying to your invitation to visit Jackson in May in the hope that we could. But at the moment Margaret is waiting to learn whether she must have an operation to remove a skin cancer from her face. Not a serious operation—she's had one before, and so have I.

———————————— I'm continuing this a day later ————
Margaret did indeed have her operation but it wasn't extensive and should be healed up in a month, so we're keeping open the hope that

we can visit you. And Avery Island. Is that the place you mentioned? Is it a bird sanctuary?

I've struck it lucky after all these months and been able to order from a book dealer in San Francisco a copy of Henri Coulette's first book of poems—*The War of the Secret Agents*—which I'll be sending you soon. I believe the long title poem may interest you as it did me.

You ask me whether I like the jacket of *Sleeping Beauty*. I think I do, though it's kind of pretty in an Aubrey Beardsley sort of way. But it's precise. I didn't see it in its final colors. Copies are promised within the next month. I hope *you* will like its appearance.

Love,
Ken

Eudora Welty to Kenneth Millar, March 17, 1973

Dear Ken,

I was glad to get your good letter, and to know that all was going the way it should with Margaret and she'll be fine again soon. And it was a delight to have the present from you of your friend Henri Coulette's first book—a happy thought and a happy inscription, and thank you, for tracking it down (a 1966 book, particularly a 1966 book of poems, must have been *hard*, these days) and for sending it to me. I've been reading the poems with a great deal of pleasure. First the title poem, which you spoke of, and then in order the whole bookfull as they came, and through to the notes and down to the last words, "Ross Macdonald."[17] A highly entertaining poet as well as a good one, isn't he? The quality that most delights me is a swiftness on the order of legerdemain—I feel I'm being let in on a spell, or almost let in, maybe not quite—in the act of reading, moving from image to image, or line to line—I always love magicians. I guess I should have said *put under* a spell. The range and diversity of his powers, of thought and feeling, are so wide—all in these brief, compact, & orderly poems—(not really *few*, as I was about to write, for the number's generous—) Their form is lovely to me, and there are some that are evocative (in their form) of the loveliest in the language and that goes especially for "The Wandering Scholar" and the early Yeats—the "Song of the Wandering Aengus"—But of course Henri Coulette's are his own, individual above everything, and in the wit and the spirited, spontaneous life they have I feel this most—"The War of the Secret Agents" has it in essence—I find it above all else so hilarious—It has a dark underside to go with it, and that wonderful cast—It's not just every poem that's got T. S. Eliot in it—in *person*, that is—along with Jean Gabin and every other ingredient that ever went into a spy story or movie, it's *packed*.[18] If you think I may be on the wrong track, Ken, about this poem, I want you to clue me in—It's so allusive and so high-speed—I'd hate not to know all. The Fuller novel he has the note about, *Double Webs*, is unknown to me.[19] (I'm not well up on any spy novels much except E. Ambler & G. Greene) It was lovely to come upon *your* line! I'm not near through reading these poems over again, I'm thanking you out of the middle of them, just in a burst of pleasure.

It was so nice of you to write me when I was sad about Elizabeth Bowen—and about Diarmuid—to whom I wrote and told much of what you'd told me about Ireland and his father—was that all right? I knew it would give him pleasure & interest him. It interested me, of course. I believe you and I must have fallen in love with the same country at about the same time in our lives. I was 18, a junior transfer to the University of Wisconsin, reading all those Irish poets where I opened the books, standing up in the stacks, and though it took me longer than you, I was at last in Dublin too, & knowing nobody, but *that* part didn't last, owing to luck. It was so amazing to be in the country in summertime and see that "the white roads" were really white, and know how Yeats & AE and all of them could really have walked all night long and seen all the world in the moonlight—There was only the draw of their poetry and the reason of their poetry that made me go, but I think all the same Ireland set me free of something too—

It is fine to know that it just *may* be possible for you and Margaret to come in May. I do want you to know that I am much in tune with that feeling of something coming up like a trip that can begin to hang over you—don't let Margaret be fretted by it, or yourself. Because you are welcome here any other time as well as in May, and if it turns out to be easier for you to travel at some other time, I would think that would be fine here too. Spur of the moment is always fine with me—I don't quite know what this May 2 will turn out like, myself, but if I get more idea of it as time goes on, I'll pass you a word. It is so nice in the meanwhile to think it really just might happen that you & Margaret could join in & be here with the others—Thank you for the letter again and the book—I'm trying to find a book for you too, but you may already have it—

Love,
Eudora

Kenneth Millar to Eudora Welty, March 25, 1973

Dear Eudora:

I think your reading of Hank Coulette is exactly right. Though he makes the ordinary seem strange—"The Blue-Eyed Precinct Worker" (to which I contributed that one line) is essentially an account of an evening walk in Pasadena by a precinct worker who was the poet himself—and allows the strange to appear in all its strangeness—"The War of the Secret Agents" is a somewhat fictionized account of an actual spy circle in wartime Paris based on a factual book by Jean O. Fuller, *Double Webs*, which I haven't read and the reading of which seems unnecessary, like Shakespeare's sources. Coulette is one of those unusual modern poets whose works can be read straightaway, then reread for emotionally accruing depth. His method is close yet distant, classic in intention I'd say. His poetry is kiln-dried: he is proud (and sorry, too) of being the only Ph.D in the U.S.A., probably, who never attended high school. He had to leave school at age 14 to support his widowed mother, working as a printer's devil, then a printer, but at age 20 or so was admitted to Cal State L.A. on the basis of a written examination, took his doctorate at Iowa and returned to Cal State L.A. to teach. I'm so glad that his poems brought you a "burst of pleasure." He's working on another volume, and your words which I'll pass on to him will give him a 'burst of pleasure,' and of imaginative energy too.

You are so wonderfully understanding of and responsive to other human beings e.g. me and Margaret, in the words you use to speak of our intended trip to Jackson in May. We're grateful that you want us, in spite of our sometimes inconvenient inability to follow through on set plans. But I am beginning to believe that we'll see you May 2, and am answering Mrs. Gillespie's beautifully written invitation to that effect. It's a once-in-a-lifetime occasion, isn't it? for everyone concerned, and we can't let it pass uncelebrated. I think, by the way, that celebration is the word for what you do in all departments of life and work. Did you use that word in one of the interviews you sent me?

We have a good deal to (changing the meaning a little) celebrate. Our grandson Jim has well survived his mother's death and grown into a fine little boy, no longer exactly little. He's the terror of the bikeways and of the checkerboard, though by exerting all of my mental force I can stay ahead of him on the latter. Jim is a delight to have around (as he is most weekends) even if he does talk each of our ears off in turn. I brood hopefully over his future, and say nothing. Jim and his father Joe P [. . .] are deeply fond of each other.

Margaret is calling me to come and watch the Tony awards on television. We're both interested in show business, and together know all the popular songs since 1928, or once did—I the words, M. the music. Thank you for your wonderful letter.

Love,
Ken

Eudora Welty to Kenneth Millar, March 30, 1973

Dear Ken,

Thank you for that lovely news—I was so delighted to know that you and Margaret really do feel you can come to Jackson. It is just wonderful of you. I just hope you will like it all right when you come. I wish I could tell you there were going to be some out-and-out marvels of birds you'd never seen before flying constantly through the air. I thought you would like a swimming pool. Today I made you some reservations at a motel that has one outdoors, instead of indoors, is that better? Tay Gillespie just brought over letters she'd got and I did what you said. Two rooms at the Sun and Sand (downtown, not a grain of sand) from May 1 through at least the 4th and I hope it will be OK. (I'll send you the confirmation when I get it.) I think Reynolds Price is going to come and he'll be at the same place, also my dear friends from Santa Fe who are coming. But I hope it will be good & quiet on the back and there are a few little green places with trees near, the Capitol grounds and a little park and a cemetery that has a lot of big old trees, so it was the best I could do about birds. (I'm trying to get onto some help about them.) I really can't imagine what that day of the 2nd is going to be like yet. Such a wonderful thing also happened in that Diarmuid Russell, who is ailing and frail, as I expect I told you, has decided *he* is going to come. He and his wife Rose, for all the times I've visited them, have never been here to see me. I'm terribly moved. They will of course be staying with me, and this means I am not asking other guests to stay at the house too—so although I did want you and Margaret to stay here if you could and would, I feel it's better all around just to have it this way, don't you? On May 1, the day you come, I am going to have all the out-of-town friends over for the evening, here, and then we can make some other, quieter plans. I do hope you can stay a little while after the hurly-burly. I'll write again when I know more, but meantime if there's anything you'd like me to do or tell you, let me know.

It was fine to read what you wrote me about Henri Coulette. And that fine boy your little grandson is growing up to be—I'd celebrate too.

I have to go to Washington for 4 days next week but otherwise will be here getting ready for I just don't exactly know what—but it sounds glorious! It really is so generous and so wonderful of you and Margaret—thank you for wanting to come.

Love,
Eudora

Isn't it almost time for that first sight of your book?

Kenneth Millar to Eudora Welty, April 4, 1973

Dear Eudora:

I've had three tidings of you in the last couple of days, the fine review of *The Optimist's Daughter* in *TLS* which I enclose; a photocopy of what I take to be your *Paris Review* interview, sent to me by Dick Lid, which I've only had time to skim over and won't attempt to comment on, except that it sounded very much like you, more than any other interview I've read; and, third, your lovely letter.[20] I'm a bit embarrassed that you should have been put to the trouble of reserving our motel rooms, but I'm glad you did, because the situation sounds just right, what with the state Capitol and the cemetery and all, and the outside pool. You're quite right not to attempt to put us up—you're going to be busy enough, and we wouldn't have dreamed of doing it. This splendid occasion coming up shouldn't be one where you wear yourself out assuming responsibility for your friends, except of course for Diarmuid. Rather you should take on for once a divine irresponsibility matching your other good qualities, and let the chips fall, the sparks fly, as they may—somewhat in the fashion of the Greeks, who set the style for civic celebrations, particularly of poets like yourself.

I said I couldn't comment on your interview but I was struck as I read through it by your homage to Chekhov, the *nonpareil*, and your feeling that his society corresponded in some sense to yours. I had a similar feeling in re-reading Gogol recently, about the kinship of Gogol with Mark Twain, say, and it encouraged me to feel that Russia and America may learn to understand each other in terms of literature and each other's past.

Jimmie *did* have a fine birthday, in the course of which he visibly put on stature, *knowing* he was now ten, and connecting: "Only three more years." "Until when?" "Until I'm a teenager." All four of us, Jim and his dad, M. and I, celebrated by going on a Bikecology bikeathon to raise money for bikeways: we all covered thirty-five miles, and

Jim finished strong, riding his yellow ten-speed birthday bike. Three hundred of us participated.

You *should* have a copy of *Sleeping Beauty* by now but my publishers are slow and stingy, sending me one copy by air which I am reading for errors, and the rest, it appears, by fourth-class mail which is getting slower and slower. But I've asked my agent Dorothy Olding to expedite a copy to you and I'll send you an inscribed one when it arrives here. I'm sorry. The book seems to me physically very well done. Your name looks good on that page.

We're delighted to hear that we may see Reynolds Price in Jackson. I've just been reading some segments of a novel by him in *Esquire* which seem to me extraordinary imaginations of the past, which moves like an ocean under our lives.

We look forward eagerly to seeing you and your city. Take it easy.

Love,

Ken

The enclosed clipping from the local paper may amuse you. K.

Eudora Welty to Kenneth Millar, April 13, 1973

Dear Ken,

Sleeping Beauty arrived, my copy from you with your beautiful inscription, and on my birthday—today, Friday the 13th—You took the curse off and put a blessing on—I came home from Washington last night and the mail came this morning & there it was.[21] (It seems to me it's when I come home from a trip, every time, that something good to do with you & your books is timed just right to meet me.) I'm so happy to see it and have it, and I think it's a very handsome book, don't you? I do like the jacket—by the same one who designed *The Underground Man* but following the new book with the different mood. I hope all good things happen to it—Of course I'm at once starting to read it again—And I thank you again—I cherish my copy.

It was fine to get your letter and I do hope the motel will be OK— But there won't be any terns there—On the evening you arrive (May 1)

I'm having the out-of-town guests to my house for drinks & buffet, I guess around 8? (I haven't thought of the time yet.) (I'll get you word.) Will you let me know what time your plane gets in, because even if those girls are meeting everybody, if I can I want to meet them too.

No terns, and no Mongolian lamb stewed in lotus blossom juice either—It was a pleasure to read about it, though, in your clipping about the picnic for Herb Caen[22]—at which you & Margaret evidently provided the most of the excitement by *coming*—And look how far you're coming to my picnic. I always enjoyed Herb Caen so much in the Chronicle while I was out there, & he must be an interesting person to talk to—It was fun to see your pictures there—and also I like the new one on your book jacket by a Boucher—kin to Anthony?[23] (No, I remember now that was a pseudonym.)

It was so thoughtful of you to clip & send me the TLS review of *Optimist's D*—It *was* a generously understanding one, which I wouldn't have otherwise seen—And again you took a curse off for me, because the *Observer*, which I subscribe to, had come with a review that gave me 40 whacks. Thank you for sending this healing one—

That *Paris Review* interview took place about 3 years ago, as nearly as I can remember, anyway it was before *The Optimist's Daughter* came out—I'm glad if it reads all right. All such are ordeals for me, but this was a rather sweet young lady who came to do this one, Linda Kuehl. I do remember the tape recorder wasn't working the whole time, & we had to do it over—

It will be lovely to see you and to meet Margaret (I enclose the reservation slip)—It's wonderful of you to come, and so far—Thank you for this too—And always for *Sleeping Beauty*—

Love,
Eudora

Margaret Millar was most comfortable within a fixed routine, and it was rare for her to leave the confines of Santa Barbara. "I live in the most beautiful place in the world," she was wont to say. "Why should I travel?" Yet when chances for trips arose, she was sometimes tempted to participate.

As the Welty celebration neared, Margaret's decision as to whether or not she'd attend changed from day to day.

Kenneth Millar to Eudora Welty, April 23, 1973

Dear Eudora:

Thank you for your warm and welcoming letter, and for the reservations at the Sun-n-Sand. I'm disappointed to have to report that I'll only be needing one room after all. Margaret's blood pressure has been jumping around—it was over 200 a few days ago—and she's been advised not to make the trip to Mississippi. This doesn't mean she's ill—in fact she's remarkably strong—but it seems best for her to stay within her routine limits. So I'll be coming solo.

My airline reservations call for me to arrive in Jackson by Delta at 5:20 on Tuesday, May 1, but there is no reason in the world why you should come to the airport to meet me and I urge you not to. Strong as you are, there will be great demands on your energy before the week is out, and you should conserve it, if you'll forgive my saying so. I'll be seeing you Tuesday evening and I understand the following evening as well. What a pleasure that will be!

I'm so glad you like the appearance of the new book. Doesn't your name look just right up front, precisely as though it belonged there as it does? We seem to go in for joint coincidences.

Your friends Tay Gillespie and Jean Turner have been in touch with me. I'll write to the motel and narrow down my reservation. My airline reservation calls for me to leave Friday at noon from the airport.

All this is very exciting, isn't it? Please don't feel let down because Margaret can't make it. That is a possibility that is always involved with our plans, and we have learned to live with it. But she's sorry not to see you. Perhaps you'll return to California one day?

Yes, Herb Caen was charming. Funny, I'd sort of thought of him as the Grand Old Man of west coast journalism. He turns out to be a year younger than I. Ray Bradbury brought up the subject of you, by the way, and mentioned how much your early stories had helped to open a way for him.[24] Two of the stories he named were "Petrified Man" and "Death of a [Traveling] Salesman," which I told him as you'd told me was your first story.

Don't you love the way everything moves in enormous meaningful circles? You (and Faulkner) have made Mississippi home, or homing, territory for all of us.

Love,
Ken

Ken Millar, sans spouse, flew to Jackson, Mississippi, for the Eudora Welty celebration and the Mississippi Arts Festival the first week in May. Millar stayed in Jackson at the Sun'n'Sand Motel, where, for at least one day of his visit, the outdoor marquee read: WELCOME MR. KENNETH MILLAR.

Here was the town that had always been Eudora's home. Ken made a proper inventory of it. To his Knopf editor, Ash Green, Millar would write that this trip to Jackson was "not unlike visiting the birthplace of a saint in her own lifetime."[25]

The public centerpiece of this celebratory week came in the Old Capitol Museum on May 2. Eudora, wrote Nona Balakian in the New York Times Book Review, *was "obviously pleased, her blue eyes as unguarded as a young girl's." Surrounded by five hundred fans, including Mississippi governor William Waller, and batteries of radio and television equipment, Eudora read three scenes from her novel* Losing Battles, *one about the heroic schoolteacher Julia Mortimer, one set on the morning of Granny Vaughn's ninetieth birthday, and a third describing the end-of-day love-making by a long separated husband and wife. Millar was impressed by her performance and by her choice of material, especially the third scene: "Eudora boldly read aloud," he wrote the English author Julian Symons, "in that same chamber where secession was first declared, and in the presence of the current governor, a passage from* Losing Battles *celebrating the sexual life."[26]*

("She put her mouth quickly on his," Eudora read of her character Gloria Renfro, "and then she slid in her hand and seized hold of him right at the root. And so she convinced him that there is only one way of depriving the ones you love—taking your living presence away from theirs."[27])

There was a buffet supper for out-of-town guests on May 1 at Welty's house—here Millar met Diarmuid Russell and other close associates of Eudora's. The next night a grand Arts Festival gathering followed a performance of The Ponder Heart, *and, finally, later in the week, a small dinner party took place back on Pinehurst Street, after which Ken and the other few guests sat and talked until midnight.*

To his friend Julian Symons, Millar would describe his "demi-week" in Jackson as "altogether a lovely experience"—adding then, in his astonishing yet still-discreet manner, that for him it had been "the biggest week since a week in June 1938 when M. and I got married."

Welty, discreet in her own way, would say of Millar's visit to Jackson in those hectic days: "Not till I took him to the airport when he left did we really get to be by ourselves. He had a good time, I think. He said he did. He's so shy, and quiet. And it didn't matter at all."[28]

Kenneth Millar to Eudora Welty, May 8, 1973

Dear Eudora:

Your invitation to visit you was wonderfully generous, and so was the treatment I received from you and all your friends, who seem to constitute a great part of the city of Jackson. That came as no surprise. I never saw such a completely and spontaneously happy group of people as those (including me) who came to hear you read in the Old State Capitol. Even the governor was happy. I was particularly happy about *what* you read, celebrating dawn and the triumph of old age, mortal love (that was a bold and excellent celebration) and intellect and character. There must have been many such devoted teachers as she abroad in the land (indeed, your niece is one of them) to have made so many people able to be happy in your art—not that your art is difficult, but it's available only to readers (and playgoers). I agree with what you told the interviewer yesterday, about the necessity of reading. Civilization is a thin solution of books, and I was continually struck by the depth of civilization I found in Jackson, where it was [nursing] still an openness to possibility, as if the south were having a new birth of freedom. If it is, you and your friends are having a lot to do with it, I think.

The forces of your society haven't gotten beyond human control, as we sometimes feel they have here.

It was a most pleasant privilege to see you (and your friends) every day for several days. It made me wish the United States was much smaller, perhaps a city state where one could live within walking distance of you. And it made me sad to leave you. I hope I'll see you before too long.

Meanwhile I know exactly where and approximately how you live, and I know you, approximately and exactly, and take great pleasure in the various knowledge. Thank you again.

Love,
Ken

P.S.—The enclosed clipping, complete with typos, is from the Santa Barbara *News-Press*. Congratulations again. No one has ever deserved that prize more.

K.

The postscript to Ken's letter congratulated Eudora on the Pulitzer Prize, which had just been awarded to her novel The Optimist's Daughter. *More important to her than the Pulitzer was the impact that Ken had on her life. She ultimately stored the prize with assorted memorabilia in a cardboard box in a closet; Ken's letters were upstairs, carefully labeled and filed, in her study/ bedroom where a rare picture of Ken and Eudora together would eventually join photos of cherished friends—William and Emily Maxwell, Reynolds Price, Katherine Anne Porter, Mary Lou Aswell, and Elizabeth Bowen—atop a bookcase overlooking her writing desk.*

Eudora Welty, "Friday, on the train," to Kenneth Millar, [May 11, 1973]

Dear Ken,

Before I leave Mississippi, which I am rapidly doing (for a train traveler) I want to tell you how much it meant and means to me that you came here—It was wholly generous and good and kind of you to make the long trip—I was glad to think you knew the happiness your being here would give to me. And you must have seen how much pleasure it was for so many others to get to meet you. Diarmuid in particular. He said to me he took most to you of anybody—"a man with a great deal of tenderness in him, it seems to me." And Reynolds got to talk to you surely—that was in the cards. And all my friends, and it was nice for me to know of my town that it is thoroughly packed with your admirers (The whole staff of the Jackson Mississippi Library came for you—to name one group.), with the ones who'd wanted to speak to you most the most tongue-tied, they've told me. But to me—it was so lovely to have you in my house. I went to your party in New York when we first met and now you've come to my party—Naturally, but like a dream too.

The thing was of course like nothing I've ever had happen to me, & wonderful for being that—it was all the *presences* of those I care for and all around me—Only private conversation couldn't happen very well, the most wished-for part—But you can't see people all together and one by one too—you can just clearly know they're in the room, each one singly, & indelibly, and dear. And it wasn't really necessary to do the introductions I'd wanted to, was it? Or to point out things—not to the best eyes and ears I know. That night you and I had dinner in New York, I asked you—it was so on my mind—about the chances of a vanished young man's being found, knowing your sympathy for the young and knowledge of them, and you said you'd imagine the boy would make himself known if and when he got ready—Well, that was Mary Lou Aswell's son, your diagnosis was correct, and that night I saw you and Mary Lou sitting side by side in my house and I think she was telling you about Duncan— Another circle—Did you know? (I hadn't named him to you.)[29]

Will you tell Margaret for me that I still hope to meet her, and some day it will be easy, don't you think? Whenever it's the best time for her and you. And you'll know to tell her that my house & my life really are quiet and we could talk and play records. The things I like best too. And walk in the open.

Thank you for your telegram. I was delighted at what you said and by hearing from you & Margaret (so I knew the plane got there). The Pulitzer news was out of the blue and wonderful. Nothing was so meaningful though as the presence of my friends here a few days before—That was the real prize and the real treasure—

We're in Alabama now, winding up a shaggy old mountain—The blackberry bushes are in flower along the track.

I want to give *Sleeping Beauty* to everybody, and soon it will be publication day, won't it—while I'm in New York this coming week? I will find a way to observe it. My feelings of pride and deep joy for my name being on that page are with me every day. When I read the novel again on the printed page, it was to see again the qualities that put it among your very best. (I think you have more than one "best"—they aren't competing.) But Sleeping Beauty has in a specially beautiful way given dramatic form to our darkest & most serious moral problems of today, and this time, more than ever before, it seems to me, in your marvelously constructed & marvelously connected story, they become in action the dark & the fiery forces they are, and the relationships are in place in every possible respect, and the proportions are kept, and the writing is all as ever precise and immaculate, and the feeling in it is like home base to me—If that sentence didn't come out exactly clear, we just went through a tunnel. You know I love this book. Its dark & deep & brooding colors I can see in my mind on this inland and lovely green landscape going by my roomette window—It's a valuable book, Ken, & not only to me. But it is so very much to me. Thank you for it, for coming, for all—

Love,
Eudora

Eudora's high opinion of Sleeping Beauty *notwithstanding, a number of prominent reviews proved harshly dismissive of the novel. Millar was enough of a scholar to know that critical blame often followed great praise; and he'd been expecting a public backlash against the acclaim awarded Macdonald's previous book by reviewers like Walter Clemons, Ray Sokolov, and Eudora Welty. But the sardonic, even vituperative critiques of* Sleeping Beauty *shocked him—as did their being used as a forum to insult Ross and Eudora both. Crawford Woods in the* New York Times Book Review *indicated that* Sleeping Beauty *was written with an inflated "self-regard" that rendered the novel's prose "nearly inedible." Anatole Broyard, in the daily* Times, *found it "difficult to see—as so many others apparently do—what sets Macdonald apart." An anonymous* New Republic *scribe mocked the way "no less a figure than Eudora Welty" had made "deepthroated music" about Macdonald on the front page of the* New York Times Book Review.[30]

There were many positive and celebratory reviews, too—in Newsweek, *for instance, and in the* Los Angeles Times, *the* National Observer, *and the* Chicago Tribune. *And Millar would have the satisfaction of seeing his novel climb high on the bestseller charts of the very journals which had knocked it most: # 9 in the* New York Times, *# 7 in* Publishers Weekly, *# 3 in* Time. *But the bad notices rankled, especially Crawford Woods's— and most especially the ones that mocked Eudora's generous judgment. Ken brought the matter to her attention, gently and almost in passing. Eudora was already aware of the situation, though, and would respond in a forceful, tough-minded fashion.*

Kenneth Millar to Eudora Welty, May 23, 1973

Dear Eudora:

I've been warming my hands all week at your marvelous lyric letter. It's not only in fiction, but in the living world itself, that your imagination creates around you an illuminated world very much like a lighted room where everything is known and loved and in its place— very much like your living room in Jackson except that it's portable, existing close around you even when you leave Mississippi (I loved your feeling that you wanted to write before you left Mississippi: it gave *me* a feeling of how deep your home feelings are) and wind "up a shaggy old mountain" in Alabama, and following you even on the streets of New York and up in the rickety old Algonquin elevator at the doors of which I first saw you in the flesh.

I'm so delighted that the new book continues to please you. I know it can't be as good as you think it is, that your responsive imagination invests it with brightness and depths not its own, but I'm content not to quarrel with your feelings about it. It might never have been written without your support. It's started well, with good reviews from a number of different journals, including one in the middle west which caught the idea of "sleeping beauty" as a dormant quality of the people in the book. And a couple of rather schizoid reviews which you unfortunately will probably see, in *Time* and *NYTBR*, and which put a rather queer spin on my dedication to you, as if it were a means of coming up in the world. But you are a veteran of such games, and won't be unduly bothered. I'm writing to Ashbel Green, my editor at Knopf, that the NYTBR reviewer did a great job of reviewing the dedication but not so well reviewing the book. In fact he misquoted me twice, and surrounded his quotations with distorting contexts. Still I'm content. It's such a relief to be out of the Crime Corner which I used to share with six or seven other crime writers jammed together like prisoners in a tank.

Margaret is well—will see the doctor tomorrow to confirm it—and shares your desire to get together. Our family news of the month is that my son-in-law has moved with grandson Jimmie into a new apartment, near UC Irvine, in Fountain Valley. This is the first move that they've made since our daughter Linda died, and it means a step into freedom and futurity for Jim, and his father, too. They'll be within walking distance of a good school and of Joe's work at the Casson Calculating Co. Joe is something of a saint, if you can imagine an engineer saint, and he has brought Jim up to be a fine and happy boy.

Our whole family—the four of us, that is—took a boat trip to the islands the other Sunday. The Channel Islands lie only 25 miles offshore but a voyage to them takes you deep into the past. Mastodons used to roam there, and there are hundreds of sea lions on the stony beaches and the ledges of the cliffs. The cliffs look like old stone walls after a siege. And there are birds to be seen, black and American oystercatchers, and one sub-species, the Santa Cruz Island Jay, which exists only on that island—too heavy to fly to the mainland. In fact it's a somewhat closed environment, like Darwin's Galapagos. Jimmie had a whale of a time. It was too late in the summer to see any whales, by the way, but we did see one porpoise.—I remembered during the voyage what you had said about *To the Lighthouse*, which struck me with similar force many years ago.

Love, Ken

P.S. Please remember me to Mrs. Gillespie and if you see them Mr. and Mrs. Turner. K.

Kenneth Millar to Eudora Welty, June 4, 1973

Dear Eudora:

Not having heard from you for two or three weeks (probably you're still away from home) I've been reading over the wonderful undeserved letter you sent me in response to *Sleeping Beauty*, treating my hopes for the book as though they were achieved and encouraging me to go on hoping that perhaps they have been, partly. As you must know, your response has been the most important one to me, and I hope to respond in turn with another wild mystical book. (Those adjectives were applied to it by another good friend and reader Peter Wolfe.) As I noted in my last letter, there has been some critical reaction, in which I apologize for your name being involved, but it didn't come from any source that one has to pay strict attention to. In fact I think that sort of thing may help to liberate a writer; of course it costs some pain.

We've had a good month in spite of these distractions. I swim in the cool gray ocean in the mornings and bike with Margaret in the cool gray evening air, mostly around Hope Ranch—a hilly 2,000-acre ranch by the ocean which about half-a-century ago was transformed into a "development" which holds now about 600 houses and will eventually take 1,000. It's a fine place to live—our house is almost in the middle of it—partly because it's sparsely settled with people and partly because it's thickly planted with trees—the developers planted

50,000 of them, eucalyptus, cypress, pine, oak (but most of the oaks are native and old). There is a golf course and in the middle of the golf course a 30-acre lake, mostly natural, and on the lake gulls and ducks and herons and sometimes migrating birds like Canada geese. This is not a typical golf-course suburb, though; just up the street, for example, lives Dean Wooldridge who with Simon Ramo *et al.* invented the modern technological factory which is one of the essential differentiae of California and has made the state more productive than the whole of Britain. Wooldridge retired before he was fifty to write books. I've never met him. Just down the street in the other direction lives Jack Northrup, the aircraft inventor who was a leader in the previous generation of technical revolution. Apart from Clifton Fadiman and some other scholarly sorts, there aren't too many writers in Hope Ranch but the surrounding woods are full of them—more than 300 in the Santa Barbara area according to a count by the local library. Some of us meet for lunch every two weeks in a local restaurant—William Campbell Gault, Michael Collins, my best friend Robert Easton who wrote a factual book about the oil spill. But mostly I stay at home or out in nature.

This account is a poor substitute for such a visit as I had in Jackson, but I felt like writing it. I loved Miss Balakian's piece about your Day, your week, in the NYTBR. She spoke with lovely feeling and for all of us, Love, Ken

P.S. Please convey my respects to Diarmuid, that noble soul. K.

Eudora Welty, New York City, to Kenneth Millar, May 18, 1973.
Despite its date of composition, the following letter was not mailed until June. Eudora enclosed it with part of a June 4, 1973, letter from Reynolds Price to her and with her own June 7, 1973, letter to Ken.

Dear Ken,

The review of *Sleeping Beauty* in the coming Sunday NYTBR is a shameful piece of work, not really a review at all of course and not worth being a cause of pain to you, but how could it help but be. Does the reviewer's name mean anything to you? It doesn't to me— but he was clearly wanting to take you down because your books have been too well received in the past for his comfort, and whatever your new book had been like (and he never found out, starting with the title which he didn't read either) he wanted to say these stupid and derogatory things about it—or rather about you. His deliberate attack was so obviously what it was that no reader could miss the motive behind the words, and even if a reader didn't know your work for himself, as being none of the things this man says, he'd know to take this review as the opposite of the truth. My impulse was to reply but I realize it would be unbecoming in the dedicatee (a word?) and besides would draw attention to something best ignored. If it is any comfort to you in companionship, I have had the exact same charge made against me, of trying to do something out of my bent, because of a dedication, which was to Elizabeth Bowen—It was a book of stories laid in Ireland, Italy, etc., and I was advised to keep to something I know and not try to be so pretentious as to write about anything outside Miss. and Elizabeth's name was used against me, just as mine was against you, and just as without reason. I was also, just the other month, attacked in the London *Observer* for even trying to foist a novel (*Optimist's D.*) on the public, with my impossible female name and my appalling part of the country—So I know something of your feeling now, but I hope, knowing, as you certainly must of the steady admiration from all over everywhere that you've long since had and will have, you'll just let this man go to hell & forget about him—Of course *I* hate it and just wanted to let loose for a minute. More later—

On June 4, 1973, Reynolds Price wrote to Eudora expressing similar sentiments, and in her next letter to Ken, Eudora enclosed Reynolds's comments on the subject: "I hope Ken Millar isn't depressed by the two or three ratty notices I've seen of Sleeping Beauty—Sunday Times *and* New

Republic. *I really don't think it was responsible of the* Times *to have run the one they did; it all smacks so much of 'He got a little too big for his britches (sez we) so we'll whittle him down.' I say it's wicked, and seriously so. I admired the book very much—one of the best three or four of his novels, I think—and as soon as I've given it a slow second reading, I'm going to write him and say so."*[31]

Eudora Welty to Kenneth Millar, June 7, 1973

Dear Ken,

It was lovely to find your letters here when I got home, and I want to answer them with a real letter and not a scrap—soon too. Meanwhile here's a piece of one I wrote you in New York, expecting to add to—that was the day I went over to the Book Review office to say hello and got the advance copy with that stupid review of Sleeping Beauty in it. And here's the last page of a letter from Reynolds which is about Sleeping Beauty—(you can let me have it back some time if you think of it). And separately I'm sending you my copy of Diarmuid's Irish Reader, to read at leisure, just some day let me have it back if you will—I tried all one morning in the second-hand shops down on 10th and 11th Sts. and B'way and 4th Ave to find a copy to give you, and couldn't.[32] Would you mind signing a Sleeping Beauty for Diarmuid—I'm sending it to you—he'd so much like to have it. He read it while here as he must have told you and liked it so much, and Rosie was reading it and said she would like to borrow mine to finish on the plane going home but I said No, and Diarmuid said "Quite right. You shouldn't let that copy leave the home." Jackson just got its copies in yesterday, for some reason, so now I can give presents—just gave one to Elizabeth my niece, who came in while I was writing this.

I'm glad Margaret's feeling fine again. I loved hearing about the sail to the Islands. I'll write soon. A lot of duties came down on me to do, and sometimes I do them and sometimes I just listen to the

Watergate—if it comes on there at 7 AM I doubt if it's as galvanizing to the Millars. A whole new, bad vocabulary.

New Stage is putting on "John Brown's Body" now, and imported a guest star, Inga Swenson, who it turns out is your constant reader. A lovely young woman.

Love,
Eudora

Later—I'm so happy to have just received your letter that tells me about your house and all that's surrounding—Thank you for just what I would have wished to know—

Eudora Welty to Kenneth Millar, June 10, 1973

Dear Ken,

Yes, I felt very glad of all your letter told me about where and how you live in Santa Barbara. I felt I could see it clearly, and understand a little how rewarding that life must be for you—not lonely, because you're reflective. The imagination needs all that room and peace—*it's* so thronging. And how beautiful, all that surround. It's no wonder I always feel the physical world, the landscape and weather, so near & real when I read your books. At the same time they're all happening in a landscape of the mind, their own place, as all stories do—(the two) Seen together—no, working together. I put with what you told me the wrong house, the one in Margaret's "The Birds and the Beasts Were There," which I *know* is not the same as the one you live in now, but I can't help it, that's the one I see. Also I put with it remembered (I hope correctly) things of my own—the smell of pepper trees & eucalyptus and the sea, the sense of the edge of a continent—to which your own books speak. So now I have some things put together.

The new oil spill made me feel bad for you, & Margaret. After the first news of it, I never heard anything more. Even any definitely assigned cause for it. Is it being helped any?

It's Sunday, I've been reading all day (Willa Cather—"The Professor's House"). After I got home from NY, where I stayed less than a week—mainly to attend a little gathering of old friends & clients for Diarmuid on the occasion of his retirement, given by Tim Seldes, who's taken over the agency—& whom Diarmuid has all confidence in. I came home by way of Charlotte, N.C. (a little girls' college there gave me an hon. Degree, and everything took 3 days) then *flew* home, which I am not good at, and found I was tired for the first time.[33] All those things that had never happened to me before, and all had really overwhelmed me. I found the name of Ross Macdonald in the newspaper I was reading on the plane, and as far as I'm concerned, that's what kept it (the plane) coming and didn't let it fall. Here's the review, I tore it out for you, you've surely seen it—It has some perceptions, don't you think? I'm trying to track down some other reviews in our rather sparsely provided library. I saw Newsweek—Walter Clemons sadly said P.S.P. carried off the book which came while he was out—Wish I could review it (*The Underground Man* review I did is going in my non-fiction book that I'm about to tackle now.).[34]

Are you really onto a new book? Say no more if you feel it's not good luck. But I hope it is a fact—that would be at dazzling speed—wonderful news though, whenever it comes.

This is as you see the book I would be so happy if you'd sign for Diarmuid—and then next time you go to the P.O. drop it in. I didn't feel you would mind—and I do thank you—

Forgive me for letting a young woman who has just opened her own bookstore here have your address—She wants to ask you to sign her book, but it's not just an idle request—she has really been so crazy about your novels for a long time and has never asked an author for an autograph before. (I don't count, I live here & know her mother.) I won't do this again though. The Irish Reader is coming too and no hurry a bit about reading it or letting me have it back—I hope you like it!

Thank you again for writing to me about Hope Ranch. Love to you,
Eudora

Now you've been in the Jackson paper & I've been in the Santa B. one. I'm glad you liked Nona Balakian's piece—it was lovely of her to write it—I cherish it.

Kenneth Millar to Eudora Welty, June 11, 1973

Dear Eudora:

You are a helpful person, and most generous, too, as always, in telling me about your own contretemps with the kind of people who chose to make an issue out of a dedication offered in a quite different spirit from that suggested. Your understanding is so complete that it clarifies mine and gives me a different reflection of the event: I see past it to you. And Reynolds' opinion, which you passed on, is worth a good deal to me, too, as is his friendship.

Still I may decide to answer Mr. Woods. His documentation is quite faulty, including two misquotations of my text and three obvious distortions of my context. In a word, I didn't say what he says I said; and my editor Ash Green seems to feel that perhaps the NYTBR and its readers should be informed of this. Apart from the New York backlash the book has been doing well throughout the country. It is seventh on the current PW list, and most reviewers seem to agree with Reynolds that it's among my best books. I'm grateful particularly because I dedicated it to you in that hope, and in the knowledge that I might never write another one as good. But now I feel I will. I've turned that corner, too. I see past it not only to you but to what you see, and feel greatly blessed by your moral companionship.

One of the things I liked best in Mississippi was the chance to look through your professional memorabilia, over which I spent a happy couple of hours—not just because they were yours but because the whole thing added up (not that the final addition has been made) to a joyful statement of how to live, wait, work, endure; all gracefully. It was with that exhibition in mind that I took the liberty of advising you to let your letters stand for the future. They have an absoluteness and delicacy of moral line which the future will need even if it doesn't desire.

You're right, Watergate doesn't jerk me out of my bed at seven a.m. but we usually catch some of it later, and then would willingly let it go again. A "new bad vocabulary," as you say, anatomizing the new bad structure of our society. Still the anatomy lesson has to be taught. (Goya recurs to the mind.)

Tomorrow we're off to be witnesses at the trial of a bulldozer-operator who is up on a charge of battery for trying to run down a group of protestors against an oceanfront apartment building near here.[35] I'll tell you how it turns out.

Love, Ken

Reynolds' page enclosed. Many thanks. K.

P.P.S. (June 12)—I have got off to Diarmuid the copy of *Sleeping Beauty* you sent me, inscribed: —

"To Diarmuid Russell, a lovely man,

on the occasion of his retirement and

in respect for his excellent career."

I'm very glad I had a chance to meet him and come to know him, and can imagine how important he is and has been in your life. A lovely man indeed.

We lost our court case. It was twisted into a contest between old and young, short hair and long hair, property and passion, and property won. But within the same twenty-four hours the environmental lawyer Mark MacGivens whom M. and I help to support, won a stay order against the same oceanfront apartment building in the Los Angeles appellate court. The world is changing, I hope fast enough to keep itself from being destroyed.

K.

Eudora Welty to Kenneth Millar, June 22, 1973

Dear Ken,

You know what my feelings are about your work and about *Sleeping Beauty*—and how I think your fine gifts have never been under more sensitive and sure control, and that they are being brought to bear more and more on the subjects that count most for you. You speak of turning a corner, and you would know, though it seems more to me like just going straight forward on your way, the way an arrow flies. The important thing is that it flies, and that's the surest thing there is about whatever direction you want your next book to take. Thank you so much for writing in Diarmuid's book—he was so pleased, and I'm glad you told me what you'd said because he thought I'd seen it (and, I guess, had sent the book from here), and it pleased me so that you felt this. I felt happy about your getting to meet each other—it was one of the things about that occasion that seemed most happy and most right. You and Diarmuid have in common one of the rarest things in the world, which surely you recognized in each other—you mean exactly what you say.—What you said about letters seemed to apply to something Diarmuid told me in New York when I saw him last, that he had all the letters I'd written during the 32 years he'd been my agent, and asked what he should do with them. I might have said on first impulse (in my sorrow for him now) to just get rid of them, but the thing is, I have all the other half of that correspondence, and it is really the whole factual story of my working life, and so to me it would matter to have it—I just never would have thought of it objectively that way. I don't suppose there's a word in any of the letters from either of us that isn't just exactly how it was.—But would other people care, or should they care, that's something else and something I shy off from too much to think about. Of course the letters are also the letters of close friendship. I can tell you the exact truth, if it had not been for Diarmuid I doubt if any of my work would ever have reached any general publication. From the start, when he and Henry began the agency, they never took on a client whose work they did not like and believe in—regardless of how well or how little they might be known. I was the prime example, completely unknown, and the first client. Diarmuid spent two thankless years trying to get me into the Atlantic Monthly, and I remember his writing me once "If Ted Weeks doesn't take this one, he ought to be horse-whipped." Enough to make me write another story overnight! He has guided me toward, and protected me from, more than I knew, and never once pressed me. All the years I didn't publish anything, before I got Losing Battles done, he never once was anything but compassionate. He never had to say much about a story I'd send, he never did say many words, but "It's good" would be pure gold to me. He *knew*—he told me that a story I sent in was really chapter two of a novel. It was, too (Delta Wedding, my first novel). It is sweet of you to be interested in the letters and what happens to them. It's just a jump-shift in my thinking to imagine any eyes reading them but those they were meant for, and the understanding they were meant for. I rely so heavily on the other end.

I'd held back from mailing my letter to you about that lowlife Woods, as you may have noticed, in worrying that I might have taken his review for more than it was worth and that this would just add to your pain about it. Also, I can't remember if I told you, I wrote to Woods myself but finally didn't send the letter because such a one as he would see in my words only the fact of the dedication which was the matter with him in the first place. It was the unfairness of the review that stung. Those inaccuracies must have been only deliberate. I can understand that you would want to answer him, it would be hard not to, and maybe not right not to. I have a deep skepticism, all the same, about answering a reviewer's ever doing any good. You would do it so well, hitting the nail right on the head, that I would really be gratified to see it, though. And it must gratify you to see how well the book's doing all over the place—I look in the NYT Book Review and Time for their best seller list every week, and am pleased to hear about the one in PW. I think it must be pretty well established all over the country what a good book we've got on our hands. (Jackson is selling a lot of copies! So the bookstores tell me. Also as you no doubt know, speaking of the Archives, *Sleeping Beauty* has been purchased to go in the Welty papers, for the dedication.)

I had a lot of letters to write, so I guess I'd better stop. Thank you again for signing the book for Diarmuid (the letter inside was for you, I guess you found it). Love,

Eudora

Kenneth Millar to Eudora Welty, June 28, 1973

Dear Eudora:

You have enlarged my life in several ways. Your letter has added an extra dimension to it, and now I am hearing from your friends. John Prince sent me the Lew Archer–cum Martha Mitchell parody from the Washington *Star-News*, which I thought was funny enough to send along to you (please return).[36] I had a delightful note from Mary Lou, who hasn't forgiven me for not enjoying my one night in Santa Fe and wants me to return and report. I've heard from Nona, having written her how much I liked her report in the NYTBR and how true a picture it managed to give of your day, your week. And now I've had a sweet and gentle greeting from Diarmuid, almost in the same mail with your exceedingly interesting letter about your long friendship and professional relationship with him. (I did find your letter, of course; and I'm greatly pleased that *Beauty* is sneaking its way into the Welty papers via the dedication.) In the light of what you say about that career-long relationship I can't help foreseeing a time when the letters that record it will be of the very first literary and historical importance, more valuable I should think than the Fitzgerald-Ober correspondence which my friend Matt Bruccoli did recently. It's an important book, basic in its new field, but the Fitz-Ober relationship wasn't really imaginative or creative. My own feeling is that it led Fitzgerald away from his best self, if only by providing opportunities to evade it. And I might add that the Ober relationship—I knew Harold Ober, but dealt primarily with Ivan von Auw—wasn't a particularly happy one for me. It's happier now that Ivan has retired. But what you say of your working life with Diarmuid sounds just perfect, exactly what you and your work needed and deserved. It's sad that it is ending. But the work remains, and so do the letters.[37]—Do I sound like a monomaniac? I'm merely a scholar, a rather wandering scholar. (But I think the mystery novel is a rather scholastic discipline, don't you?)

Beauty is doing quite well, in its fifth week on the *Times* best seller list, and probably its last. The competition is very stiff this month.[38] But

Knopf has shipped close to 40,000 and will probably, after remaindering, have sold thirty or so. All of which gives me what I value most: freedom to write what I like next time around, the same freedom I've always had really. As for the book itself, apart from the politics of the game, I feel pretty good about it and am so glad you do, too. It would be terrible to dedicate a book to you and have it turn out to be a flop.

Love,

Ken

Kenneth Millar to Eudora Welty, July 18, 1973

Dear Eudora:

Here is a copy of the letter I wrote in answer to Crawford Woods' review in the NYTBR. I've sent typed copies to the editor and also to Nona Balakian, who expressed regret about the review. It isn't what I would call an eloquent letter—I found myself unwilling to argue the literary issues with a wholly hostile critic, and confined myself to showing the weakness of the scholarship on which his critical judgments were based—but I hope it will teach him to be more careful in his handling of other writers' words and sentences. Do you think the mistakes have been further compounded by the writing of this letter? I do regret having had to write it, but in the end I felt compelled to. One consequence is that the great millstone in one's head which turns only when the stream runs has turned in me, and I have had some dreams approaching nightmares from which however I seem to have awakened refreshed. Aggression comes hard to me, as I know it does to you. I do hope you won't feel that my sending you this copy of the letter means, or is intended to mean, that you should in any way become involved in the issue, but I thought you might like to see it after the event. (That last sentence may betray the fact that I have been reading fairly late Henry James, *The Wings of the Dove*, which until I got a stronger pair of glasses had been a closed book to me, at least in the paperback edition which I own. It's a terribly poignant novel, but at this point I'm not quite sure of it. I started it once years ago, but didn't get through it, though I love James. This time is different: it holds me in more kinds of suspense than one.)

The summer is proceeding at bicycle pace, a coolish summer with quite a lot of fog which I have learned to regard as a blessing, for one reason because our old dogs breathe so much more easily. We've started going in the ocean again, together I mean, since I never really quit. There's still some oil floating in the water, but nothing serious.

Herb Harker and his wife just this month, as I write, blew in from Calgary in a rented truck with all their furniture (hers from Pocatello where she taught in the state college) and are setting up housekeeping here in a house which they are buying. Herb's making it back here is a great satisfaction to us, not to mention to him. (He spent the last several years in Calgary.) We lose so many friends to distance. Which reminds me to ask you to please remember me to Reynolds, whom I wish I could see more of (though I read him with excitement in *Esquire*) and to Mary Lou, whom I owe a letter to—I hope all is well with you, Eudora—I know this is a hard period for you.

Love, Ken

Eudora Welty to Kenneth Millar, Sunday morning [July 22, 1973]

Dear Ken,

Thank you for your good and warming letter—I've been thinking of you but have not written because my best friend in Jackson suddenly died—was found dead [on July 14]—and I've been feeling bad about her. Rosa Farrar Wells, called Dolly—She'd have been at that big party one of a crowd to you, but was an admirer—She and I were friends here from schooldays, then she went to New York and worked in publishing (Harper's) for years, got tired of all that, & came back home (3 blocks from me)—We normally saw each other two or three times a week, had a drink & watched the news at the end of a day. She lived alone, and dying alone was the sad part. I guess the good part is that a heart attack is quick. I miss her not only for herself but because of my friends here she was almost the only one who liked to read, & the only one who knew the same friends I knew in New York and here too, and we also had shared a trip in Europe—we both loved boats the best thing in the world, and had been planning a possible trip in the fall if we both could manage it. She liked picnics the way I do and we've been on many of the same good crazy ones a small crowd of us (we began it in the penniless, jobless days of the Depression) always had this time of year on the spur of the moment—So many falling stars is how I set the time of them, the ones that fall all through late July & August—Perseides?—Of that little crowd, three have now died. It's the time of life I've now reached, I know—But your *feelings* don't change—

I did copy out this page or 2 of *Uncle Vanya* for you, in place of a letter, wondering if you'd read it again lately enough to remember its beautiful and extraordinarily apt speeches about conservation—I hadn't read the play in ages, but the book of Chekhov's letters sent me back to it—Have you read *those* lately? I love him above all the short story writers ever born—do you?

Thank you for sharing the clipping the Princes sent—it's pretty good, I agree, so much more amusing than the last one I read that missed every point about Lew Archer—A parodist should realize that work is just as precise & succinct and concentrated and *difficult* as what he's parodying,—as I think you earlier said to me!—Of course this isn't a real case of parody—Buchwald had a funny column on slightly the same subject of the wild complications of Watergate, only he used the Forsyte Saga instead of Lew Archer, did you come across it?[39]

The news of how the book's doing is welcome & good & not surprising, and I hope it continues that way which is the way it deserves. (I'm pretty sure this review from the Jackson paper last Sunday, which I cut out for you, must be a syndicated one, but I send it just the same since it's ours & since it's pretty well done, don't you think?)

My own love to the book & my own knowledge of how good the work is—you know you have that, and my thanks that go right on. You must feel the kinship it has with the bit of *Uncle Vanya*.

Love,
Eudora

Eudora Welty to Kenneth Millar, July 23, 1973

Dear Ken,

I just got your letter and the copy of the one you sent to the Book Review. I'm glad you let me see it, and I hope it will appear soon. What you said was said well, of course—with restraint which meant a good deal to accomplish I know—and with nothing but the facts to speak for you, which were all that were needed to show that man up. The quotes from your book in their proper form and context—*and* the quotes of *him*—the combination was very eloquent. And how could you argue a literary issue with a man who'd written those things about you? What makes me so sorry is that anything came along to take away any of the pleasure in the book for you—and that it's bothered you and even troubled your dreams. Please do begin to feel that since there was nothing of truth or value in what this Crawford Woods said, and since you have set the factual correction to this down on paper, you can leave it behind you now—Don't mind if I say this, since the book is close to me too. My mother had a saying when she wanted you to dismiss some offender like that, "He's not worth an inch of your little finger," and indeed, Ken, he's not. So I hope what you're doing is getting the feel and the joy of a new book in you, that's the best change in the world, don't you believe? And that you won't let this stupid man take away your rightful good feeling about *Sleeping Beauty*, to the least degree—You know that wouldn't be right, to let him get away with his attack, which is so clearly one of ignorance, envy and malice. I feel sure it didn't come easily to you to write that letter—you could have done it more easily on behalf of somebody else—Do you want me to return you the copy? I'll watch for it in the paper. Just tear up his rotten review—I hope all goes well with everything, and how good that your old friend Herb Harker has come to live close by—Do you think I should try The Wings of the Dove? I gave up the first time too—

Love,
Eudora

Kenneth Millar to Eudora Welty, July 24, 1973

Dear Eudora:

Not having heard from you for a while I had begun to wonder if all was well and now you tell me that it isn't. I am so sorry you lost your dear friend Dolly Wells, and grateful to you for telling me something of your lives together in Jackson and elsewhere. It's a hard thing to be moving as you are, and I close behind you, into the time of loss. No wonder as we grow older we like to live in the more populous past. My father-in-law Henry Sturm, who is in his ninetieth year, almost blind but full of memories, has almost no coevals left. But he has one good niece (about your age) who keeps in steady touch with him, and makes him happy, if that word can be used for a man who is almost blind and almost ninety. Henry would have made a character in *Losing Battles*: he left school in the fourth grade and went to work in the (Ontario) fields, to such good effect that he became mayor of the city of Kitchener, a city not wholly unlike Jackson though its core population is German and Pennsylvania Dutch. I'm impressed by the strength and courage that makes such a man as Henry dare to grow very old, outliving [my] wife Margaret's mother by forty years. I wish you strength and courage, but not such lonely longevity as that, though you have your nieces, too, and so many friends.

I hadn't looked at *Uncle Vanya* since I was in graduate school and even then I hadn't come far enough along to recognize Chekhov's complete relevance to our concerns. I do now, though, and the passage you so kindly typed out for me points it up. And the answer to your question do I love Chekhov best of all story writers is yes. I'll never forget the first time I read *The Black Monk* and now I learn from his letters—yes, I've just bought his letters, too—the Karlinsky and Heim selection, not the Yarmolinsky—I learn from his letters that if he hadn't become a writer he would have become a psychiatrist. (So might I.) I think his life was exemplary as well, noble and sweet and above all intelligent for everyone but himself.

Yes, I saw Buchwald—the Watergate Sage. I'd also seen the review from the Jackson paper which you so kindly sent me. I don't use a clipping service but I have a friend in Florida named W.T. Bresson, a true-crime writer who for reasons of his profession buys dozens of papers from all over the country, and when he sees a friend named he lets us know—a wonderfully generous man.

S.B. is still being shipped, at the rate of about 800 a week. I enclose the June wrapup from *PW* so that you can see where it stood, though it no longer does of course.

Margaret sends her love, with mine. Our thoughts are very much with you. Thank you for writing. As ever, Ken

Kenneth Millar to Eudora Welty, July 29, 1973

Dear Eudora:

I'm grateful for your warm and strong support in the matter of the Crawford Woods review, which now that it is answered, and in your opinion properly so, I can forget and almost already have. Jimmie and his dad were up for the weekend and we had a fine time in and out of the ocean and at the dog show. One of the lifeguards took Jim for a ride in his dory—used for rescue—and J was in seventh watery heaven, and I recalled my own first experiences with the Pacific, on English Bay in Stanley Park in Vancouver. I think that blue oceanic dream (you have it, too, being crazy about boats) is a good one to have through life. As for the dog show, our favorite part was the obedience trials, with the deep and subtle and differing relationships between the dogs and their masters. My favorite dogs in that event, and usually the winners (though I once saw a Welsh Corgi take the first ribbon) are the German Shepherds like my own old dog Brandy who was also obedience-trained, up to a point. I think the most fun Margaret and I ever had was when Brandy was young and the three of us would go swimming in the ocean. Brandy is too arthritic to go in the surf any more, but we're not.

Joe, Jim's devoted father, is looking himself again for the first time in the nearly three years since his wife and our daughter Linda died. For the first time he looked at the light as if it didn't dismay him. At the same time he's always been perfect with his son—I've never seen such complete understanding and respect between a boy and his father. In fact we all get along very well, and fly high on bicycles.

Having diligently read my way through *The Wings of the Dove* I think I can report that it is safe for you to give it a skip. Line by line it's marvellously wrought but somehow overcharged with electricity that fails to flow from scene to scene, and by emotion which is elaborately known but not quite felt, like a model of the circulatory system without any heart attached to it. Or, to name what it is, a novel of seduction told in purely cerebral terms. James avoided his subject in more ways than this. Milly Theale is a portrait of the artist as a dying young woman, but we never get to know what really killed her, or what killed or attenuated James' immense talent. I think I can guess, though. Between *The Ambassadors* and *Dove* the American tie which held his imagination in place was somehow cut. He ascended like a balloon.

I'm sending you a book, a very thin book published by an old friend and former student, in which a couple of essays about detective fiction which you may not have seen are reprinted.[40] It's dedicated to Donald Davie because we were close, literally and fig'ly, the winter I wrote *The Galton Case*.

Love,
Ken

Kenneth Millar to Eudora Welty, August 7, 1973

Dear Eudora:

I found when I opened my New York Times Book Review that a remarkable thing had happened which I must share with you. My letter had been printed, but as I started to read it the language didn't seem entirely familiar. In fact it had been improved. It struck me as I went on that someone at the Book Review had edited and revised my letter, strengthening it and putting teeth in it. And it seemed to me that John Leonard himself must have done the deed, or at the least authorized it. Whatever, I took it as a strong direct personal message which pleased and encouraged me, and has had the effect of putting the whole unfortunate matter behind me. (If you should wish to compare the two letters, you have a copy of my original, I believe.)[41] Life continues full of surprises. Another was a very late hatching of quail, long after we had given up on them for this season, so that there are ten "walking walnuts", as M. calls them, spending a good deal of time in our back yard. We're doing a good deal of hiking and swimming these days against the day coming on when I have to stay home and get to work—which I'm starting to look forward to now.

Love,
Ken

Eudora Welty to Kenneth Millar, Sunday morning [August 12, 1973]

Dear Ken,

It was a comfort to get your letter about the losing of my friend—but I know I'd been self-indulgent when I sent my letter to you—you were so kind and so quick to write to me. Thank you for your wishes. I've been owing you more than one letter, and have wanted to say how very much I prize the book you sent me with your two pieces on writing. I've never seen the first, "The Writer as Detective Hero," and had seen the second, on writing *The Galton Case*, in the volume called *Afterwords*, which Reynolds Price sent me some time back, because both you and he were in it. (I read it in your new little book and in the Afterwords collection too, together, seeing that you had left it without changing a word—and why would you have, in its excellence?) And I went back and read your Introduction to *Archer at Large*, which you gave me, which even before I'd met you I found so personally moving, just to see them together. It's good to have the real thing being said about a writer's work, and working, by the writer—when he can do it, which not all writers can at all. To me what you say about plot in the first piece is the best I know. Those four clear probing sentences, in their concentration of knowledge and wisdom—I rejoiced when I read them. Of course the essay itself is full of imaginative and sane and just comparisons and distinctions that you're the exact right one to make in your account of Poe and Doyle and Hammett and Chandler and you, and your detectives—(I say "just" not because I think I know more than I do, but because I know it can't help but be just.) It is good to have, and the two pieces together ought to always be available to readers—though of course it's a great pleasure to have them in this handsome form—thank you for the present of the book, and for the inscription in it, which I shall be taking good care of. I thought at several points in reading it how well it would have served me in my year or two with my writing class at Millsaps College here—I did use the detective story in my efforts to illustrate the vital elements of plot which could be learned there, in its strictest form. The piece you've written is now a help to me. I've been trying to get a short piece written on time in fiction,—the kind of thing that I can learn a little from in trying to put down. So it was timely, your book, as well as welcome.

Yes, I'd seen the altering of the first paragraph of your letter to the Times B-R, and I wondered who. You are probably right that it could only be John Leonard. I hope it was. It had seemed rather a poor thing to do on his part to let that review be published—although of course I realize an editor does stand behind his reviewer (he's done that for me), still he owed you the much greater debt, to have your book honestly and fairly reviewed—and his admiration of you and your work is certainly long since proven and known. Maybe all the while he's hoped you'd write and give him some little chance to say he's sorry. Anyway, the letter read fine, and it's on record now. I've been meaning to return your draft of it to you, it was good of you to let me see it.

Things sound so nice there—the peaceful days and the excursions in the cool evenings on the bicycle. I'm glad to know you feel as you do about Jimmie and his father. And of course glad it is so for Jimmie. He is doubly fortunate, he has you—and I think of how what was your own right as a child being taken from you has only made you so giving. (My mother used to use that word. She would say you were "very giving.") To more than your family, to your friends too, and your students—as Mr. Noel Young says. Don't mind my saying it, I've often thought it.

By the way, did you safely get the little Irish Reader that I sent off to you a while back—things get so lost in the mail. It's not that I'm anxious to have it back any time soon. But now, the book man I know in NY has succeeded in finding me a copy second hand that I'll send you to keep—though my original wish had been to get Diarmuid to inscribe it for you, and I don't know about this now—he's in Maine, with Rosie, till after Labor Day, all going well, but says he does get these spells of tiredness—his word. I want to go up to see him in September, if he feels like it. Anyway, I thought you might like to have a copy to keep. One of my favorite things in it is the letter from Connemarra by Maria Edgeworth—isn't that wonderfully wild?

I've written too long a letter and let the beans burn dry, I bet—

Please give my love to Margaret too, and thank her for her message. Nice news about the quails. I believe you told me once they were your favorite bird. I saw a hummingbird early in the morning today, away up high in my oak tree. What was he drinking—the dew?

Love,
Eudora

Kenneth Millar to Eudora Welty, August 12, 1973

Dear Eudora:

I've been approached to put together a mystery and suspense anthology, a fairly thick one comprising novels, novellas, and short stories. The emphasis, my editor Ash Green says, is to be on suspense. If any nominations spring to mind, I'd be glad to have your help. The book as I see it will be divided between English and American work. At the moment I'm re-reading Graham Greene's "The Basement Room" which seems a likely candidate—I don't think familiarity is an objection in a book not aimed at aficionados.

I'll tell you more about this assignment as it proceeds, if you are interested.

The enclosed review, written for the *S.F. Chronicle* about 15 years ago, turned up in my files and I send it on to you because it ends up with Chekhov. Nona Balakian (speaking of reviews) wrote me a warm friendly letter on her return from her vacation, enclosing a clipping of my letter to the Book Review and saying I should have put it even stronger. It's almost worth having a review like that, to have one's friends old and new rally round.

We have ten brand-new quail in the yard as I wrote you—or is it twelve, or are they two separate families? We can't tell yet. Love, Ken

P.S.—Immediately after writing this note I went to an unfrequented bookshelf and picked out a book apparently at random and then saw it was edited by Mary Lou Aswell—*The World Within*, a psychoanalytically oriented literary anthology which includes not only "Why I Live at the P.O." but Chekhov's "The Black Monk," and which I have been recurring to for years but not recently. This seems to be a kind of coming-together time. So now I must write to Mary Lou. K.

[also includes *Detroit Sunday News* review, May 27, 1973, of *Sleeping Beauty*, written by Peter Wolfe]

Thought you might be interested in this, too. Somehow it just reached me. I don't vouch for all of it. K.

Peter and his two young sons are visiting here next week.

Eudora Welty to Kenneth Millar, [August 1973]

Dear Ken,

I'm sending you my first thought [Patrick O'Brian's "The Walker"][42] though it might not be any good to you as a possible candidate—Do you know it? What a pleasure to think of your doing such an Anthology—

"The Basement Room," which I too like makes me think of Ralph Richardson in the movie of it, remember "Fallen Idol," who makes me think of Chekhov—the best Vershinin that could ever have been—

I want you to have back your draft of your letter to the *Times* too—have been waiting to come by an envelope. Letter next time.

Love to the quails too,

Eudora

Thank you for letting me off The Wings of the Dove

Kenneth Millar to Eudora Welty, August 24, 1973

Dear Eudora:

I did receive the *Irish Reader* you sent me, long since, but while I wrote to Diarmuid about my enjoyment of it I evidently failed to mention it to you. I'm sorry. It's a very good collection: I'm glad to have been told about it and would be very happy to have a copy to keep, since you are so generous, with or without Diarmuid's signature, as it falls. If you do see him next month, please remember me to him. I never saw a more pure or direct light in a man, and it was a great privilege to meet him, a privilege now perpetuated by his book, which I'll return to you soon.

You probably make too much of my very small book, but I'm so glad you like it! In allowing it to be made I was carried away by the purely personal (as Noel Young was in his introduction)—the idea of a hometown product put out by two old friends, one of whom is a rather elegant printer. Noel has since acquired a kind of fame with his book "Hot Tubs" about communal bathing in the Santa Barbara hills, which you may have seen written up in *Newsweek*. It seems to be an innocent sport but I prefer the solitary ocean, and bicycle twosomes. Though it's getting a little warm here—nothing like Jackson, but we had a hot dry Santa Ana wind last night—but M. and I are still getting out on wheels every evening, coming home just as night falls, with the last of the birds (except the owls, who stay out later than we do—barn, screech and great horned owls, the latter contemptuously imperturbable in the presence of human beings.) I asked Margaret, by the way, if hummingbirds *do* drink dew. She thinks they do, but get most of their liquid needs in the nectar they drink. A nice life, humming around and drinking nectar. But my favorite birds at the moment, as I may have mentioned, are the various kinds of terns—Caspian, Elegant, Forster's—that are fishing these days in our channel. They have such beautiful lines and such a deep emphatic wing-beat, as if they were leading an orchestra. Our greatest find, though—not ours personally, though we got in on it—our best find this summer was a couple of roseate spoonbills who turned up in our local slough, a first sighting for S.B. but not for California. Yesterday my brother-in-law snuck up within seventy-five feet of them and took their pictures 24 times. The last spoonbills I saw were off Corpus Christie, flocking in such number that the island they were sitting on looked like a pink island.

It was good of you to take the trouble to send me "The Walker." It's a terribly powerful story—one of those stories that stays with you forever, I suspect, like a terribly bad dream—and I hope to use it. The deal for the anthology isn't quite set yet, I'm told; I'll be content, whichever way it goes. Meanwhile I'm enjoying the reading, rediscovering Ambler, Christie, Greene, Stanley Ellison.

Tomorrow, camp having ended, Jimmie comes to us for ten days, and it'll be a threesome on the bike trails. Love, Ken

P.S. I look forward to your piece on time. K
P.P.S.—I didn't think your letter about the death of your friend was in the least self-indulgent, and I was glad you felt able to speak to me about it. Like the trees in your yard we lose limbs but still put out new leaves. K.

Late in 1973 Eudora and Ken both sought the convergence of their professional lives; if they were not to be together in person, they could be together in their work. In September Eudora asked for Ken's reaction to her essay "Some Notes

on *Time in Fiction,"* and in October she sent him her essay *"The House of Willa Cather."* He responded with admiration and appreciation for both, and both would ultimately appear in the collection of nonfiction pieces Ken was urging her to compile, a volume that she would dedicate to him. Eudora certainly thought of Ken as a serious novelist, not just the talented genre writer whom some reviewers wanted to keep in a ghetto. In fact, she saw "mystery" itself not as a separate genre but as lying at the heart of fiction. "Relationship," fiction's primary subject, Eudora contended, "is a pervading and changing mystery; it is not words that make it so in life, but words have to make it so in a story. Brutal or lovely, the mystery waits for people wherever they go, whatever extreme they run to."[43] Just as she saw mystery as part of Literature, with a capital L, she recognized Ken as a serious student of literature; widely read though she was, he had the graduate training in literature, she did not. Her graduate studies had been in business in deference to her father's belief that she needed something practical to fall back on.

For his part, Ken asked Eudora both to suggest texts he might collect in an anthology of suspense writing and to respond to titles he already had under consideration. Eudora was delighted that Ken wanted her advice and was eager to comply. Collaboration and consultation provided one way of transcending the 2,000 miles that separated them.

Kenneth Millar to Eudora Welty, September 17, 1973

Dear Eudora:

Your "notes on time in fiction" are superb, and I'm grateful to you for going to the trouble of making me a carbon, not to mention writing the piece in the first place. It's a long time since I've read any essay in criticism which ranged so far and wide and deep, expressed itself so eloquently and justly, and made so many absolutely final statements. It's virtually a philosophy of writing. And it ends powerfully with your tribute to Faulkner, who of all American novelists came closest to wrestling our beloved enemy to a draw. I do congratulate you on this wonderful piece of writing, which I hope will be widely seen. It deserves to end up in *Familiar Quotations* e.g. "It can expand a single moment like the skin of a balloon or bite off a life like a thread." "In the sense of our own transience may lie the one irreducible urgency telling us to do, to understand, to love." "Distortion of time is a deeply conscious part of any novel's conception . . . it matters continuously, and increasingly, and exactly as the author gives it to us." Which has never quite been said explicitly before.

I hope your trip was pleasant and satisfying; and that all is well with you. We're having a cool September, which we both like. I'm nibbling at the edges of a book but haven't taken a big bite yet—a book I've had in mind, and in my notebooks, for almost twenty years (and have probably already written at least once, but no matter). Have also been reading along through Diarmuid's splendid anthology, with a consciousness of being in direct contact with his fine and various mind. The love that goes into such a book is stronger than death, too. In contact with you, as well, through that book with its green wrapper so well worn. But it's time I returned it to you.

Love,
Ken

P.S.—Working on the anthology, too, if you can call reading work. That story you sent me, "The Walker," is just about the most frightening thing I've ever read, the more so that its ending has a dreadful subjective quality, the reader having been gradually betrayed into complicity.

K.

Eudora Welty, on the train, to Kenneth Millar, September 25, 1973

Dear Ken,

This is on the train, in the Georgia hills headed for Birmingham. I've been in N.Y. a week and spent Saturday & Sunday with Diarmuid & Rose in the country. Unalterable in mind and spirit, but so frail and very tired now. I'm glad he felt like having me come. I took greetings to him from friends—and yours brought him a smile of pleasure. I'm glad that you and Diarmuid got to meet each other, at no matter what point. I didn't ask him to sign your book, though, after I saw him, knowing it would be just as good either way, and will mail it on one day soon. He would be made to feel cheered, I think, if the last wildflower volume would come out soon—it is due to. Did I tell you (or did he? but he would have been too modest about his part in it, which was to start the whole thing, and attend to all the publishing details—just out of love and thinking a copy of the book would be nice to have) about the magnificent undertaking of the *Wildflowers of the United States* published by the N.Y. Botanical Garden & edited by that Mr. Rickett who knows everything about flowers, absolutely authentic & complete & every flower with its own color photograph—before it's bulldozed out of the earth for good—Each section of the U.S. has its own one or two volumes—and Texas has 2 all to itself—just as with the birds, I believe you told me, things live there that aren't found anywhere else[44]—Anyway Diarmuid knows & loves wildflowers the way you and Margaret love birds. He has a gift for getting them to grow for him too.

Nona & Joan & Olivia Kahn, too, send greetings, and so do John & Catherine Prince, whom I saw in Washington after the meeting I went to was over.[45] Oh, God! I had to meet Pres. Nixon! We (the Council on the Arts) were all taken over to the Oval Office (in the rain) & made to go in a line to shake hands with him. I felt a bad hypocrite to touch him. (I who had never missed a session of Watergate.) He had a soft handshake & very feverish looking brown eyes. Make-up, I thought (& we all had to be photographed with him, our hands being clasped, "a copy will be sent to your hometown paper"). He seemed unreal as a man and poor as an actor—very jerky-jovial. All the same, while I resented being asked to look on this man as a fellow human being, who must in fact be suffering, we don't know how much, this *was* the case—I hated the whole thing. We were given souvenirs from trays as we went out—pens, Nixon's signature on same, & a pin with presidential seal on it, & cuff-links, with seal. They've been loading down my suitcase. In the Oval Office there was a perfectly smooth bare desk, and on a little table beside it a tape recorder. Yes there was! Nobody was offered *that* souvenir.

I haven't properly told you how much I liked your piece that had such telling things to say about Mann. I will stop this though because I can't ask you to read the terrible writing. How is the anthology coming along?[46] All the thoughts I had were really no good to you because my favorite & most admired examples are detective stories & not suspense (I'm not quite sure how you divide them, since they overlap, don't they?) Yes I think too that little story "The Walker" is powerful & terrible—It has stayed with me for years. (Somehow I haven't thought of it as much since passing it along to you!—Not really so, of course). More later on—

Love,

Eudora

At the head of the letter's first page on Algonquin stationery, Eudora has written: Every morning early & every night late, a large spotted common cat with short hair comes out into the only clear space in the Algonquin lobby & washes itself from head to foot making everybody go around it. Nobody minds.

Kenneth Millar to Eudora Welty, September 29, 1973

Dear Eudora:

Thank you for the news of your trip, the good and the bad. I know how difficult it is to see an old friend dying, especially a man as splendid as Diarmuid. I think of him often, too. His face is in my mind, and of course I have no need of his signature but will be most pleased to have his book from you. I hope Diarmuid lives to see the last of the wild-flower volumes, and then goes quickly. He has such heartbreaking grace.

President Nixon, I gather, does not. The penalty of fame, which you paid when you touched his hand, is stiffer under this administration. But I think I prefer him punchy and diminished—he is more likely to seek and take good advice, and we never had a president who needed it more.

I'm sorry (for my own sake) if I gave the impression that my anthology will exclude detective stories. On the contrary, it will probably start out with a Christie (what do you think of Miss Marple? I like her, and as of now propose to use *What Mrs. McGillicuddy Saw*, which moves beautifully.) and, if I can get away with it, include a Margaret Millar. I'd be most grateful for any nominations you might have, English or American, long or short.

It was so good to have your letter. I don't count the days but am acutely conscious of the time that passes between your letters. That same time which you wrote about so eloquently in your essay. All seems well here. Jimmie is enjoying school, and I am enjoying being out of it. The Fall bird season is starting. I must have told you about the roseate spoonbills that appeared here this last month, a first Santa Barbara sighting. And swimming in the ocean I saw a Xantus's murrelet, very rare so near shore, probably sick, probably from the underwater oil which continues to run.[47]—Incidentally, when Nixon flew here to inspect the oil damage in 1969, a crew was sent ahead of him to *clean up the beach*. Gogol, thou shouldst be living at this hour.

Which reminds me that some time ago I read in the paper about the death of a man who had travelled with circuses and carnivals as the Petrified Man.[48] I believe he died in Texas, which isn't so very far from Mississippi.

Thank you for the greetings from your friends. You have friends here, too, who love to know that someone in Santa Barbara (me) is in touch with you.

Love,
Ken

Eudora Welty to Kenneth Millar, September 30, 1973

Dear Ken,

Thank you for reading my paper with so much warm understanding—I was proud of your good opinion of it, and I hope you would have told me any misgivings you had, too. You know a lot more about time than most people I can think of, including me—it's just that I'm so interested in it, from a writing point of view—and reading—and had tried hard on the paper, so I wanted you to look at it. I'm especially glad you thought the part about Faulkner didn't do anything too outrageous. This was boiled down from a long piece I tried to do on time and *The Sound and the Fury*, which has never ceased to fascinate me. No, I don't suppose many people will see it in print, as I did it for *The Mississippi Journal*, put out by Miss. State U., an edition supposed to be about some of my work, I understand, edited by Lewis Simpson from The Southern Review, do you remember meeting him here? I wanted to thank them in some way. You and these editors are the only ones I showed it to (I'm a very nervous writer about any new piece). They have accepted it.[49] Now working on a lecture I must give on Willa Cather next month in Nebraska—it was a joy to read her all straight through. Your friends the Knopfs will be at the thing—it's a centennial—a nice note came from her, saying they'd had lunch with you and Margaret (recently?) in Santa Barbara. He is to speak of his reminiscences about W.C. Leon Edel is to lecture.[50] I'm the only non-academic, I take it, and my lecture will be in keeping—Don't you like this, from *My Antonia*, remember it: "More than anything else I felt motion in the landscape; in the fresh, easy-blowing wind, and in the earth itself, as if the shaggy grass were a sort of loose hide, and underneath it herds of wild buffalo were gal-loping, galloping . . ."

It's good to know you're nibbling around the edges of a new book—and I won't ask you any at all how you get along because of my feeling that it might be bad luck (this just applies to fiction!) but I hope you have good luck. We all write the same things over again, I guess—If I can find it, here's another thing Willa Cather said. It's from *O Pioneers*—"Isn't it queer, there are only two or three human stories, and they go on repeating themselves as fiercely as if they had never happened before; like the larks in this country, that have been singing the same five notes over for thousands of years." And "the old story writing itself over . . . It is we who write it, with the best we have."

Thank you for sending back the Irish Reader, which came safely, and I have meant to put the copy for you to keep in the mail before this—I am glad you like it as you do. It was comforting what you said about Diarmuid.

Love,
Eudora

What you say about "The Walker" & the reader's being trapped with complicity expresses or explains the awful hold it has, which I could not have put my finger on, or never had.

It rained a little—Mockingbirds singing in a renewed burst.

I hope all goes well with you both and all you do—

Eudora Welty to Kenneth Millar, October 14, 1973

Dear Ken,

I was so glad of your letter, and thank you for it as I do for all your letters. When I'm slow answering, that's because it's the way I am—you might not believe what a horrible reputation I have as a letter writer. The thing is, I *want* to write, and don't manage the right way. Forgive when I'm late, knowing I think of you and things I want to remark on, or ask you, or tell you.

Did you see the Xantu murrelet again? (Mental picture of that is as amazing as I can make it. In the house I don't have a shore bird or western bird book, but I now and then see one in the library—I'd better correct my vision. I did see the roseate spoonbill's portrait.) It must be lovely to see this whole world of birds stream through in the fall of the year—and you must be the one they (not the birds, the bird people) depend on most to report the rare and far-from-shore ones that they themselves would miss. The hummingbird never came back to my tree for more dew, it must not have been Grade-A. But I've seen some passers-through here in this not-too-quiet yard, even, especially while the sprinkler is on, and heard warblers etc.

How is your anthology? I've been reading over people I like, without seeming to hit upon the very book I like—I forget all books' titles. Julian Symons's "The Plain Man" I just read and started "The Belting Inheritance" again—it was*n't* "The Color of Murder"—I wonder what it was. Yes I do like "What Mrs. McGillicuddy Saw," that's the train one, isn't it—also I like "Mrs. McGinty's Dead"— do you remember that's Poirot *and* Mrs. Ariadne Oliver—Christie is endlessly diverting to me. I haven't tried her again but did you ever think anything of Elizabeth Daly? I like "The Book of the Lion"— well, all of hers. I re-read a dreadful Ngaio Marsh—whom I enjoy mostly—which was maybe the first one, where Alleyn goes home each night from his case in the family Daimler sent by his mother, Lady Alleyn, and sits on her bed and lets her guess what's happened and pronounce on who couldn't possibly be the murderer, while they drink sherry and call each other "Darling." He is just meeting Troy in time—I've already forgotten the name of the book.[51] I read some favorite John Collier stories, but I suppose they cross the border into fantasy, and I read some Sheridan LeFanu again, whom I relish, but of course they're long, long—"Uncle Silas" and "Green Tea"—I love that Irish Victorian. (Do you remember Elizabeth Bowen's brilliant preface to an edition of "Uncle Silas"?) Another Victorian with suspense is Algernon Blackwood, do you agree, and there they all are on my shelf but I haven't re-read—I did try Saki and thought NO—and what about Bradbury, and Roald Dahl, and William Samson, for short stories—don't know how they'd stand up to test. Some others I've had in mind—I've just tried to think of the ones not in your own field, but what delight for you to be reading all those with the new purpose and perspective. Of *course* Margaret Millar's got to come in! Do you know which one?

My time before going to Nebraska to read a paper is getting short, and I've been working hard—and slowly. I have to finish this week. Mary Lou came through and spent from 4:18 PM one day till 1:25 PM the next day here—it was lovely to have her. She was on her way to visit her children, one in Atlanta and one in Oswego,

N.Y. She was fine and in high spirits. We spoke of you. ML said you might come to Santa Fe some time and she would ask me too. That's a nice idea.

We celebrated Gershwin's birthday here with a fine show down at that little converted church, New Stage, where you were—5 young people singing & dancing the songs and one more at the piano—the young people *loved* that music (which is in my very nerves) & did it just right—"Nice Work," "My Man," "Of Thee I Sing, Baby," "Someone to Watch Over Me,"—all of the good ones with "Rhapsody in Blue" for while they were getting their breath. I hope all goes well with you, in all ways,

Love,
Eudora

Kenneth Millar to Eudora Welty, October 21, 1973

Dear Eudora:

Your letter was most welcome, as always, and I was glad to be reminded of Elizabeth Daly, though I haven't found any of her books yet. Glad, too, that you should mention Margaret whom I'd like to include simply on her merits—perhaps *Beast in View*, which I've just recently read and consider very strong. Also read, and was impressed by, *The Big Clock* by Kenneth Fearing, a poet who wrote only two mystery novels. To give you some idea of the variety of my reading, yesterday I read *Dr. Jekyll and Mr. Hyde* (which still has power to scare, and reminds me of a more elegant but smaller Dickens; it interests me, by the way, that *Dr. Jekyll*, Jack the Ripper, and the first Sherlock Holmes stories, occurred within five years of each other, in a London which was a terrible city in those late Victorian days) and today, speaking of terrible cities, I'm reading W.R. Burnett's *The Asphalt Jungle*—not a *good* book but a very powerful one, and the source of the movie in which Marilyn Monroe had her first featured role, as the old lawyer's (Louis Calhern's) girl. Margaret knew Burnett when he was writing *Jungle*—they were both employed at Warner Brothers in 1945–1946, Burnett at $1500 per week, but with three wives to support, two exes and the current wife, so he had to work *all* the time. Writers do strange things to themselves, especially in Hollywood, which M. left quickly and I have stayed away from. (But there are a couple of movies on the way—a TV movie based on *The Ferguson Affair* which I sold years ago, and one based on *The Drowning Pool* which I sold this year. The *Underground Man* movie seems to be bogged down but may eventually come to life.)

I did see the Xantus's murrelet several times, but then it disappeared. Its place has since been taken by half-a-dozen western grebes (before the oil spill we had many more) and in the air by one or more Pomarine Jaegers, a rare bird like a kind of hawkish seagull whose unpleasant habit it is to chase the terns and steal the fish they have caught right out of their mouths. Why are predators in so many ways highest in the order of nature, swiftest and strongest? Is nature Nixonian, is its history Agnews? But then I think of the swift and strong and rather benign cetaceans, or among the birds of the condor which flies, did you know, thousands of feet high, and preys only on the dead. The beach these days is alive with smaller shore birds moving en masse as if the sand and stones had grown small invisible feet, and blessed winter, as we laughingly call it, begins to be in the air. But the sea is still warm enough to swim in, and tarry enough to get well blackened in.

I'm glad to hear of the celebration of Gershwin. He and Cole Porter and Ellington were great celebrators and deserve to be celebrated. The other night, for the first time in three years (since Linda died) I got out some Ellington records and played them. Linda's boy, our Jimmie, is flourishing, reading like a streak and swimming like one too. We'd be sad indeed if it weren't for him.

Did I mention that Diarmuid's *Irish Reader* arrived in good shape?—a book I'll treasure both for your sake and his, and its own sake.

Love,
Ken

P.S.—When I wrote you some time ago that I wished Diarmuid a death not too long drawn out, it may have sounded inhuman but it wasn't meant that way. I've sat through the last days of old friends dying of cancer, and wished them Godspeed and still do. One of the dearest and one of the first gone was M. M. Musselman the humorist who wrote the Ritz Brothers movies and was Hemingway's best friend at Oak Park High School in Chicago. Mussy spent his last years here in Santa Barbara and in the last months of the last year I saw him every day. That was twenty years ago.

I'm glad you mentioned Julian Symons, by the way. He and I are good friends and have visited each other, quite a feat. I haven't found any one book in which his great talent shows itself fully, though I enjoy everything he writes—the most recent one as much as any.

Speaking of visiting friends, I'm glad you had a quick visit from Mary Lou and I do hope to see her again. We have a hard time getting anywhere, for various reasons. For example, a couple of weeks ago we were all set to go to Yosemite and Mammoth. Then Brandy had to have a tumor removed from his belly. He's fine now. I don't complain. A good dog is worth all the mountain scenery in the world. Did you ever read *The Day the Mountain Fell*? K.

Eudora Welty to Kenneth Millar, October 24, 1973

Dear Ken,

I seem to be in a sort of habit of sending you what I'm doing—this is my Willa Cather paper, which, for better or worse, I'll be delivering out in Nebraska on Friday night. (I leave early in the morning on a plane.) It would be good to know what it seems like to you—I don't know whether or not you care for Willa Cather, but you have read so widely and thoroughly in American literature that I'd like to know just fine if you thought I had fitted her in in the right place and with the right feeling. No hurry though to read this—I know you're busy with reading of your own. Of course I finished typing it in haste and expect I'll give it some more work. I'm looking at a table full of stuff I left out—

Do things go well with you? I hope so. Maybe the season is really changing there, as it is here, without much of a sign—we have a long slow gentle fall—cool morning & evening air, warm sun, hardly any wind, gently falling leaves, and a wonderful sky after sunset, broad rose and blue halves of the western sky, and the moon comes up HUGE!

My news: Mary Alice, my niece the schoolteacher, whom you met here, had her first child last Friday night, a son. All went well, and they're home from the hospital now. His name is Donald Alexander White, like his father, and he's being called Alex. So relieved I was still here.

I read a mystery every time with thoughts of what you're looking for, as I imagine that to be, in view—I have a lifetime habit of reading them, and am really re-reading. But with the fondest memories of a book—such as Andrew Garve's "The Cookoo Line Affair"—I come to the conclusion none of them are good enough to mention to you. These are the books I've kept on my shelves as the best—I can only think I've been too easy to please. Learned from yours!

Love to you,

Eudora

Kenneth Millar to Eudora Welty, October 28, 1973

Dear Eudora:

It was thoughtful and generous of you to send me your essay on Willa Cather. From the very first page it opened her up for me as she never had been before. She opened *you* up, too, into a further breadth and eloquence of statement, which should set to rest forever any doubts you have expressed about your right to speak out strongly on these matters. Your own profoundly faithful practice of the art of fiction has given you an eye for its largenesses and depths which couldn't have been acquired in any school. I was overjoyed by the clarity and reach and strength of your statement.—You know, Alfred Knopf considered Miss Cather his greatest native author, and I believe he would love to see this tribute to her work. Indeed, I think a lot of people would.

Turning from great things to lesser, I have to admit that I share your disappointment in rereading some of the mystery fiction I used to consider first-rate. Helen Eustis' *The Horizontal Man*, for instance, turned out to be quite a disappointment. Chandler stands up less well than Hammett. But Kenneth Fearing's *The Big Clock* still has power to interest and excite. And an unambitious police-procedural like Hillary Waugh's *Last Seen Wearing* seems to have more meat on its bones than Charlotte Armstrong's novels, say.

I do appreciate your re-reading some of your books on my behalf, and hope you won't hesitate to mention any possibilities. Fortunately the enterprise isn't tied to the field of detective stories, but can range through the various branches of suspense. I'm enjoying the reading, but am beginning to look forward to some real work.

That's great news about Donald Alexander White II, who must come as a splendid fruition to you as well as his parents.[52] Congratulations to all three of you, and to Donald for being born into such a loving family. (There's something about aunts, may I say? I'd have perished long ago without my aunts picking up where my poor parents had to leave off.) And you will have the same grateful pleasure in watching him grow and learn to walk and talk and become a boy, that we have taken in Jimmie. All goes well with Jimmie and with us. He's such a good boy that it sometimes brings tears to my eyes—a goodness based on his love and respect for his father. Some relationships are so valuable that one hesitates to look too closely at them, or describe them, and their love is one of these. "I wouldn't want to go *away* to college—I wouldn't want to leave my dad." But of course I hope he will, and he probably will.

We're having a late summer, bright and warm. Yesterday there were four red-shafted flickers on one of our palm trees. The ocean is 62°. I trust all is well with you. And thank you again for your Cather, some of which made my hair stand on end.

Love, Ken

Eudora Welty, New York City, to Kenneth Millar, November 17, 1973

Dear Ken,

Your generous and warm feeling about my W. Cather paper did me much good. I'd of course worked hard & long, and had hoped

I'd managed to get down what had emerged as central for me in her work—What I know so little about is the generality of American literature, which I've read spottily and not chronologically and entirely to please myself—I've missed a lot, and missed the background knowledge that I felt I owed to this. I know you have only recently been reading systematically the whole stretch of American novelists and this makes me still more pleased that you saw worth in my paper. I gave it in Nebraska, and you'll be interested, after what you said, to know that Alfred Knopf was in Nebraska too, for the same celebration—he and Helen—and I got to see quite a bit of them[53]—They asked me to go along in their private car on the day's trip to Red Cloud, W.C.'s childhood home—which I will tell you about some time, when I have a typewriter, or when I see you. Anyway, Alfred was feeling fine in Nebraska, attending everything (he said of some of the speeches "BOSH," and he *did* say he liked mine, so I came out all right with him) and at a luncheon in his honor he rose from the table and gave a 30- or 40-minute talk, from a few memos in hand, about his publishing life with Willa Cather from 1918 on—you can imagine how succinct and pertinent and how valuable all he said was—nobody else could have known or said it. I was most moved to be present. I'm sorry I've been so long in thanking you for your letters, but I haven't written any letters, owing to Nebraska, then the U. of Chicago where I gave a reading, then the flu—in bed (at home) for over a week, from which I got up to come to New York where I had been asked to give a talk at the Museum of Modern Art (imagine!) on my little photograph book—a slide lecture, no less. I got through with it OK, in spite of the current strike going on in the Museum—the picketers were yelling "Eudora Welty is a liar!" "Eudora Welty, read your book, and you have betrayed us."[54] They had threatened over the phone that they would do this unless I withdrew my lecture from the Museum and delivered it to the strikers in another place. I was not informed on the issues, and thought it was only right to keep to my engagement, made months ago. It gave me a trip up here so I can go out to see Diarmuid, as I'll be doing tomorrow, if he feels like it. What you said about his going quickly is what I fervently feel too, and what he has said himself about his friends in these same circumstances. Diarmuid had to watch his partner, Henry Volkening, die of lung cancer, and learned of his own right after.

I read again 8 or 10 of the mysteries in the house that I've cherished as "best" while I was down with flu and *none* seemed good enough for you. I would have thought too that *Horizontal Man* would stand up (!) It's good *The Big Clock* does—As I recall Kenneth Fearing's other mystery was a disappointment when it came out, wasn't it?[55] I made a little packet of 3 Elizabeth Dalys to send you but didn't get to mail—but not that I think they're strong enough to be candidates, probably, but because she's a nice writer and I like her work—Only I can't send you the one I think may be her very best one because I no longer have it, & can't find another copy. *The Book of the Lion*—Joan Kahn gave me Julian Symons' new one yesterday which I'm anxious to get into—[56]

I've had a nice few days here, & seen some of our mutual friends— Joan, Nona, Walter Clemons, Dick & Tessa Ader, & I hope I'll be seeing Diarmuid & Rosie tomorrow[57]—Then home for Thanksgiving, with the girls & their families—the new baby—and thank you for your good wishes for Donald Alexander—I hope you have a fine Thanksgiving with Jimmie and his father coming to be with Margaret and you. He sounds so very fine.

Love and thanks to you, from Eudora

Kenneth Millar to Eudora Welty, November 19, 1973

Dear Eudora:

I was so happy to get your letter today—had assumed that you were moving around quite a bit, and indeed you have been. The trip to Nebraska sounds like fun. I know how much you must have put into the preparation for your paper on Willa Cather, and it's so good that Alfred got to hear it. Indeed you got to hear each other.

Margaret and I had a bit of a shock last week. I hasten to add that it was nothing *really* serious. Our fine old dog Brandy was supposed to die long ago, but hung on well with the help of cortisone and butazolidin and other drugs. But last week he got into a dog fight, was chewed up by a couple of black Labrador retrievers and, though his wounds weren't terribly serious, he died two days later, here with us at home. He was completely fearless and probably died perfectly happy in the thought, or in the assurance that he had defended his territory one last time. We miss Brandy like hell, though we still have our little old spaniel, *apxt.* 13 ½, and are looking for another German shepherd pup; in fact we're going to look at a litter tomorrow. But Brandy's rather irreplaceable. We were never separated, except for the few times when I had to go out of town.

One of those times is coming up in December. I forget whether I told you that the Popular Culture Association—I think I did tell you—is going to give me a "merit award," their first, at the MLA meeting in Chicago on December 27. The idea pleases me abstractly but I'm not looking forward much to the actual event. Four scholars are going to address me and I am supposed to respond. From here it sounds almost ludicrously strange and difficult but it can't be any worse than my doctoral orals, when people kept asking me questions about things I hadn't read. At least this time I'm familiar with the material. But it bores me.

I don't know where you got the impression that I have been systematically reading my way through American Lit. (Can K.M. be as E.W. is reputed to be, in N.Y. artistic circles, a *liar*?) Perhaps I impressed you by getting through *The Wings of the Dove*. But apart from that noble effort, I'm the least systematic reader around, and the gaps are immense. I don't really care, either, having so many good things to look forward to. Mostly novels, with enough criticism to keep me semi-alert. Right now I'm still reading crime stories, in the hope of finding something new and good, but not too new to be reprinted, and not too good to be usable. It does look, by the way, as if I'm going to get away with using a very long fine story by Patrick White, "A Glass of Tea," from *The Burnt Ones*. Most of my short selections are not detective stories or even crime stories in the routine sense. John Collier and John Cheever instead of Ellery Queen and that sort of thing. The four novels, as of now, are the Christie I mentioned—yes, the "train" one, as you remembered, and one of Dick Francis' thrillers, *Bonecrack*, or possibly Le Carre; but the thing about Francis is that he is in every respect quite fresh, and his mature style now is clean and strong. With *The Big Clock*, on the U.S. side, goes probably either M's *Beast in View*, which I am pushing, or *The Far Side of the Dollar* which my publishers say they want. Am I repeating myself? Anyway, I'll soon know how it turns out. The main virtue of the collection is that it won't reprint too many over-familiar crime stories, but ranges outside the fence a little. Fortunately I was asked for a *suspense* anthology not a detective one. Probable title: "Suspense and Surprise." Though I didn't peek until I'd made up my list, I find I have one overlap with Joan's [Joan Kahn's] *Trial and Terror*—Flannery O'Connor's "The Comforts of Home." But it can stand the exposure and I'm leaving it in, of course. The rather broad range of choice, aimed at variety rather than fitting a definition, makes the introduction rather hard to do, I find, so I'm falling back on a kind of historical introduction telling the reader about what *preceded* the material I've collected. This introduction will have the advantage of making the stories which follow more interesting by comparison. I must thank you again for that explosive story "The Walker"—probably the most original and least known.

It rained half-an-inch yesterday and today was really chilly. I love to feel the winter, as we call it, coming on. Happy Thanksgiving, dear Eudora, and my best to Donald Alexander and the other good people of Jackson. I hope you were able to see Diarmuid.

Love, Ken

Kenneth Millar to Eudora Welty, December 9, 1973

Dear Eudora:

Just a note to let you know that all is well. Fortunately just before the energy squeeze was officially announced (environmentalists have been predicting it for years) we bought a small German car, a BMW, which is supposed to do 22 m.p.g. I'm hoping the various freezes will bring this country out of the wild last-days-of-the-Roman-Empire spree in which it's been indulging these last years. But it's going to be tough now to save the Santa Barbara Channel from the oil lords.

The great old ghost of Brandy still haunts our house, but scampering in its shadow is a new German Shepherd pup, very lively and full of nuisance value, named Macduff Macdonald, Duffy for short. Yesterday he weighed 34 lbs, tomorrow he'll weigh 35. We love him. So once again we renew our somewhat tattered youth.

The weather was very bright and warm today, typical for December, indeed for no other month. We often think of you, in your beautiful life, and wish you a happy holiday with your dear friends and nieces.

Love, Ken and M.

Eudora Welty to Kenneth Millar, December 10, 1973

Dear Ken,

Every day—this is true—I start out meaning to write letters, and then the whole day turns into an interruption. I think it's making me pretty neurotic, I can't get to sleep for thinking how I have failed. It's because it means a lot to me to keep in touch with them (my good friends)—and they're not all that many—and I miss writing and miss hearing. But I had such a good letter from you when I got back from New York, and I do want to write, no matter how poorly.

I was sorry to hear about Brandy—ever since I've been hearing from you I've heard about him. You must both miss him like fury, and I hope by now you have a new pup to take up some of the empty space, even though not that same space. His end sounds like a soldier's or a hero's, though, and coming properly at home, with you and Margaret by him.

Have you got the Patrick White story you were hoping for?[58] I hope all the permissions and such come through without too much load of letters and work (I remember Diarmuid telling me what a headache his anthology permissions were—nobody answers, etc.). I must say that from the idea you've given me of the contents it sounds full of interest and variety and vitality—very much a personal collection, which is what will make it worth the effort, and will make me want most to read it. I'm sure the publishers are insisting on your putting you in—it would be like Gershwin having a party and having everybody else play but not playing himself, if you didn't. You really ought to make it in 2 volumes, maybe—then you could be in one and Margaret could be in one, and the guests could be divided spaciously—like two rooms for the party. I'm glad Dick Francis is probably coming in—his work I like very much indeed. (He always has so much pain in his novels, though, real damage and suffering—which I guess he should know all about, from all the falls and bone-cracks he's had to take in his life. Isn't it a remarkable life, too—the two gifts, both excellent, and quite unrelated, you would think.) I wondered about Joan's anthology and yours, coming not too far apart—that's amusing, you both picked out F. O'C, and the same F. O'C. story. Who was ever better? I remember your talking about her stories, first time I saw you. I'm pleased you think well of "The Walker," enough to want to include it. Did you happen to notice a short review of a new novel by Patrick O'Brian in this week's NYTBR? It's so sad to think that he's never realized his powers, apparently—just writes run-of-the-mill historical or adventure books, or according to the reviews that's what they are.[59] Did you hear from him yourself, I wonder, and I wonder what sort of man he sounds like to you.

Yes, I did get to see Diarmuid. The Sunday before I left NY Monday, I went out to spend the day. He was about the same, in Rosie's estimation. He was of course in command as always, and it was good to be with him. I worry some about the heating oil shortage, because it gets so cold up there, and he is just not able now to be cold too.

Donald Alexander II is a laugher, even laughs out loud (at his parents). They were pleased to get your good wishes.

Have a fine time in Chicago. It does sound as if anything might be expected out of those four scholars firing remarks and questions at you, but (all aside from being a PhD like them) you are used enough to the academic world to take such in stride. (I'm not.) Watch out because when I was in Chicago, a young woman (who for all I know will turn out to be one of the scholars) was asking me questions about you, and she was trying to hitch you onto Nabokov by some flick of the wrist. Not being a reader of him as I am of you I didn't follow. But it is fine that they are going to give you an award, and the first of its kind, and that sounds as if from now on the award will be one with prestige attached because your name was on it. I'll be in touch again before it's Christmas. This is when I should say Happy Birthday! You're a 13ther like me. Many happy returns,

Love,
from Eudora

Eudora Welty to Kenneth Millar, December 17, 1973

Dear Ken,

It saddens me to tell you, but I thought you'd want to be told, that Diarmuid died yesterday afternoon—Will, his son, phoned and told me last night. I do feel glad for him that it is over. He was valiant—The word you used—noble—that was right. Your card that said a contribution in my name had been given by you to the Cancer Society did something good for me, that's present now. Thank you.

Transportation and weather problems make me not sure I'll get to go to Katonah in time for memorial services on Thursday—What matters to me is that I did get there to see *him* when I did. And it was wonderful, wasn't it, that he came here in May.

I hope all goes fine with you—I'm glad about your great huge puppy—Write soon.

Love,
Eudora

The loss of Diarmuid Russell was a devastating blow for Eudora. Four times during 1973 she had visited him in New York, and he in an incredible effort of will and in the face of intense suffering had managed to come to Jackson for

Eudora Welty Day. But on December 16 he succumbed to lung cancer. Ken's words of comfort in his next letter—"certain souls live on intensely in their work and in the minds of people who knew them"—would be resonant ones for Eudora. She would echo them in her autobiographical Harvard lectures, given shortly before Ken died in 1983, and in the 1984 published version of those lectures, One Writer's Beginnings: *"The memory is a living thing—" Eudora said and later wrote, "it too is in transit. But during its moment, all that is remembered joins, and lives—the old and the young, the past and the present, the living and the dead."[60] Ken was destined to lose his memory, its comforts, and his life to Alzheimer's disease; Eudora's recollections of him would be needed to sustain her in the wake of those losses. But for now they found sustenance in letters from each other.*

Kenneth Millar to Eudora Welty, December 20, 1973

Dear Eudora:

I hope you will have been able to get to New York for Diarmuid's memorial service. It helps to share these losses, doesn't it, and you are good at sharing everything. I don't know of anyone who has given more than you have to other people, or has more love resurging back to her. Such considerations are not terribly comforting, I know, when you have been bereaved. But that long friendship and creative partnership with Diarmuid is the living truth of the matter, and won't die. While I don't believe in the immortality of the soul—neither, I doubt, does my friend Bishop Corrigan (*Right*-Way Corrigan)—there are certain souls that live on intensely in their work and in the minds of people who knew them. Diarmuid's is certainly one of them. And he will live on, as he would have wished, in the work of you and other writers which he helped to bring to birth. There is a great deal, too, to be said for an end to suffering. I hope your own suffering won't be too hard to bear. You've had a difficult season. But you've had long joyful seasons—you've left a full record of them; you're the most irrepressibly joyous person I know—and you'll have other good seasons and know what to do with them, too.

Here we're having what I consider a pretty good season, de-em-phasizing the Christmas spirit but trying to make the most of every day, including Christmas. Jim and his father will be with us for four or five days, and I hope the good weather holds. As in some other years, we're having a week or two of bright December weather—shirtsleeve weather—and I've been walking on the beach every day with my pup. Yesterday I sent you a picture of him (together with Margaret and me) but the picture was taken a couple of weeks ago and no longer represents him adequately. He is now a teenager. I measured his neck today, and it's size 14 (mine is 16 ½) and at three months he weighs forty pounds. He actually grows and changes in twenty-four hours, like a flower.—We had our Christmas bird count last Saturday but it was a comparative failure—some 15 or 20 species fewer than usual—so for the first time in some years we won't be in national contention. We had one unusual bird over Santa Barbara, though—a California Condor which ordinarily doesn't leave the mountain fastnesses. The deep sea birds, the murrelets and murres, were missing from the coast, either because the wrong observers went to see or the oil in the chan-nel has been getting to them. Margaret rescued an oil-trapped murre on the beach a couple of weeks ago and sent it back out to sea again. Which is a good image to end on. I wish you voyaging; not necessarily away from home.

My love (and Margaret's)
Ken

P.S. A parcel came from you. I haven't opened it, but I suspect it's a record. You are too generous. K

Eudora Welty to Kenneth Millar, Friday night [December 21, 1973]

Dear Ken,

That was such a sweet thing to do, to send me the picture. It was like having all of you appear tonight, all swiftly, cheering like a visit. I was glad to see you, glad to see Margaret, a little better than I did in other pictures, and glad to see Duffy—ready to jump right out of everybody's hands and the picture the next second—he's a huge pup, all right, and hugely appealing. I have the picture propped up on my mantle shelf up here in my room, where I'm looking at it now, and where it'll be a bright spot in the morning.

Thank you for it, and my love to you both. I hope Christmas is good—and Chicago not too cold—We have had snow too. A beautiful Baltimore oriole came his first and only time to my feeder while I happened to be watching.

Love,

Eudora

Kenneth Millar to Eudora Welty, December 26, 1973

Dear Eudora:

I'm so glad you liked the pup picture and I hope one day you'll come and see him in person, not to mention the rest of us. The only thing missing was Jim, who wasn't around that day, but we're having the pleasure of his company this week. His presence is a double joy because it's exactly two weeks ago that he fell off a piece of playground equipment and suffered a concussion which put him in the hospital for several days, and is still being watched. But he's coming along fine, is back in the water swimming (which he is good at) and gaining weight which he can use, being small and slender. He's a darling boy, full of gung-ho helpfulness. His favorite study, for some reason, is very ancient cars. His father Joe P [. . .] is a computer engineer, Italian in family background, a devout Catholic, which means that Jim is, too. Our daughter Linda never joined the Church but sang in the cathedral choir in Los Angeles—we have an LP record of their voices.

Speaking of records, it was most thoughtful of you to send me the New Orleans jazz record, which I am crazy about—such celebration of sacred and profane matters—indeed the sacred profane (which now that I think of it is one of your main subjects, at least in your comedy). It's a most welcome addition to my little collection, much the more so that it came from your hand and generous heart. (Incidentally I've ordered the Smithsonian jazz album which was reviewed in the *New Yorker* a few weeks ago.) I almost feel that listening to jazz can renew my youth and it almost can. Not that I want to go through all that again. But I'm ineluctably drawn back and back to autobiography, what I call autobiography, anyway.

Dick Lid the F.M. Ford scholar came up from Northridge where he teaches, for lunch today, and showed me a couple of the short educational films he's been making for the feds, as he calls them. He gets young people, grades 10 to 12, talking—they talk better than their teachers—about such matters as "The Mystery of Poe." Though I liked the films, they're not as brilliant as his criticism by a long shot and I must find a way to tell him so, or not. He was a boy wonder at the U. of Chicago in Hutchins' day, went in at sixteen and in a sense never came out, and I had to give him a late education, which never entirely takes. He's a good and lovable man, deliberately stepped down last June as the head of his department in order to do more important work.

Day after tomorrow I'm off to Chicago. Rubin of the *Progressive* had ten hours delay in traveling yesterday from Madison to here, on account of fog. I hope the fog lifts for me. I hope all is well with you.

Love, Ken

P.S.—Duffy is now in the King of the World stage, insufferable!

K.

P.P.S.—The daughter of friends in Quebec, Roberta Langford (now married to Dr. Eddie Cone) just completed at Duke her thesis on "The Comic Sense of Flannery O'Connor." I wonder if Reynolds knows her.—Weren't those beautiful cards Reynolds designed and translated and sent out?—he seems a many-sided perfection. K.

Millar took pleasure in his new friendship with Reynolds Price, the forty-year-old North Carolina writer sometimes referred to as Welty's protégé. Reynolds, having been introduced to Ross Macdonald's work by Eudora when she gave

him The Chill *to read as Price kept her company during her final edit of* One
Time, One Place, *was now a devoted Macdonald admirer—one who made
his appreciation known to interviewers, listing Ross Macdonald (along with
Bernard Malamud, John Updike, William Styron, Saul Bellow, and of course
Eudora Welty) as being among his favorite living writers. Price had initiated a
correspondence with Millar, which pleased and touched Ken. Then the two men
met in person in Jackson in May, during the week of Welty celebrations.*

*Price, like Millar, had been lodged at the Sun'n'Sand. On evenings when
other events were not planned, Ken and Reynolds got together at the motel for
whiskey and conversation. One night over drinks, Ken Millar said something
to the younger writer that almost knocked Price out of his chair. As Reynolds
would recall, "We were talking about Eudora and what a wonderful person she
was [. . .] And Ken stopped me and said, 'No, you don't understand. [. . .] You
love Eudora as a friend. I love her as a woman.'"*[61]

CHAPTER FOUR

"If one of your letters could be rotten there'd be nothing sound left in heaven or on earth."

———— ❦ ————

1974

AT an event at the Palmer House, in Chicago, near the end of 1973, Ken Millar received the first Award of Merit from the Popular Culture Association, whose members were in that city for a Modern Language Association convention.

The PCA had pioneered academic study and acceptance of popular literature. Ross Macdonald was their heavyweight champion: a genuine artist, a PhD, a genre master, and a bestselling success. Macdonald novels were being or would soon be taught at Ivy League schools including Yale. Kenneth Millar, the born-poor but brilliant son of a Canadian sometime poet, was grateful for the praise and attention he received at the Chicago event; but it also made him uncomfortable. He was much more at ease back home in Santa Barbara, soothed and stimulated by the passing seasons as he assembled in his mind the pieces of a new book, swam in the ocean, biked with Margaret, walked his dogs, and penned letters to friends.

The letters he wrote and received from Eudora seemed to mean the most to him, as perhaps did his to her. Often, when one of the two of them was traveling, the other would send a letter ahead to be received at their friend's destination, from the Algonquin Hotel to Oxford University.

Sometimes they dreamt of each other, then shared those dreams in letters. A few times they dreamt of letters written or received by each other. In waking letters, other dreams perhaps were revealed or concealed between the lines.

Eudora Welty to Kenneth Millar, January 11, 1974

Dear Ken,

Thank you for the letter you wrote about Diarmuid, full of thought and kindness. I know you and he only got to meet for a little but there's the gift of the short-cut (or it may be the long-cut), by which you were friends. I felt—Diarmuid told me long ago he believed that people who would like each other always eventually came together.

How have things been going there? I hope young Jim is perfectly all right again and you no longer need to be the least uneasy. Did you have your Chicago trip, and was it interesting? The weather I know was horrible. It's been doing the same thing in Southern California as in Mississippi, for days, I noticed—raining. But there are narcissus bloom-ing in the yard here and at night I hear the peepers calling in Belhaven Lake across the street (invisible from my house—really just a pond, on the campus of the little college). I hear lots of birds singing and I can't tell you what birds, as I'd like to—(Except cardinals & white throated sparrows. The cardinals with their spring song.) Mockingbirds so far shrugging off starting to sing. (They know.)

Did a man called Frank McShane get in touch with you? I hope it was all right—he telephoned from Columbia as a friend of Bill Smith's (I've only just met him but he seems a very nice man) to ask if I'd give him your address as he'd like to consult you about Chandler.[1] I guess publishers don't give out addresses—anyway, I did and hope you didn't mind.

I'm so glad you enjoy the record. I've been to hear Sweet Emma & most of that personnel in Preservation Hall (where the picture is taken from, out front) and love them—I see the record was made up-river a piece, up in Minneapolis. Some time you and Margaret will come to New Orleans—& I'll meet you there and we'll go. We may need to hurry—I'm sort of afraid Slow Drag Pavageau may have already gone to his reward—A young friend of mine, Tommy Sancton, is one of the white boys they used to let sit in and play with them—He had his own band later on & when he went over to Oxford as a Rhodes Scholar a few years ago he got his band (or formed a band) over there & they went all over England & Europe playing New Orleans Jazz. He's teaching (English I think) this year in Paris, & still has his band, playing the way the Humphreys taught him—he plays clarinet.[2] So it goes on, handed down person to person—I do want to come your way too. It will happen. I hope the New Year is a wonderfully good one for you—Love and wishes,

Eudora

I'm cheered every day by the picture. I suppose Duffy weighs 50 by now and is that much fuller of his own say-so.

Kenneth Millar to Eudora Welty, January 11, 1974

Dear Eudora:

We loved the beautiful bird card you sent. As I may have already told you, our Christmas bird count was a bit low this year—15 or 20 regulars didn't show up—and we weren't in national competition, not that it matters. Perhaps the birds stayed away in expectation of the very wet and stormy weather we've been having for the last couple of weeks: over seven inches of rain, which is half a yearly rainfall in these dry parts, gale-force winds up to seventy miles an hour, power failures and blackouts all over town. We lost our TV antenna but we were lucky. Our neighbors lost five trees, five huge eucalyptus which were laid across the road in order as if to halt troop movements. Well, it was sort of fun living by candlelight for one night and listening to the radio. We are so spoiled. It was the first real rain I'd seen since Jackson. What an enjoyable couple of days that was with you and your friends. I'll never forget the poignant pleasure of it, or the pride I felt for you when you stood up in the Old State Capitol and read aloud. I was particularly reminded of that week today because I received from a book dealer in England (Bertram Rota) a copy of *The Ponder Heart* and I can hardly wait to read it again.

The anthology is pretty well wrapped up, I think, but not wholly to my satisfaction. The Book-of-the-Month Club, which is now actively involved, has objected to some of my prize choices, including Margaret's *Beast in View*, *The Walker*, and the Patrick White story. They're afraid the anthology might be too literary. I think they underestimate the public, and not for the first time. Fortunately, apart from M's book for which they're substituting one of mine (*Far Side of Dollar*), they didn't mess with the novelists, and there are altogether only 12,000 or so words of substitutions. But my feeling about the book has changed a bit, and I'm eager to get back to something all my own.

The trip to Chicago turned out to be quite a lot of fun. We got a fine turnout, perhaps six or seven hundred; the papers were good, and one of them, by George Grella, was brilliant, and I hope to be able to send you a copy of it some day—he said he'd give me one; and best of all was the party afterwards in a suite on the twentieth floor of the Palmer House, with scores of people (including old friends from Ann Arbor) coming by to talk. I live in California but the milestones in my life still stand back in the middle west. (You must feel this even more strongly about Mississippi, and yet you're much more cosmopolitan than I.)

I loved the record you sent, as I told you before, with all its courage and sadness. I hope that your courage is high and your sadness quotient is low. You've had a difficult year. And you are not easy on yourself; just on others.

Jimmy is fine. So is Duffy—nearly four months, 54 lbs. My best to your very young relative, and love, as ever,

Ken

Eudora Welty to Kenneth Millar, January 27, 1974

Dear Ken,

It was good to get your news, and I'm glad to know that Jim is altogether fine again, and the anthology just about wrapped up, and the trip to Chicago accomplished to what sounds like much success and a pleasure for you. I wish I might have been in the Chicago audience listening to you. You received a prize too, didn't you? A party at the

Palmer House—that's my idea of the real thing. And how fine to have old friends converging from all around & from earlier times. I'd like to see what the young man wrote, if he comes through with his paper, and still more I'd like to read what you said—if you wrote it down. (I remember it was partly to be replies to questions.)

It's a relief, I feel sure, to have the anthology off your mind after all your work, though it's annoying the way publishers seem to want to make use of your name as editor, yet don't want the collection *too* different from what it might have been with some other editor—(I've noticed that trait in other respects.) I feel sure it's a fine array you assembled, even if it isn't exactly what you wanted to make it, and I must say I'm delighted they pressed for *The Far Side of the Dollar*—A few weeks ago I read it again and believe it really is securely among your strongest and best ones—I remembered so many good things before coming to them, memories like signaling lights appearing ahead on the train track—the fine scenes with Stella (& the towhee)—the terrible farmhouse & barn scene—the very first one at Laguna Perdida, and the one near the end at the Barcelona Hotel, which seemed in a way to answer & echo each other—I just mention because it will vouch for the extra pleasure in store for all who'll be reading it again, in the anthology—it's a beauty that just gets better—What good luck for the Book-of-the-Month Club that they got hold of it to offer—and not bad for the book either, I hope.

We've had rain rain rain, like you—I hope the winds didn't come again or take any trees of yours—I've had a sort of moat around my house, the walk & half the front yard standing under a couple of inches of water, and it's good to see the sun out today—Birds are loudly singing now—the flowering shrubs in bloom, & the trees budding. I have to go north next week, though—to Washington, Bryn Mawr, Hollins College (in Virginia) & back up to N.Y. for a week before I get home again on the 24th of Feb. At which point it will really be spring here, I hope—which will make me feel ready to write a new story, I hope—And I hope you are writing a new work of your own—How good, after doing other things, to get back into *fiction*. Don't you think?

Geraldine Fitzgerald is in Jackson, doing *A Long Day's Journey into Night* in a guest appearance with our little New Stage, which is where you were that rainy night. She is a wonderful, powerful presence—and a generous person, with much help for the local cast supporting her. Love, Eudora

What will Duffy weigh when he is grown?

Kenneth Millar to Eudora Welty, January 28, 1974

Dear Eudora:

I've just been reading in NYTBR the shortened version of your talk on Willa Cather, and enjoyed it once again. Bill Koshland had just written me that it, and the chance to see you, were for him the high points of the Centennial.[3] Even from here it feels like a great occasion. I'm interested in the way the creative heartland shifts with the decades from place to place. Though Mississippi seems to hold quite steady.

I suspect that Chicago doesn't, though it's rude and rash of me to express even a suspicion after spending less than twenty-four hours there. The meeting itself was large and warm-hearted, though in some respects it resembled a funeral where friends took turns finding things to say about the departed, me. Four papers were read—the one by George Grella of the U. of Rochester was *very* good, and I understand he's writing a book—the mystery form—and then I gave a sort of multi-purpose response, which I enclose. (The title is a parody of Chandler's "Down these mean streets a man must go," in case you don't know, or remember, that essay of his.) It was intended to be mildly amusing, and got some laughs. Afterwards there was a big and long party, which lasted until 3 a.m., in the suite in the Palmer House which the Popular Culture Association had rented for the occasion. I gradually lost the feeling of attending my own wake like somebody in Synge, and simply enjoyed it: Made a new friend, John Cawelti of U. of Chicago, a pop. cult. critic. Yes, I think there must be something to Diarmuid's idea that those who were meant to be friends do get together in the end, or sooner. Perhaps it's easier for writers than for other people: our skeins blow out in the wind and touch so many others. A language or a culture can speak, or reply, almost without recourse to the human voice. The voice merely authenticates what has been said already, in virtual silence. I'll never forget those meetings in your house. It made me happy to be there, and see you and Diarmuid and your other friends. Jackson had it over Chicago by a country mile. Santa Barbara, now, is another story, but it's a story I don't know how to tell, unless I have. In the middle of all the real-estate transactions and oil drilling (still quiescent here, but threatening) and such stuff, we've distilled out of the past, Spanish and anglo, a drop of the real thing. It's really a cluster of cells: art, writing, music, a certain civility, a sense of togetherness—a city not too large. This persistence of the human scale is the essence of it, I think. We know other people, and continue to know the same people, as they change. I'm sure you take all this for granted in Mississippi, but one doesn't in California. It's almost a miracle here. And perhaps the fuel problem will save us yet a little longer from the metropolitan blues.

My Smithsonian Institute records came, by the way, but coincidentally my record player went on the blink so I haven't heard them yet.[4] We note your kind offer to meet us one day in New Orleans. New Orleans would be splendid, but anywhere will do.

Love,

Ken

P.S.—The anthology is turning out better than I'd hoped, after all. In place of what I lost, I at least got in James M. Cain's "Baby in the Icebox."

K.

Eudora Welty, Bryn Mawr, PA, to Kenneth Millar, February 13, 197[4]

Dear Ken,

Thank you so much for your letter and for the copy of your paper that you gave in Chicago, which crossed my letter asking if you'd let me read it—they came just before I left home last week. This is just a quick note and I'll write more when I get home again & have time, but I do want to say how much I enjoyed reading what you told them—"The moral life of the characters is the lifeblood of the story" and the rest of that sentence; "The assumption of the mask is as public as vaudeville but as intensely private as a lyric poem"; and "Like iron filings magnetized by (*The Maltese Falcon*) the secret meanings of the city began to organize themselves around me"—all so good, and the things I like best. All so interesting, about the ascent from the Gothic novel—I'm sure they all liked it & felt indebted to you—

It's snow & ice all the way—Four days in Washington at an Arts Council meeting, here in Bryn Mawr on a sort of personal thank-you visit to friends here, where I've worked before, and I did a reading for the freshmen—Today I go back to Washington to spend the night with John & Catherine Prince, whom I expect you'll remember, then down to Hollins College in VA., where I'll see Bill Smith (who teaches there) and Reynolds and some other friends—It's fun though I am working too—I must go—I heard a wonderful record last night of James P. Johnson, "Father of the Stride Piano,"—he taught Fats Waller—I expect you know it. The Smithsonian collection sounds superb, I read about it too. Have you heard them yet?

Love,
Eudora

Kenneth Millar to Eudora Welty, March 5, 1974

Dear Eudora:

I'm slow in answering your letter, having had some strange wild variegated days—good ones, though. Margaret and I, for the first time in some years, went to Los Angeles overnight and spent two days on the set of "Underground Man" watching it being filmed, for TV not for theatres. The aim of the producers at Paramount is to start a series, if possible, and to that end they cast Peter Graves (of "Mission Impossible") as Archer—he's quite good in the role—and will carry on with him if the series eventuates. Actually they've assembled a very good cast:—Jack Klugman (Sheriff), Celeste Holm (*old* Mrs. Broadhurst), Jo

Anne Pflug (*young* Mrs. Broadhurst), Lee Paul (disturbed gardener, who got jailbirded, like you, by shadows), and as his mother, the murderer, Judith Anderson. It was fun for two days to be around the players and share their cheerful cooperation, and hear Miss Anderson (whom we've known here as someone quite grand) called "Judy-Baby."

Then we came home and got some good news here. My anthology is set now (with the changes I mentioned to you) and no alterations are suggested in my Introduction. Which of course I tried to write straight down the middle of the brow, while trying not to bore really literate readers; but the result is, perhaps appropriately, a little dull. I'm glad you liked my other little piece, for the Popular Culture people, which was also intended for a particular audience, indeed as a response to four papers which I hadn't seen, indeed any possible four papers. I'm reminded that I quoted Frank Norris and must call your attention to a book you should have if you don't have it—*Americans and the California Dream, 1850-1915*, by Kevin Starr. It's a first-class work of cultural history, not just for Californians born, like me, in California in 1915. It seems to tell me quite a lot about my parents and their world—like walking through a country which one has formerly known only in snatches of fiction, fragments of history, old wives' tales.

My other news is that I'll be checking in at the Algonquin again on May 2, having been slated to receive on May 3 from my colleagues in Mystery Writers of America what they call their "grand master" award. I'm very happy about it, never having won an Edgar before (but Margaret did long ago)—it's so good to be accepted by the other members of one's craft. I'll be going up into Canada afterwards, and perhaps M. will join me there where her father is still living, in his nineties, well but nearly blind.

The present delight of my life is my German Shepherd pup Duffy, who's close to six months now and is getting very tall and long in the tooth but has all his puppy sweetness still, towards all living creatures. I'm taking him to school: he learns fast but forgets easy. Our lives are quickened by his.

I don't know much about James P. Johnson but Fats Waller has always been one of my favorites. Haven't been able to hear my Smithsonian jazz (which sounds like a phrase from Eliot: "that Shakespeherian rag") because our record player is still on the blink *and* in the record shop. But it's something to look forward to.

Love,

Ken

Eudora Welty to Kenneth Millar, March 7, 1974

Dear Ken,

All's going as it should with you, I hope—with everybody, and the huge pup all in good health—and with the anthology, and new work too, if you've started some—I wonder if maybe you've had a fine idea and begun yourself a new novel.

I always feel as if I've been gone so long when I take even the shortest trip. I got home last Sunday after being in Washington, Bryn Mawr (did you get a note from me there? I never believe anything mailed in an unfamiliar mailbox ever gets picked up for collection—I believe I put it down some slot in the Philadelphia train station that looked as if nothing was on the other side), Hollins College, Va., & for a brief time in NY. (It was work & play both in each place.)[5] I saw a lot of our mutual friends along the way—in N.Y. Nona, & Joan Kahn, & John Leonard, & Walter Clemons—I impulsively told Reynolds Price I would let him read your speech, then thought I should ask you first—May I? (By the way, though, do you need it back?)

It's spring here—flowering trees, daffodils,—Today the yard is full of blackbirds—It's 80°—The oak tree is full of buds, some fringing out, and in the frailest of twiggy ends of a big branch high up, a squirrel hardly more than a baby is swinging and eating the new buds, holding them up like corn on the cob—I'm looking out the window at him.

Love to you and I hope all your news is good—I'll write more soon—Eudora

Kenneth Millar to Eudora Welty, March 19, 1974

Dear Eudora:

I was properly put in my place today. A gentleman named Lincoln, visiting here from Boston, called to tell me that his eleven-year-old son was eager to meet me, having read and enjoyed my books. They're getting younger and younger, which I like to think is a sign of increasing literacy; though afterwards Margaret reminded me that our daughter Linda was reading Theodore Dreiser when she was ten. I arranged a meeting with the young man for next Sunday when Linda's son Jim, who will be eleven on April 1, will also be present. We can alternate literary discussion and building sand castles on the beach. I'll take along a volume of Kierkegaard in case anyone wants to be read aloud to.—Actually, as you know, I'm very pleased to be reaching young people. It is their elders who are bothered by the complexity; the young have been brought up in it.

I should have answered before that I have no objection to your sending Reynolds my rather fragmentary speech. I would divulge anything I knew or remembered to Reynolds Price, indeed I love him. He is so complex and complete in his candor, both spoken and written, which is all of a piece. Not the least of the glories of Eudora Welty Day was the opportunity it presented for such friendships. You know their names. What pleasure you must take in them.

You are right in supposing that I'm working on an idea for a book, but it isn't a new idea. I did get a new idea—if any of my ideas can be called new—but having developed it to a certain point I put it away to ferment. The old idea I *am* working on goes back more than twenty years, but of course I can't tell you what it is. It's about a painter, which isn't strange: there are a number of painters in my family (as I mentioned in my speech.) My late uncle Stanley, retiring from his professorship at the Ontario College of Art, went to Mexico to paint and had a show in Mexico City when he was in his seventies.[6] The strange and central secrets of his life I cannot tell you, at least not here and now—not until in my seventies I go to Mexico City and write my autobiographical novel, full of strange and central secrets. Soon I'll have no excuse not to.

Stanley's last surviving sibling of fourteen children, my Aunt Laura, is 92 and now resident in the hospital in Medicine Hat, Alberta. Margaret's father is the same age now, and in pretty good shape. I expect to see him in a matter of five or six weeks, when I go east, then north to Canada. I hope Canada will begin to surprise me. It used to be as ingrown as a toenail—forgive the expression.

My dear dog Duffy is growing in all respects, and responding well to Obedience training, sometimes over-responding. He's strong, bright, sensitive, and nice. At six months he is larger than most German Shepherds, and he already towers over the average dog, with twelve more months of (slow) growth to go. He's snoring, rather softly, behind me now.

Margaret, who is snoring, perhaps, but out of hearing, would send you her love if she were awake. All is well here. Your trip sounds like fun. I'm looking forward to mine.

Love,

Ken

P.S. Encl. clipping from today's *L.A. Times*. K.
[Cecil Smith, "Underground Man to Surface on TV," including photograph of a smiling Ken and Margaret with actor Peter Graves]

Eudora Welty to Kenneth Millar, March 22, [1974]

Dear Ken,

Your letter was full of such good news, and I was delighted to hear about the film underway, the anthology all set to go, and the grand master award waiting for you in New York, all coming upon you at the same time. All the way it should be. (I was astonished to know you'd never got an Edgar—could it have been because you were generally acting as a picker and giver of the awards, and so not the receiver?) I'm glad you think the man who plays Archer is doing a good job. I don't know his work, but am anxious to see it in "The Underground Man." And Judith Anderson! Great day! How are they going to keep it a secret from the audience that she is the murderess, that's the only question. They sound as if they've given the production a fine cast—and what fun to have been there watching them work. They must have been very proud that you came. A real holiday for you both, it sounds like, and I hope it happens again before they wind it up—they may need you, indeed. If they do start the series, will all the pictures be films of your novels as written—I remember you told me they'd bought "The Ferguson Affair" and earlier "The Drowning Pool"—wasn't it?—and if Green [Graves] does well as Archer will they put him in those, or want new stuff written? (I'm very ignorant about the way things are done for film, as you see.) All the best to whatever you would like to have happen.

I've noted *Americans and the California Dream* to look up. Our last letters, like the ones before last, crossed—and I'll write a quick line here as the result of a letter from Mary Lou. I have to be in San Antonio on May 2 (a Council on the Arts meeting) (the same day you have to be in New York, I see) and I'd told her maybe I could come the rest of the way to Santa Fe either before or after. She said in her letter that she wanted to ask you to come to see them at the same time, and she may be writing you. Since I know from your letter that if you could come, it would have to be on your way *to* NY, I could make it before San Antonio. And it would be nice if it turned out to be possible for all of us. But I'm not even truly sure I can make it at all—I *think* I can, but am so tired at the moment—a regular descent of both expected and unex-pected things. Anyway, I wanted to mention it to you, just on the happy chance. Maybe you could persuade Margaret to come along on all. I've been re-reading some of her novels now appearing in new paperbacks, just started "Vanish in an Instant." I'm reading the Faulkner biog. too. I think I agree fully with Walter in his Newsweek review. (I had to do a Times review which was an unhappy one—but a first book by a young author, I couldn't bear down on it for that reason, yet couldn't like it very well—*hard* to review a book you don't like.)[7]

All the best to all of you, Duffy included—what kind of scholar is he making?

Love,
Eudora

Kenneth Millar to Eudora Welty, March 24, 1974

Dear Eudora:

It isn't very nice, or very sensible, to reject an invitation before it has been received, particularly when it's an invitation one would dearly love to accept. But I have to confess, just to you and Mary Lou, that my blood pressure has been playing a few tricks on me again. Nothing to worry about—I've had this problem half my adult life—but it does limit the number of starts and stops that I can sensibly make. Though I'd much prefer to come to Santa Fe, and go no further, I feel I have to go to New York and then to Canada because I've promised to, and the third plan is probably more than I should attempt. I know it won't be our last chance to get together. I very nearly accepted a brief "visiting professorship" at the U. of Arkansas because it seemed within distance of Jackson. But you wouldn't have been in Jackson anyway.

I *have* been having good luck with the writing: the new book is beginning to come alive (my notes for it cover a period of fifteen years) though not yet started, and the old books continue to show signs of life. The idea of this Edgar gives me great pleasure—for some eighteen years M's Edgar has been sitting lonely on the shelf. And the television movie is rather fun. If it goes into series, I'll be paid royalties but will probably make no contribution except to read the scripts. They won't be using my books for the episodes, but simply bought two books (*Underground Man* and *Goodbye Look*) in order to acquire the movie and television rights to Archer. I hope he proves to be worth it. I understand the initial movie is turning out well, and also that the series-or-not decision may be made in the next month by NBC, who will see the movie this week. Peter Graves, though he is identified as the star of *Mission: Impossible* (for six years), looks to me as if he will make a good Archer: he's tall, lean, white-haired, athletic, middle-aged, not stuck on himself, a genuine actor (he was the German spy in *Stalag 17*) and keen on the role. The fact is, I picked him for it years ago, and though I had nothing to do with the casting, it turned out. Judith Anderson was whom I had in mind for Mrs. Snow, too. She plays it coldly, rigidly superior—the servant who judges—and may not be detected by the viewer. For Judith Anderson, I wouldn't care!

Just to make everything clear, I should explain that *The Ferguson Affair, not* an Archer book, is also being worked up into a television movie by another group headed by the writer Wendell Meyes. And *The Drowning Pool* is being made into a "theatrical" movie by Fox, who will change Archer's name. It never rains but it pours. (Of course these may not happen, in the end.)

I know Blotner—met him in Ann Arbor—and am sorry his book is being so badly received. But evidently he wasn't quite up to his subject, or misconceived his duty to it, and stumbled in the detritus of scholarship. Still his work is indispensable, as Walter Clemons suggests.[8]
Love, Ken

P.S. Incidentally, Faulkner was kind to Margaret when they were at Warner Brothers in the forties—invited her to tea and talked about his work, saying he hoped *Absalom Absalom* might have been best. Also talked about Melville. K.

Eudora Welty to Kenneth Millar, March 28, 1974

Dear Ken,

Thank you for writing me about it, but I don't like the thought of the blood pressure making itself a bother to you—I hope it'll soon be very much all right again. Of course you're being wise not to complicate your already busy and far-flung trip in May. Take it easy till then, because it sounds very exciting and fine in New York—quite properly so. I was delighted at your view of it—to get the matching Edgar to finish out the pair for the home shelf. (His and Hers.) I wish I could be in NY to hear about the evening. The Council on the Arts always meets at the wrong time. In confidence, I'm trying to get off. They do many good things, and I am for them, but I belong in another part of the program—a reader of candidates' books and projects, not a voter on the ~~cmo~~ money (can't even spell it, much less vote it by the millions). I'm waiting now to be re-placed.

Will you get to go back into deep country again with your old teacher, in Canada? It sounded very beautiful when you told me about it before.

It really *is* pouring movies on you. It sounds just a wonderful descent of good things happening. If you like Mr. Graves and think he will do well as Archer, that's the main thing, isn't it? It would be wrong all the way if they tried to start otherwise. It must have been a lot of decisions and conferrings and ponderings you've been called on for—but now that so many things all coming at once are settled and happily, you can just let them go merrily about the work of it and not give it any worry yourself (I hope). So really lovely, to think of all these good things happening.

And just at the time when it's nice to have that peaceful feeling—when you are ready to start a new book. Like coming to the place you've been looking for to spread out your picnic and enjoy your feast. No, it's not possible to talk about a book beforehand. Let me wish you luck though. (15 years is your magic number, isn't it?)

Your letter with the clipping in it crossed mine to you, but I thank you for it now, and was glad to be filled in on The Underground Man from both it and from what you described. I would feel exactly the same about Judith Anderson. *I* thought of her in *The Chill*—I can see her in those scenes, and in the last one, at the last line, her face. (Is she—she must be—a reader of yours? Probably of very long standing.)

How was the 11-year-old fan? Don't forget to tell me some time what he was like, and how he and young Jim got along and what Jim said about him, it sounds promising.

Mary Lou will be sorry you can't come this time. I'm not perfectly sure I will be able to go either, as I told you—sheer weight of things I ought to be doing instead. You are right, though, that there will be other chances to meet. I am sorry about the Arkansas thing, but I have worked there from here, and it is fairly far. (But I wasn't flying then.) If you do get a chance to come nearby any time, do let me know (ahead), and I will stay home, as I do actually most of the time. Today Reynolds phoned me about something and said he was getting ready to invite you to Duke to some kind of seminar thing, and would invite me to it also—he'd talked to me about this a good while back and probably to you too. So that might be a nice time (it's off in the Fall) to all three meet and would (perhaps) be easy. Wait and see.

It's so beautiful here! All green now, the dogwood out, wisteria, climbing roses, everything. Birds—I wish I knew enough to tell you.

Take care.

Love,
Eudora

Kenneth Millar to Eudora Welty, April 2, 1974

Dear Eudora:

Thank you for your concern about me and my blood pressure. But you don't really have to be concerned, since I have learned to live with it, and have developed a system of early warning signals, which I pay attention to. I have a good doctor and see him regularly, and he regards me as a model patient. There are even certain advantages: e.g., I get off jury duty. The disadvantage is that I don't get around quite as freely as I did when I was younger, or see my friends as often. But that is a common human condition.

Every two weeks we have a writers lunch here, as I've told you—it's been going on for well over fifteen years—and today at lunch Barnaby Conrad asked me if I knew of any brilliant women writers who might be willing to come to the Santa Barbara Writers Conference, which Barnaby founded with great success last year.[9] Knowing that you had been to California and liked it and intended some day to come again, I took the liberty of mentioning your name. I wouldn't have, if I hadn't taken part in last year's conference and found it a pleasant experience. The conference is held in Cate School, a beautifully situated private school near Santa Barbara. You would be housed in an excellent hotel, could stay as long or as short a time as you liked, and do as much or as little as you liked with the students. The time is some time around midsummer. Barnaby will be writing you in a day or two. If you should feel like making the journey, it would be a chance for you to see California, this part of it anyway, at its best, and above all for us to see you. Margaret would love to get to know you. But of course you will be governed by the needs and occasions of your own life. And as I quite easily predicted in my last letter or so, there will be other chances for us to meet, if this one doesn't work out. I'm bearing in mind what you say about the prospect of a seminar with you and Reynolds: in company like that, who would object to being outclassed?

You're right in thinking, I believe, that you belong at or near the creative end of the art business, rather than at the financial end, though I suppose sometimes financial levers *have* to be used. But there's no substitute for the books, or for the feeling that you have for them. Your approbation opened up *my* life, for example. (But now I have to close it down again and go back into the underground-man business. Fortunately I can take my dog Duffy with me: he sits and keeps an eye on me when I write, and then reminds me when it's time for our walk on the beach. Great rolling breakers these last few weeks, which kept me out of the water for the most part. Today was crystal clear, a perfect spring day, and we went for a walk with Bob Easton in Skofield Park near his house. A rapid mountain stream roars through the middle of it. We walked around the park three times in measured ecstasy.)

I have some questions to answer. My 11-year-old fan never showed up, but his parents did. They had neglected to mention that their son was in Boston. So I wrote him a letter instead of talking to him.—I don't know whether Judith Anderson is a reader of mine, but she looks and talks like one. She's a woman I admire, seventy and still pitching. Her *Medea*, which she played in our local theatre (and of course all over the world) was the most powerful performance I ever saw. She'll make an excellent Mrs. Snow, I believe. About the rest of the show, we won't know until we see it. These TV movies are shot in three weeks instead of three months, say, like regular movies; and the difference shows. Don't be too disappointed if it is rough. But I think they have given it a very good try. *Underground Man* will be shown on NBC television *the evening of May 6.* No, I had nothing to do with the script except that it was based on the book. The script was arrived at in a peculiar way. Four leading TV writers were commissioned each to do his own script. Then they picked the best one, Douglas Heyes's. I thought he managed to get the core of the plot into his brief hundred-page compass. We haven't heard yet if Archer will "go for series," but should within a couple of weeks. I honestly don't care much, one way or the other. Books are my trade, and I'm staying with this one. As you say, there's nothing like the peace of starting to get into the writing of a book.

I'll be in Canada when the movie is shown on the air, but hope to catch it. Probably won't see my old teacher this time. He's remarried and moved to his wife's house in a nearby city. I'm glad he's no longer alone: Roy Dickson was my best teacher, and he considered me his best pupil. Wonderful to know him all my life.

Love, Ken

Please give my warmest regards to Mary Lou. K.

Eudora Welty to Kenneth Millar, April 13, 1974

Dear Ken,

I was so glad to get your letter, and thank you for your reassurances about your health. I *was* reassured, and to know that the good doctor and the good judgment and good sense can take care of it is the right kind of reassurance.

May 6 NBC is written down, and I am also alerting lots of people around here who would want to be sure to see The Underground Man. You'll have to see it, Canada or no Canada! I think that's the night after I get back home from my Council on the Arts meeting in San Antonio, which will fit just right for my own chance to see it. I am anxious to. If it goes off well, and leads to more good things, how fine that will be. (Celeste Holm will be in Jackson a week from tonight to give readings at Millsaps College, and I plan to go. Mentally casting her in Underground Man, whatever she's doing.)

It gives me both delight and disappointment that the Santa Barbara Writers Conference is going to be in *June*. Delight that through your thoughtfulness I was asked (I duly received the invitation from Mr. Conrad) and disappointment that I'd already planned to be in Europe that month. You remember John and Catherine Prince—they asked me a long time ago if I'd drive with them through France, and I found I could both go and come by ship, and made a tentative reservation on the Michelangelo and the France respectively, and I guess I will go— it's really not any more final than the reservations (except the Princes have made them for me too in their itinerary plans) but now this lovely chance to come out there arrives to make me wish that nothing would be keeping me from it. I'm sure you knew it was just the kind of thing I could do fairly easily and with no pain, as far as the work went—a nice assignment and a nice list of people, too—and of course the main reason to come, the fine chance to see you and Margaret. Thank you for thinking of it. I'll have to tell Mr. Conrad that I can't come this time, but I'll sort of hope he'll ask me again. Or you will.

It's the kind of thing Reynolds has asked you and me to do that I really don't do at all, not any longer. I hope I won't be missing another chance to see you when I don't go to Duke? Reynolds really does know I have stopped visiting campuses and giving lectures and going to classes and reading manuscripts and staying a week!—I quit about 8 years ago, having done my full share of that, and finding I just couldn't write and do that too. Can you? I wrote Reynolds I had been saying a steady no to such invitations and that to say yes to Duke would make my excuse no longer true or valid to use again. I told him I'd gladly come some time just for a night, to read to the students, and not take pay for it. If you *should* be accepting, I would time it to be able to see you there, if agreeable to all.

The Santa Barbara arrangement would be, on the contrary, just what I'd like. —Well, I still think there'll be other chances. Don't you?

I'll be seeing Mary Lou—finally decided I could manage it, because the free trip as far as San Antonio wouldn't probably happen again—

and when we talked on the phone just a while ago, she asked hopefully if you might be able to join us—she had put off asking you till I let her know for sure about my own dates, which is why you haven't heard from her direct. She was so sorry when I told her you couldn't, and disappointed, and sends you her best. It isn't too incautious, is it, to count on another chance, as I do, that we'll still get to meet? Have a wonderful trip up to get your award—I'll have it in mind as I sit on a barge in the river in San Antonio on that night eating my supper.

It's raining and raining here—all green outside, and if the rain slacks up the birds begin to sing. It sounds wonderfully beautiful where you walked in Skofield Park, three times around.

Good luck on all you do, and love,

Eudora

My respects to your dog Duffy, who does well, doesn't he?

Kenneth Millar to Eudora Welty, Santa Fe, April 24, 1974

Dear Eudora:

Just a note to thank you for your most welcome letter. I'm so glad you felt that the trip to Santa Barbara which Barney Conrad and I suggested was the sort of thing you'd like to do if you weren't otherwise occupied. I like the quick spontaneous meetings, just as you do, and have no desire to resume the academic life. I did go out to the University today, though, to hear Kevin Starr (*Americans and the California Dream*) talk about more recent cultural developments—which he's dealing with in his second volume—and was happily surprised to hear my name come up. When only a few short years ago the detective story was considered beneath the notice of anyone who wished to be thought genteel. I talked to Starr briefly afterwards and we'll meet again, probably here. He'd like to live in Southern California, for his purposes as an historian, and in fact would like to give up Harvard and teach in Santa Barbara. Who would not? (I speak from knowledge of Harvard, which I once attended, as Gatsby attended Oxford, under

Navy auspices). A year from now, if our Writers Conference survives (and it seems to be), I hope you'll be able to visit it and us. Meanwhile I know how you'll enjoy Europe with the Princes, not to mention Santa Fe with Mary Lou and her friends, to whom my best, please. I know I would have, too, and was most pleased to be asked. I feel as you do, however, that the kind of week-long schedule that Reynolds proposed, which would play hell with both my work and my blood pressure—much as I'd like to see him again, and will.

Hope *Underground Man* doesn't disappoint you. It's only a TV movie, you know, with a 22-day shooting schedule instead of 80 or 90 days. But the cast is very good. Celeste Holm plays Mrs. Broadhurst senior, by the way. The movie has *not* been taken as the basis for a series, and that suits me just as well. It would have been a distraction from real work; indeed, even this much has been—I mean the movie.

I still don't know whether I'll make it to Canada. There's a wildcat airline strike up that way, on top of the postal strike which has prevented me from sending or getting any Canadian mail. But I trust it will be resolved by the end of next week.

I'm sending this c/o Mary Lou in the hope that it will catch you, and the assurance that she'll mail it on if it doesn't. M. and I are well and happy, and Duffy is developing into a superdog. At just over seven months he weighs ninety pounds (and is noticeably thin) and already is too large to be shown. Which is fine with me. He's a wonderfully gentle and affectionate dog, and anything I throw he will retrieve. I'm gradually throwing the sticks and tennis balls further and further into the surf, and one of these days he'll find himself swimming. The weather is bright and brisk these days, and our walks on the beach are heavenly. Yesterday we met one other walker and two runners, in three miles. Quite a few godwits and sanderlings and willets, though, which only enhanced the blessed solitude, just down the road from home—a combination that enchants me.

Love,

Ken

P.S.—I'll be thinking about you under the clock of the Algonquin elevator. Hope to see Joan in N.Y. K.

Eudora Welty, Santa Fe, to Kenneth Millar, New York City, [April 29, 1974]

Dear Ken,

We stopped at the mailbox on our way into the compound where Mary Lou lives—they'd met me at the airport in Albuquerque—and there was your letter. It was so thoughtful of you to send a message in place of you, the next best thing, but we all wish it had been possible for you to be sitting around the piñon fire at night having supper & talking—and you could have had Agnes's 5 dogs introduced to you, 2 of which are Ibiza (?) hounds, those lean longheaded pointed eared fast brown & white dogs that come down from the sacred Egyptian dogs that the Phoenicians carried to the coasts of Europe—Agi [Agnes Sims] says they *still* expect to be waited on hand & foot, as when they were sacred. What would Duffy think of *them*? Agi uses them as models in some of her paintings based on myths & tapestries etc.

This is just to say I hope the Mystery Writers of America do you proud and celebrate you the way they ought to on May 2. I hope you have a splendid time in N.Y. and will indeed see Joan—and the others that would like the chance, like Walter Clemons?—I'll be seeing John Leonard in San Antonio at that meeting, May 2, I gather from the list— And I hope you don't have to give up the Canadian part of the trip. Good luck on it all—

It's cheering to be told there might be another chance for me to come to Santa Barbara—Actually I was just invited to come for a semester to the U. of Cal. at Santa Barbara (by Mr. Frost whom you probably know[10]) but it's the kind of invitation I can't ever accept—a full-time job is what it would amount to with me, who takes such things hard, so I couldn't do my own work—But I was honored to be asked, and it gave me another twinge to say no to Santa Barbara. It was surely no more than your due that you were made a part of Mr. Starr's talk—or of anybody's talk on that subject that was at all serious. Give my regards to the place where you are now—I'll be home just in time to see The Underground Man—I hope *you* see it—and like it—

Love,

Eudora

Again Millar went alone to New York and was pleased to find a letter from Eudora awaiting him at the Algonquin Hotel. "We live out our lives in terms of a very few people," he later wrote her, "(you more than others, I less) and it was good to feel the touch of your mind as I entered the Cretan labyrinth of that weekend."[11] He managed to negotiate the "Cretan labyrinth" and showed up at the Essex House the evening of Friday, May 3, for the Mystery Writers of America dinner where he'd receive the MWA's Grand Master Award. But he managed to avoid doing any interviews, even hiding behind a curtain at one point in order to duck the press.

Kenneth Millar to Eudora Welty, May 8, 1974

Dear Eudora:

Your letter was waiting for me when I checked in at the Algonquin and made me feel much less far from home. Then within an hour or two I was having dinner at Dorothy Olding's house with Joan Kahn, and further good memories were renewed. My only regret was missing the Santa Fe part: Mary Lou and Agi and the Ibiza hounds and you. Life is full of different choices and near misses: I hope it will give me another chance at Santa Fe. You I know I will see again. My recent trips have turned out so well—Jackson, Chicago, New York—that I'm beginning to lose some of my disinclination to travel. Good as this last trip was, though, I have to admit that I got home exhausted. Though I greatly enjoyed the press of people at the dinner, and the honor they did me and the kindness they showed in the process, I feel more at home *en plain air* with few people around, or none, and a dog quite near. But then life would be duller without the exclamatory punctuation of those occasional public events. The whole affair was well-handled and I think well-covered. One incidental dividend was having lunch with Kurt Vonnegut whose girl-friend Jill Krementz asked me over to take my picture for a magazine: they were both exceedingly pleasant, I thought; and I've always heard this of Vonnegut.[12]

The Canadian part of my trip was cut short by external circumstances. Two hours before midnight Sunday night, having just driven back from Kitchener to Toronto, I got a tip that the Toronto airport would be shut down at midnight by a strike. There being no other way out but bus, and I unwilling to be trapped in Canada, as I was for too many years, I grabbed the last seat on an eleven o'clock plane back to New York. Then flew out here the next day. It made me realize dramatically how I felt about Canada, a place whose air is slightly difficult to breathe— bracing but untempered by gentleness or real civility (such as I was surrounded by in Jackson, where even the dear lady who Stole the Lunch did it with good manners). Canada, in short, remains the place that M. and I had to get out of. Her father, in his ninetieth year, remains a remarkable man and his daughter's father. Dim sight but perfect memory and mind: he told me how he left school, never to return, at age 12 to work in a furniture factory, a fifty-nine-hour week at two dollars a week, and, as I've told you before (and he me) rose to be mayor, and president of the Ontario Municipal Association. He told me many things, without self-pity.

I'm glad to hear that Santa Barbara isn't letting you alone—I do know Professor Frost and he is a decent man, active for many years in the NAACP before this became popular among whites, but his campus is not a very happy one: the administration lost its morale during the riots and never regained it—and particularly that we'll perhaps be able to entice you to the Writers Conference next year. It will be fun. Meanwhile you have Europe coming up. My regards to it and the Princes, and my love to you, As always, Ken

P.S.—I told the MWA that my Edgar would solve a problem we'd been having in recent years with Margaret's Edgar, who had been crying with loneliness

K.

P.P.S.—Review of TV movie enclosed. I thought it was terribly obscure, but I may be prejudiced—print-prejudiced.

K.

Eudora Welty to Kenneth Millar, May 25, 1974

Dear Ken,

I was so glad to get your letters, both—yes you did write me soon after you got home from your eventful trip. It's no wonder you were tired. What a lot of pleasure you must have given, at the same time. I hope you didn't suffer in your health though, or in writing your new book, for even a little time.

It's the way I feel too when I get home from a trip. I believe I may be more understanding about that than you know. By necessity I had to learn to cope with lecturing at colleges and all that goes with it, and I would collapse afterward when I got home, it's so hard for me. This may show you, a remark I don't believe I ever repeated to anybody because they wouldn't know what was so hilarious about it—a young man in a strange city at a party: "You're the only low-key wallflower-type celebrity that's ever visited here." (The word celebrity is what makes it the funniest of all, of course.) But I'm not by nature the social being you saw here last May—that was something I had to be keyed up to, which indeed I was, by happiness. But I like one-time things, and special and extraordinary happenings—don't you? Those are worth it.

All the time I was watching and trying to figure out what they thought they were doing to The Underground Man, I was wishing you could just get it back from the screen. They did you wrong in a whole lot of departments, which is bound to have upset you some in spite of your warning feeling that it might not be very good, had been made in such a brief time. Was all that confusing build-up, before the title even came along, something they were doing in aid of selling the pilot? And I thought they *could* have made a good movie out of it—and the way to do that was all in your book. They had only to use *your* characters play *your* scenes. That would have kept a clear, tight, intact, good movie. But they threw every chance away, it seemed to me. (I don't feel in agreement at all with that Times reviewer whose piece you let me see.) I was especially impatient with them for not holding to & following the main drive of the story—Archer's care for the fate of the little boy—who was made just an infant and then mostly forgotten about. What I did was go straight to the novel and read it again that same night—which settled my feathers. I agree, that's where novels ought to be, on the page—

Did Jill get some nice pictures? I too have met them and think they are unusually sweet people. I'm glad you got out of Canada (again) all right and in the nick of time. But so good that you went and got to talk again and listen again to Margaret's father. He sounds magnificent.

There's a mocking bird in my yard that I believe can do arithmetic. This is the way he sings—each * is a phrase:

***
***
****** (he can add)

****
***
* (he can subtract)

******
**
*** (he can do short division)

then something like this, approximate only:

******
****
*********************!

It may be multiplication, but there he loses me.

I've been putting my non-fiction book together—a lot of work and what it will amount to I feel uncertain about—I'm better at knowing whether or not stories are good. I take off on Thursday (flying) for NY and will probably finish the book up in the Algonquin, leaving the next Wed., June 5. I'll write you a letter on the boat.

Greetings to Margaret—also to Duffy & to the new Edgar—With love to you, Eudora

Kenneth Millar to Eudora Welty, New York City, May 30, 1974

Dear Eudora:

It was such a delight to get your letter, as always so kind and understanding. I'm afraid I've been spoiled by these writing years in the fastnesses of California, so that while I'm a low-key type like you by preference, I get terribly keyed up in the big city, find it hard to sleep or even stop moving. The best thing is to stay away. But the trouble is, I enjoy it. But better for me are the long slow seaside days with the sound of the waves instead of the sounds of traffic, and birds around. I spent a happy quarter-of-an hour today watching a couple of surf scoters foraging underwater in the surge around the pilings of a pier, and another half-hour or so walking my dear old 8 ½-month-old Duffy, who is getting quite enormous but is as mild as a kitten. He's already as tall and long as Brandy was, but is narrow in the beam and, under his fur, quite lean. He still has his sweet puppy smell. His intended companion, another small dog from the same kennels, was born last week and we'll be bringing him home early in July. Our hands will be full for a while, which is the way hands should be.

With all my bucolic intentions and resolutions, New York has reached its skinny arm out to here and offered me once again its dubious embrace. A reporter for *People* magazine, Brad Darrach, has been following me around this week, asking questions and getting answers, aimed at some kind of article for the magazine. Fortunately Darrach is both bright and honest, so that the process is painless, but still enervating. The funniest thing is that Jill Krementz, after taking all those pictures in N.Y., is flying out here tomorrow to take some more. I really don't complain. Publicity is one of the things a writer can use, and I am willing to be struck while the iron is hot, but it will be nice to crawl back into my book.—The comparative mess that was made of *Underground Man* didn't really bother me, in fact I had some good laughs in the course of it. My feeling is that such enterprises don't really touch the books, and that all a writer has any right to expect is, if he's very lucky, one good movie based on his work in a lifetime. I'd probably feel much worse if they had made a TV series and I had to sit and watch it every week. Books, novels, belong as you say on the page, and these fantastic interruptions only send us back rejoicing to the quiet writing life which is interrupted only by the scratching of the pen and the trilling of mathematical mockingbirds. I loved your demonstration and am prepared to accept it absolutely. Nature taught *us* to count.

Barnaby Conrad and I were filled with joy by your saying in effect: ask me again. It will be lovely for all of us, and I hope for you too, if you can come to our Writers Conference in 1975. Barney asked me to tell you that he greatly appreciated your note and that it was the sweetest rejection he ever got. This year's conference, by the way, is now filled up, with as many students as Cate School can house and handle. I enclose a program for your amusement.

Margaret is very well, and so am I. We hope you have a fun time in Europe with your dear good friends. Please do write me on the boat. I've written many letters on boats but never received one.

Love, Ken

Eudora Welty, New York City, to Kenneth Millar, June 4, 1974

Dear Ken,

Thank you for your letter, which I was so happy to be handed here, and cheered to read. I was glad to hear all your news & to see the prospectus of the coming Writer's Conference. I'll hope for that later next year—

Watch out for a photo of me that Jill Krementz is sending you— She picked out *her* choice, and sent it over by messenger to be inscribed—It's one she took at 7:30 AM when she rushed upstairs without warning into my bedroom—I could have picked you out something a bit tidier.[13]

My boat sails tomorrow and I'm still finishing up errands that ought to have been done in Jackson—Excuse this awful writing—it's being done on my knee in the lobby—

Good luck with everything, including the new puppy when he comes.

Love,
Eudora

Eudora Welty, at sea, to Kenneth Millar, June 14, 1974

Dear Ken,

This is our ninth and last day of the crossing—with smooth seas for the most part, the days some sunny, some overcast—but to me all good, for being on a moving deck with the Atlantic rolling by, & just reading or just breathing the good air—The Raffaello itself—herself, I guess— is the most casual & confused ship in the running—For example, I had to change my cabin 3 times the first night out—getting thrown out of one & guided to another one, no reason known. This is tourist class, but some acquaintances upstairs tell me it was the same there. Slightly comic opera, but I just go on reading Lord Byron's Letters and the autobiography of the Emperor of China, and on—an old friend from home who now lives in Italy is meeting the boat in Genoa & I'll go home with him & friend for the weekend, near Pisa—Then John & Catherine Prince & I will connect—they're heading toward Italy from Greece—It ought to be the nicest, easiest trip—back roads & good food—they've already cased the way—We'll postcard you.

I hope your work goes well—That everything goes well. There's a beautiful German Shepherd who made a safe trip over—I saw him embark in N.Y., & heard his voice at night from my cabin, & saw him disembark at Naples yesterday—Entering that Bay & sailing out of it! It's as hypnotic & lovely as ever—

This may be mailed in either Genoa or *France*—I'm told any letter mailed in Italy can take a month. My letter to my friend near Pisa took over a month to reach him, air mail. I read a mystery by Alan Hunter, new to me, that I liked—"Innocents" was in the title. (I can never remember the title of any book, just the contents) I'm wondering if you approve of him? Love from the Mediterranean,

Eudora

Eudora mailed this letter to Ken from Riparbella in Tuscany near the home of her old friend and flame, John Robinson. She and Robinson had been involved in a long and complicated romantic relationship between 1937 and 1952. The relationship had ended when Robinson either told Eudora or she realized that he was in love with a young Italian named Enzo Rocchigiani; the two men would be together until Robinson's death in 1989. For a time in the 1950s, Eudora and Robinson were alienated, but their friendship ultimately endured, as their romance did not. In her letters to Ken, Eudora never mentions this part of her history with an "old friend from home."

Meanwhile, in Santa Barbara, People's Brad Darrach witnessed the bleak tension often apparent in Ken and Margaret Millar's union. "I had the feeling he was manacled to his wife," Darrach would recall much later, "and maybe she to him. I was aware of the ravine in their marriage: something very fundamental had happened between them, and I felt it had reached the point where there was barely civility[. . .] And it all centered around the daughter, I'm sure."[14]

In August and into the fall of 1974, writer's block became of concern to both Ken and Eudora. She had published no fiction since The Optimist's Daughter (1972) and he was struggling in the wake of Sleeping Beauty, which had appeared early in 1973. Ken hoped that Eudora's 1974 trip to Europe might prompt her to return to fiction in the same way that her 1949–1950 trip to Europe had inspired some of the stories in her book The Bride of the Innis-

fallen *(1955). And for his part, Ken sought inspiration by traveling to the San Francisco Bay area, where he and his family had lived from 1956–1958 while sixteen-year-old Linda was on probation for driving a hit-and-run car that left one young man dead. Guilt-ridden and grief-stricken, Ken had during these years in Menlo Park undergone intensive psychoanalysis. Now he looked back at that difficult time as a possible source of new fiction. It seems that Eudora, instead of turning to her recent travels, hoped to discover ideas for new work in uncompleted stories she had abandoned in the more distant past.*

Kenneth Millar to Eudora Welty, August 5, 1974

Dear Eudora:

I enjoyed your bulletins from Italy and France, and envied you not only your experiences there but the blithe spirit in which *you* enjoyed them, but I got a particular kick out of your most recent letter announcing that you were once more on native soil and heading back to even more native soil. You'll be counting over your experiences and perceptions for many months, and the familiar stimuli of home will be absorbed into the game as you play it hour by hour and minute by minute. Everything will be refreshed for you, and perhaps there will be a collocation of images that will strike sparks and start a new story. I wish it for you, though it isn't necessary to you. I'm really just indulging myself in the thought of your beautiful mind in flight again and stooping like a falcon—a benign falcon which doesn't hurt its prey, at least not so very terribly.

I, on the other hand, am the victim of my books, and have recently spent several days in San Francisco and Palo Alto, revisiting some of the more painful scenes of my life, in the hope that mad California will hurt me into prose again. She will. I have a rather grim story in the planning stage, and my trip will help to flesh it out. San Francisco was rather fun, though it's becoming overbuilt and has more skyscrapers sticking out of its poor bones than a chicken has feathers. I enjoyed the Bay scenes, though, and the crowds where you could see any kind of persons and feel a certain fraternity with them. It's important to me to be reminded of the urban poor, and I took long bus rides with them.

Altogether it was a good experience. Perhaps next year, when I get my book done, I'll hie my way back to Europe. I spent most of a year there when I was twenty and twenty-one, and would like to repeat the experience, though not for so long. Of course I have more responsibilities now. My wife, my grandson, my two young dogs. Margaret is physically well but unable to write for several years now. She doesn't need it, but she used to enjoy it and depend on it. Now she has people. Grandson Jim is one of the people, and a good sort, strong and bright and in key with the difficult times which he handles with humor. He is a good student and, at eleven, thinks nothing of biking twenty-five miles in a day to swim in the ocean, at Huntington Beach. He's been in the house tonight, went to bed laughing. I wish my very young pup would go to bed and stay there, but at ten weeks he can't hold his water for more than a few hours, so I get up in the middle of the night—sometimes, quite often, too late—but there are worse things than puppy pee on the floor. This pup is the best one I ever had, doing by instinct already everything that a dog should do, and more. At ten weeks he weighs twenty-six pounds, is black and red, very beautiful, very friendly, very assertive, very rugged, "holding his own" with his hundred-pound ten-months brother MacDuff. His name is Skye and his father was the best German shepherd in the U.S.A. a couple of years ago. So we have made it into the aristocracy and as for living, our dogs will do that for us. I am looking forward to seeing you, on one coast or the other, surely within the new year. My love, as always, Ken

P.S. Speaking of Skye, Macdonald country, thanks for the mysterious clipping about Ross.[15] K.

Eudora Welty to Kenneth Millar, September 2, 1974

Dear Ken,

I hope you are fine, and everything going well. I got your letter safely, right after I got back to Jackson, and was glad to know your news, and have been thinking about you going about and working on your new book. I hope you haven't given up ever getting a letter from me and would readily guess the reason for the snag—the pile-up of *things* that overwhelms you when you've been away from home. (The pile-up of the things you went away in order to get out from under in the first place. —I was just speaking of myself) I've felt unable to write a letter to a friend or do a lick of my own work—what bad management. I expect you would never be guilty of such a thing, and guilty is the right word for the way I feel. And unhappy, not to be doing the two things that give me the most pleasure. Enough of that. Maybe today will break the spell, for the weather's changing. I've been looking out the window to see if I can spot any new birds in my tree.

Have you finished the moving about your book has been asking for, so that you've been able to settle back into your good working life at home, with its walks? And two dogs now. The puppy sounds unbeatable. Very beautiful too, and with a beautiful name, Skye. The two of them running together must make quite a thunder in the house. (Coming out of the Skye, I didn't realize.)

I too look forward to coming out there next summer—is it June? It seems to me a lovely prospect. I don't want it to interfere in any way with your book, which is clearly an important one to you and one long in the making—but I trust it won't. June is a long way off.

If I may, I'll wish for Margaret that she will have found her own good way back into writing again.

Sometimes only the doing makes me believe I can do it at all, even a line. I do know what it is to be unable and to miss it.—Have you read Midnight Oil, by V.S. Pritchett? (One of my favorite writers.) A marvelous autobiographical book.[16]

With love,
Eudora

Kenneth Millar to Eudora Welty, September 7, 1974

Dear Eudora:

I'm so happy that you've mastered the world of things again and settled down at peace with the realities of home and are waiting to be struck by benign lightning. Happy too—and so will many of us be— that you remain fixed in your intention to come to Santa Barbara next June. (Barnaby Conrad will be writing you later about times and arrangements.) I really enjoyed this year's conference, particularly Ray Bradbury and Joan Didion. There were 62 full-time students, not including dozens who came out from town for the lectures. I think you'll love Cate School, where the conference is held. Santa Barbara in the summer is very heaven. And we'll be so glad to see you.

Margaret may or may not write again. She ran into a severe block after Linda's death, and sat for months in her room trying to get past, sentence by sentence, the middle of a tragic book. Finally she couldn't write at all. She needs writing to complete her life, but it is still a rather full life, full of talk and friends and several interests. I regret her silence. But as you imply, we all write on the verge of silence. When the words come, they're pure good luck, like rain. My own words have been coming slow this year, but I haven't run out of them yet.

Yes, I've read *Midnight Oil* and like V.S. Pritchett very much, admire his short stories. Also his previous volume of autobiography, *A (Hansom?) Cab at the Gate* [actually, *A Cab at the Door*] or some such title, which interested me particularly because so many of the members of my family, though they started out as Mennonites and Presbyterians and whatever, ended up as Christian Scientists. My mother was a Christian Scientist, and I had almost as hard a time as Pritchett breaking away from that unreal world. Fortunately Mother became reconciled to my apostasy before the end of her life (in 1936, aged 58) and was content to see me go my own way, out of churches altogether.

If Christian Science could do what it claims, I'd be calling on it now. My seventy-year-old brother-in-law Clarence Schlagel, husband of Margaret's sister Dorothy, is in the final stages of a four-year contest with cancer. He lost his larynx years ago, and now is losing his life. But he is going not unhappily. Dorothy is a devoted wife, nearly twenty years his junior, and she also happens to be a very good nurse, and she's taken leave of her job (head of the X-ray dept. in a local clinic) to nurse Clarence through his final illness. She can't save him, not for too long, but she can ease his passage. The very close careful direct physical attention ruled by both science and love that she is giving her husband is beautiful to watch, more beautiful than any ballet. She goes home exhausted at eleven and comes back fresh, or fresher, in the morning. I can't express my admiration for the courage and devotion of such women as Dorothy. Night after night she battles with the Fiend himself and licks him. My mother, who was also a nurse, Winnipeg General class of 1900, nursed my father in that way in his last days, and temporarily said to hell with Christian Science.

Love, Ken

P.S.—Eudora, I hope I thanked you properly for signing Jill's picture of you. K.

P.S.—I gave my friend Brad Darrach the journalist your address so that he could send you his book about Bobby Fischer in Iceland in the thought you might find it amusing or instructive or both.[17] It's a kind of comic saga done mostly in dialogue and monologue. K.

Eudora Welty to Kenneth Millar, [October 8, 1974]

Dear Ken,

I hope you are fine, and the book going steadily on, and all keeping well with you. As you've found out, I'm the worst correspondent that could ever be wanting badly to write and failing to, with the attendant feelings of guilt—the last thing I see when I turn out my light at night is all my unanswered letters on my desk—*cherished* and unanswered. I truly cannot seem able to get past the stupid (to me) daily demands of things I don't care about at all, to the real things of my real life, like my writing, like my friends. This sounds as if I'm in a bad way, and maybe I am, but I'll still lick the problem, I hope. People

[The handwritten letter breaks off at this point, and Eudora begins anew on the same page, using her typewriter.]

Dear Ken,

I'll try again. I wanted to ask you about the new oil slick—when the news came one morning that it had happened during the night, I felt distressed for you, and Margaret, and of course Santa Barbara and once more your birds, and then I never heard a single follow-up report. Oil slicks don't just go away, do they, any more than other troubles? Somehow I felt this would be the worst time one could happen, because isn't it a migratory season? But I will hope—maybe this isn't a bad one?

Thank you for your letters, and for telling me more about your family—And I think I do know about the long experience, almost impossible to conceive of until you are given it yourself, of nursing the long illness of someone you love, and I feel able even from away off as I am to send sympathy.

It was interesting to get the book about Bobby Fischer, and thank you for asking your friend Brad Darrach to send it to me—he also sent a very nice letter, which I must reply to, in which he told me he was the one who had interviewed you for the magazine *People*.[18] This I missed because I was away, and our library doesn't get it. Would it be asking too much if you would send me a copy to read—I'd send it back. Ordinarily I shy away from reading interviews of my friends because they seem superficial and full of error (not Christian Scientist, just the plain kind) by their very nature. But you and he must have achieved something better, and I would also like to see the pictures Jill took. You must have been rather a change from Bobby Fischer! What a character—how unbelievable he'd be in a book of fiction. I agree with you that this young journalist did his job well, and that must have been a harder job than the job itself.

I did enjoy the *New Statesman* parodies—was delighted you sent me the page. The Wasted Land was a prize one. I also like the one on Amis and Betjeman, didn't you? (I ought to be ashamed to send you the note I'd started, on the other side, but will write on the back of it feeling better.) I have a clipping somewhere for you, too.

Mary Lou has been here lately, and stayed a week which was grand. The local ETV station is giving a prize for the best documentary and the best fictional film entered from around the country, and asked me to get a jury here and be a judge with them. Originally 40 entries—they had 7 left to judge. We got a good one, I think—called "Glen Rose, Texas." When it's shown (I suppose it will be) on PBS I will let you know, I think you would find it worthy. What they showed was good, and then they made something with it, in filming, recording talk—the real thing—and selecting. A work of art, really. The judge representing TV was Curtis Davis (unknown to me), of NY, who I thought might have met you—but he hadn't—since he had produced that program about the Louds (I never saw it). He hadn't been the one who'd gone to see you, hadn't gone to Santa Barbara. But he was a nice man, anyway. After the ETV things, Mary Lou stayed for a little visit, and I enjoyed her so much. She asked about you—and she said what if I could stop off in Santa Fe when I went to Santa Barbara.

Before this, the State Council on the Arts had the National Council on the Arts people—Nancy Hanks & Co.—to Jackson, and I had to help, wanted to of course—I had to make a speech, and after they left I felt so bone tired from nervousness. Crowds of people—I was not built for doing my civic duties, and maybe I ought to quit trying. I feel you understand these things.

For the last two days I've been trying to write a story, pick it up where I left off a month ago. This is the way to get back on the track, for me. Please forgive such a rotten letter. I do hope all is well with you.

Love,
Eudora

(over)

I thought you could enjoy this: My niece Liz has just entered her daughter Leslie, age 3, in nursery school. She came home yesterday & said, "I was the leader for today."—"What does the leader get to do?"—"Push."

Kenneth Millar to Eudora Welty, October 10, 1974

Dear Eudora:

I greatly enjoyed and have read over and over the letter which you unaccountably consider "rotten"—if one of your letters could be rotten there'd be nothing sound left in heaven or on earth, regions which you seem to take turns inhabiting: weekends in heaven, weekdays on earth. But of course your feeling of distress is not really unaccountable: you are a writer, and too many duties and occasions have been getting in the way of your writing. I wish you some clear space to work in, and a renewal of the selfish dedication that used to be our armor. I include myself, because I've been suffering from the same dissipation of my energies. We are not lotus eaters, but we are duty eaters, and we must return to what my friends in college used to call *the higher selfishness*. I am willing to cooperate to the extent of sacrificing one of my greatest pleasures and suggesting that you not answer this letter at all.

These past months have been not unhappy but rather broken up, so that while I have been able to do a great deal of planning and note-making towards my new book, I haven't actually written any final copy. But as the fall comes on, I'm beginning to feel something stir, like Frankenstein's monster. Brad Darrach, who for ten years was movie reviewer for *Time* magazine, has recently been doing a profile of Mel Brooks, and tells me that Brooks' new Frankenstein movie, starring Cloris Leachman, is one of the funniest things he's ever seen. I hope you didn't mind hearing from Brad, and seeing his book. We spent a solid week together and became good friends. He is the only glossy-journalist I ever met who struck me as a truly simple and virtuous man. But he isn't young,

as I too supposed he was when we first met—I spoke of "his generation" and "mine," and he announced that he was 53. But his attitudes
are youthful, and the Bobby Fischer book is his first. I admired the way
he told his story almost entirely in accurately overheard language. I
am sending you his piece for *People* magazine, which is also generally
accurate, except in the matter of earnings. Jill's pictures are good, don't
you think?

A friend of Jill's, Susan Sheehan of the *New Yorker*, was here earlier
this week to interview me (and Judith Anderson) in preparation for
her biography of Alfred Knopf. Apparently I was the only author so far
who came out unreservedly on Alfred's side as a man and as a publisher.
I did not of course become involved in the Alfred-Blanche controversy.
I knew Blanche slightly, and respected her; and respect her more since I
learned—this in confidence—that she had left behind a written tragic
cri de coeur among her papers, explaining and lamenting. Suddenly, for
me at least, the dreariness of that life and broken marriage fell away and
revealed a flash of Racinean splendor which redeems all. Miss Sheehan
expressed such a warm and intelligent and friendly interest in you that
I suggested she give you a ring next time you both are in New York. If
I am too free with such suggestions, stop me, please. But I believe you'd
like her, as I did. She does a good deal of "Talk of the Town," she told
me, though she lives with her husband in Washington.

The oil slick which was given such publicity was not a serious one,
just one of the many that occur off these shores, in no way comparable
with the big spill of 1969. But we like the publicity, and it is an index of
how seriously people here, and now even the authorities, are beginning
to take this problem. A little late, of course, but we'll slow 'em down.
Knopf has just published *Supership* which is about the really great threat
of the future: the mishandling of oil tankers in the world ocean. The
author's conclusion is that if present practices continue, the world oil
pool will be depleted and the world ocean will be dead. Which means
that life on earth will become virtually impossible—that is the price for
fifty years of oil. It's a frightening book. But now you don't have to read

it. I'm glad that by sheer happenstance—living in the right place—I got in early on what is now the central world issue, I suppose. I don't mean to brag, but do you know half my books, starting with *Moving Target*, deal with the oil dynasties of California and Texas—without, in the early books, any very conscious propagandistic intent. Well, there's no oil in the new book coming up, but there does seem to be a giant copper mine blighting its landscape. (My father worked in the silver mines at one time.)

Dear young Jim joined the Scouts last week and came home carrying his Scout Manual. "I love this book," he said. He fills me with joy as your grandnieces do you. I wish you more joy in Jackson, and so does Margaret, who is back among the birds full tilt. Our love, as always, Ken

P.S.—It will be great if you can do Santa Fe *and* Santa Barbara in a single swath next summer. K.

Eudora Welty to Kenneth Millar, Thursday [October 17, 1974]

Dear Ken,

Thank you for your letter—all kindness. You couldn't be hard on your friends, I suspect, or on anybody (unless it's yourself). But I just don't manage right when I can't reply to letters better than I do—the letters I really *want* to reply to. Not the professor who wrote me today asking what reason I had to give him for not having any diabolism in my stories. (Is he the Devil, I wonder? He sounded provoked.) It's good to know that all your interruptions haven't done any harm to your book—you probably carried it all in your head right straight through those people's interviews and all. By this time I hope you've got down all you were waiting to get on paper—I mean begun to get it down, with a good clear road ahead. You have indeed made the strongest dramatic use of what the oil dynasties are doing to your country and all the life in it—and not because of happenstance, living in the right place, as you put it—you were *knowing* in the place where you happened to live—and *seeing*, and because of that you had a subject for your talent to work with. I look forward to seeing what comes out of your copper mine.

Yes, I read about *Supership*—frightening it must be—I expect you were about the first one Alfred K. sent it to—

Your words about him to the woman who came about the biography are bound to give him a lot of pleasure, in reading her book. He was telling me himself about the book's being written (and so was Helen K., about the lady's being underfoot!) when I happened to see him at a party in N.Y. in May. He seemed to have much confidence in her, and you when you saw her liked her. I hope it *is* a worthy book—he's an extraordinary man, isn't he, and undoubtedly the last living great publisher—a man who knows *and* loves *and* publishes the best, and would not have done otherwise. Of course I don't know him personally very well, yet I feel so much his kind interest in regarding me as a friend, in being a friend as I am of yours and of Elizabeth Bowen, and when we were together in Nebraska for the Willa Cather thing, we really did get the chance to talk a little. So I, too, want to see him done justice by, as a friend. It is touching, what you were told about Blanche. Touching and strange—How warm and good Helen is now—wonderful to see them together. She told me about what he said when after days & days of lying unconscious after his stroke he opened his eyes & saw her sitting beside him—"Never underestimate the power of love."

Sure, I'd be pleased if Susan Sheehan wants to call me—that was nice of you since you liked her.

Thank you for letting me have a look at the interview in *People*. It was an unqualified delight to see the pictures—they *are* good. I do think Jill's photography is more sensitive than Brad Darrach's reporting, in the case of you! He likes you, clearly, but I just wanted him to say everything better—about your work—and I felt in some respects he had too much brashness—in place of perception. But the pictures said what the writing wasn't able to—Or this was how it struck me—

carper that I am? No I'm not!—And of course you were so nice to him—I'm returning it separately—putting with it a little item I did by request for a mag. starting up at Chicago—(the offprint is how they paid me).[19]

Jim sounds finer & finer all the time—"I love this book"—What a joy he must be.

Thank you for your good wishes for my work. I need them and feel better for having them. It's that good fall feeling here too—Beautiful, clear, cool air, warm sun—sweet smells—Both some thrashers & some mockingbirds are courting again, maybe they know what they're doing but it's nearly November. Got a new bird book out of the library, opened it to Barn Owls, & read: "They may be frequently encountered in castle ruins"—Oh?—Then some finches were said to go as far as Siberia—Of course it was a Czechoslovakian bird book!

Love,
Eudora

Donald Alexander White will be one year old tomorrow.

Kenneth Millar to Eudora Welty, October 21, 1974

Dear Eudora:

It was most thoughtful of you to send me your beautiful short piece about "A Worn Path." It matches the beauty and simplicity of the story itself, yet seems large enough to stand as a credo. I'm so glad you wrote it.

There is a book I believe you would enjoy—I am in the middle of it now—Iris Murdoch's *The Sacred and Profane Love Machine*. I have not always greatly liked her novels, but this one is extraordinary even for her, succeeding in translating her philosophy into binding plot and very interesting people. It makes me green with envy.

Brad Darrach called, and I was able to pass on your pleasant words about his Bobby Fischer book. It is being quite well reviewed. Though this is his first book, and he is young in heart, Brad isn't really young— early fifties. He was *Time's* movie critic for ten years, in those great days when the modern masters were showing their hands. Brad once did a cover story on Bergman.

I am struggling with my plot which as you remind me means: struggling with my meaning. I think it is that a very strange and difficult and even terrible life can feed an art. But where can the emotion derive from? I hope "the poetry is in the pity."

I was glad to be told of your visit from Mary Lou—such a delightful woman. A young girl student and budding writer, aged twenty—first sale at age sixteen!—named Lorna Clymer visited us yesterday. Lorna is the daughter of our neighbors who are educational writers, and a student at St. John's College at Santa Fe. I gave her Mary Lou's book "The World Within" with a double purpose, to introduce her to some good, old writers, or reintroduce her, and possibly to introduce her to Mary Lou, with whom I suggested she get in touch. I hope Mary Lou isn't upset if Lorna turns up on her doorstep. She loves animals and is almost preternaturally well behaved, so much so that I fear for her spontaneity, a faculty with which Mary Lou has no problem. I hope *her* son is well and reasonably happy.

Our new young pup, aged five months old and weighing sixty pounds, is an absolute darling, ready to lick his weight in wildcats but he couldn't catch them. He's a deep dense black, except for red-and-tan paws and underparts. I think he will be our personality champion, his elder Duffy being our sweetness king. The two German shepherds love each other and are in constant physical contact, even when sleeping.

We are both well, and hope you are the same.

Love, Ken

Kenneth Millar to Eudora Welty, November 16, 1974

Dear Eudora:

That was a most interesting piece you sent me of Miss Jacobsen's, about the transmigrations of a poetic line.[20] I don't have anything comparable to *riposte* with. So far Knopf have sent me only one copy of the suspense anthology and I was wheedled into giving it to a friend who is about to leave on a Mediterranean cruise. The book is very large and heavy for such purposes, but quite handsome. I'll send you a copy when I get some more. Not much in it will be new to you. I do enclose a clipping about Katherine Anne Porter which you may possibly not have seen. What courage she has, always had.

Tomorrow, displaying some courage of my own, I am flying off in the teeth of the winter gales to New York, to try and do the anthology some good. I leave behind about a quarter of a draft of a book which I'm glad to get away from for a few days but can hardly wait to get back to: "Portrait of the Artist as a Dead Man." It's a bit different from the others, perhaps lighter, though they never seem to turn out that way.

Margaret is well. She bought herself a fur coat then bought an imitation fur coat so she won't wear out the real one. Do you like Brian Keith? He's going to play Archer on TV beginning January. We'll see how it goes. Love, Ken

Eudora Welty, New York City, to Kenneth Millar, November 21, 1974

Dear Ken,

I'm here again, for just a few days—having come by way of Sewanee, Tenn., where I attended a celebration of Allen Tate's 75th birthday, and going home by way of Washington over the weekend, a Council on the Arts meeting. The time at Sewanee was very whole-hearted in praise & affection for Allen—I enjoyed the conversations more than the papers read, though they were substantial & scholarly, I know. Still leaves on the trees in the Valley, & snow powdering the mountain that we were on top of. Poems were written & sent by old friends of Allen like Robert Penn Warren—and poets present read their poems at a banquet. William Jay Smith thought all this up. It was moving and poignant too—Allen is in very frail health—but responded to the occasion with his old wit—I was so glad I got to be on hand—(I had breakfast before leaving with a big fan of yours, a member of the English Dept. named [William T.] Cocke.)

N.Y.'s blowing with an icy wind. Today I saw your old friend & mine Joan Kahn. She was telling me about the World Congress of Crime Writers in London next fall & said she bets she could get me in on it some way—She said some will be going as crime writers and others as nothing, and I could go as a nothing. What a fine idea even if impossible. Do you plan to go? I love the idea of a cocktail party at the Old Bailey! Joan is fine. I had lunch with Walter Clemons, who is fine too.

Is it about time for your anthology to appear? On the chance it was, I looked for it in Brentanos but didn't see it yet. All goes well with the new novel, I hope. And with all of you. I just wanted to say hello from here. Love, Eudora

Happy Thanksgiving!

Eudora Welty to Kenneth Millar, [December 1974]

Dear Ken,

We arrived in New York on the same day! When I got home & found your letter I felt awfully disheartened. If you checked in to the Algonquin, and were anywhere near to room 900 between Sunday & Friday morning, I'll feel worse. I wrote you to California while you might have been next door reading the paper.

Did you have a good trip? I hope so—and I look forward to a sight of the Anthology—And I can give copies for Christmas, too. Good news about Archer if you approve, & if you like the man. My nieces know what he looks like, I don't—They said the way they thought of Archer was a man who looked like you—We all had a good Thanksgiving—I hope you did too & came home to find all well and the new novel (I think your title is wonderful) safely waiting. (I'm always worried that a ms. isn't safe if I'm out of the house—But of course you've got a fine guardian who could swim out of a flood with it in her teeth or get it back from a raven who tried to carry it away, like the car keys that time.[21] This is silly sounding because I feel unhappy to have missed you. *Isn't* it absurd!

Love,
Eudora

Kenneth Millar to Eudora Welty, December 3, 1974

Dear Eudora:

I am wreathed by irony and regret and feel that it is absurd indeed that you and I should have been lodged on nearby floors (9 and 12) of the Algonquin week before last, and never know it. It was stupid of me not to check for you at the desk, but it never occurred to me that you might be there. Accidents balance out in life, and probably this is the price I have had to pay for the most happy accident of meeting you, for the first time, in the Algonquin lobby. I did have a pleasant time in New York, part work part play, but do wish I had seen you. The best of the play part was hearing Marian McPartland play the piano, which I'd never heard before. At the end of the week, Friday, I went up to Canada for a couple of days and saw my father-in-law, who was recovering from pneumonia and feeling, at ninety, the first real desolation and chill of old age—the hospital did it to him; his first illness since his appendectomy in 1919—but he still has a few years left in him. I greatly enjoyed your account of Allen Tate's seventy-fifth birthday, having long been an admirer of his, prose and poetry, and the man himself. There are common feelings that draw together southerners and Canadians, I think, feelings for tradition and for the land, so that Tate meant quite a lot to me when I was young, in his anti-megalo-American way. Which reminds me that flying home, over Lake Michigan, the lady beside me, a Quebec educator, announced that her ancestor Nicolet was the first white to explore that lake. She was also proud that Nicolet had married an Indian.

I came home to find Margaret in good shape and my dogs somewhat gentler than when I left. The six-month pup is black and red and low and wide and strong, and will possibly be beautiful. He has a fine nature. His name is Skye. My grandson Jim, who is eleven now, is developing a fine nature, too, his face shadowed for the first time this fall by a hint of adolescence. He is both serious and cheerful, like all the most fortunate people. Nor can I think of anyone who is more serious or more cheerful than you.

I appreciate your continued interest in the anthology and wish to send you a copy but so far have not been sent any. I must shake up my editor. Had lunch with Alfred and Helen, with some feeling that it might be, for Alfred and me, a farewell lunch. He's well enough, but not strong; he's grown almost sweet-natured in his age and his fortunate marriage.

Love, Ken

Eudora Welty to Kenneth Millar, December 21, 1974. Note card reproducing Mary Cassatt's "Feeding the Ducks."

Dear Ken—

Many wishes to you and Margaret for Christmas, and a lucky and benevolent and busy and productive New Year—that'll take in the new novel.

It was fine to see the Anthology listed as a Book-of-the-Month Alternate Choice, and I alternated to them by return mail. And your editor has just sent me a copy. So I'm bountifully fixed for Christmas, and am delighted to have the good reading ahead. I've only had time to read the good & provocative preface you wrote, and one story—Margaret's, which I had not seen before—most rewarding—A lot of them I do know but I want to read them again plus the new. A handsome book indeed—

I'll write a letter I owe you, soon, and I'm away behind with everything because my furnace went Boom the day I got home from NY and had to be dismantled & hauled out and a new one put in—it's taken all this while—I've felt hamstrung & unwarm & can't talk about anything but plumbing. One of the funny circs. is that there had to be 2 new furnaces (to take care of all those old vents) and they have fans (they use gas), and so they've been fanning each other's pilot out! Anyway, as of Friday, all seems to be well, and warm now.

Next time I go into the Algonquin, I'm going to look. Happy New Year to you both—and to Jim—and to McDuff & Skye too—& the book. Love, Eudora

CHAPTER FIVE

"Simple but infinitely complex expressions of love and courtesy"

———— ❧ ————

1975

AS Ken worked in 1975 on what would prove to be the last Lew Archer novel, his private-eye character was brought to small-screen life in a short-lived television series. An earlier work by Eudora received a more satisfying adaptation when The Robber Bridegroom *became the basis for a musical in the repertoire of John Houseman's City Center Acting Company. Eudora labored sporadically on a story and eventually had high hopes for a new one. But the non-writing highlight of 1975, for both Eudora and Ken, was her visit to Santa Barbara for its now annual writers conference and for a week in the company of Ken Millar, his wife, and his closest friends there. It was the first time Ken and Eudora had seen one another since Eudora Welty Day in 1973—and the first time Eudora had met Ken's wife. Margaret Millar felt that having Eudora in Santa Barbara was a "special privilege" and urged her to return. Ken did the same. The occasion enhanced the closeness he and Eudora had established in their letters and provided opportunities for the extended private conversations they had missed when Ken came to Jackson.*

Kenneth Millar to Eudora Welty, January 12, 1975

Dear Eudora:

I'm getting into that point in my book where it's starting to get seriously interesting (to me)—I'm so glad you approve of my title, you being the only one I've trusted with it, and I'm depending on it to prop the book up—but must come up for air and a chance to tell you how greatly I enjoyed your account of Elizabeth Bowen's last book. There is nothing better in life than to see a good writer take up and handle carefully the work of another good writer. Yes, there are two better things in life. One is to be the one writer who is spoken of—and I have been that, thanks to you—and the other is to be the writer speaking. Anyway, I love these simple but infinitely complex expressions of love and courtesy. You continue to give so much. You gave the same measure of tenderness and justice to the ladies in the bird pageant which of course I remember from your book of photographs but am so glad to have the words now, rescued from that ancient *New Republic* (which I started reading a year or two later, I think, and still subscribe to.)[1]

I was reminded of you in another context, when the Carol Burnett Show did a parody the other week on that television series, The Waltons. At the end of the scene, all the Waltons got into bed together, innocently enough, and their parents said goodnight to them: — "Goodnight, John Girl," "Goodnight, Eudora Boy." I hope you don't mind that your name was taken in vain. Speaking of television series, I believe I've already told you that "Archer" is going to replace "Ironsides" on January 30, and I hope it turns out better than the Peter Graves version of *Underground Man*. I'm going down to Beverly Hills for a news conference next Saturday. But my heart will remain behind in Santa Barbara, with the books. Writing books on whatever level is a lucky way to make a living, isn't it?

Do you like Doris Lessing? For years I tended to slight her but as I read further into her it seems to me that her vision enlarges, and into what seemed a single theme she introduces a strange and wonderful variety of life, and what seemed coarse at first ends by seeming humane to me. Perhaps I'm learning something as I grow older. (Reading *Golden Notebook*, belatedly, and some of the stories.)

Certainly Jimmie is. He's knocking himself out, qualifying for merit badges in the Boy Scouts and taking a strong bite on life. I never saw a more willing boy. Skateboarding around the pool tonight.

Glad you liked the hummers. Like other people who give a great deal, you're so appreciative of very small things. I finally got my copies of the anthology, too late to send you one. It's going well, by the way, and should sell out the first printing (10,000) in another month or two. Thank you again for your encouragement and help.

Love, Ken

Eudora Welty to Kenneth Millar, January 25, 1975

Dear Ken

Wasn't it lovely, to get to talk on the phone? It was such a happy surprise when you called, and thank you for giving me the message from Mr. Conrad—Thank you indeed for setting this in motion in the first place, and I hope I can do what they ask well enough so you won't be sorry. Now I'll wait patiently for Mr. C. to send me along the address, but it's something that gives me pleasure even in January looking forward to Santa Barbara.[2]

It gives me pleasure to think your book's going well, too—Many wishes—For its sake, anyway. How fortunate you didn't have to interrupt it to go to Beverly Hills—and maybe for Archer's sake too. We'll never know now, I guess, but what happened to *The Underground Man* was pretty forbidding if that was any sign—He belongs on the page and in words that are all yours, and I for one feel better about him just where he is right this minute, in your "Portrait"—

Speaking of film, here is a piece out of a stranger's letter sent to me by a friend in Texas about "Chinatown" (which I haven't seen— have you?)[3] Others may have said the same thing, of course. I didn't see the Carol Burnett parody, either, hadn't heard about that—sounds amusing, and it would have made all the Eudoras laugh—there ain't many of us.

It made me feel reassured to have you say my review of Elizabeth Bowen's last book seemed to speak my feelings. You weren't reading it exactly as I wrote it, for they cut and took out quotes and transposed it somewhat, so I couldn't know what effect was left. This was my fault, for I overshot my space, but I cared a good deal about the piece—it was personal with me, of course—~~I guess only the writer of the piece would've noticed what they'd~~ (Sentence didn't make any sense!) It did me good to have you say you found it an "expression of love and courtesy"—nothing could have comforted me more, in the circumstances—

I must try Doris Lessing again—Like you, I decided earlier in that she was clumsy & coarse, but unlike you I hadn't given her a second chance—I'll look into the *Notebook*—

I thought of you when I was doing another review, *The Cockatoos* by Patrick White, because didn't you at one time say you thought of using one of his stories in your anthology? *He's* a strange one and a powerful one, isn't he? I'll see if I can find a copy of my review, or better, a copy of *The Cockatoos*, if you'd like to see it. I am not quite certain I know the handle to pick those stories up by—But they are potent and heavy & throbbing stuff, like hunks of fallen meteors or something cast upon us from another orbit.[4]

I thank you for your thought of sending me your anthology, all the same, and it was your editor, after all, who did send it—Heavens, I must thank him directly—And I got some from the Book-of-the-Month Club too, for presents—I've just finished reading dear Agatha's again—The book introduced me to James M. Cain, whom I'd never read—"The Baby in the Ice Box" was great fun, so I read *The Postman Always Rings Twice* and *Double Indemnity*—both of which I thoroughly enjoyed. I can remember, in the 30's I guess, my mother, a great mystery reader, saying "That old James M. Cain! I wouldn't give you 2¢ for all he's written!" (Well, you know the times—she was reading S. S. Van Dine and Mary Roberts Rinehart along then) and strangely enough I didn't take her up on it & try for myself. Till now.

Now Ken, you won't be going east in February, will you? I've got to go to a Council on Arts meeting in Washington Feb. 6-10, and just might on the off-chance go to NY, and if you're going to be there I'd want to know it. But I don't look forward at the moment to ice & snow. The camellias & narcissus & quince are blooming here—The birds are singing—It must be balmier still where you are—

Love & luck,
Eudora

Kenneth Millar to Eudora Welty, January 28, 1975

Dear Eudora:

That was a most interesting and multifaceted and delightful letter that you sent in answer to my phone call, and I got the impression that you are happy about coming to Santa Barbara, as happy as we are, almost, that you are coming. I enclose an ad from last weekend's *L.A. Times*, which lists *last* year's professional participants, many of whom will be turning up again. Everyone seems to enjoy it. I believe you will too, or I wouldn't have suggested you come. You can do with the students pretty much as you choose—perhaps an informal talk (or formal if you like) followed by questions from the audience, which is what I did last year. And of course there are chances to talk to people at meals and in one-to-one encounters. Whenever you want to get away from the Miramar Hotel where the Conference will be held, you can retreat to my cabaña at the Coral Casino which is not far away, and enjoy a perfect solitude watching the sea. It will be such a pleasure for M and me to have you here for a while. (Guess who was at the Coral Casino yesterday! Ingrid Bergman, escorted by Baron Rothschild. I missed her.) The dates, as the ad says, are June 13-20.

Thank you for the clipping-from-a-letter re *Chinatown*, which I have seen (twice) and enjoyed but am not sure you would. The very beginning and the very ending are crude, and there is some crudity throughout. But the movie really moves and has a sense of life. I do think the writer (Robert Towne) got some help out of my books. *The Drowning Pool*, by the way, is now in the can but while it has its merits, to judge from the script, it's far from being a *Chinatown*.[5] These script-writers are so concerned to shock and titillate that they lose their seriousness, without which powerful drama is impossible. What makes *Chinatown* valid is its historical basis in L.A.'s great water war, which still continues.

Yes, I'm just as glad I missed the press conference in Beverly Hills the other week. Brian Keith has since recovered from pneumonia and announces that if the Archer show is a success he's going to move it next season to Hawaii, where he lives. Fortunately I learned some time ago never to take television, or *anything* in the movie industry, seriously. I lie in ambush behind a screen of books, and occasionally throw a rock.

I am touched by your loyalty to the anthology and feel that it has served its purpose by introducing you to James M. Cain. He's still writing, in his late seventies, and will have a new book out this year, with Knopf. At his peak he maintained the fastest narrative pace I've ever seen in the *genre*. The ones you've read are his best.

This letter is mostly chatter—backchatter to your letter. I must get in the fact, though, that my new pup Skye is the nicest dog I ever had, and possibly the smartest. He's going on 8 months, black and red, 85 lbs.! Cold here—32° last night—but it will be warm in June. Happy days! Love, Ken

P.S.—Doris Lessing always disappoints me in the end, but *The Golden Notebook* has great things in it. She just doesn't know where to quit or leave out.

K.

Eudora Welty to Kenneth Millar, February 19, 1975

Dear Ken,

Thank you for your letter, which rode with me in the plane to Washington and back because I thought I could answer it there—(I like to take letters, and a book or two I'm already reading with me on a trip for continuity's sake or something, do you?) But they (a Council on the Arts meeting) didn't leave us time to ourselves. It was good to have your added words on the Conference—I do think it sounds enjoyable because of the people there—and for me because of where it is, and the prospects of seeing you again and getting to meet Margaret. It is so very thoughtful of you to say I might retreat to your cabaña at the Coral Casino when I want to get away from the crowd and just look at the sea—thank you for the kindness of that thought. It gives me a feeling of security.

Your book goes well, I hope. And everything else too. It must be a bit hard on you to have to follow the TV "Archer"—even if it were the best thing in the TV world, it wouldn't be the real thing for you. I must say it isn't right to me as a reader either. This "Archer" doesn't use the mind, and he doesn't use much of anything else either—he's not in the least bit active. He's lazy! The whole tension of one of your stories is a result of the concentration of Archer, which never drops or loses its force or direction, and he's its sole agent—don't those writers and so on know that? Oh well, you don't need me to add my complaints. I hope it's not too painful and distracting for you but it must seem so foreign to your books that it doesn't connect very much at all—maybe in the light of the series so far it would be just as well if Brian Keith *did* move *his* "Archer" to Hawaii. (You could run an ad in the personal column that you are not responsible for the claimant in Honolulu.) I've seen them all and since they're all different, I try to keep hoping they may hit the right note somehow. I did think they got Archer's car right—Did they?

It's been so mild here, everything's leaping into bloom ahead of itself—even the oak tree is budding today—I can see a little kinglet finding this out now. It was cold in Washington, down in the 'teens. The best part of the trip was getting to go after hours to the National Gallery and have the great Chinese Exhibition all to ourselves. In the calm and peace of those halls when the chime of the nine temple bells were struck, the sounds might have been coming to you all the way from the fifth century BC. The famous star-part of the exhibition is the Flying Horse, whose touchdown from the air is only by one hoof, and that rests on the back of a swallow—Marvelous indeed but hardly anything there is not marvelous. Nothing they used, not any pot or cooking pan, or lamp, or anything in all those centuries, was not beautiful. I liked the little domestic things—two bronze leopards inlaid with gold—both would have fitted into the palm of the hand—curled up with the most catlike spines, and jeweled eyes in their masks—these were made as weights to hold down the silk sleeves.

I was interested in what you said about Chinatown (in the non sequitur sense!) and should like to see it—especially in connection with your own treatment of the scene. It's what "Archer" *ought* to do, had the chance to do, & owes it to you to do. What's on next for me is Murder on the Orient Express, which has just arrived in Jackson. What did you think of that?[6]

Did you get sent the galleys of Reynolds' novel [*The Surface of Earth*]? I expect Reynolds wanted you to have them early, though I know you are busy and they are hundreds of pages long—I just got them and haven't begun, just felt the weight—and am longing to begin.

With the spring I hope to do some work too—I feel there's so much I would like to write *simultaneously*—there must be a word for that trouble, or joy—But I had better just get to it, a little at a time—

Love,
Eudora

Eudora Welty to Kenneth Millar, Sunday [February 23, 1975]

Dear Ken,

Before it gets away from me—I had a dream last night that you were in, although I didn't get to see you. The one I saw was Ring Lardner!—whom I never saw in the flesh—and the scene was Venice—I think it was Venice, Cal. (though it could have been Venice, Italy, only Venice I know)—strings of lights along the water's edge, seen from the door. There beside me I recognized Ring Lardner. In the dream he looked something like [Canadian actor] Ned Sparks, remember him? He quoted Flannery O'Connor to the shoe clerk—commendingly—Then he told the shoe clerk he was in the city to meet you and was on his way to keep the appointment very shortly. End of scene—Isn't that a good dream? I knew all through it you were moving around out there somewhere out of sight—what a piece of luck, I thought, to overhear what Ring Lardner said (again commendingly) to the shoe clerk. I woke up thinking I had something to tell you—Well, who knows, it might be a good sign—of something!

Love,
Eudora

Kenneth Millar to Eudora Welty, March 5, 1975

Dear Eudora:

I don't know what your dream means, either, but it was a lovely dream and it makes me happy. What more could a storyteller ask than to be associated with Ring Lardner, in your mind! Perhaps the dream had its source in our circuitous walk back to the Algonquin after Alfred's party, when we talked about London and I quoted among other things:

Night and day under the bark of me

There's an oh such a horde of microbes making a park of me[7]

which I think is one of the best couplets in the language, the American language, that is. And Venice is on the sea, like Santa Barbara, though a different sea. (It's a less beautiful city than Venice, which I haven't seen, I suppose, but it has its own persistent excellence, continually being enhanced, as Venice was, by the people who come here and create its beauty with their intelligent eyes and minds—a place takes so much of its beauty and value from the people who have been there—which is why I'm so glad you're coming.) I forget whether you saw the television version of *Underground Man*, alas, but if you did you may remember that Archer lived in Venice, California. Now again, I'm glad to report, he doesn't live in any part of television, the ill-fated series having been canceled but not before poor Brian Keith had facial surgery to beautify him for the role. No wonder he looked rather pained and distraught. I probably did, too, as I watched those pitiful episodes of Archer's brief career on the air-waves.

Meanwhile the book is growing, approaching two hundred pages; it feels as if I'm coming to the end of something; I hope and trust it will mark the beginning of something else. This week we had a mini-beginning, when I found an abandoned puppy on the beach and brought her home—a sweet lively little silky terrier-type dog weighing about fifteen pounds who takes on my ponderous German shepherds in bloodless combat and in effect drives them into the sea. It's pleasant to see two hundred-pound dogs (Skye is nearly that now) avoiding any violence or harm to such a midget. She's a female, which helps. It was time Margaret had someone to gang up with.

Speaking of women reminds me of the novel I've just finished reading which, in spite of some of the language which you might find offensive, I really do recommend as an illumination of the present lives of intellectual young women: Gail Godwin's *The Odd Woman*. It's quite devoid of the heavy monocularity which you object to in Doris Lessing and is what I consider one of the best novels I've read in recent years. I hope you can read it because I'm eager for your opinion.

All well here in spite of days of rain, welcome after a rather dry wet season.

Love, Ken

P.S.—I neglected to answer some questions:

No, I didn't much like *Orient Express*—I thought it dragged—but Albert Finney was remarkably forceful and spry.

I haven't heard from Reynolds, but am most happy for him.

I liked Archer's car better than Archer.

And that Chinese Exhibition sounds magnificent. I'd like to get to Washington—have never been. K.

Eudora Welty to Kenneth Millar, March 9, 1975

Dear Ken,

You've most likely seen this letter to the Times already, but I thought it was worth sending to you anyway. All goes well with you, I hope, and with the new book.

Did you happen to be looking at the national news the other evening when they (NBC) showed the unprecedented visit of Ross's Gull to the U.S.A.? (Didn't they say it was from Siberia?) A group of bird watchers on the New England coast was waiting for it to put in an appearance, and it did. The camera caught it too—a little gull, walking about unconcerned with the locals (gulls!), who were big & heavy by comparison. Of course if Ross's Gull was coming to our shores, he was on the wrong side of the country to see (and be seen by) Ross—But I hope you were at your TV—

It seems I'm about to have something dramatized too—my short novel called "The Robber Bridegroom"—did I send it to you once, a sort of fantasy? It's going to be a musical put on by John Houseman & his City Center Acting Company—a touring company—opening in July in Saratoga.[8] I don't exactly know what to expect—but I highly regard Houseman & feel lucky it fell into his hands. Maybe, unlike Ross's Gull, it will be seen in Santa Barbara before it's over. You could observe it in flight.

Reynolds is coming here next weekend on Arts Council business— we will be thinking & talking of you—

Love,
Eudora

Kenneth Millar to Eudora Welty, March 12, 1975

Dear Eudora:

That's thrilling news about *The Robber Bridegroom*, Houseman being one of our very best directors. I *hope* it comes to Santa Barbara, but doubt that it will. We lack a theatre of adequate size, though once long ago I saw *The Glass Menagerie* there. By the way, I read *The Robber Bridegroom* when it first came out, with great delight.

Didn't see the Ross's Gull on TV—Margaret did—but I saw a picture of it. Today's excitement here was an escaped *lapis lazuli* finch. Can that be right? It's the way I *heard* it, anyway.

Thank you for the NYTBR clipping—I get mentioned in some surprising contexts. The new book is coming along, about 2/3 through the first draft. It's less of a generational chronicle than usual. I don't know exactly what it is but await the outcome calmly.

The Canadian producer of the movie being made in Canada from *The Three Roads* phoned from Toronto today to report progress and ask me to read the now finished script. The director is Peter Glenville (sp?) who did Becket, and it will be shot in Quebec in the summer with a French star as the female lead—one of Canada's first big international pictures, he says. (Bret becomes a journalist, Paula an architect) Because of the Canadian aspect and because the book was written, really, out of my Canadian background, I'm rather excited about the prospect, the first time I've really felt thus about a movie.

My love to you, and to Reynolds, too. I'm eager to see his book published.

Ever, Ken

Eudora Welty to Kenneth Millar, Monday [April 14, 1975]

Dear Ken,

—A *lapis lazuli* finch? It sounds like a bird that flew in out of Yeats, or fairyland. I wonder if they caught it? Should we wish they did or hope they didn't? Maybe it got away to that lovely island out in the Channel.

That's wonderful news that *The Three Roads* is to be a film and in such good hands, —Peter Glenville, and with the plan to give it such evident serious attention. I'm delighted for you, and can imagine the fresh and stimulating impact it could very likely make on you when you see what comes of transposing the story from California to Quebec—all kinds of forces joining. I hope the script is heartening to read. And that you'll be happy with what they do. I read *The Three Roads* again when I got your letter, and of course the novel is as far as I can imagine—Canada being a place I don't know, just to start with. Good luck with these people. They do sound like a promising and exciting group to trust your story to. I must say after all that messing around the *Underground Man* and *Archer* productions did with your work, you deserve double all the good things they can bring about with this new film.

And meanwhile, I hope the new book is being brought to a fine flourishing close.

It's been a while since I wrote, I know, because I'm just now coming up for air after a three-week film project here with three Californians—all from around San Francisco, Richard Moore, Philip Greene, and helpers doing a PBS thing on my work. It was really a pleasure working with them, even though it was night and day without a stop, because they're so interesting and expert, and showing them around and responding to their questions etc. gave me all sorts of new things to learn and see—I don't know what the end product will be like—all this work will have to be edited to something half an hour long—we shall see.[9]

It won't be long before I'll be coming out to Santa Barbara, which I look forward to so much. I have to be gone some in May, but if Mr. Conrad gets worried at not finding me home or something, tell him I am not forgetting. One trip is to Seattle, May 1—so I'll be on your side of the country but I guess not close enough to wave my handkerchief—a Council on Arts meeting—

By the way, Mr. Houseman sent an itinerary of the City Center Acting Company's current tour and it will play Santa Barbara, at the University of Cal., April 22-24—next week!—doing one of their shows, Marlowe or Shakespeare or Chekhov or Becket or Saroyan or Goldsmith. I want to talk to you about Reynolds's book—but just send this line now, hoping all's fine with you and Margaret and all, and how is the little new dog and the great big ones that are playing with her so gently?

Love,
Eudora

Eudora Welty, aboard an airplane, to Kenneth Millar, May 5, 1975. Mailed from Jackson and written on Washington Plaza Hotel stationery, which sports an image of the Seattle hotel's circular tower. Beside the image, Eudora has written "(Some day they may have to change its name to the Washington Pisa.)"

Dear Ken,

This is on board a Northwest Airlines 747 to Chicago, where I change for the flight home. I've been up the curve of the coast from you since Thursday, on an Arts Council meeting. John Leonard was on hand part of the time, & when we spoke of you, he said he'd seen you not long ago in N.Y. on your way to Canada. Perhaps you went up to see about your film? I hope your news about that—and about everything else too—is good. Can you attend to your novel?

I know the Cascades are under me—and I saw them in splendor, coming out—but this morning there's just one limitless ocean of white cloud below, and just one bossy & white-whiskered seal head poking out of it—Mount Ranier. I can see why it was you brought an alarm clock to Jackson—I'm only two hours out of my home-time, the other way, and I faithfully wake up at quarter to five in the morning and feel that it's three oclock the next morning when I'm getting to bed. I needed an un-alarm clock. I love the world on this side of the Great Divide, and am glad I've been here before on the surface of it—years ago by train—From my hotel room I could see Puget Sound and the western & southern quarters of the city & the ring of the mountains. I wanted to take the boats! Though we had to sit in meetings & so on, & be inside from 8:45 AM till sometimes late at night, there was early in the morning & sometimes late in the afternoon to see all this, in the long slow changes of the light. Here it was very northern in feel. I look forward so much to seeing and being in your country, your South.

Mr. Conrad sent me a tentative schedule where I see I'm on the first evening and you're on the last, and I hope it will be OK if I stay for this *finale*, which will be one of the things I'd come for. Later news for the Conference will probably follow. In between now & then I am supposed to bat around the country like a loose balloon—it has a vulgar sound to say it, but I'm to be given 3 honorary degrees in 3 days—Really I am proud & excited to be given them, and in confidence the 3rd one is from Yale. Also, I am going to be in the Algonquin Hotel May 20-27 or 28—not to run the risk there of ever missing you again. Then home until time for Santa Barbara.

All this is just about me, and I hope for news of you. And the word that it is properly good and is making you happy. Though extra busy I expect. Still clouds below. I'll mail this as I explore my way through O'Hare. (A mailbox is something they have on the ground—isn't it? Like North Dakota.)

With love,
Eudora

Writing, the thing Ken most liked to do, had become much harder. Coming up with the introduction for that suspense anthology had taken him six weeks. When he'd begun just making notes for this new novel, his blood pressure had soared. Once into the manuscript, he'd had a lot more difficulty than usual pulling its elements together. Still, the pages and chapters accumulated, though he sometimes drank a modest amount of alcohol to stimulate their flow.

But he indulged more in distractions that took him away from work. He and Margaret went to Toronto in April, for the purpose of Ken publicizing the film to be made there of his 1948 novel The Three Roads. *After visiting relatives in Ontario, Ken went on to New York for a few days, while Margaret (no fan of Manhattan) returned to Santa Barbara.*

Kenneth Millar to Eudora Welty, May 7, 1975

Dear Eudora:

Having spent the second half of April in the east—I think my longest sojourn away from home since I left Ann Arbor for the last time in the summer of 1951—and the last week in getting back into my book, I'm slow in answering your letter of mid-April. In accordance with your cheerful wishes, the Toronto people did turn out to be extremely pleasant and also well-endowed with intelligence—the young writer who did the script is particularly talented, I think—Tom Hedley—and Margaret and I had a fine time and stirred up some publicity, too. An example of the hospitality we were offered: the producer Jerry Simon insisted on lending us his own car for the drive to Kitchener to see Margaret's father—a visit that turned out most happily, by the way. As for the film, one never knows until it's made, but I particularly like the completing of that circle in Toronto where I did my first published writing, for Toronto *Saturday Night*, and where M. studied the classics at the University of T. She prowled the campus for four days and went home on the fifth. I went back to New York where I had the extreme pleasure of presenting an MWA Grand Master's award to Eric Ambler, who is thin and grey and witty and arthritic and delightful.[10] The previous week, by a lucky chance, I was present at Alfred's ante-penultimate farewell to publishing.—We're looking forward keenly to seeing you here next month. Remember to tell me what plane.

Love, Ken

P.S.—The new pup, Misty (short for Mistinguette) is now the mistress of the household.

K.

Kenneth Millar to Eudora Welty, May 17, 1975

Dear Eudora:

Your letter written enroute from Seattle and the Washington Plaza (which I have seen but never dared to enter) was one of the most delightful I've ever received, even from you. This won't be a proper reply, partly because most of my writing energies these days are going into an effort to get a draft of my book finished before June 13. I think I can see the end of it now, but I can also see that I'm in for some rewriting; the sin of complexity is growing on me.

Not only I am delighted at the imminence of your visit here. Your name and the memory of your work arouses the warmest responses in people—this will be hardly news to you by now. I'm so glad you are thinking of being able to stay a week. What comes at the end of the week (moi) will hardly justify it, but I trust the week itself will, among friends both old and new, here at the start of the fresh summer season. It will be such a pleasure to show you Santa Barbara.

The Conference this year, its third, promises to be such a success as it has never been before. In fact the limit (100 students, I think) has long since been reached. Of course people are invited to come out from town for individual lectures, or talks, or whatever. I make a practice of giving a short prepared talk and then answering questions, which I enjoy. But everybody has his own approach. I've been asked to introduce you. I'll probably say: I love Eudora Welty in spite of the vulgarity of receiving three honorary degrees in three days: on the fourth day she rested. Did you, by the way, see the mention of you as a photographer in a recent *New Yorker* review of Wright Morris' "About Fiction," by John Updike.[11] It sent me back to your photographs, and I never saw such a steady moral eye. (*See enclosure*).

Alas, I had my days at the Algonquin in late April, the occasion being Mystery Writers of America's annual gathering. (I had the pleasure of handing a Grand Master award to Eric Ambler, who is modest and witty and urbane and very nice.) But Santa Barbara, I hope you'll agree, is better.

Love,

Ken

Eudora Welty to Kenneth Millar, [May 17, 1975]. Written on a newspaper clipping showing a picture of Canada geese "silhouetted against a full moon as the birds wing northward over Baraboo, Wis." Mailed in a letterhead envelope of the Monteleone Hotel, New Orleans.

Dear Ken, did your paper carry this marvelous sight of your Canadian geese?

Love,
Eudora

Eudora Welty to Kenneth Millar, [June 2, 1975]

Dear Ken,

I was happy to find your letter when I reached home—and it was more than kind of you to write it when you were right at that point with your novel. Luck and love to it, all smooth days and no interruptions—I hope it goes where it's safely headed just like a bird.

This isn't to interrupt either, but only a line to say how glad I am to be coming so soon. Mr. Conrad sent me the ticket itself, which is very generous of them—it says I'm to arrive on Friday the 13 at 4:35 PM on United 864. Of course it would be lovely to see you there but not unless you get your novel to where you planned, this is understood. I'll see you soon, at any rate. It's so strengthening to know you are going to introduce me—thank you for that one more act of kindness. I'm so delighted at the prospect of all I'll see and hear and take in about Santa Barbara—nothing like it has ever come my way, as you know.

Thank you for the copy of John Updike's review, which I had not seen—I'll read it tonight but I wanted to send a line on to you now. My best to "Portrait"—and to all going well.

With love,
Eudora

Eudora arrived for the Santa Barbara Writers Conference on June 13. Ross Macdonald and Eudora Welty were conference headliners and introduced each other to the participants. In the course of her comments, Eudora described Ross Macdonald as "a supremely moral writer" who "cares about the welfare of each human soul in his novels." Ken delivered the following introduction of Eudora:

I have never been given a more pleasant task than that of introducing Miss Eudora Welty to a Santa Barbara audience. She is a woman who illuminates her surroundings, and she does so in a quiet way, without fireworks. Her being is as quiet and shy as the moon. Only afterwards do you realize that the light has changed.

For Miss Welty is one of the most completely articulate women who has ever practiced the art of letters in the United States. Her range of expression is remarkable, unique, extending from broad humor through tragic emotion. The underpinning and undersong of all her imaginative work seems to me to be her respect for, her fealty towards, our common humanity. She is one of those aristocrats of the arts who has never turned her back on common men and women. There is a profound equalitarian and religious quality which informs all her work and sets it apart. Miss Welty celebrates human life in all its conditions.

This was evident in her earliest stories of Southern life which she began to publish in the thirties. I believe she was the first Southern writer, perhaps the first white American writer, who was able to give her unreserved imaginative love and care to blacks. The incorruptibility of her eye and thought is evident in her photographs of poor Mississippi people—photographs which have recently been compared with those of Walker Evans in *Let Us Now Praise Famous Men*. Miss Welty took those photographs with a plain box camera and no other paraphernalia whatever—just the light of day and the light of her mind.

There is no need to dwell on the long list of her accomplishments, the long list of Universities including Cambridge U. where she has taught, and the long list of public honors she has won. Miss Welty is modest to a fault. She did admit to me that on three successive days this spring she was given honorary degrees at three universities, but she would have considered it vulgar to name those universities. Still she cannot conceal the fact that her most recent and most brilliant novel, *The Optimist's Daughter*, won the Pulitzer Prize, and incidentally conferred new prestige on that award. She is an active member of the National Institute of Arts and Letters, and was given its Gold Medal in 1972.

The important thing is not the honors, but the work. Her stories are among the best and saddest and funniest and [most] humane in the whole range of American literature. They will never go away. She is a first-rate playwright and novelist.[12] Her body of criticism is brilliant and still growing, in size and depth, recent additions to it being her essays on Willa Cather and Elizabeth Bowen in *NYTBR*.

I don't want to burden Miss Welty with the appellation of our best living writer. But I do suspect that, line by line, word by word, that may be what she is. She has taken possession of the language as if it were her own invention, and given it back to us refreshed, clean, brand new, with a kind of half-heard musical accompaniment, and joyous laughter in the wings.

Miss Welty stands unassumingly at the peak of one of the great careers in American letters. It seems to me a kind of miracle that she should have come from Jackson, Mississippi, to converse with us. I can think of only two comparably miraculous visitations on this Miramar shore. One was Scott Fitzgerald. The other was Ty Cobb.[13]

After this introduction, Eudora delivered remarks drawn from her essay "Words into Fiction" and answered questions from the audience.[14]

Eudora Welty to Kenneth Millar, June 22, 1975

Dear Ken,

I got home last night, about 9:30 our time, but I go on thinking of Santa Barbara—and of being there. I treasure my visit and what it meant to me to see you again, & meet Margaret, and your dear grandson, & his father,—and Margaret's sister, and the close friends about whom you had spoken in your letters—and to be in your house & with your dogs, & see the garden, and your view the circle round—The rides and the walks you took me on were beautiful and I was seeing the sea and the mountains as you showed them to me not as a sightseer but as a friend who had learned & was learning more each day of what they had meant to you—I felt so happy being shown what was important to you and your life—It was not just the compliment to me, though it was a great one, but it made me feel how well you knew me and my wishes, and I was glad of that. It was the truest welcome I can think of.

And when I was close enough to it I could see too a little of what you and Margaret are doing for Santa Barbara, working to keep alive what is so beautiful and valuable and humane there—What you mean to *it*.

When I think of the pleasures, the cabaña & the Coral Casino, the Botanical Gardens, the Museum of Natural History, the mountain roads and the waterfront, the gliding kite-man & the seismograph, the Courthouse and its goings-on & its rooftop—the books for every night, the trees over the road to the beach, the other houses (I do have a sea shell picked up on your beach)—How can I say just one thank you. And I'm glad I came home with your introduction of me to the Conference— So much joy & pride I have in it. I wish I also had a copy of what you said on Thursday night—But one day I can see & read it in print, I feel sure—It was very fine to hear it, & your answers.

And oh yes, the Conference itself, to which I owe my chance to get there—I thank you for that too. You couldn't have made it happen in a pleasanter, more agreeable way, to enable a friend to get from Jackson to Santa Barbara. And, as I think you did too, I enjoyed the young people & the good discussions—

The first thing I should have thanked you for, I guess, *was* the first thing—meeting me! And late as I was, but I was happier than I was late. And I should say last too I was grateful for being seen off, and I was—only sad to go. I hope we all see each other again not too far away from now.

The Sausalito part of the return trip did not impinge on the entity of my memory of Santa Barbara at all. It was all the daylight time inside a closed projection room. Interesting to see how the men worked, and the only finished job—that on Janet Flanner—was splendid, very sensitive, it caught an essence, I felt. What a strong minded soul came across! There's been no editing done on mine, it was just sequences of landscape & other sequences of readings, etc. At night, a party at Muir Beach—It looked wonderful, sea & the Midsummer Night's Eve full moon, but cold—& we had the picnic inside—They're fine people, both, though, & their wives nice—one is Italian.[15]

I'm sending you my copy of *Uncle Silas* (you keep it) because Elizabeth Bowen's introduction is in it, which I'd like you to see. She, too, would have liked you to—she always had a strong admiration for you—we used to exchange your books, so a number of them ended up in Ireland—(You wouldn't mind!)

It made me very glad that you showed me the family pictures—those other faces I would have particularly wanted to see. And yours & Margaret's in earlier times. In return for this, & the snapshot of you, here's a few from here—The Welty grandfather is the "Pennsylvania Dutch" (more accurately German-Swiss in Grandpa's case, & Amish ancestry) element we have in common, along with some other ones.

Thank you again for so much, and when you do finish that waiting last chapter, and have time again, please write & let me know if all kept fine and went well and nothing suffered harm for your being away from it and thinking of a hundred kind & good things to do while I was nearby.

Love,
Eudora

Both Margaret and Ken were as grateful as Eudora for the time she had spent in Santa Barbara, and both wrote to say so, Margaret first, telling Eudora: "Your visit had a peculiar effect on me. I want to start writing again after a long layoff in which I told everyone I'd retired.[. . .] Thanks. Really thanks."[16] Ken's thanks soon followed.

Kenneth Millar to Eudora Welty, July 8, 1975

Dear Eudora:

I have been putting off answering your letter until I had the time to do it justice but, that day never having come, I'll write as I can. I greatly value your expression of feeling for Santa Barbara and the people you met here. You must know how thoroughly it was reciprocated. It was a great week in the life of this community—you must know I mean this literally, for the cultural life of a community is made up of such weeks scattered over the years—and it will never be forgotten. The community aside, for the personal is even more important and more central, I dwell with continued pleasure and the hope of its renewal on the times we spent together and the places we went. You're such a keen observer and enjoyer that you enhance a place by looking at it, and you strike notes that do not cease to vibrate.

I was right about needing more time for my book. I'm letting it go on a bit and unless I cut it drastically on rewriting, it will probably be my longest book, and a little different from the others. I seem to be yielding finally to change, and I suppose it's best to do it voluntarily. It looks as if the first draft will run well over 320 pages.

My friend Ralph Sipper the rare book dealer liked Reynolds's book so well that he phoned from San Francisco to tell me about it. Though I've only read a part of it, I think the book will find its readers now and in the future.

Santa Barbara is hot and blue-skied and blue-sead and will never be quite the same again. I hope you won't be, either.

Love, Ken

P.S.—Thank you for that rich trove of pictures. Surely you want them back?

P.P.S.—I've been playing my Smithsonian Jazz album in remembrance of you.

K.

In April, when Eudora had read the proof of Reynolds Price's The Surface of Earth, *her assessment of it had been less generous than Ralph Sipper's, but she had praised the novel's craftsmanship. Then in June she was shocked and angered when Richard Gilman in the* New York Times Book Review *ridiculed Reynolds's book not for the quality of its writing but because of its genre. The "family saga," Gilman proclaimed, was "a great lumbering archaic beast," no longer viable as an art form. Eudora wrote to the* New York Times Book Review, *decrying this restrictive decree defining what a writer might attempt, a decree very much akin to the one that had two years earlier been applied to Ken's novel* Sleeping Beauty. *On July 20, Eudora's response to Gilman appeared in the* Book Review.

Kenneth Millar to Eudora Welty, July, 1975

Dear Eudora:

We have been slow in thanking you for the beautiful cookpot you sent us. M. has been starting a book—inspired by the Writers' Conference and you (*she*, not the book, inspired by the conference and you)—and I have been finishing one. Today I wrote the 327th and last page of a first draft of what appears to be my longest book. Have already started rewriting, which it needs.

I still haven't had a chance to read Reynolds' book, except for the part that appeared in *Esquire*, but I do agree with your criticism of the NYTBR review—as if a writer had to obey the "rules" of his decade. Usually the writers who don't, stand up best in the long run. Speaking of *Esquire*, I am told that John Leonard has in the current issue a light piece which refers among others to you and me.[17] I'm complimented by the juxtaposition, and hope you don't mind.

I wonder if you realize what an impact you made on Santa Barbara and our conference, which will have been permanently elevated and inspired, I believe; and what an efflorescence of good will you planted behind you. Please give me a hint as to whether and when we might get you back again between these mountains and this sea.

Love, Ken

All well here. How are you, dear Eudora?

K.

Eudora Welty to Kenneth Millar, July 23, 1975

Dear Ken,

Thank you for your letter and you don't know how many times I've gone back in my mind to when I was there and wished that we could talk again and take one more ride.

I'm glad to know the news about your book, and I hope you will go happily fully as far as it leads you. I trust it! And you, as ever, in whatever you choose to do. All the best of luck all the way.

I've gone back to your letter, along with my memories of the time in Santa Barbara as a kind of refuge—A terrible thing happened in Jackson—Frank Hains, a good friend of mine was found brutally murdered in his home, a week ago Sunday. I haven't been able to write because of the grief and horror I have been feeling for him—I think the chances are good that you will remember him. He was the arts editor of our newspaper and a strong moving force in the arts in our state—Talented in so many ways. He was my neighbor (4 blocks away) and we had been friends for over 20 years. He's the man who wrote & directed the dramatic version of "The Ponder Heart" which you saw here, down at our little New Stage—

In a day or so I might send you some of the things that have been in his paper, because I think you might—that you would—care about what happened. The people concerned are really the whole bunch that you met here—It was more than ourselves that felt it, too—For instance, yesterday morning Geraldine Fitzgerald, who'd worked with New Stage in 2 productions and knew Frank in the course of it all, phoned me (she'd seen a note about it in the NYT) from the Eugene O'Neill Center in Connecticut, where she is appearing, to find out more and talk about it—He was just 49—

I've been trying to meet a deadline on a rather foolish article I'd rather foolishly promised—But I stopped it to write this note to you—I didn't mean, when I said at the beginning I wished we could have one more ride, to be ungrateful—The way it was, it was perfect. I love being able now to imagine it, blue-skied and blue-seaed. Love,

Eudora

P.S. I was so glad to get the letter from Margaret and will write her—The good clippings too—And I look forward to the Biltmore photograph.

PPS I wanted you to have the little snapshots if you would like them.

Kenneth Millar to Eudora Welty, July 28, 1975

Dear Eudora:

I am profoundly sorry to hear of Frank Hains' death not only for the loss to you, and the dreadful shock it must have been and still be, but the loss to the whole state of such a civilized and creative spirit. There is really nothing to be said in the face of such a disaster except to wish you well in the bearing of it, and in turning your mind to all those positive and creative currents in your life, which leave you not quite defenseless even against such things.

It's good that your mind should be turning to Santa Barbara again. Though we have our share of disaster we have a full share, too, of good people and good luck. The good people keep asking about you: the Freemans send their love, and just this weekend I ran into the Conrads at the club. They are already thinking about next year's Conference and excited by the hope that you may come again. We all are, I particularly—there is a great deal more to be seen and said; and other things to be said and seen *again* here.

Margaret sends her love with mine, and thank you for the pretty gift of the pot. It wasn't necessary but its presence in the house is a nice reminder of you. Do take care of yourself and be easy on yourself for a while; it takes a while to absorb such a shock as you have had. Please do send me the clippings when you can. Eudora Welty Day made me a kind of Jacksonian democrat.

Love, Ken

P.S. Glad you crossed swords with Gilman, as I've already said, I think.

K.

Eudora Welty to Kenneth Millar, August 10, 1975

Dear Ken,

Thank you for your letter and what it said in its feeling and kindness about the death of Frank Hains—I thought you would remember him,

and you'd remembered him well—Here are the clippings I cut out for you (and there won't be any more news printed now that an arrest has been made) and I don't know anything except what's here. What I think is that it was completely random and senseless, and that the poor soul plainly needed helping a long time ago—and the strangest & saddest thing is that Frank (who never locked his door) was a person who would have tried to give help if he could, & especially to a black person in trouble. For instance, he ran a summer workshop for young people in the theater in the poor part of town to keep them off the streets—very successful.

I hope everything's fine, and you didn't get any unwelcome attentions from that earthquake, like the water coming out of your swimming pool again. Where were you? (I thought of the needle on the seismograph.) (If you were writing it might have left a record on a page of your novel, the same way.)

My best to the novel. And to Margaret's, that I'm so glad to know she has begun—

Of course I'd like so very much to come back to Santa Barbara—I can't think of anywhere I'd rather. The Conrads did mention asking me to the Conference again, and if they'd again let me just non-lecture, and not pay me for the non-lecture, to keep my record clear*, maybe that could happen.[18] In the meantime, maybe you & Margaret could come my way. If you see a possibility, of a time or an easy way, will you tell me—then I could ask when it's just the right moment. (*I had to decline a lecture invitation to Whittier, Cal. lately. The only time I broke my rule was for Willa Cather's 100th birthday celebration—*Nobody* could say no if asked to represent the Female Novelist! (Nobody female, that is.))

I'm glad you thought my letter to the *Times* was all right about Reynolds' critic. (I'd copied it to send along to you, but hadn't done it.) I'd like to know your thought on the novel when you do get time (it *takes* time!) to read it—I'd felt a relief about my own difficulties with the novel after our talk about it. Reynolds sent me a number of the good reviews it's gotten elsewhere, & seems in good spirits about it.

Isn't that a nice picture Miss Virginia Kidd came up with, taken at the Conference?[19] I'm so glad to have one, and thank you for letting her know I'd like one—it's exceptionally good, and nice to have it nearby. —On the mantle piece.

Such nice letters from your friends—Don Freeman, & Robert Easton, & Herb Harker—How far that welcome reached. I'll write to Margaret soon, please tell her with my love.

I am doing some writing—which indeed does help as you said in your letter—Not very good yet but something that looks possible—

With love,

Eudora

Just before Eudora left Santa Barbara, Frederick Zackel, a young writer who had attended the conference, spent several hours with Ken, Margaret, and Eudora. Ken had asked him to the Millars' Via Esperanza home, with the promise of a ride to the airport in four hours' time. On the journey to the house, as Zackel recalled in a 1999 essay, no one said anything in the face of Margaret's "bat-out-of-hell" driving, and the only person Zackel described as speaking once the group arrived at the Millars' home was Ken, who to the young writer's amazement offered to help him with his fiction. Eudora, a brilliant conversationalist, a writer who took pleasure in helping young people, made little or no impression on Zackel. It seems likely that she was as ill at ease as he; she may well have sensed what she would later learn: Margaret did not want visitors in her house; it was for family only.[20] Nevertheless, this tense afternoon could not and would not dim Eudora's happy memories of Santa Barbara.

Eudora Welty to Kenneth Millar, August 23, 1975

Dear Ken,

I'm sitting here looking at Santa Barbara—the beautiful aerial view you sent. It's so all-encompassing, with everything visible and showing those lovely relationships of mountain and sea & sky, and the clarity of the light, and the distances—It's so much pleasure to have the contours

of the place brought back before my eyes, and to see it close to as azure in its photograph as it is in my mind. It's a picture of many rides. Thank you so much—I am so glad to have it.

Is everything going fine with you, and with Margaret and Jim? And novels, and dogs in all their motions? I hope so—I'm all right & trying to get a story on the right track & keep it there. It's been going through some misguided notions.

John Houseman's Acting Company is opening the musical of "The Robber Bridegroom" in Ravinia (Chicago) Tuesday night and I decided to go up & get a look at it. It opened before this in Saratoga and I didn't go, but saw some reviews which were "favorable." I gather it's lively and fairly full of 4-letter words—So I want to see what else it is. Houseman I consider a good man to trust.

I read John Leonard's piece you told me about—Have you had time to? It was odd to see what has its personal meaning turn up in the version of an anecdote in Esquire but John is a nice fellow and he made a good story out of it, perhaps in the course of it taking more of the credit than belonged to him—it still belongs right where it started, with you writing your good books. Have you any idea what kind of detective novel *he* might be able to come up with? He must be really not at all lighthearted these days—Had you heard, as I had from Reynolds & Nona, that his marriage has broken up—This & leaving the *Times* too, all at the same time, must make writing anything pretty hard for him—

I hope to get back from Chicago the next day or the one after that and if there's anything interesting to report, I will. I have to get up & *vote* before I go—about 6 when the polls open—very crucial run-off in the Democratic Primary for Governor—a Good Guy versus a Bad Guy, literally & scarily.[21] I will write better next time. But I wanted you to know how happy the view of Santa Barbara has made me—I put it with mine.

Love, to you both,
Eudora

Eudora Welty to Kenneth Millar, [September 3, 1975]

Dear Ken,

I hope life goes well, and the novel too—The novels—

I work here, and am about to get a draft of a long story done—The stage where it's in pins & Scotch tape but all scratches—

It was hard to tear myself away to Chicago overnight (2 nights actually) to see John Houseman's musical of The Robber Bridegroom but I had too much curiosity not to—You know better than most what changes happen to a story when it gets taken up off the page and put into another medium altogether—This was no longer what it had been, but I found I didn't really mind, because the performers were so young & sparkling & full of bounce, & the direction seemed inventive to me, and the music OK, so it has a life of its own—the real test, isn't it? I don't know whether they'll keep it in that repertory (along with "Arms & the Man," "A School for Scandal," & "The Cherry Orchard"!) or not. We shall see—

Have you read "Rag Time"?

My yard was full of 24 visiting robins early this morning—They must be starting to travel these days, and so eventually fall will be here—It's so hot now—

Take care—good luck with all—to both—

Love,
Eudora

The Chicago lake front was not like the coast of Santa Barbara.

Eudora Welty to Kenneth Millar, September 8, 1975

Dear Ken,

Are you quite all right? If you were a poor letter writer like me I wouldn't feel so concerned, but you're a good letter writer—and a letter from you hasn't come since July—I know you're working hard at the revision of your book, maybe extra hard because my visit interrupted the first draft—So I hope all is well with you and with all of

yours. What I said about missing the letter isn't to complain, but just to want to make sure you're all right—& the way I saw you last.

Love,

Eudora

Even as Eudora was writing this worried letter, Ken was apologizing for his long silence. Their letters crossed in the mail.

Kenneth Millar to Eudora Welty, September 8, 1975

Dear Eudora:

It was most thoughtful and generous of you to continue to send letters into this epistolary emptiness. It's always so good to hear from you, and to be assured by your voice that you are recovering from your shock and sorrow for your friend. I've been released now from just under a year's steady writing, having got a copy of the new book off to Dorothy Olding over the weekend. Though this is not usually the case with me, I have no certain idea of where it stands in relation to my other books, for one reason because it was more difficult to write. One other reason is that I spent too long, intermittently, on the planning, which went on over a period of thirty years. It seems to me quite different from the others, not so tight—either structure or style—perhaps a transition book to something else. You may be interested in the title, The Tarantula Hawk, which is a wasp that preys on tarantulas in this fashion: the female wasp lays her egg on a tarantula which she has paralyzed with her sting and which is available for the young wasp to eat when he hatches. There are roughly two such (human) situations in the book.—My final week on it was blown merrily along by Jimmie's breezy presence in the house, his last week before school starts. We actually did go sailing one afternoon, with a good wind hurrying us along, and for the first time in several years I saw the city and the rim of mountains behind it as Dana saw it c. 1835. The sea is a good place to look at the land from, don't you think? Do you recall Dana's glorious account of his entry into San Francisco harbor, with the wild deer running on the wooded hills?

Jim had spent the previous week in Yosemite with his father and had changed when he came back, having acquired a bit of the pride and certitude of adolescence. He beat me at checkers, twice in a row, and learned to handle his surfboard. It is such a pleasure to see him come along, and gently too. Last year when I was visiting an old friend—indeed my oldest friend, we met when we were five, lived three doors from each other in Kitchener, Ontario, where he still lives—last year Clay [Hall] showed me a camping picture of a group of boys taken when I was eleven. One of them looked like Jimmie. I realized that it was me, then, and that he somewhat resembled me in appearance. But the inside of his head is quite different: mine swarmed with words and stories, his with technical information like his engineer father's: I think you and I were very lucky to be brought up in cultures where the language was paramount, don't you? The physical world is a thankless and even dangerous god which we are consuming in a giant grotesque parody of Mass. For Jim the structure is alleviated, I believe, by the fact that he is a Roman Catholic and will have access to a more traditional Mass. But for me, and probably for you, the English language is the repository of nearly everything good.

I've probably long since told you that Margaret is writing again, morning noon and night, with an obvious gusto she hasn't felt in years. About Baja California, where she has never been; but then Santa Barbara is thirty percent Spanish-speaking and its real heart is Mexican. I think your visit and your influence had a good deal to do with bringing Margaret back to her work—just one of many many people whom you inspired here. I hope Santa Barbara is reciprocating in a way.

I'm in a kind of limbo at the moment, waiting for a first reaction on my book, and waiting also to be taken up by my travel plans which haven't quite seized me yet; they don't seem to be quite real. But I have a reservation to fly from L.A. to London on Oct. 1 for the International Crime Writers' Conference, where I'll be on a panel with Eric Ambler, Dick Francis, and Stanley Ellin, which should be fun. Before the Congress I hope to get down into the west country, as far as Cornwall, where my friend Ping Ferry and his wife will be castle-looking in early October and I may be able to join them. I haven't been in Cornwall for 31 years. Love, Ken

P.S.—I gather you sort of liked the dramatization of *The Robber Bridegroom*, will look forward to it. K.

Ken had had and would continue to have an unusual amount of difficulty finishing and revising the manuscript of what would prove to be the final Lew Archer novel. When he showed his work to Robert Easton to critique in advance, as was their custom, Millar's friend was shocked to find uncharacteristic lapses in tone and diction; he suggested various revisions in word choice and even structure—changes Ken made (again uncharacteristically) without complaint.

Kenneth Millar to Eudora Welty, September 12, 1975

Dear Eudora:

I'm sorry I caused you anxiety and should have explained earlier that I was rather completely absorbed in getting my book finished. I was afraid it might get away. The last six weeks or so I was rewriting ahead of the typist in the daytime and preparing final pages for her in my spare time. Well, the whole thing got done and went off to Knopf this week, and I am retracing my steps back into civilization. It's the longest book and it took the longest time of any of mine; over twelve years in the planning, also twelve months in the writing. I hope it turns out to have been worth the effort. You know, on a larger scale, how hard it is to keep a book alive and going over a long period of time with so many interruptions. But somehow, when a book survives such delays (as *Losing Battles* triumphantly does) there's special reason for thanksgiving. I'm celebrating my own small private thanksgiving (enhanced by the fact that Margaret is writing again as you know— and you really did help with this, too. We're creatures of emulation who love company.)

Next month when I'm in England after the Crime Writers' Conference in London I hope to get down to Cornwall with Ping Ferry and his wife, am starting to reread *Women in Love* by way of preparation. Suddenly I'm moseying around in a vast acreage of time. There's no fun comparable with getting a book in, is there?

My friend Matt Bruccoli, MATTHEW J. BRUCCOLI, the Fitzgerald (*et al*) scholar, has just written a good strong solid first-biography of John O'Hara, Matt's first.[22] Having enjoyed the work, he's looking around for another subject. He's a Chandler scholar, too, but Chandler has been pre-empted by two other biographers working separately. Matt asked me for possible subjects. I thought of James M. Cain and Nelson Algren, but of course they're both alive. Do you have any nominees?—recent writers who deserve but have not been given biographies. Matt teaches at the University of South Carolina and could probably handle a Southern subject. I think he's one of the great enthusiastic scholars of our period—he's lit more fires than any other scholar in his field, and I never knew anyone capable of such sustained cheerful work. All this just in case you think of someone interesting and deserving. Albert Erskine is Matt's editor at Random House. It occurs to me belatedly that you may know Matt Bruccoli—I think his FS Fitzgerald collection is the largest in private hands.

All's well here. Forgive me for alarming you. I should have at least dropped you an explanatory card. I guess I was in a writing madness like Zelda's dancing madness, and it never occurred to me that you might be concerned. You know, Eudora, if I was *really* in trouble I'd get in touch with you right away. But my life seems very lucky at the moment. I hope yours is the same, and the work goes well.

Love,
Ken

P.S. The photographer, as of course I intended he should from the beginning, is making a copy of the lunch picture for you. K.

Eudora Welty in the cover photo for a 1941 publicity pamphlet announcing her first book. *Photograph by Chestina Welty, used courtesy Eudora Welty LLC.*

Ross Macdonald (Kenneth Millar) photographed by publisher Alfred Knopf in Knopf's New York City office, 1965. *Photograph courtesy of Alfred A. Knopf.*

Eudora returning to the Algonquin Hotel in New York City, just before meeting Kenneth Millar on May 17, 1971. *Photograph by Paul Matthews.*

Kenneth and Margaret Millar at the opening of the new Kitchener, Ontario, public library in May 1971, just after Ken and Eudora met in New York City. *Photograph courtesy of Kitchener-Waterloo Record Collection, Dana Porter Library, University of Waterloo.*

Eudora Welty and Walker Percy being interviewed by William F. Buckley Jr., December 12, 1972. *Photograph courtesy Eudora Welty LLC.*

Ken, Eudora, and artist–author Don Freeman in Santa Barbara. *Photograph courtesy of Eudora Welty LLC.*

A protective Ken with grandson Jimmie at the Hope Ranch pool, in a picture posed for *Esquire* magazine in 1972. *Photograph by Mike Salisbury.*

Ken and Maggie with Peter Graves, who played Lew Archer in the 1974 TV movie of *The Underground Man. Photograph by Hal Boucher.*

Ken, Maggie, Eudora, and *Los Angeles Times* arts editor Charles Champlin at the 1975 Santa Barbara Writers Conference. *Photograph courtesy of Mary Conrad.*

Eudora seeing "all those Constables" at Yale University, October 1977. *Photograph courtesy Eudora Welty LLC.*

Kenneth Millar in Santa Barbara, 1980. *Photograph by Trevor Clark.*

Eudora Welty at her upstairs window in Jackson, 1977. *Photograph by Angela Hederman.*

Bits and pieces of scenes, written on both sides of an October 1981 document, for Welty's never completed story "Henry." *Images used by permission of Eudora Welty LLC and courtesy of the Mississippi Department of Archives and History.*

Ross Macdonald
and Eudora Welty
at the Santa Barbara
Writers Conference.
*Photograph by
Virginia Kidd.*

Eudora Welty to Kenneth Millar, September 14, [1975]

Dear Ken,

I rejoiced in your letter—all that good news! (I saw it sticking out of the rest of the mail, from upstairs at the typewriter, as the postman brought it—I'm sorry I got the wind up and wrote you the note that crossed it.) It's such happy news that the novel is finished and sent off—there's nothing quite like that feeling, is there? Especially when a book has taken, needed, a long time and put many questions to you along the way. I'm eager to read it. I have every belief in the good of its differences, too, because it's the writer whose control is sure and tight and tested like yours who must be able to judge with the most sensitivity when it comes to giving it leeway. I'm so glad you've brought this one about. And thirteen years is a long time—pressure enough on its own.

"The Tarantula Hawk" is a pretty galvanizing title. (But you won't throw away that other one you had earlier, "Portrait of the Artist as a Dead Man"—that's still in the bank) Your word "available"—what the tarantula is for the young wasp when he hatches—goes *on* being galvanic—and I can see that the symbolic possibilities there are good and strong, and rightly scarey.

It's like a reward, to have the trip to London come right on top of finishing—all as should be. The panel you're to be on is about the best they could have possibly gotten anywhere any time, surely—at least to this reader. It ought to be full of pleasure for you—especially seeing Eric Ambler again, after you presented him with the award in NY. I just read "Knockdown" and thought it fine, as Dick Francis always is, didn't you like it? All the best for the trip in every way, and Cornwall sounds magical (well, that's what it always was, isn't it?)

One reason I was getting anxious to hear from you was that I'm getting ready to go off for a few weeks too, and while I'm away from home usually the P.O. just holds my mail, and so it would be a long time. I have to go to Washington on one of those Council on the Arts meetings, and then John Houseman was planning to open The Robber

Bridegroom in NY around the first week in Oct., so if that still is on, I'll be in NY from Sept. 27 till Oct. 8. You'll be flying over, I guess, while I'm down below. I'll think of you as vertically near on that day.

Mary Lou is coming this Saturday for 4 days, on her way to see her son who is living in Atlanta. We'll think of you here. Everybody's well in my family, and yours sound all well and happy and busy. It's so good that Margaret is working and enjoying the work—I know it is a lot easier to go off to London when she is having a fine time at home with her book.

Please give her my love. Thank you again for your good and happy letter and please forgive my anxious note. My mother used to chide me out of giving in to such.

Love,
Eudora

Eudora Welty, New York City, to Kenneth Millar, October 1, 1975

Dear Ken,

I was so sorry to hear from Joan Kahn tonight that Margaret had had an operation and that you were not going to England after all— Joan said she understood (from Dorothy Olding?) that Margaret was doing well, and I do hope all's going along all right now. What a shame this had to come along—and just now.

I'd been thinking today that this was the day you were flying from L.A. to London. I'm in the city between a 4-day meeting of the Arts Council in Washington & the opening of The Robber Bridegroom here on Tuesday night. The meeting was a bit exhausting—so many people talking for so many hours about so much money, though in a good cause. Today I went to see "Ah Wilderness" at Circle-in-the-Square, mainly to enjoy the performance of Geraldine Fitzgerald—we'd got to be friends in Jackson on her visits to work with New Stage—and to go back-stage afterwards and talk. I'm reading "Middlemarch" which I'd never read—You have, I expect—I was always sure it was worthy but that hadn't made me read it—maybe I should say and that hadn't made me read it. And how delicious it is—I look forward all day to coming back here to it at night.

I have a feeling that all the signs point to your new novel being one of your best—The feeling you described of the last weeks of work, which I have sometimes felt too, I trust—It's evidence, I think that something has received the best you can do at the time. I'm eager to read it, of course.

I hope Margaret can get back to hers soon. My sympathies to you both, and love,

Eudora

Kenneth Millar to Eudora Welty, October 5, 1975

Dear Eudora:

I was supposed to be in England this weekend and ensuing weeks but a bit of an emergency came up which has been enough to keep me at home. Margaret had a cancer removed from her nose last week and it caused her some trouble both physical and emotional, so I decided to stay. I can go to England another time. Margaret is okay, you don't have to worry.

In lieu of the trip I'd planned, I've been reading various things about England e.g. Lawrence's short stories and your short essay on Jane Austen in *Brief Lives*, which will send me back to *her*. I read her novels at one fell swoop years ago, and haven't since, I must confess. But now is the time for rereading.

The book I've been working on is substantially finished but runs a bit long and may need some cutting. I'll get back to it shortly. The reactions of readers here and in New York have been good, and I think I have a good title—"The Blue Hammer," referring to the human pulse, from a poem by Henri Coulette. Jim and his father are here this weekend and Jim is full of tales of adventures, his own, on sea in canoes, sailboats, and on his surfboard; fortunately he is equally enthusiastic about his new school. His father, after several years of quiet mourning, has at last turned outward, grown a beard, and got a new look in his eye.

We are having our normal hot later summer—over 100° last week. I rather like it.—*Here at long last* is the picture taken at lunch: both the photographer and I have been unconscionably slow in producing it.

Love, Ken

Eudora Welty, on a plane, to Kenneth Millar, [October 8, 1975]

Dear Ken,

A note from the middle of the air. I'm on the return trip to Jackson. And as I was checking out of the hotel whom should I see but Don Freeman standing next to me. He wasn't staying at the Algonquin but was there to meet someone for lunch. We had time to talk for a few minutes and it was so nice to see him—10 minutes one way or the other I'd have missed him. I expect he'll call & give you my greetings when he gets back to Santa Barbara—he hadn't known about Margaret's trouble or your giving up of your trip. I'm hoping all goes along satisfactorily there—and I'm very sorry about it all.

My show of "The Robber Bridegroom" opened last night, and I enclose the 2 reviews that had come out before I left. It was really a most cheerful & enjoyable evening—It had taken me from the performance I saw in Chicago till now to get used to it, somehow—The best thing about it was the quality of the performers themselves—a young, ardently devoted & accomplished group of talented kids, with the most ambitious repertory—Marlowe, Shaw, Chekhov, what have you—and the same cast in those august plays was cavorting in "The Robber" in the form of a country musical—It was different, in spirit & style from my book, but it had a valid life of its own in those terms. And I loved those kids. If Don gets his tickets as I hope, he'll see it tonight & can give you a first-hand account—and his own impressions.

I've seen some of our mutual friends of N.Y. too—Joan, as I told you, & Walter Clemons (who was along last night) etc. And what did our dear Algonquin do but have a bottle of fine champagne in a bucket of ice waiting in my room when I got back? (I had already been to the cast party, so I'm taking the bottle home in a sack for some time or other.) I'm reading Middlemarch & steadying myself to fiction where I belong after the Broadway excitement. I hope all is OK in Santa Barbara, & many wishes to you both—.

Love,
Eudora

Eudora Welty to Kenneth Millar, October 9, 1975. Written on reverse of a postcard with image of a Jane Austen letter.

Dear Ken,

Your letter & the fine picture of the lunch were here at the p.o. when I went for my mail this morning. I'm glad to know Margaret is all right and I hope she will be fine & back at her novel soon—

The picture was a lot for you to bother with at a time when you had so much on your mind. Thank you for it. I'm glad to have it from that happy time. (And here's Don again, whom I just saw yesterday in NY).

In N.Y. I went to see the Jane Austen mss & some letters at the Morgan Library—The only p.c. was this one of her backwards letter to a little niece. There were some where she began a page this way and these ended this way [writing in a cross letter style]—I just read Persuasion again—moving and beautiful in a way all to itself among her others—It's good to be home & hear the birds again—Love, Eudora

Kenneth Millar to Eudora Welty, October 19, 1975

Dear Eudora:

That was a rich assortment of messages and information you sent me last week. The good reviews of "The Robber Bridegroom" were particularly cheering. (I enclose another which you've doubtless seen but may be able to use another copy of.) And it was such a pleasure to have your report of meeting Don Freeman at the Algonquin, soon amplified the other day at lunch by his report of meeting *you*. These not entirely random chimings of the lives we care for are the very essence of the enterprise, aren't they? I know you think so, because your whole life moves to that music.—Speaking of Don reminds me of Ann Pidgeon who has just sent me a note of appreciation for the Cather book which you gave me and I lent her and she is now sharing with friends at the University. What a wonderfully evocative book, with everything in it including Mesa Verde which I hope to see one more time before I go hence—go *thence* before I go hence. And from Willa Cather it isn't too great a leap to Reynolds Price. I think I've got my own book under sufficient control, having rewritten the start but not yet the ending, to dare to read his, and I'm well into *The Surface of Earth* now. I find it engrossing and liberating and am thrown back powerfully by it into my own first and last theme, the father-heart. In all its delicate and gross detail it seems to me strong and original, very much Reynolds' own, as well as ours now. Though it was written in the unavoidable aftermath of Faulkner, no shadow falls on the page. The knowledge has been absorbed. It's wonderful to live in a period when such books as Reynolds' are being written and such defenses as yours of it are being made. It is not only the South that is still fighting the Civil War—the New York reviewers, or some of them, are, too.

There are other things I have to thank you for, Eudora. Among them is the Oriental pot which now handsomely contains what Margaret tells me is a Celethea Roses Lineate; and Jane Austen's backwards writing, so young and sweetly human. We've been having pleasant weather the last few days, warm enough for types like me to swim in the ocean, which is in the low sixties. Had lunch yesterday on the Conrads' verandah with Oakley Hall who teaches half-time at UC Irvine, is head of their creative writing department. The other half of the year he lives at Squaw Valley, presumably for the skiing. Each to his taste. But he is an admirer of yours, and seems rather a nice man.[23]

Margaret is quite well again and working on her book, approaching what looks like the halfway mark. I think your visit inspired her, you know. We both hope (along with dozens and scores of others) that you will repeat it.

Love,
Ken

P.S.—What appears to be the final title of my book, I hope, is "The Blue Hammer" — a phrase referring to the human pulse in the wrist or temple which I stole from a new poem by Henri Coulette, with his permission.

K.

Eudora Welty to Kenneth Millar, November 4, 1975

Dear Ken—if you'll excuse this [lined] paper—anyway it's a pretty sea color, and it makes me think of Santa Barbara—It was good to have your last letter—the one about Reynolds' book among other things—which I have been wanting to thank you for and write back about. So many daily interruptions—one good one, I'm writing a new story—I've felt so happy to be back with a story, and have been wanting to send you a letter out of that happiness, too. I'm hoping you're feeling the same way with the last work on your novel.

The thought and understanding you brought Reynolds' book moved me—You are as understanding and good to a book as you are to a friend. I wouldn't expect you to be any other way—but I felt the force of your insight and belief in him in your words about his treatment of that theme you have here in common—You know that he felt he had learned from you. He did. He would be made very happy to know the book made you feel so strongly aware of his deepest intentions and of their carrying out—When you have finished reading it. But you know he would. I haven't written to Reynolds for too long—but I guess he is back at teaching this semester—

You asked me recently if I could come up with any ideas about a Southern writer as subject for Mr. Bruccoli to write about next, but so far I haven't been able—I've read the reviews of his O'Hara book, all finding it good but the NYTBR which sounded somehow as if the reviewer didn't *want* to like it because he'd liked this other man's, Farr's—(contrary to the prevailing opinions)—I'll be interested to read Mr. B's book myself—I've had such respect for him since that astonishing feat he did on the Fitzgerald mss for Tender Is the Night (I have your copy, do you remember?) I was glad to see your quote for it.

It's lovely & soft, the day here, November though it is—I have to leave everything, including my story, to fly up to Mt. Holyoke College this weekend, but am coming right back Monday—(Almost embarrassed to tell you, it's another hon. Degree—I will have to do some work, though, so it will seem more orderly & more according to how I was brought up, not to take the diploma just wantonly.)

I've been reading *The Instant Enemy* again, in lieu of the new novel not printed yet, and I am now positive that it was this of your books that I wrote you the fan letter I never mailed you. (before we ever communicated) As I read that chapter of going to the Krug Ranch, I knew. It is superb—on every count. I thought again, all through this novel, but here most, that the tension of action and feeling in one, really one, that comes precisely of its structure and building and motion and compression & its long beautiful curve as its goes, and all very purely out of its inception & dramatic necessity made it as far as I could see and feel a quite perfect thing. (Do you think I'm repeating my fan letter? I don't remember my words, just what caused them.) The whole book has an intensity of dark—tragic—feeling about it that stirs feeling, all the way. It is also, in its visual landscapes, beautiful. Archer seems very close to the nerve of all your books when he says "Everything matters."

Many birds now—I heard the white throated sparrow sing for the first time this fall last evening after the rain stopped—My best to Margaret too—and Love,

Eudora

I went to the toy store, & what did I see—a sign in the window:

CALIFORNIA SKATE BOARDS

ARE

HERE!

I hope your Jim has come to like his surf board better—

Thank you for sending those Robber reviews!

Kenneth Millar to Eudora Welty, [November 1975]

Dear Eudora:

It was so kind and good of you, on the eve of my attempt to make something for film out of *The Instant Enemy*, to remind me of the sense you got of its feeling and its shape. I sometimes think other people may see our stories better and more clearly than we do ourselves. Certainly, in your case, more generously. But with your help—and how happy it makes me that you should like it, still—I can in some way like it, too. I tried to get into it some of the disorder and early sorrow of my child-hood. The aging man in the Mission District hotel room who once mined silver in Nevada represents my father (who once mined silver in Nevada). Part of the new book is about the people who run a *copper* mine in Arizona. I sometimes think fiction is the smoke that reveals, and conceals, the fire. But not much really gets concealed in the long run, and that suits me.

I'm afraid Matt Bruccoli got some pretty unfriendly reviews on his O'Hara book. I still consider it highly interesting and done with honesty and strict scholarship—in many ways a model of what a *first* biography should be. I was accidentally sent an extra copy, by the way, and will send it to you. Correct me if I'm wrong: I'm always glad to have an opportunity to praise a friend. There's one thing in Matt's book that gives me particular pleasure, I hardly know why: his report of O'Hara's attending a luncheon in Princeton in the Lambert (LISTERINE) house,[24] which Margaret and I rented in the summer of 1944 while I was going to Princeton as an officer in training. It made me feel like a retroactive Gatsby I think. Which reminds me that the third movie Gatsby is going to appear on TV in a few min-utes. Warner Baxter was the first! Alan Ladd the second. I'm afraid Robert Redford may have been the worst of the three, but there were many things I liked about this third production when I saw it last year in a theatre e.g. the Daisy, the jazz scenes, the L.I. settings, the middle, the endings.[25]

Yes, Jim has pretty well turned his back on skateboarding and he *is* becoming—a process that takes years—a dedicated surfer. I think time spent in the surf is well-spent, not only in building the body but the spirit and its relationship with the world. We get from it the nearest thing to a live response that inanimate nature affords us. Which reminds me that I published the other day, in a short note on "Sense of Place" in *South Dakota Review*, the following: "This ocean, with its great spatial and temporal continuities, its currents and recurrences, its destructions and renewals, represents a changing constant in my life and fiction. It is the nearest thing in my fiction to an inescapable and memorable place." You know, Eudora, a friendly black lifeguard in Vancouver rolled me into the surf when I was three, and I sort of never came out.

This is a scattershot letter but it represents the condition of my mind. I'm relaxing down after just completing a little over a week ago my final revisions on *The Blue Hammer*. It took me thirteen years in the planning and eighteen months in the writing—in all that time I should have been able to produce something bigger and better—but still I hope you like it and find it fit to be read as a sequel to *Enemy*. I'll send you a copy when I can, at present have only the one to keep track of corrections in. Thank you for your lovely letter. All well here.

Love, Ken

Eudora Welty to Kenneth Millar, December 9, 1975

Dear Ken,

Your letter went on two trips with me—to Hartford, Conn. & back, & to Washington & back—Having it by me—it was such a fine one—wasn't the same as answering it, I know. Thank you for it—

I didn't know till you told me in it that you were about to make something for film out of *The Instant Enemy*—I'm glad it's you that's doing it. Are you working on it now? I would love to see what you come out with. What others make of your books seems all wrong, consistently so (I have to differ with your friend Mr. Chamblin (?) on the *L.A. Times* who liked *The Drowning Pool* movie—I thought it lacked absolutely everything the book called for, the first thing being even a suggestion of the quality of the original. I really hated what they did to it.) But *The Instant Enemy* is something else as a novel and I hope you find translating it (or is it re-seeing it all?) into film an interesting experience—To me the two closest cousins are fiction & film—I hope to try a film myself one day—Don't you think they are alike in many ways—not least in ways of technique?—I was glad to know what you told me about the background of *The Instant Enemy*—some of which I had surmised when I read it this time—I agree about the smoke & the fire—

Thank you for copying out for me what you wrote for the *South Dakota Review* about the ocean and its meaning to you in your life and fiction—This can be felt—You couldn't help making others feel what you feel so deeply. An ex-writing class student of mine is in the English Department of the U. of *North* Dakota, just wrote to ask me to do some little thing for him and I wrote him then to please send me the *North* Dakota Review with your piece in it—the wrong Dakota. If he's any good he'll think that's just what I did, & get me the right one. There's a quote I want to send you but I ought to type it—

Thank you so much for sending Mr. Bruccoli's *O'Hara*—I'll read it with pleasure, I know from what you say about it & from that good note in the *New Yorker*—You asked once if I'd met him—no, just almost. I walked into Albert Erskine's house in Westport and was asking if he had a certain book and he said "I *had*, but Matt Bruccoli has just left the house with it under his arm."

All the chores I had to do before the end of the year are just about done—the kind of thing you've agreed to do away back and finally the reckoning comes—The only one left is being one of the fiction judges for the Pulitzer—Books have been arriving box after box, and I unpack them in rows on top of the piano & under the tables—I've got one going in almost every room of the house—I'd got way behind—and have far to go. The good ones seem ever so far between to me. Then I read those slowly and hate to give them up. If they're bad enough, I can read as many as 3 a day & depressed as I can be.

Alfred Knopf sent me his book of photographs which pleases me deeply.[26] It was kind of him—He knew, I think, what would make me happy to have it, that I had my own friends in it. It holds three dear friends. Elizabeth Bowen, Bill Maxwell, and yourself. I cherish it. The one of you is eloquent! I like it more than any of you I've ever seen—

It's good to know *The Blue Hammer* is all really done—after thirteen years of planning and eighteen months in the writing. You aren't feeling bereft without it, I hope—Dear Ken—Happy Birthday on the 13th—I remember it because I'm another 13th—With love—and give my love to Margaret. I'll write better next time—

Love,
Eudora

P.S. Reynolds came up to Washington to see me one evening while I was there for an Arts Council meeting. We had a fine long evening of talk—We spoke of you—He seems very well—A good reunion.

Eudora Welty to Kenneth Millar, December 12, 1975

Dear Ken,

The quote I was thinking of when I wrote you I'd have to copy it out on the typewriter wasn't long at all! I'd remembered it as very long,—you can see why. Anyway, it's something Dostoyevsky said, quoted by a writer of a book on sea birds (Louis J. Halle, *The Storm Petrel and the Owl of Athena*).

"Everything, like the ocean, flows and comes into contact with everything else: touch it in one place and it reverberates at the other end of the world."

(And a strange thing to say itself out of the middle of Russia, isn't it? Proving itself.)

You probably remember Charlotte Capers, a good friend of mine in Jackson—She just got out a little book or booklet (by me), through the Miss. Historical Society, and I sent you and Margaret one to be a

Christmas card to you—It's very local, but we count you in, here. The tear-sheets are a little piece I did for Esquire—not thinking you'd likely see it I wanted you to have it simply because it's true—[27]

Beautiful clear bright days here—

Love,

Eudora

There're some other things in that issue of Esquire (December) you'd like to see too—I ought to've sent it all.

Kenneth Millar to Eudora Welty, December 15, 1975

Dear Eudora:

I subscribe to *Esquire*, which has turned out over the years to be just about our best general magazine now, don't you think, and so I had the pleasure of reading your memory piece several days ago. Still I'm glad to have another copy which I can pass on to a friend, and it was thoughtful of you to send it to me. Too bad you were restricted, by your conscience, to the exact truth, because I'd dearly love to know what happened to the proprietor of the store, and only you could tell us. It seems to me that in the days of our childhood, our lives were full of such mysteries and disappearances. I'm still trying to figure out some of them. Others I would rather not know the solution of, but do. I know what happened to my father, for example—a Dostoyevskian fate.

His son—I'm still his son, though I celebrated my sixtieth birthday two days ago (which is more than he lived to do)—has embarked on a very new and very brief career by writing, or starting to write, a movie treatment which seems to be going well but probably isn't. It couldn't be that easy. But it seems one can throw overboard the burden of style— excess baggage. The style belongs to the man behind the camera. As I think I've mentioned, I intend to get my feet wet but not go overboard myself. My producer is a very bright young businessman from Chicago named Burt Weissbourd whose father is a noted builder and whose wife has just taken her doctorate in psychology with a dissertation on Henry James Sr. and his son William—a dissertation that will eventually become a book, I'm sure. Her master appears to be Erik Erikson, that most Dostoyevskean of psychiatrists. Thank you for the wonderful quote from Dostoyevsky—about the endless oceanic reverberations of life. I know I have to spend some of my remaining years reading and rereading him, and have been working back in that direction by way of Chekhov. Have you seen the English movie of *Three Sisters*? it sticks unusually close to the play.[28]

Today in the mail I received two envelopes which looked at first, from the handwriting, as if they had been addressed by the same person. You were the author of one of them but you'd never guess who wrote the other. You may know him. Certainly you know his books: Julian Symons. I enclose the two envelopes to prove my point. Isn't it remarkable that a Mississippi lady and a London man should write so very much alike? The London man, as the postmark of his card will tell you, is at Amherst this year, teaching writing at the college. Julian and his wife spent their first few days in Emily Dickinson's house—a lucky thing for another poet if not for poor great luckless Emily. Apart from a couple of recognized saints, who present unfair competition, I think Julian is the best man I know. How often has an autodidact turned into a novelist and critic and poet?

Last week some fifty of his friends here celebrated the birthday of W.H. Ferry, his 65th, by [drinking] and contributing money towards a coin-operated laundry for a laundryless southwestern village—the money paid for laundry to belong to the village. I think it was Ferry's own idea, it's typical of him.

Have a good Xmas, dear Eudora.

Love, Ken

Kenneth Millar to Eudora Welty, [December 1975]

Dear Eudora:

This is a combination of a Christmas greeting and a miniature version of the letter I owe you, it seems, for some time now. I emerged from the new book only to plunge backwards into the old one (The Instant

Enemy) from which I am now trying to wrest a screen treatment—not bad fun, but I won't vouch for the outcome. The *best* parts of these days are the late afternoon hours in which I walk my two bigger dogs on the beach. It seems to me we've had an extraordinarily clement fall, with the mountains more persistently clear than I've ever seen them. Between those mountains and this sea I can lose myself in nature, but then quickly find myself again. I never get far from the sound of a human voice, or a bird voice for that matter. Our most striking out-of-town visitors among the birds this fall were three white pelicans on our local lake: they're normally found no nearer than a hundred miles south of here.

I must have told you the happy news that Margaret is well past the middle of her book, and going strong (ASK FOR ME TOMORROW (Mercutio) is the title). We wish the same for you, and trust that your Christmas will be a happy one and that, with luck, we may see you in the new year.

Love, Ken

CHAPTER SIX

"I dreamed I was sending you the dream I was dreaming."

———— ❧ ————

1976

THE imminent publication of Ross Macdonald's eighteenth Lew Archer novel, The Blue Hammer, *had already been trumpeted in trade-paper ads by the house of Knopf, but Ken Millar was still hesitant to sign off on it. When the book's proofs arrived for correction early in 1976, he asked longtime Santa Barbara colleague Bill Gault (*The Bloody Bokhara, Million Dollar Tramp, Thunder Road*) to read and critique it. "I thought, 'Well, what do I know about this intellectual prose?'" Gault would say later. "So I took it home and read it, and some of the things—I just couldn't get the connection.[. . .] Certain things I didn't understand. Well, he didn't say anything. But when the book came out, the stuff I'd suggested he take out was sorta taken out."[1] Millar dedicated* The Blue Hammer *to William Campbell Gault.*

Kenneth Millar to Eudora Welty, January 9, 1976

Dear Eudora:

Please forgive my silence, which this note will barely break. I've been doing income tax, writing my *Instant Enemy* treatment, seeing it and M's new book ("Ask For Me Tomorrow") through the typist, etc.

I think you'll like M's book: the plotting and the dialog are brilliant: and I'm so glad to have a book of hers after six silent years.[2] It changes the whole atmosphere. Indeed it appears that I have nothing at all to complain of, so I won't.

My neighbor Ted Clymer came across the enclosed mention of you in PW, p. 14. It reminded me, though I don't need reminding, how lucky I am to know you. *Santa Barbara* misses you!

I'll try to say more in my next. This is just to remind you that I'm in the land of the living.

Love,

Ken

Eudora Welty to Kenneth Millar, January 12, 1976

Dear Ken,

Wasn't the mail service wonderful in Victorian days? I've been reading *The Woman in White*. You go downstairs and drop your letter in the post bag, and even allowing time for Count Fosco to open and copy it, it gets to London and the answer is back by next afternoon—by gig from the station, if it's urgent.

I'm glad you quietly continue to use your airmail envelopes, and believe they may do some good—How long does it take a letter from NY to reach you in Santa Barbara? To Jackson it's about 6 days—for a book, a month.

I was thinking of you through the holidays and hoping they were good with you—they must have been busy, with both of you in the midst of work. Along with wishing you and Margaret a happy New Year I was sending you my thanks again with a feeling I'll never lose for the happy visit there in the year just over—I was working here—on the reading committee for the Pulitzer in fiction, and I'd got desperately behind. Now that the 3 of us have gotten together (on the day after Xmas) we still don't know what the ultimate judges at Columbia will decide—Well, it caused me to read books I'd never have chosen to read for myself, so I guess that was good for me—There were some bright spots, and, to be fair, a number of abysmal ones (to me)—All 500 pages long.[3]

A nice family time here, anyway—Christmas dinner with my family—4 babies now! (happy & good). One of my oldest & best friends, John Robinson, was here on a visit from Italy—a country he fell in love with when fighting there in World War II and now lives in with full commitment. A novel I wrote that long time ago (Delta Wedding) I wrote & sent him in installments—the Delta was his home. But I may tell you his story some time.

Just now I heard on the news that Agatha Christie had died. Was she a friend? I remember hearing from Elizabeth Bowen, who came to know her well, what a marvelous person she was. She really was an era all in herself, wasn't she? Her life sounded very contented and benign for her—I hope it was so.

To go back to "A Woman in White," it was the perfect antidote for some of my Pulitzer chores—the form & shape of it, the control, the delicious sensation of seeing the way he unfolds his plot—the suspense of it, which is perfect, is somehow kin to the solidity of it—& all the minutiae *counting*—Well, I care about such things and they make me happy—It was like the peace of an ocean voyage to go off on such an excursion—I think Julian Symons's foreword (I always prefer to read forewords as afterwords) was just and interesting and certainly it told me things I didn't know that really got me, such as the fact that Collins & Dickens, to provide installments for "All the Year Round," thus furnished "A Tale of Two Cities" and "The Woman in White"! That last scene concerning Fosco, with mobs of the curious crowding the morgue to view his body, has the impact of some archetypical crowd-performance of Victorian life—don't you feel?

And I wonder if you happened to read a *modern* novel *about* the days of the Empire, "The Siege of Krishnapur" by J. G. Ferrell (Harcourt '73). You'd think well of it, as I did, I think—(If you want me to I'll send.)

Oh, Julian Symons' handwriting! Indeed it is similar to mine, which isn't too good a thing for it to be, and as far as I can tell not very similar to other "English" handwriting—? Since he's somebody I've long admired, it pleased me to see it, and you're probably the only person in the world who'd have noticed it.

How is the film treatment going? They'd better let you have it your way. Is there a better eye to see it for us than the one that saw it for us to begin with? I like the novel such a lot and don't want them to mess it up. I guess I find it hard to trust them. More power to you, my feeling is.

I had the announcement from the Santa Barbara Writer's Conference with a line saying they would like me to be there again, and I was pleased to think that might be. If you are free of the film and whatever else you'll be doing after that and if Margaret has her novel all done, it would be joyous to me to see you, you know, and I could see how the idea works out. I've turned down a number of other things sort of in the hope I could make it there if conditions allowed—We can see—

It's been cold there and here, I guess. I hope what the news said about the Riverside oranges doesn't apply to the flowering trees & shrubs in your garden. It went down to 15° here—from 75°—& stayed very cold for several days, which isn't the normal pattern. I found 2 birds frozen—a white throated sparrow in the front yard and a little towhee in the back.

Jan. 13

Before I got to finish & send this, your letter came (dated the 9th) which had fine news in it of work getting done & through the typist— It's good to know. I'm delighted to have the prospect of reading "Ask for Me Tomorrow" before long—a lot of people are going to be glad about that, and I'm glad for Margaret's sake & can imagine how happy it makes you—

Thanks for the clip from PW, which I hadn't seen, & to Ted Clymer too—(a little mystifying, the clip.)

Lots of wishes about the work, works, and love to you both, and thanks for your letter, out of the midst of all you are doing—

Yours,
Eudora

Kenneth Millar to Eudora Welty, January 25, 1976

Dear Eudora:

I am slow in answering your lovely letter, having knocked myself out on the *Instant Enemy* treatment then taken a week off just ended. Tomorrow I start a rewrite. The work is easy compared with fiction— or perhaps I don't know enough about it to make it hard—and my young producer seems to like what I'm doing. The main task is to simplify, and cut the number of chapters to about half, while keeping the feeling of the book so far as I can. It's a bit like translating, not into one's own language—The season has been brightened for me, for us, by M's finishing her new detective novel *Ask for Me Tomorrow*, and getting it in to Dorothy Olding in New York this past week, with a favorable response coming right back. M., who never does anything by halves (including her six-year retirement), is now at work on her second book this year! It's going to center in the Coral Casino, she says.[4]

We're both so pleased and happy that you will come back to Santa Barbara next summer. Our time together last summer wasn't nearly long enough, and I speak not only for us but for everyone I know. (Don't worry about your visit interfering with work—I won't be working, and M. gets up early and finishes her stint in the morning.) Don't worry, either, about preparing a formal statement for the conference unless you want to. Your presence alone will give it a tremendous lift as it did last year. This is really fine news.

So is your liking *The Woman in White* so well.[5] I think it's the class of the field, showing all of us right at the start what a suspense novel could become. No, I never knew Agatha Christie except through her books. I think she wrote well, don't you? People I know who have known her have nothing but praise for her courtesy and goodwill. She was even modest. Her early life, by the way, was marked by what was for her a tragedy. Her first husband left her for another woman, and she was so hard hit that she was unconscious for a week. Then she came to and (not long after, as I remember) began to write her detective stories.[6]— You know, one nice thing about us detective-story writers is that there are so many different kinds of us, and we don't envy each other, though we compete.

We were both sorry to hear about the cold spell which killed some of your birds. Our current problem is the opposite, an unseasonably warm winter made worse by a total lack of rain this season. In spite of that our Xmas bird count was 202, which last year was the number that came in first, but not for us. Our nearest competitor this year at 201 was the Point Reyes bird sanctuary above San Francisco. All this is assuming that none of our birds are disallowed.

Everyone here is well, including Jim and his dad who are part-time (weekend) residents these happy days. Jim will be a teenager in two months and acts it (this is a compliment—I can't fault him). Still reading books on World War II on which he is becoming an expert: I've ordered him a book on King Tut in the hope it'll change his track.

Love,
Ken

Eudora Welty to Kenneth Millar, February 23, 1976

Dear Ken,

It's been so long since I wrote, I feel, and I just must send a line however brief to say I'll send a better one soon. It's just work, the reason. But I've thought of you with such a good feeling because your last several letters sound so happy and full of good spirits. I'm so glad.

And though I haven't written you, I've read you—Mr. Green sent me the galleys of your new book [*The Blue Hammer*], which was so kind. I read it with admiration as I always read your work, but this time of a special kind, because I was watching how you were allowing yourself a little freer rein, more ease of the old strictness but still keeping the tension, and nobody knows better than you do how much that matters in plot and all its branchings—and more scope, and more length. I applauded it all. It was an interesting subject and I thought you made the painting story and family story and murder story astonishingly believable in their multiple connect-ings and connections—I said astonishingly not because I was astonished at your doing that, but meaning the result of it on the reader. It must have been hard using a painting, though—an object, not a live human being—as the original object of search. Of course it didn't stay not a human for long. I've read the book twice and know the scene I think most powerful—it's when Gerard Johnson shouts in the street. It's marvelous.

When I was in Washington the other week at one of those meetings I wished very strongly for you one night—we were taken to the Hirschorn [Hirshhorn] Museum and the director took us backstage to the working parts, to the "storage room." Temperature control, white, antiseptic, bare. He reached down and pulled a handle out of a rank of them in the wall and out came a long drawer. You know what I thought of. And rising from it was a 10- or 12-foot high screen on which paintings were hung, on both sides. The work of a painter's life was hung up there in a drawer in a cold room and could be rolled out for inspection and rolled back. At the time, I hadn't read your novel, but I thought I was looking at an image of it from what you'd told me was its first title, Portrait of the Artist as a Dead Man.

Is the film treatment going well in the rewrite, or have you finished it? I hope it pleases you, and I hope to see it.

It's lovely here now—daffodils in flower, crabapple tree too, pear tree too, and the camellias still heavily blooming. Birds singing with all their might. About a million (I counted as many as 24) robins are at present abiding in my yard. A little kinglet is just now flitting through the still bare oak tree outside my window, feeding on something no doubt an elixir to him but invisible to the human eye.

I've been working on a story ["The Shadow Club"], begun some time ago and interrupted—it's going all right, well, I think, but is maybe going to turn into something longer. I too have a Mildred, also a Ralph, and a Gerard (as a last name), and I too have a greenhouse, in which the major critical event took place and in the past, though it wasn't a murder exactly. A sort of murder. This won't surprise you.

Did you know that the Chairman of the literary panel of the Endowment for the Arts is mailing out copies of the South Dakota Review, the issue on Place, which carries your article? You sent me a sentence or two from it, which I loved, and I was so glad the whole piece came to me. And to the young writers to whom the issue was being mailed. (I got it because of being on the Council.)

I work so hard (I don't stop till end of the day usually) that I'm absentminded and if I have to go out on errands forget to shift gears. A good thing I don't operate on your Freeway, in second gear—I can just imagine how I'd get whanged from behind, probably by Margaret Millar! Tell her how glad I am about her two, repeat TWO, new books. And I'm glad about yours.

With love,
Eudora

Kenneth Millar to Eudora Welty, [Early March 1976]

Dear Eudora:

You sat down to write me a note and ended up sending me a full beautiful letter which I only wish I could match. But then I don't have to. The sympathetic vibrations of your letter spoke for me as well as to me. It's not a new thing but I still marvel at your ability to work all day on your own story—and I gather you are working wonderfully hard—then take up mine into your thought as if it were your own. You are a profoundly generous woman.

And I'm so glad you liked the *shouting*, and felt for Gerard. He is not I, but he is not unlike me in putting together a working life out of unlikely components. I started drawing when I was three. A number of my first cousins are artists. My maternal Uncle Stanley managed to combine schizophrenia and painting and had a one-man show in Mexico City when he was over seventy. But I really haven't done Stanley's story justice in anything I've written so far. One beauty of this mystery-series method is that you are permitted to go over and over the same material until you get it right, or even wrong. I am beginning to hope, to *have* to hope, that this may be a way to write a novel, on the curve of its possible manifestations. Laurel, for example, whoever she is, keeps cropping up. I think she may be, partly, a combination of my excellent Aunt Laura who died at 95 last year, and of the laurel that we all seek. Well, your letter was my laurel, all I need, more than I deserve.

I have another reason to feel relieved. Having completed the treatment (first draft) of the *Instant Enemy* and been asked to write the second draft i.e. first-draft screenplay, *and* the final-draft screenplay, I saw clearly that it was not for me and bowed out. I don't know whether my treatment will turn eventually into a movie, let alone a good movie—a good screenplay is one out of which a successful movie *has* been made—but I don't really care. I'm out. It doesn't suit me to work with anybody else at all. And money should not be too easily earned. I sound like a tyro just learning the rules. Well, I am. This was my first movie effort. I'll show it to you sometime if you wish, but not right now. It *isn't The Instant Enemy*; there simply wasn't room in a movie for the long curve on which the book depended; and it was necessary to make the detective more central to the story, make it in part *his* story.—In the course of my researches I did have a chance to read a brilliant script—KLUTE—which was turned into a very good movie with Jane Fonda, but not as good as the original script. I hope the reverse for mine.

Nona Balakian, as secretary of the book reviewers' association [National Book Critics Circle], has invited me to join a panel on reviewing in New York April 20. I'm glad to be asked, and intend to go; have done enough writing for the immediate present. I'm glad you're at work, dear Eudora, and envy your great surges of creation. May they be oceanic, like your generosity. But don't work *too* hard! The Two-Book Kid sends her love along with mine. Ever, Ken

Eudora Welty to Kenneth Millar, [April 15, 1976]

Dear Ken,

I'm glad I'll be seeing you before too long now—I hope?—so as to catch up in talk, because I've been such a bad correspondent all spring. Thank you for your fine letter, with all it told me about, and around, Gerard. (I just read in something Robert Penn Warren wrote, "A man doesn't find himself, he creates himself.") And about deciding not to write another line of a screenplay for the movie of The Instant Enemy—which sounds so absolutely wise and utterly reasonable a decision. I agree with your attitude and also rejected an offer to me for the same reason, since last I wrote you. I can't work with anybody else at any stage of the doing, so even if I wanted to try a screenplay I couldn't. What I hope is the results of your first draft will show up in the end enough to make the difference—but how *could* it be The Instant Enemy, which is a novel. Getting out of it must be a lovely send-off to you starting on a trip to NY—have a fine time there. Nona and many others will be made happy by your coming.

I've been working too hard, I think, and fighting off distractions too hard, because I'm tired and realize the work is showing it. I began dreaming in manuscript form, revising, and writing in the margins as I went—ruining the dream. Yesterday I took off and went to hear some music—the Mozart Requiem being sung in a church—wanting not only the music but the washing away of words, but they handed out the texts to us and I couldn't take my eyes off it—in Latin, so I had to work on it besides. The marvelous hour and a half of the music won over everything though, of course. It's beautiful here now, and it's beautiful there always—I look forward to filling up my eyes with it—Maybe what I need is a good long breath of that Pacific Ocean air—

This isn't to say I've done nothing but write—there was a weekend in Oxford, and there were visitors coming through Jackson—my dear friend Robert Penn Warren among them—And I'm happy writing, as you are too—I just don't want to ruin anything—

Maybe your book will come out while you're in New York? All my very best to it—Also to our mutual friends. Ken, I will write better soon—My love for now to you & Margaret.

Eudora

Kenneth Millar, New York City, to Eudora Welty, [Late April 1976]. Written on Algonquin Hotel stationery.

Dear Eudora:

Margaret told me on the phone the happy news that you will be coming again to Santa Barbara this summer. I'm so glad, and it seems appropriate that I should be telling you so on Algonquin stationery. I've been here in New York ostensibly to do a couple of chores at Columbia—still another connection with you, and indeed I met your friend the poet Smith there the other day—but also to promote my new book which I'll be sending you soon. At present I'm having a marathon interview (third day, and three or four to go) with a rock music critic named Paul Nelson who writes for *Rolling Stone*. He wears dark glasses and never takes off his flat cloth cap even in a dining room but seems remarkably bright and comes from a place in Minnesota just over the line from Winnipeg. I love these temporal and geographical reverberations.

SEE YOU! MUCH LOVE, AS EVER, Ken

Though Ken was in New York promoting his new book, Eudora had no new book to promote. She worked hard at writing but brought no fiction to a conclusion. The 1973 death of Diarmuid Russell, her most trusted advisor, surely contributed to the difficulty she found in "hewing to the line" of a story.[7] Perhaps Diarmuid's advice over a thirty-two year span had come to seem indispensable. And in 1976 Eudora faced the prospect of writing without the counsel of the two editors upon whom she most relied.

Eudora Welty to Kenneth Millar, May 5, 1976

Dear Ken,

I was delighted to get your letter from the Algonquin, and it sounded to me as if you were having a very busy good time. Fill me in with more of the details when I see you. Maybe you can connect up with Julian Symonds if he's still in that part of the world? Did you get to catch your friend Don Freeman's show, down in the Village? (I'd love to have seen it too.) Nona remarked in a note to me what an asset to her panel you were, "saying more in his quiet way than others who made more noise."[8] I wish I could've been in the critics' audience. And you went to the Plaza. Did the Rolling Stone man roll everywhere you went, even into (who knows?) the fountain at the Plaza and still with his cloth cap on? I hope the interview comes out while I'm in NY, where indeed I'll be this time next week. I've found myself at the point where my Random House editor, Albert Erskine, & my New Yorker editor, Bill Maxwell, are both now retiring (Bill's already done it, & gone to Egypt & back with his wife to celebrate it). These are both old and dear friends, and we need to talk a lot over—I'm taking some work too but may not get to it—anyway, shall be back in Jax on the 20th, and the next thing I know I'll be flying to Santa Barbara—& on the right plane, too. I'm so glad you and Margaret think it won't interrupt work, I hope this is still so. You mustn't "do" for me, just let's be together the easiest way when we can. Can we ride some more to the same places? I can see them when I try, in my mind.

I look forward so much to seeing your book—books?—& to read in the place they were written in, which really is a different experience, isn't it?—and of course to *seeing* you both & all of you—I have the date down as June 18–25, is that still right? Well, we'll find out more later— Oh it cheers me!

Reynolds will be here this weekend, when the literary panel of the Arts Endowment meets in Jackson. I'll attend their meetings, then jump on a plane at an hour it would give you pain to hear, to go to NY by way of Chapel Hill—N.C.[9] I'll be seeing an old Virginia cousin (she is also Bob Woodward's aunt!) of my mother's, now in her 80's, & her journalist daughter—darling people, and it's keeping in touch as my mother would & always did—her family's way and I feel it's mine—

I wrote you an earlier letter but I guess it missed you before you went East. Forgive what a bad writer I've been—and thank you for writing to me. Love, to you both, & see you soon—

Eudora

Kenneth Millar to Eudora Welty, May 18, 1976

Dear Eudora:

I didn't get to do all the things I wanted to do in the East—see Julian Symons on New England soil, for example: but I did see a lot of people, more than I needed really, like a hermit drunk on company. I especially enjoyed coming to know Nona better. It was she who set the ball rolling that tilted the map and slid me eastward, and it is she whose image, now that I am home, stays clearest and warmest in my mind. Such a steady light burns in her. I owe my knowledge of her to you.— For once I stayed in New York long enough to get some sense of what it is to live there (though I couldn't, not any more) and I covered several hundred blocks on foot. But not one of my walks contained so much laughter (or, fortunately, such melodrama) as our Broadway walk that first night. I *did* get down to Freeman's show and took great satisfaction in it—something that he had been hoping for all his life and that I had wished for him. Well, his life is rounding out. While I was in New York Don was in Budapest and Zurich, where his son is studying at the Jung institute, and, I believe, painting, too. Which leads me to the fact that M. and I are planning to go to Zurich on our own business in the Fall— Diogenes Verlag are reprinting some of our books—and also to England, where the *new* books will be coming out.

I must hasten to explain that the *Rolling Stone* interview, in spite of the six or seven parts of days I spent with the putative writer of it, is still just words in the air. He plans to come out here to Santa Barbara and doubtless will, before he sets pen to paper. I don't mind. He's a gentle soul and can tell me things about music, which is his main subject. He went to St. Olaf's College in Minnesota, wears a cap most of the time, and has decorated his rather nice bachelor apartment with large movie posters and tends to work at night, sometimes all night. St. Olaf's is just a hop skip and slide across the border from Winnipeg where I went to boarding school. On this vast continent, that just about constitutes an introduction, even a shared background. Perhaps between the two of us we can understand the compulsions of popular art a little better.

My current contribution to pop art shows signs of doing well e.g. a strong favorable review (except that it refers to the slow start, which I wasn't able to get rid of no matter how I tried) in *PW*, and indications that the publisher will give it a good try. They gave me a nice party at the St. Regis on my last night, so nice that I didn't even feel self-conscious, and Alfred and Helen came, as at that other party in their apt., but you didn't. Well, I'll be seeing you here in Santa Barbara in a month, and that is better. I'm looking forward keenly to your coming, and so are Margaret and your other friends here. Yes, the conference starts on June 18—I have it well-marked on my calendar.

Love,
Ken

Eudora Welty, New York City, to Kenneth Millar, [May 20, 1976]. Written on postcard of Algonquin Hotel and mailed in a letterhead Algonquin envelope.

Dear Ken,

Hello from my own slot in the A. It's a good visit—I was up at Rosie Russell's in the country Sunday night[10]—Saw Joan—Walter—Nona—we all spoke of you, and in N.Y.C. they'd seen you, of course—

Had an unexpected pleasure in meeting Dick Francis & his wife when Joan K. asked me to join them for a drink.[11] You probably know him—Such a merry face—I liked them both—

I'll be home on the 20th—and then before very long, I'll be in Santa Barbara & seeing you & Margaret, as I hope—a good & glad sight.

Love,
Eudora

Eudora Welty to Kenneth Millar, Sunday [May 30, 1976]

Dear Ken,

Meet my new typewriter, which I went out and bought on my birthday, to talk back to it maybe. [Eudora has drawn an arrow from "it" to "birthday."] The anticlimax was they had to back-order it because today nobody wants a manual typewriter. But here it is now, on my table, ready when I am.

But what it's to tell you is I'll be on the plane on June 18, coming in on United flight 984 that gets in at 1:55 PM. That sounds in the middle of lunch. If you'd like to meet me, could you do it easily? Anyway, I'll surely see you soon! This is lovely to look forward to—I want to hear all the new news of you and Margaret, and more of what you wrote me, which promises all kinds of good and rewarding things. And more about your stay in New York. I'm glad you had that visit, long enough to let you range out and make your place in it as you liked, and relax and enjoy a world that was glad to see you and would be happy to see you more—you know this. I found your traces here and there and wish we might have coincided, but I don't complain because of Santa Barbara ahead. I continue being amazed—

Thank you for your letter, which came just after I'd got home. There's a lot I must do before I come so I'll begin on the chores. It's wonderful here now—that is, when it's not threatening. One night 7 funnels were travelling overhead above Jackson, but forebore to touch down. Next night the trees were alive with the flashes of the first lightning bugs and everything smelled of mimosa and honeysuckle—it's like the little girl with the curl in the middle of her forehead, when our weather's good it's very very good, and when it is bad it wants to take the roof off.

I'll write Barnaby Conrad presently but wanted to send this on. Is there anything you or Margaret would like me to bring you? I hope everything's going the very best way with you.

See you soon!

Love,
Eudora

Kenneth Millar to Eudora Welty, June 3, 1976

Dear Eudora:

Your brand-new typewriter delivered crisp and clear the message that you will be here on June 18, and I'll be happily waiting for you at the airport. I think you do well to exchange your native funnels for our local problems, even if they do include oil derricks. (Which for some reason reminds me of: "Milton had his daughters; I have my Dictaphone" [Wyndham Lewis].) Current horrors include a plan to put multi-storied commercial buildings on the Santa Barbara wharf. But I somehow doubt that it will ever come about. In spite of all the assaults on her integrity, Santa Barbara remains essentially unspoiled, I think; and the preservers keep increasing in numbers.

I did enjoy New York, but not in the easy way that I think you do. However, the trip was enough of a success to persuade me to have another go at England and Switzerland—London first for the publication of *Hammer* on September 17, I think, and then to Zurich which we've never seen: Our German publishers are there; so is Roy Freeman, Don's son, studying at the Jung institute. Mainly we hope to get out into the English countryside, and up into the Swiss mountains. Our earlier attempt was abortive, partly because we made the error of flying direct from here to Heathrow. *This* trip, we'll break enroute in Canada.

Have you ever read any of John Franklin Bardin's (BARDIN) three mystery novels?[12] Julian Symons sent them and I'm reading them now. A little nutty but highly original—not so very different from M's earlier psychological thrillers. Speaking of which, I've already started to think about a new book which I hope to get some more Canada into—the last place I'll discover, no doubt.

It will be such a pleasure to see you again here and soon. I can't think of anything you should bring except your dear self, and a list of *drives.*

Love,

Ken

Eudora Welty to Kenneth Millar, June 9, [1976]

Dear Ken,

How glad I was to get your letter and to know you'll be there to meet me, feeling as I do that the first face I see I would so like to be yours. So, a week from Friday!

The Times Book Review just came with its piece on *The Blue Hammer*—had you seen it before now?[13] I was delighted that it led off as the Number 1 novel under review this issue, right where it ought to be, and that it got a lot of space, and that it yielded some satisfactory quotes, such as "the best work Macdonald has done in a number of years." It could have been a little more knowledgeable and discerning, but it made good and strong points and was certainly roundly in favor. He's properly calling the novel brilliant, but I resented both for you and for your readers his feeling free to give away a key part of your plot. And in doing so calling it a "flaw" which is quite the opposite to what it is. I also resented the gratuitous and unreasonable slap at *Sleeping Beauty*. (My book!) But anyway, he knew he had hold of a very good Macdonald indeed here, and I hope it's only the first review of a long line of very shining ones. (The Library Journal and PW ones I would like to see and am glad they pleased you. I thought the novel's start was paced and set forth in keeping with the larger structure it would be holding up this time.)

It will be lovely to see you. Then I can listen and ride and see and breathe, and while it'll be nice to hear about the European trip you and Margaret have ahead, this is the nicest thing I can think of: seeing again in the time that's almost here that beautiful place where you are right now.

Love,
Eudora

At the 1976 Santa Barbara Writers Conference, Eudora delivered a reading of "Where Is the Voice Coming From?" a story written in 1963 in horrified response to the assassination of Jackson civil rights leader Medgar Evers. "This kind of thing is not easy for me," she later wrote to Margaret, "and the support of you and Ken and Jim all there in the audience made the difference."[14] Gratitude not withstanding, Eudora's 1976 visit to Santa Barbara proved to be full of the same tension that had characterized the afternoon of her 1975 departure. During Eudora's second stay, Ken regularly took her to the Millars' home, which Maggie considered "a special island away from society" where guests were not encouraged. "She was nice to me, when she saw me there," Welty later told Ken's biographer. "On the other hand when she got mad, there wasn't anywhere to go. It could be pretty explosive; [. . .] And every time, Ken would just back off, impervious in a way, and make whatever change it was she wanted. Well, what else could you do?[. . .]

"For no reason at all once she said to me, 'When Ken is away, of course I open your letters to him, but only to see if there's anything in them he needs to be informed about.' I don't know why she told me that, but—I don't think she'd ever have found anything in any of them to give her pause."[15]

When Eudora wrote to thank Ken for the Santa Barbara visit, she made no mention of these tensions.

Eudora Welty to Kenneth Millar, July 2, 1976

Dear Ken,

I thought I had much of it by heart, but it was being there, not just remembering, that was marvelous all over again. It was so lovely to be riding in the mountains and along the sea, walking in the town, and all. When I think back, I see that last year and this year came to something more than the two visits added together. Did you ever look through that device called a stereopticon? You see two pictures of the same place as one, and what appears new through the combination is depth and perspective and rounding out—it brings you nearer. Anyway, I felt I had been brought nearer to where your life is, Ken. Thank you for doing so many thoughtful and generous things for me—meeting me, & seeing me off, & all in between. It was fine to see Margaret and Jim so thriving—Jim in spite of that painful spill from the skateboard, and he did look all well again when he did me the honor of coming to say goodbye at the airport. How did he like his first plane ride? I'm happy for Margaret about her new books in particular—From now on all is bound to go easier, with the new start once behind—as indeed the second new book is already evidence for. I hope for both of you that the beautifully planned trip to Zurich & the English countryside will be a celebrating one.

I do thank you for sharing Herb Harker's manuscript with me—&
for the trouble you took to mail it to me—It safely arrived. Herb must
feel good to know that all the time he'd been fortified and helped by
your criticism (I got to hear a sample of it—exemplary—in that session
at the Conference) has yielded the piece of work that can make him
proud and you too. The 200 pages I've read so far showed an originality
and a confidence, if that's the word, that really won me. I'll finish it &
return to him—I have his address.

I did so especially enjoy that impromptu visit to the Eastons, that
good afternoon—the good talk—It smelled so good, too, didn't it,
arriving just after all the plants had been watered? And I was glad you
took me to meet Ralph Sipper and see his fine bookshop & admirable
collection and hear about his plans—and I like where it is.

I went back to The Zebra Striped Hearse to find the beach house
again that you showed me. Of course I kept on reading—I do think it's
one of your best, do you agree? I remembered as I came to them things
that had struck me with such pleasure before in the writing, from the
careful way your eye had looked at whatever you showed us—the baby
asleep (and I guess now this was Jimmy?)—and the hawk—which was
used to extraordinary effect in that scene, but was a living wild creature
first. People every one are seen carefully because with care, and however the characters fulfill their parts in your complicated plot, they are
understood, and treated, as human lives. It's not the only way your work
is of a different order from Chandler's but it's an important way. The
way of seeing, the point of view, the view of life, the vision, in every
writer, how can these things be separated? I should have said the *act* of
seeing. The action, really.

Mary Lou liked your pieces on Crime Writing so much, and they
were new to her—she was writing to you at once, she said. It was a fine
weekend. Mary Lou is well, though tired I think—you know this is the
tourist season there and she always has company and flings herself into
everything. My old friends Mary (your fan) and Aristide Mian (he's a
French sculptor) were back in their house there, and their daughter
Mickey was flying in from Geneva at the same time I was flying in

from Santa Barbara—so it was luck on top of luck that I could see them too.

And when I got to Santa Fe, I accidentally received a magnificent corroboration of my belief in the sight of the polar bear running under the plane—it was from the grandson of William James. You couldn't beat that! He was telling me about his son who is making documentary films up near the Pole—he's photographing wolves from a plane. So I told him about the polar bear and the commercial pilot and he said oh yes, it would have been easy, because there are no mountains, just flat snow, and no plane needs to fly higher than 1000 feet and can easily dip down if it wants. And he agreed: how could it be made up? So I pass the word back in all its lovely coincidence.

His ties to Santa Barbara belong to 1919, he said. He remembers Montecito as wild and sparsely settled. He has lived all over the world, was a painter. A few years ago he lost half the forefinger and all the middle finger of his right hand in an accident with a piece of farm machinery (he and his wife lived out in the country from Santa Fe). Now he has made himself a new life as a maker of violins. He put himself to learn this under masters and is working hard, still learning, deeply engrossed, and believes now he will be able to do it well. A whole new world has opened up, all kinds of music makers on the contemporary and popular scene have come into it. He said if he had not lost his fingers none of this would have happened, the learning of another whole art. I was seeing them for the second time, and all this has happened since the first time. —He has That Profile. There was a portrait he had made of his daughter on the wall—it was sensitive and full of feeling.

By now you may have been to meet another visitor at your airport, Mr. Symons. I was glad to know he is to head up Penguin, and delighted that he wanted to bring out Mr. Bardin and give him the chance at rediscovery while he's still living. (I wonder how difficult, as well, this could be for the subject of rediscovery?) Maybe Julian Symons might know something about Kenneth Hopkins [1914-1988] of, She Died Because . . ., and Dead Against My Principles, all going back to 18 or 20 years ago for Holt, Rinehart & Winston. I'm so glad you took

to him and apologise for having nothing better than a library book to
show you.

I'll pursue the Chandler biog. [by Frank MacShane] from here, and
will be interested to read the Dahlia film script.[16] When it turns up and
is easy, if you'll let me see a copy of the film script of your novel, I'd like
to see it, and get it straight back to you. And best wishes to the book on
your own work that Twayne is to bring out, as long as you've kept an
eye on it. The writer of the musical on my story "The Robber Bridegroom" now rehearsing in L.A. says 2 of the main characters have just
been combined into one—I guess this has to be expected? But these
two characters are Mike Fink and Little Harp—one a real legend and
the other a real-life villain. Now how will I ever get them back? And
who is that *one*?

As you can see, this was written at different times over a couple of
days, and it got too long before I knew it. It's the Fourth of July! & the
tall ships are moving up the River—Lord, so beautiful! I miss you and
send love—And love to Margaret, to whom I am writing too—

Yours,

Eudora

Eudora Welty to Kenneth Millar, July 28, 1976

Dear Ken,

You are all right and things go well there, I trust. Today I was thinking
how much you would like the Constable Exhibition Catalogue—I
remember your feeling for his work, which would probably increase,
like mine, with the sight of these sketches from his notebooks—repro-
duced by the scores—Pocket-sized, some of them—2 ⅝ by 3 ⅜!—and a
sketch that might be scribbled over by one of his children—London from
Hampstead, in a view from "our little drawing room"—& that would
include the dome of St. Paul's—Did you know that when the Houses of
Parliament were burning, both Turner & Constable were watching in the
crowd? I once saw, & you might have too, in the big Turner Exhibition,
his sketchbook of the Fire, one after the other, fast as fast, keeping up with

it—But Constable had brought his two little boys, so his hands would have both been held.[17] This Tate catalogue is wonderfully informative about his life & his family & his travels & letters & the contemporary scene—he was a very complex man with such volatile spirits, and such a need for his landscapes to be *populated*—as we can see—he was so lonesome & homesick in Wordsworth's Lake country, but he stuck it out. His only years of real serenity & stability were those in the lifetime of his wife. One of the things that struck home with me was that he painted Willy Lott's house (one he saw every day) simply all his life—and that Willy Lott was living in it when Constable was born & still living in it when Constable died—And the same ferryman turned up in many a painting, poling his way. Our subjects remain the same. The anecdote I like best is that in the Academy on varnishing day, a rival named Chantrey (indeed) told Constable his foreground was too cold, & right in front of Constable picked up a brush and put "a strong glazing of asphartum" all over that part of the picture, and Constable said, "There goes all my dew."[18]

It's really hot here now—I've been working on a story that I hoped would be good. I tried writing some things I'd been feeling for the last year into a new scene that I introduced into it but hard as I'd worked I knew it honestly didn't belong and so I've just taken it out. It's hard to keep things hewing to the line in a short story—or it proves so for me.

The paper this morning said that just prior to the big earthquake in China, all the dogs barked. Is this a known phenomenon?

I hope everything's fine there and everybody well. I have to fly to Washington Friday to an Arts Council meeting but will fly home again Sunday. When you have time, a letter would bring me cheer. Take care.

With much love to all,

Eudora

Kenneth Millar to Eudora Welty, August 1, 1976

Dear Eudora:

The world has been too much with me recently. But now it seems to be receding a bit and letting me live in the past, not my own but the timeless past which you reminded me of with your comments on Constable (and Turner). Your reminder was an act of wise friendship. I must be after all a Romantic writer, with piped-in English weather in my head, and it was no accident that I spent those years of my life on Coleridge, searching for the source of my fantasy, learning to identify my own with a general past.

These past few weeks have been occupied with a new form of that enterprise. A young man named Paul Nelson—have I mentioned him before?—has been sitting with me through the afternoons and trying to reconstruct with me a story of my life which will make sense to his editor at *Rolling Stone* and its readers. The best thing about it for me is the opportunity to learn a younger man in the same depth that he is learning me. Paul is a music critic by trade—a *rock* music critic—and he put me in touch with a couple of rock composers.[19] I find I like them and feel safe enough though a long way from home. (Home is Ellington.) Paul attended the U. of Minnesota, wears a cap at all times, and tinted glasses, and is a highly (as well as lowly) literate book collector.

Though I write about some of the complexities, the simplest things in general seem best to me. Swims in the ocean followed by a good lunch with friends or relatives, preferably both as today. Or Jim who today was the missing relative at lunch, Jim staggering in a few minutes ago at ten o'clock at night after a day spent a hundred miles away at a swimming meet at which he won no medals but improved his time in the hundred—now 71 seconds, which means more when you recall that Johnny Weissmuller's world record time a generation ago was just under a minute (now it's just under 50 seconds). Jim staggered in, drank a lot of milk, and went to bed happy, still wearing his swimming shorts. Happy as I am for and with Jim, I don't live through him at all so far as I can tell. To the extent that a boy should be at 13 he is on his own, and he has a father of his own, who loves him.

My life is going through a change which I am slow and unwilling to define because definition would tend to determine it. I am more at peace with the world but less with myself. I'd like to take a further step but perhaps have taken not enough previous ones. I am woefully ignorant but not sufficiently concerned about it to educate myself. Still I love to work and am waiting to be able to, in my fashion.

It was wonderful to see you here again. We love you, dear Eudora.

As ever,

Ken

Eudora Welty to Kenneth Millar, August 14, 1976

Dear Ken,

I was so glad to have a letter come from you—to tell the truth I had been feeling a little uneasy. When I was with you I had had the sense of that not-being-at-peace you speak of—and hadn't had the wits or the right trust in my instincts to let you know my awareness if it would have made a difference. In some ways I am a very shy person—and I revere the privacies—But reading your letter, so sweet and kind as ever, I feel the uneasiness still and I hope whatever you do think now of doing, taking a fresh turn, will be good and restoring and go positively to make things the way they ought to be for you—If this hope sounds vague, it is really strong and even precise. You must use my wishes whenever they fit and as you will—but this may make you smile: I dreamed I was sending you the dream I was dreaming (not a letter dream, the dream itself) and that as I dreamed it you got it. Part of the dream. When I woke up I felt happy—I couldn't remember my dream because it was wholly gone from me and you knew everything.

It's been terribly hot, with violent electrical storms in the afternoons—I have signed myself up for some jobs, the kind I have been declining to do for the past 8 or 10 years, because I find I have to put a new roof on the house & other such like, and need a good way (surer than my fiction) to pay for it, so I decided to take the next lecture offers that came along—I'll be writing lectures & going to give them or do other stints at Cornell & Smith & Denison U. & Agnes Scott—because if you possibly remember the roof on the long slope, of my house, I have an acre of shingles! I like the subjects I'm doing, the greatest of which is Chekhov. Barney Conrad asked me if I might do a workshop for him next summer, but I watched Herb Harker do his for a week and I know I have not got the stamina. (And will have used up what little I have in "panel" work already by the time he was ready to start.) I told Barney I could do as before if wanted, but can't do workshops. I also lack some other prerequisites Herb has got—He is fine. (I must go back over & write him on his good novel.) In addition to lecturing I of course hope to finish my real work of the stories I'm wrestling with—which I still do, through the thunderstorms.

It's good to be able to do this real work, isn't it? I hope yours, whatever it will be, goes well—whether it's about Canada or California or Xanadu or where—I send it love, and you—I am trusting in outcomes. As ever—Eudora

When you can, do let me hear again. Take care.

At last Ken revealed to Eudora what he'd not shared with any other correspondent: the lapses he'd been experiencing with his memory, a problem made all the more clear to him during his long talks with interviewer Paul Nelson.

Kenneth Millar to Eudora Welty, August 15, 1976

Dear Eudora:

I was rather depressed when I last wrote you, and indeed for some weeks before that, but now that I feel some relief I hasten to assure you that all is comparatively well here. I was suffering from a failure of the memory function which is probably within the normal limits at my age but which, because I had usually had a nearly perfect memory, scared and depressed me. I got a psychologist to give me a series of tests, got through with colors if not flying ones, and with a combination of luck and cunning persuaded myself to accept the change and did. The sharing of the pressure with a professional really helped, and so did my return to work, if you can call revising a screenplay work. I refer to the "Instant Enemy" screenplay, which is now in process of being passed around to directors. The first one who has seen it, Alan Pakula, was interested enough to come up and talk about it—very intelligently—and he has not yet made up his mind whether to do it or not. If he does, I'll revise it under his direction but in the meantime I'm going ahead by myself. It's so good to be able to work, isn't it?

We've had a pleasantly eventful summer, much of the action being supplied by Jim and his swimming-team-mates. It was sort of climaxed today when Jim's father (and therefore Jim) joined the Coral Casino as out-of-town members. They plan, as the summer ends, to spend a couple of weeks in canyon country—Grand, Oak Creek, etc. Our plans, as you know, are even more ambitious—London and Zurich. I'm looking forward to the change, and so is Margaret. We'll go by way of Canada and visit her father on the way. He lives near Toronto. I find as I grow older that more and more of my thinking and remembering recurs to Canada. It would be a pity not to put some of my strange early life on record, of course as fiction—I can never tell a straight story.

But I love to read one, and it seems to me that William Maxwell's *Ancestors* hews so close to the truth as memory and research can come. What a good book it is, so full of humane feeling and understanding. So many of us are remiss in our duty to our lares and penates. I know you are not remiss, either there or in other places. You give us all our due, and more than our due, in your generosity of mind; as I am reminded whenever I hear from someone we both know. Just tonight as I was talking to Barny Conrad on the phone he mentioned your generous praise of Herb Harker's conduct of his writing class. I'm so glad you feel as I do about Herb, who has come a long way and is going further yet.

The ocean has been violent this weekend. It overturned and destroyed the diving raft, but then after a time it grew reasonably quiet again. So have my unquiet spirits. I hope and trust my silence didn't alarm you. I prefer to mention problems when they are on their way to being understood or at least controlled. And, you know, my life has been fortunate, and so continues.

Love,
Ken

Eudora Welty to Kenneth Millar, August 18, [1976]

Dear Ken, this is letter 2—I'm glad you are feeling some relief—I hope by now *more*—but you've been in torment—I'm sorrier than I can tell you for what you must have been going through. Heroically. It's good that the psychologist helped by taking some of the pressure off— Of course I know that what the memory means to you of all people is what made this hurt most, and made it hardest on you to deal with. (That you showed no bitterness about this made me want to cry.) And you're dealing with it in every good good strong way you know, of course—

I hope you will not mind if I try to say the only thing about it I know enough to—it's from knowing *you*. You have had such a long, deep, searching, truth-seeking, truth-learning relationship with the function of memory, full of recognitions & discoveries & encounters with its mysteries (and maybe this is, in its course, another one) and you *solved* them—you *solved* them—You are so versed in them, its mysteries have aided and abetted you. And why not again? This is what I feel, that you are going to positively come out all right again *because* of the deep nature of memory and of you—And the strength in both—

I won't say any more now except, how good a journey I'm wishing you and Margaret—and soon now. The change, new scenes, sound full of refreshment to the spirits and what a beautiful time of year to be flying over the Alps, & walking in England—love to you both— Thank you for letting me know how you are. There is no friend for whose welfare, past, present, & future I care more—For whose dear life—Eudora

Kenneth Millar to Eudora Welty, [August 1976]

Dear Eudora:

I wouldn't have written you about my memory problem if I hadn't known that you would in any case notice the difference with words and concern. But I'm glad I did write you. Part of the problem is a sense of isolation (cause or result?)—a sense which simply evaporates when

I am in contact with you. Your letter, your letters, were so beautiful in their feeling and understanding—and your dream about dreaming a dream for me so supernaturally right—that I think there is no end to your loving intelligence, your intelligent love. I think the memory is not a separate faculty but something which the mind is meant to do, a variation in warmth which sustains a movement like the Gulf Stream's in its ocean. There is more warmth there now than there was, thanks to you, and less anxiety now that I have spoken not only to you but the psychologist who tested me and found me mentally normal in most respects, and my loss of memory within the normal range.

I'm not really grieving, you know, nor have I any intention of not working. In fact I have been working, though not yet on finished writing. I count my blessings, too. When my father was sixty he could neither talk nor work. But he could still write, a little, and did, in the manner of Robert Burns and Sir Walter Scott. His father came from Dumfries to Ontario and formed a small-town newspaper there, so that he was a writer, too. The paper still survives after more than a century.

I'm so glad you came to know Herb Harker well, and liked his book. I've never known a better man, or one with greater capacity for growth. As is true of all of us, I imagine, the source of his virtue is also the source of some of his writing problems. I mean Mormonism. But a good novel, such as I now believe him to be bringing off, will solve these and other problems, and also make him an intellectual leader in a Church which needs more of the life of the imagination.

I wish you good luck with your speaking or reading engagements. Don't worry about me, dear Eudora. My life, particularly in its second half, has been exceedingly fortunate on the whole. I've been allowed to do a full stint of work and am not finished with it yet. Your professionally intelligent concern, as accurate as a shadow, suffuses my mind with heat and light.

We're off to Europe via Canada on September 9—Canada because Margaret's father is still surviving there in his ninety-first year, but not in particularly good shape. From Canada to London, thence to Zurich. We have books coming out in both those cities this fall, and our trip will be partly a working one. We'll be back in under three weeks, which is as long as Margaret can survive outside Santa Barbara.

Jim's summer with us has been most pleasant for all of us. Yesterday the swimming, and his sailing lessons particularly, came to a head when he took a small sailboat out to sea in a wind, came back into the harbor, then turned around and headed out again. "So mean I."

Love,

Ken

Eudora Welty to Kenneth Millar, [September 2, 1976]

Dear Ken,

I'm glad you found you could write to me about it—it's so understandable that the sense of isolation would come with the memory problem and—cause or result—would have been the worst of it. Your letters both moved me so. I wanted to help—as I always would—and your beautiful letter made me feel today that I had—you'd put yourself in my place, even in your trouble, and knew *this* would comfort *me* too. It was a letter full of such giving—of belief and trust in the feeling out of which I'd written to you—you made me feel I had made something easier—The thing is that you do feel better now—

And of course you're working—How could you not be writing? The next book, when you come to that, is a good challenge, (I like one, don't you?) since it will follow the long and different and long-in-the-evolving *Blue Hammer*—And best wishes by the way to the British *Blue Hammer* and the German—And to Margaret's new one too—

What you said about the memory, that it is something the mind is moved to do, sustained by a variation in warmth of a Gulf Stream moving through the ocean of the mind, I felt to my fingertips must be a truth—It could only have been reached out of your troubles—but or maybe thus it is like a vision—I shouldn't say "like," I think it is a vision.

As you well know, and have shown, in the memory nothing is really lost—It's there, somewhere—And that's so in just the common memory—not yours, which is not in any way at all common. As time gives it its chance and your writing does what your writing can do, I believe your whole memory in all its phases will light up for you when you wish it, as bright & endless as that other stream, the Milky Way (we are in that too). But nearer than that, I am taking both your hands to tell you, never feel isolated any more—

I hope the trip is all you'd like it to be—I hope they get a rain in England before you come—For the sake of the birds too that you'll want to see—The best of good luck—The possibilities sound lovely— Just walking in London sounds lovely to me—

Your letter took a whole week to come after its postmark! But it came—Thank you—

& Love,
Eudora

I can hardly tell you how much your writing it meant to me.

Eudora Welty to Kenneth Millar, October 15, 1976

Dear Ken,

I'm home again from a work-play trip up East, and I'm wondering if you're home again from your much longer one—I hope it all went as planned and you had a fine time and the good refreshment of a change.

My trip was to two colleges—Smith and Bryn Mawr—where I'd worked before, and so it was being among friends—and the countryside was so beautiful! I love seasons—and in New England, in October, you're conscious at all times of the season's happening, can smell it, in the air, and walking through the leaves, and see it in the light. In between the 2 visits, I spent a few days at the Algonquin. The musical made from my story "The Robber Bridegroom" was finally, after 3 years in the workshop, opening on Broadway, and I wanted to see it.[20] A high-spirited, young, energetic affair, moving with great speed—lots of music—I liked the young people a lot. There'd been a change from my book, by necessity—it's now sort of Blue Grass and hoe-down. But it has its own existence as it is—The leading man, Barry Bostwick, had a rope to break with him in rehearsal, just before the play was to open, pitching him 12 feet to the floor—The poor man broke his arm in two places—But he went on, with his arm in a big leather sling that managed to look like part of his robber disguise.

My sister-in-law Mittie came up for it—wasn't that sweet of her? Reynolds came, too, on his way to Oregon—but couldn't stay for the show when it got postponed after the accident—He was in his usual high spirits—Nona was, too, she was at the show. Rosie Russell was with me, so was William Jay Smith, he & his wife, down from Vermont to see it. So I had people to clap. Here's the Times review, if you'd like to see it—I cut it out for you.

The other clipping, about more amazing things—the Monarch butterflies & where they go—the Maxwells gave me & I thought you would like it. I'm so glad you like his *Ancestors*.

I had a nice letter from your friend Ralph Sipper, with a review he'd written of *The Blue Hammer*, which I was glad to see and thought sensitive and good—He's been so nice and very quick about finding some books for me.

I did a review of Virginia Woolf's Letters, Volume II, for the *Times*.[21] And turned in my collection of non-fiction to Random House—and so *now*, I hope & trust, I can work on *stories*. Only I have to go to Ohio first & earn a little more time by a lecture.

This is all my news—

I so hope all things go well with you and all belonging to you— They *must*.

Love,
Eudora

Kenneth Millar to Eudora Welty, October 17, 1976

Dear Eudora:

I got back from Europe over two weeks ago, and it's time I gave you some account of my trip and of myself. One thing seems evident, and that is that I've made some recovery from the tiredness that has dogged me for quite a few months; which is just as well, because I'm slated to do a revision of the *Instant Enemy* script in the next couple of months. The first producer-writer who saw the earlier version, Alan Pakula, decided to make the movie, whether as producer or director he has not yet decided. As you can see, I'm not exactly carried away by the prospect of movie work but I'd like to write one movie and see it made, and this may well be it. Fortunately I feel myself beginning to stir in other directions, too, for instance the direction of Winnipeg in 1929, where and when I think I became aware of evil in the world. But it begins to appear, even to me, that these lines have some of the flaccid self-centeredness of someone who is recovering from an illness, or an uncertainty, and I had better change the subject, or come to it.

The trip to Europe was a good idea, and on the whole it sits well in my memory. But the first week overseas, the week in London, started with a disaster—not my disaster exactly, but partly mine. My dear friend Julian Symons' twenty-year-old daughter, who had been seriously ill for much of the preceding year, committed suicide the day before I arrived in London and for reasons that you will understand it set me back on my heels. Since Julian was the one person in London I really wanted to see, and he wasn't really seeable, I spent most of the week by myself walking the London streets and trying to come to terms with Julian's loss and the memory of Linda's death seven years ago. Perhaps one never does come to terms with these matters. But as I walked the London streets I kept remembering a walk I had taken the previous week through the streets of Kitchener, Ontario, where Margaret was born and Linda spent her first two years, and where the past rose around me not threateningly but lending some support, as water supports a swimmer. I spent most of a sunny day walking those old familiar streets, to the hospital where my father spent much of his last years, to the high school where I was a student and then a teacher, to the old stone rooming house where I spent a happy week or so in my seventh year with my father. There and then, and later in London (where I had spent the best month of my twentieth year) the difficult past sustained the difficult present and I even found a name for both when I walked down the short ugly red-brick street which was and is named Strange Street—this in Kitchener.

From London I went to Zurich and didn't much like it at first. The people I'd come to see were, most of them, at the Frankfurt Book Fair. For once in my life I did something unexpected and took the surprisingly short flight from Zurich to Venice. I'd never been in Italy, let alone in Venice, and I found the place exhilarating, to put it mildly. Back in Zurich, I found my German publisher Daniel Keel of Diogenes a man of wit and learning and dedication, surrounded by young people like himself and by some older people of the same sort—notably Ruth Liepman our German agent. She lives with her office staff, young people some of whom are married to each other, in a large oldish mountainside house which also serves as their offices, and do their business through a nearby branch post office, though they don't *live* there.[22] From Zurich I went to Amsterdam, where my room overlooked a canal, and so home after a three-week absence, my longest in many years.

I think on the whole I did well to go: the world is realer and larger than it was. But Margaret did well to stay.[23] Travel gives her no pleasure, except for the kind that Thoreau did in Concord. At the present time she has a touch of flu which does not, however, interfere with her pleasure in the reception her new book is being given (her first book in six years.)—I have more to tell you but have rambled on enough for tonight. We trust all is well with you. Love, as ever, Ken

P.S.—Your letter, somewhat cheerfuller than mine but I'm getting cheerfuller by the minute, especially since your letter came—your letter, as has happened before, crossed mine in the mails or would have if I'd mailed mine yesterday when I wrote it. That's fine news about "Bridegroom," and an excellent notice from Clive Barnes. It must give you great satisfaction not only on your own behalf but for all the good people who put the play on. It must be thrilling to have worked for and with such a fine group of people.

Margaret, who sends her love and congratulations with mine, has herself recently had kind words from the *N.Y. Times*—from Anatole Broyard who the other day gave her new book one of his very rare rave reviews. I enclose a copy. And a souvenir of the Tate.[24] K.

Eudora Welty to Kenneth Millar, [November 3, 1976]

Dear Ken,

I was so glad to hear from you after you got back—First, I'm so glad you went, for the refreshment and rest that a change can bring. But that was a hard thing to happen, when you arrived in London to the news about Julian Symons's young daughter. And not to have been able to give or take comfort, there in the same place with your dear friend. I'd imagined you walking in the London streets, but in the pleasure of being back there, not from grief. I hope the rest of the journey brought something else, when it opened out with the sight of Venice—and a new sea for you—What a wonderful idea, to go there.

What I think of when I think of Venice is the sea—washed stones in the floor of San Marco, the real and actual belonging-in-one of the city & the sea. And the light there. Also the feeling that the night & its moving lights there give you. I was there in a summer season, but it must have been the same feeling of being surrounded with the story—history—fantasy—dream—maze—of the place, while it's real all the time, carrying on in a big Byzantine racket—Was there a smell of roasting chestnuts, among the others? I wonder if you got on a boat and rode out to sea & to Torcello? A bell older than Venice rings there. That big sheet of gold mosaic on the wall of the old bare country church.[25]

What was it like for you?

It was fine to see the excellent review of Margaret's new book, and to know the rest of the reviews have been just as glowing. It must have made her feel very good indeed and you too. Broyard as we know is an unmitigated rat but that doesn't keep his review, in that slot, in that paper, from doing a lot of good, or of course keep the review from being *right*, and it sounds very right. I'll be reading the book for myself soon. Congratulations to Margaret—

Thanks for your good wishes about my musical—though I had nothing to do with its writing, it just took off from my book as it liked, which was what it should have done. I think you have much fortitude

doing the revisions of the film script of your *Instant Enemy* for them—
But I hope it's interesting enough to reward you for it. I too think
writing a movie would be much worth doing—what seems so difficult
to me is writing a movie of something you wrote in the beginning as a
story on paper. Good luck on it—On everything—

I'm just back from Ohio.[26] It was 20° there & snowing—But in that
pleasant small college town (Granville) the trees were still bright with
fall colors—maples mostly—and inside the house, fires were burning,
and after a long hard day's work with classes etc., there was that fire to
sit around in small pleasant company (I'd worked there 3 times before)
including a young Sheltie pup named Bonny, who thought the fire was
her enemy & ours, and having a drink (the humans) & talking about
Fats Waller. Now I can get back to writing a story—

I am so happy to have one of Constable's Dedham Mills—Thank
you for thinking of how I love him in the Tate—I put it on my mantle.

Love,
Eudora

Eudora Welty, Washington, DC, to Kenneth Millar, November 18, [1976]

Dear Ken,

I think of you as writing hard on your film treatment. I hope
revising it goes smoothly, and that everything else does too.

A glowing review Margaret's new book got in the New Yorker!
Leading off in the Sunday Times, too—So satisfying on all sides—

This is in Washington—I'm here for the Arts Council meeting, and
so is Reynolds—We both got in this afternoon (before work starts
tomorrow), and tonight we're going to dinner with John & Catherine
Prince in their house in Georgetown—like a little reunion of that May
evening in Jackson, and I wish you could be here.

I've been working hard myself. A long story that's tantalized me is
slowly finding its shape, I believe—and my hope is that when I get back
home (Sunday night) I can bring it off, then. It's a hard one, but the hard
parts are all new, so I very much want to solve them as well as I'm allowed.

The birds at home are full of energy, the cold bright days—The feeder I have hanging in a crabapple tree is innocent of all seeds by the end of the day. Many winter transients & visitors—And that long, high, living path of birds endlessly going to roost at sunset each evening.

There was a long shining jet track in the sky, like the bar the Blessed Damosel leans out from—[27]

My love to you,

Eudora

The long story that had "tantalized" Eudora was one she called "The Shadow Club." Begun a year earlier, it focuses upon two crimes but not on detection. Instead it deals with concealment. As a young girl, the middle-aged schoolteacher protagonist has been asked by her mother's lover to conceal the murder-suicide of her parents. And now as the victim of rape, she chooses again to conceal rather than report a crime. Then she learns from an elderly neighbor with dementia that her mother's lover was also very probably her father. The crimes, the past haunting the present, the present repeating the past—these concerns were not new to Eudora's fiction, but whether by confluence or influence, their appearance now linked her work to Ken's ever more strongly.

Kenneth Millar to Eudora Welty, November 25, 1976

Eudora:

What a lovely letter you wrote me the other day from Washington—the writing of a woman whose spirit seemed tuned and ready. I can't make quite the same claim but I'm gradually working myself back into shape, doing little writing jobs. The most fun has been revising (somewhat) the short talk I gave in Chicago in 1973 to the Popular Culture Assn—revising it for Dan Halpern's *Antaeus*—I was very glad to be asked.[28] The least fun was trying to write out for a nice but journalistically inexperienced lady professor from Indiana State who interviewed me early this year for *Writers' Digest* (which I haven't seen for years)—write out the reasons why I write detective fiction. The fact is I don't think I know why I write detective fiction, and that is the reason it's *detective* fiction. No doubt another reason is that I refused to be bettered, or worsened, by my education and chose not to rise very far away from my origins, just far enough to breathe. But you can't say things like that to *Writers' Digest*.

I envy your seeing Reynolds, whom I often think of, in such terms as that if there were princes in America he would naturally be one of them. I have been reading his latest book (*Surface of Earth*) with great interest and attention, and it seems to me profound in feeling and in detail, too. I wish I could write such a book. My father's life in all its strangeness, all his strangeness, all life's strangeness, deserves a book and it may not be too late for a *short* book. It takes a lifetime to learn to love what we have been hurt by.

Contrary to my expectation I am not yet working on the final version of the *Instant Enemy* screenplay, but am still waiting for the deal (director + producer) etc. to be consummated. My secret hope is that it never will be. I have scarcely as much desire to write screenplays as to become a chiropractor. So how did I get involved with this one? Well, I wrote a treatment and it interested a director whom I admire (Pakula) and I was drawn by a combination of faith, hope and vanity into the film web. But really not very far, I tell myself—six or seven weeks at most. And as for waiting, it's really rather refreshing to think about possible books and not have to start one.

We've had quite a lovely fall, warm and bright with one lifesaving rain of several inches. A new bird, a Harris's sparrow, came to one of our feeders the other day. Which reminds me that Margaret is in fine shape, the best in years, having at long last (*six* years) written another book and had it well received, as you noted, by the *New Yorker* etc. It's gone into a second printing and M. is writing a second book!

I'm looking forward to seeing in print the story you are working on—the process of which you so beautifully described or evoked, in your letter, in all its difficulty and necessity and newness, with the élan and strength to put together a new shape.

Love,

Ken

Eudora Welty to Kenneth Millar, November 29, 1976

Dear Ken,

Thank you for your letter—and I'm glad to know you're working again—Good wishes to all of these pieces—

I hate it that those hurts have come to you—You have so resolutely and honorably worked to learn and understand from them, and you have learned and understood, even come to love where most people couldn't—but I wish they could give you a little rest, release—you have earned much more than rest. We somehow do learn to write our stories out of us, however disguised and given other players who can move and act where possibly we can't—and all, but in the end, if the hurt still stays, that's wrong—It's been a good deal on my mind, but when your letter came today I wanted to ask you *now* if there is any way you know of that I could be any help? Of course you have written around and about it—your father's (I know no word—his doing)—and into it and out of it, while you yourself have made a whole life that is good and truly good, aware and *un*hurting and understanding of others, a shining way to have dealt with what was done to you—But it hasn't seemed to have been enough for *you*, to bring you real peace of mind. Would it be any use to you to write about this to me? Trying a new way if it came to you? You have written about it to me in letters, you know. The time I first thought of asking you this was when I read your letter about walking in Kitchener—that you wrote when you came back from your trip to London. The old stone rooming house where there was a happy week or so in your seventh year, with your father—I know you've thought and thought, so much and so long, about putting it down—and have worked it out in many circuitous ways. Maybe there are endless circuitous ways. I know I may be out of my depth. You will understand, though, what makes me try—I would try to be a reader of understanding and imagination and safety.

When we were little we were so very far away, but now we are growing old (not in feeling, I hope) but are close—perhaps both are reasons, when taken together, why you might some day try this, if the spirit moves you. It would help that we share a sense of continuity in life, and that there's a continuity that we have between us of caring and concern.

It's been terribly cold here—sleet, snow, and the thermometer down in the teens—I had enough birdfeed, though—I haven't been able to back my car out of the garage. Today is fair & bright & up to 24°—The poor camellias were showing color in their buds.

That earthquake—seaquake?—you had there didn't come near Santa Barbara, I hope—And I hope the rare Harris Sparrow does come near—nice & regular.

Love,
Eudora

Kenneth Millar to Eudora Welty, December 9, 1976

Dear Eudora:

I'm really not in bad shape and you mustn't worry about me. I believe I'm a little spoiled by, among other things, the ease with which I wrote the middle books. In any case I'm getting back into the work again and beginning to enjoy it; and trust in a year or so I'll have something to show you. Margaret is working hard and with great zest. The weather is cold and clear. The night is quiet except when my dogs move. Tomorrow I go to a lunch on the Riviera (S.B.) signalizing my sixty-first birthday. When do I grow up, dear Eudora?

Love, Ken

Kenneth Millar to Eudora Welty, December 20, 1976

Dear Eudora:

I've been reading over your recent letters and really should regret the tremor I caused in your strings, except that the sound it made was so beautiful. I am grateful for your love and caring. I wasn't in such bad shape as I may have seemed to be, and certainly am not now, with memory improving and urge to work returning. Also I think I've traced the cause of my malaise, or one of the causes, to that movie work I did early in the year, and then the long wait to finish it. Much to my relief, as I may have told you, the deal I was waiting on fell through and released me into my own life. I hereby vow never to get involved with movies again. It seems sinful to me, to let anyone interfere in any way with what I write, or to wait on anyone's approval. I don't mean editing; I mean a forced or even a borrowed vision. This has to do simply with me: robuster imaginations can bull it through. But offhand I can't think of any writer for print who benefited by writing for the movies. And I can't tell you what relief I experienced when United Artists told Alan Pakula that they didn't want him to make "The Instant Enemy."

This is a terribly self-centered letter, with 'I' in every sentence, it seems. Let me report that Margaret is happy and well, except that she has itchy eyelids and wonders if something is biting her. I suspect it's an allergic reaction. In any case it doesn't seem to interfere with the work on her new book, which like the one before is about Tom Aragon. I haven't read any part of it, and won't until she's finished with the book.

I'm in the middle of Borowitz' *Innocence and Arsenic* which Joan Kahn sent me (and perhaps you?) and think it's extraordinarily well written, simply loaded with carefully shaped historical insights which would seem to me to qualify it as a university textbook; and intellectually witty. Another thing I've been enjoying is Donald Davie's Clark Lectures on Dissent which have been (partly) printed in some recent *TLS*'s. With these lectures, and his Pound book, and his own recent poems, Davie has become a central figure in English intellectual life, and done so by becoming simply (and complicatedly) himself, and personifying that whole great England which was excluded from the centre and its controls, until now. But England has lost Davie. He'll be back at Stanford, evidently to stay, next month—in the poetry chair which he inherited from Yvor Winters.[29]

No, I don't have much nostalgia for the halls of ivy, preferring at least in these later years just to do the one main thing with all the energy I have left. No politics.

Thank you so much for your recent letters, indeed for all of them. Is it too late to wish you a happy Christmas?

Love, Ken

(M. sends her love, too. K)

Eudora Welty to Kenneth Millar, December 29, 1976

Dear Ken,

Thank you for your sweet letter—it came Christmas Eve—and how forbearing it was, when I realize what a mistaken way I must have put something. I wrote from a feeling that you were—not in bad shape at all, far from it—but perhaps casting about for a new form for a piece of work, and I was wondering if I might possibly do for you what someone had done for me. When I was working on my novel Losing Battles, which was a new form for me, and life at home grew very difficult—my mother's long illness, and my brother's—I needed for this novel to stay real and grow the way it needed to for me in spite of no time or way to work, and my dear friend William Maxwell suggested I send along what I could and his secretary could type this up for me. (I have to work with a typewriter, for objectivity and for the ways I revise). My mother could not bear the sound of the typewriter if I began working late at night, she thought I had forgotten her. Bill Maxwell never offered a word about what I sent, though I invited him to read it if he felt like it, he just provided me with a confirmation at a distance of what I was doing, if that expresses it at all, an objective guarantee that it was alive. I had never shown anyone work in progress and never have since, and perhaps it was only the angelic sensitivity of Bill that made this possible. He read it and didn't say anything, and I took a great deal of comfort from it. You of course don't *need* this, as I needed it, but I guess something came over me, what if I could do for you what was done for me, but I would never have had the impertinent idea of "criticising"—I'm sure you were horrified, as I am, to think of it. I love your work, and wasn't offering to do any more. But I can do that when it's in print.

We all had a nice Christmas here, as I hope you did there. I got up early! to see the little ones come downstairs to see their Santa Claus—little Andy, my niece Mary Alice's 18-month old, spotted the red motorcycle that he *knew* was for him, it *spoke* to him straight, and he pushed through all the rest, mounted it in his pajamas, and rode it right out from under the tree and through the house, never letting a word fall. I got some kind of flu the next day but feel all right again now. I'll write a better letter next time, but just didn't want you to think bad things from what must've been a confused letter.

With love and lots of New Year's wishes to you & Margaret,

Eudora

CHAPTER SEVEN

"Sometimes your insight is so dazzling that I have to shut my eyes."

———— ❧ ————

1977

AS 1977 began, the musical version of Eudora's novella The Robber Bridegroom *was still enjoying a Broadway run, and during the year she would take her own show on the road. Colleges and universities were eager to bring her to their campuses. She made thirteen trips over the course of eight months in the year and received three honorary degrees, one from Harvard. Both happiness about the play and her reason for making these appearances were at least in part financial. Her income had waned while household maintenance expenses had waxed. Bill Maxwell offered to help with her expenses; Ken would offer as well. But perhaps Eudora's peripatetic existence was also motivated by her inability to complete a story and by her sense of time's urgency. That sense of urgency sent her on a long trip— first to see Ken in Santa Barbara and from there to see Mary Lou Aswell in Santa Fe, the second time in two years she had taken this route. The death of her lifelong friend Frank Lyell shortly after she returned from the West surely confirmed the wisdom of such travels. "More and more I prize the present," Eudora had declared as the year began, "and if you look at the strange device on the banner I'm carrying 'mid snow and ice, it's CARPE DIEM."[1]*

Ken though was less and less able to seize the day. He became Margaret's support and caretaker when she had surgery for lung cancer in the spring, and he sought help from a psychologist when his memory problems intensified in the fall. Through all of this trouble, however, he drew comfort from his correspondence with Eudora.

Kenneth Millar to Eudora Welty, January 2, 1977

Dear Eudora:

Today was a fine grey day and not too cold for us but cold enough. M. and I celebrated by taking a swim and eating a hearty lunch, you know where, with Ted and Lois Clymer, whom you will remember. They are in the process of arranging a divorce and for some reason it, or the prospect of it, has enabled them to become good friends again, and convinced me of what I didn't use to believe, that divorce could be a suitable end to a marriage.[2]

I should have answered sooner your kind offer to let me write out to you what I remember of my own early family life. But I've been thinking about it and decided I'd better not. It will have to be done in fiction. Which, like all my fiction, will be aware of you as the most responsive imagination I write to. That sounds sort of boastful but is really meant to be thankful. Seem to be coming to life again.

Have I mentioned Donald Davie's Clark lectures, partly printed in several recent issues of TLS? I think they're strikingly important and will give England a fine forward shove, and show us ourselves in the bargain, all us dissenters.

Love and a happy new year, dearest Eudora, ever, Ken

Kenneth Millar to Eudora Welty, January 7, 1977

Dear Eudora:

Sometimes your insight is so dazzling that I have to shut my eyes. But you must not feel that it has ever hurt me to be touched by it. Your rays are wholly benign and leave no mark. The fact is—if I may step to one side and comment simply as an innocent bystander—the power of your empathy is so great that it fills me with glee on behalf of the whole human race. I'm sure you understand me, you always do. Too well indeed except that your perceptions are *always* benign and never harmful. And if there is some unease in my letters from time to time, you are never the source of it, merely a witness. And always, dear Eudora, a witness for the defense.

I'm moving from position to position on my internal map, trying to get a fix, or a series of fixes, on my early life which is the so far unstated source of all my fiction. For some years now I've been thinking about Winnipeg in 1929 and may do it next. I'd better hurry. A professor at the U. of Manitoba recently semi-predicted in *The Nation* that Canada was going to break up into two or more parts. At any rate the west will be freed from the destiny of the South.

Well, things are evoking. I can't tell you what a joy it was to feel that I live in your world, as you live constantly in mine.

Love,

Ken

Eudora Welty to Kenneth Millar, [January 27, 1977]

Dear Ken,

Thank you for that letter you last wrote me, with its feeling so deeply kind and delicately understanding. And I was, am, so glad to hear that the work was going so well—That's exciting—

I've been working too but the kind of thing with a deadline—have done a couple of reviews for the Times lately (both books of letters, Virginia Woolf's and now Faulkner's[3]) and need to finish now as soon as possible the remaining essay for my book of non-fiction, which I agree to have ready by February 29. This is a piece on Chekhov—I'd rather read him than anybody, but what I could come up with about him that's the least bit fresh or new, as from the point of view of a short story writer—my assignment, from Cornell—I can't think. I've promised, though. How long has it been since you read "The Duel"? It's miraculous—

We've had our share of the nation's winter, which only California can cock a snook at—It was 6° the other morning—We've had both a snow storm, and an ice storm—Everything just stopped. Children sledded down the middle of Pinehurst Street on cafeteria trays from the schoolhouse—I don't really mind being holed in, as long as it's just for a few days. The only good thing about cold waves in the South is that they don't last long—Today, instead of 6°, it's 60°—and camellias coming back into bloom—They warn us, "Not for long!" about the mild weather, now.

I had a fine time with Margaret's book, tell her, which I'd been trying to get hold of. The true expert, and fine handler of the sinister scene, the splendid dialogue writer that she always is, I thought this novel just about her best. It was interesting to see how she was making Mexico, at least partly, out of bits of Santa Barbara,—wasn't she? Tops— Congratulations to her again—

Did you happen to see Reynolds's piece in *Time* about Plains, Ga.? In the issue with Carter as Man of the Year [January 3, 1977]—Anyway I tore it out for you in case you missed it—I think it's fine—

I'll write when I'm out from under—For you I hope every thing is going wonderfully well—Thank you for your letter—your letters—

With love, always
Eudora

Kenneth Millar to Eudora Welty, [January 28, 1977]

Dear Eudora:

I don't want to alarm you but it would be pointless to write you without mentioning what is most on my mind. Margaret has been coughing and breathing with some difficulty for weeks now. Of course she's been going to doctors but they haven't given her a thorough examination until today; and they found a spot on her lung. We're naturally concerned, since M. was a heavy smoker for many years, and keeping our fingers crossed while further tests are being made. Please cross *your* fingers, too.

We've both been working, M. more advanced than I, as usual, until the last couple of days. I'm trying to invent something out of my childhood, and she is writing a sequel to TOMORROW.[4] It's been cold here, even here, but not by more eastern standards. Rather than use too much gas, we bought a half-cord of wood, seasonal oak, and have been enjoying fires in the fireplace.

In renewing my subscription to ANTAEUS I had a chance to write your name down for a free subscription and did so. If you already get it, pass it on to someone else. For the current issue, on popular fiction, I cleaned up the speech I gave in response to the Popular Culture award several years ago.

I hope and trust all is well with you, dear Eudora. You are more in my thoughts than any other absent person. Love, Ken

Eudora Welty to Kenneth Millar, Monday morning [January 31, 1977]

Dear Ken,

My fingers *are* crossed and you know I'm sending my love and hopes—I'm so sorry this trouble has come down on Margaret and you—and I hope the next news you get will ease it and the worry in some way. It's good to know you're there where there must be wonderfully able and wise doctors helping.

That fire going sounds nice—I'll think of you with it burning steady & long and smelling good and cheering the whole house, with the dogs to lie about it too—up on the raised hearth, if that is not too hot for German Shepherds, or for Misty either.

That's just what I wanted to find, *Antaeus* with your piece in it— you'd mentioned letting them have it. I used to take the magazine but my subscription had run out so I'm pleased to have it renewed for me—Thank you—

Like you and Margaret I've been busy working—Doing a piece on Chekhov, which is absorbing as well as hard—but yesterday, the story I've been writing but had to interrupt for this, made an appearance again in my mind like a fish leaping in the river when

I thought it was quiet and I wrote on it again for about an hour. Anyway I took it as a sign the thing was still alive. And I hope yours is the same—

Dear Ken, I think of you and send my love to you & Margaret—I'm going to walk up the street & put this in the mailbox—we're all under a new fall of snow here—when people can't drive. It's beautiful—it was beautiful falling all night. I hope to hear soon—

Much love,
Eudora

Kenneth Millar to Eudora Welty, February 1, 1977

Dear Eudora:

Thank you for your letter and the enclosure which I had missed. Reynolds, by dwelling on the simple and not so simple facts, has expressed better than anyone what Carter and the Carters may mean to us. Last night on national television we saw a vision which also made us think of you—a vision of Jackson blanketed with snow. I'm ashamed to say that we're having an embarrassingly sunny winter, so mild that we've been able to do without our furnace entirely. Wood fires in the evening, though.

Margaret is in somewhat better shape, both physically and emotionally, than she was when I wrote you the other night. The cell tests she has taken show no sign of malignancy and that is relieving. She'll be going back for further tests next week, but her doctors don't seem alarmed.

All my life I've kept coming back to Chekhov and I remember the initial impact of *The Duel* when I was a very young man. But I must confess I haven't read it lately—made a search for it tonight but couldn't find it. Robert Payne omits it, no doubt purposely as not a short story, from his "forty stories" of Chekhov. I quite agree that nobody has ever written so well as C., not even you in the full white heat of your powers.

Love, Ken

Kenneth Millar to Eudora Welty, [February 7, 1977]

Dear Eudora:

Today I was lucky enough to hear from you twice: once in your public voice and once in your private voice, in your review of Faulkner's letters and in your letter to me. These two voices are not very different, and what rings out in both of them is the generosity of your support to other human beings. Your statement on Faulkner is strong and simple and built to last, like the first story of a large building. As for your letter, your dear letter, it's a great comfort as always to have one's feelings corroborated and supported by yours. There is a definite improvement in the way Margaret feels. Next week, as I mentioned before, she'll have repeated and additional tests, about which I'll let you know. M. isn't letting this interfere with her pleasure in life which rests as you suppose on such things as burning logs and yearning dogs (yearning to go for a walk), and she's looking forward to her imminent sixty-second birthday. (She's ten months older than I am.)

I'd been reading Strindberg's one-act plays (to the translation of which Shaw donated his Nobel Prize money, wisely) but your special current interest in Chekhov derailed me back into nineteenth century Russian literature and I've been rereading Pushkin to see over again how that miracle came about. There's so much to be grateful for, is there not?

Love and gratitude,

Ken

P.S.—I had a talk with Barnaby Conrad the other day, about next summer's local writers' conference. He is eager to have you come again if you can, as we all are, but the growing expenses of the conference (the hotel has increased its rates considerably, etc) would make it difficult for him to pay your fare. I know that you have had some unexpected expenses this year and it would make me happy indeed if—as a matter strictly between you and me—you'd let me help with the fare. You needn't answer the suggestion right away, but please in the end say yes. You and Santa Barbara need each other. She's growing more nearly civilized every year, but will never make it without your continued help. Nor I!

P.P.S.—Bob Easton shared my feeling that Reynolds on Carter was the deepest statement yet. K.

Eudora Welty to Kenneth Millar, February 16, 1977

Dear Ken,

It was lovely to have your letter—I've been so glad to know that Margaret was feeling improved all the time in health and spirits, and hoping this would all be proved out fine by the tests as she finished them—And that you'll both be relieved and comfortably back to work soon—

We must talk about the Russians when I get there—I feel now I can come—if all bodes well. It was so deeply thoughtful of you to write as you did about the ticket. It's true I've had unusual expenses, but I'm taking on some extra work, and in the same mail with your letter another chance arrived to add to it—I haven't answered Barny Conrad's invitation yet but I will—

How does Pushkin go? Do you know I've never yet read him? Even worse, I've never read Tolstoy. (Not many people know this about me.) It's just that I gravitate so strongly toward Chekhov & Turgenev that I never deserted them for that grandeur—I feel I still have time—which I guess I'll go on feeling till it's every bit gone—

But working as I am, hard every day, I feel on the contrary I have no time at all—Trying to do reviews, Chekhov & my new story (which may be more than a story, as of now) & various chores—yet I feel happy, as I always do when working—and I know you feel the same—

Thank you for reading my Faulkner review—*Antaeus* has come—thank you again. But just the announcement copy they sent saying the subscription was to start, which has a piece your friend Matthew Broccoli found by Fitzgerald, I know you saw it, but not your article yet. Reynolds told me you'd written him a wonderful letter. I felt so glad that you saw that in his *Time* piece, that insight into its Southern meaning. But you understand us. I'm glad Bob Easton liked it as well. I'll be seeing Reynolds on March 17, when I read at Duke—He seems in very good spirits.

I'm hoping everything will go fine & keep on going fine—I'm glad you think it's a good idea—my coming to Santa Barbara again. I can be thinking of it. Love, Eudora

P.S. I see that, not surprisingly, Herb Harker's novel is dedicated to you.[5] I tried to do a bit for the jacket or whatever for Random, which I hope will suit, because I like what he did—

Kenneth Millar to Eudora Welty, February 21, 1977

Dear Eudora:

It's good and heartening news that you feel able to come to Santa Barbara again this summer. I mentioned it to the Conrads and they are of course delighted, and will take care of the cost of your hotel room as before. And I'll be glad to help as needed, and as you know. We'll all be so happy to see you, especially me.

Margaret is definitely feeling better and seems to have lost the wheeze which was her most bothersome symptom. Her doctors are going to look at her with a bronchoscope on Tuesday (Feb 22) and, I hope, determine the cause of her symptoms. M. isn't wholly sanguine nor is she afraid, either; nor do the doctors appear to be. But we'll be glad to have the puzzle solved. Today we had a lunch in celebration of other good news. My son-in-law Joe who has been out of a job for three months—he's a corporate engineer—got a new job last week, with a better firm, and at a twenty percent raise in salary. I never saw Jimmie happier, and Joe's celebrated further by swimming about a mile in heavy surf.

I'm glad Reynolds felt my letter was okay. I wanted to thank him for his beautiful work in several fields on behalf of all of us. He remembers that we are a young country, and reminds us, like Chekhov, to take care. Like you, I prefer Chekhov to Tolstoy, almost to anyone. (So, surprisingly, did Thomas Mann.)

Our love, as always, and please give my warmest regards to Reynolds when you see him in March. Ever,

Ken

Eudora Welty to Kenneth Millar, March 3, 1977

Dear Ken,

Of course every time I think of you, it's with the hope things are all right—that the news Margaret gets from her doctors is reassuring, and that she's kept on feeling better as time goes on. No one can help feeling anxiety where the lungs are concerned until the reason for any trace is known, of course, so I hope you both have been relieved of that by now—

I was glad to get your letter—It was fine to know of other good luck in the family, your nice son-in-law's new and better job, and Jim's happiness over it. In this crazy winter weather, I try to keep up with what it's doing where my friends live, like keeping up with a barn-yard of distracted chickens—so I keep up with your rains, and so on. Somebody told me Santa Barbara doesn't have the droughts the more northern parts have, and this seems proper. Santa Barbara is different and more deserving, I feel personally, and deserves every drop.

Here we have the more usual gamut. One day I was breathing all the topsoil of Oklahoma when I stepped outside. We had in Jackson in three days, tornado watch, tornado warnings (escaped this), flash floods, and a hail storm and a dust storm. The local TV weathermen described the dust storm as "an unusual phenomenon." (The other things were usual phenomena). Today it's raining, windy and dark, with a tornado watch. I'm only nervous to think it could blow all my story away. But in Miss. we live under the possibility of tornadoes as you do to some extent under earthquakes—So!

Ken, I did deeply appreciate your thoughtfulness of me about the ticket. I wouldn't have hesitated to accept with thanks had I needed that help, or any other. But having taken on these lecture jobs, I am OK. It's really a piece of marvelous luck that the colleges still ask me, because I'd said no to all for a good many years. But it's working out fine.

And I didn't take on *too* many. Enough is enough. And I'm managing to get my writing in. I was planning on paying for my hotel in Santa Barbara anyway, as I did both years I was there. (My conscience wouldn't let me stay at the Conference's expense though they offered, because I stayed for the chance to see you.) So this year it will be just a swap, between them & me.

Your letter must have meant a great deal to Reynolds. The fact that you sat down and did such a thing is so warming to think about. That goodness is so much a part of you. I am due in North Carolina 2 weeks from today, the 17th. Reynolds has asked me to come out & stay with him for the last part of the weekend, when the work's over, and I probably shall. I have some kin there, too—some of my mother's Virginia cousins, who're dear to me, and I'll have the chance to see them too.

A very nice letter to me came from your friend Ralph Sipper—he said he liked my Faulkner review.

I don't know if you think anything of Joan Fleming—she is uneven as can be—but one I just finished last night, *To Make an Underworld*, I thought so well done, and I also distinctly got the feeling she'd been reading Henry Green.[6] He's very catching—

My best wishes for everything to be fine there—

Much love,
Eudora

The next two letters crossed in the mail.

Eudora Welty, Durham, NC, to Kenneth Millar, [March 19, 1977]

Dear Ken,

I'm writing this in Reynolds's house—just to say we've been speaking of you a lot and to send love. Through the literature panel on the Endowment, one of whom had asked you about a project over the phone, we heard that Margaret had had surgery—and both of us are so sorry, and hoping things are going now in the very best possible way there—I wish I could help.

It's lovely in this part of the country—the spring is about 2 weeks behind Jackson, so I'm seeing that first veil of gold & green in the treetops—Reynolds's house is right in the woods—he has forsythia out, and daffodils in bloom all under the trees—He's a good cook. The record player is on Mozart. I did 2 jobs at Duke, read for the Friends of the Library and answered questions etc. for his writing class—Nice people he has round him here, and they value him in a very satisfying way to me.

Love to you and all good hopes for things to go well now with Margaret—please tell her for me. Take care of yourself too. Reynolds sends love. Don't try to write when things are pressing—You know we're in touch.

Tomorrow is the first day of spring—A good sign—

Yours ever,
Eudora

Kenneth Millar to Eudora Welty, [March 1977]

Dear Eudora:

I have been slow in answering your loving letter. It is not for want of news but because things have been happening quickly here. Margaret's lung operation was completely successful according to the surgeon and other doctors. After ten days in the hospital, which terminated last Wednesday, she was sprung and came home. We decided to go it alone with the help, of course, of regular medical visits, and as of this Saturday night it appears to be working. Margaret is moving well though rather painfully around the house and the flat places of the yard. She has her birds around her, and her dogs, and the promise of years of life. According to the several doctors involved, the cancer in her lung was excised completely and requires no further treatment. If she continues to build up her strength, as she will, she can swim in six weeks. Her only outward mark is a slanting foot-long scar across her back which I find rather attractive. Of course she's in considerable pain but she stands it well. She loves her life. So do I. And by the time we see you here in Santa Barbara, the whole painful thing will be in the past. I'm so glad you're coming! Love, Ken

Eudora Welty to Kenneth Millar, March 21, [1977]

Dear Ken,

Your letter so filled with relief and rejoicing brought the good news about Margaret—I'm so glad to know how very well it's all turned out—and how happily things are arranged now so that she can recuperate completely at home, with the right birds around her—and everything. Soon she'll be swimming—and soon be going back to her book (if she hasn't already).

I have a little background in this because my brother Walter had a third of one lung removed and I went down to New Orleans to be with him and his wife during that time. I know it's a hell of an operation. So I know how fine this news really is, and I can feel with you in that too. And do.

This is just a line but I wanted to say how happy I am that all is well—Love and wishes to you both,

Eudora

Eudora Welty to Kenneth Millar, April 20, 1977

Dear Ken,

It's a morning of soft rain, not torrential the way we had it earlier—I'm sitting in the car and finding it nice just to sit & listen, and look into the green light of the trees just come into their full leaf—(I'd started work so early.) (But a mockingbird was earlier—he woke me up singing at 3:45 AM!)

All keeps going well there, I'm hoping and trusting. It's good to know that all the painful time & the worry and all are behind you now. I hope Margaret is getting back her strength faster all the time.

My travels and assorted tasks are keeping me at it without a stop these days—Atlanta (Agnes Scott College) is where I was last. Beginning May 5 I go to Cornell, New York, Georgia again, Washington (Arts Council meeting) & back, the 15th, all work but for the 3-day breather in New York. After that I have 3 more places to go before I get to come to Santa Barbara. I'll hear from you before then, won't I, to be sure it's still going to be a good time for seeing you & Margaret—I'll be so glad to see you.

Now I'll get back to it—Is it the Peter Principle that says everything takes just exactly as much time as the time you've got to do it in? That's the case with my Chekhov paper—I've had a year to do it in, but I bet I'm still typing the last of it when the morning comes to take off. I don't care, because I love him. I'll bring you "The Duel" when I come. You don't have much extra time now to read, I can imagine, but by June *everything* will be easy I hope. My best wishes for her good breath to Margaret & love to you both, Eudora

Kenneth Millar to Eudora Welty, April 27, 1977

Dear Eudora:

There is no reason in the world why you shouldn't come to Santa Barbara for the Writers' Conference, and from our point of view every reason why you should. Margaret and I love to see you. And while M is not completely back to normal—final healing takes longer than the two months she has had since her operation—her somewhat less than normal is, like yours, quite awe-inspiring. She's swimming and biking and looking after the house and keeping track of her friends and getting up early (like you!) to write her book. And we're both looking forward keenly to your visit, along with the many other friends you have made here.

Just had a phone call from Bob Easton, back from a long weekend in the mountains in search of condors. His party saw no condors, though they still survive back of here, but did see three golden eagles. Have I mentioned to you that U of N. Mexico Press is reprinting Bob's early novel, *The Happy Man*, about life on a western ranch. I think you might like it; I think it's a quiet masterpiece.

So far I can't fault Jimmie [Carter]; I like his style and brains and ideas. He'll change the country back to itself if anyone can.

Our own Jim is now fourteen and very nice to have around, as he was this past weekend. Putting on inches and getting serious, but not too.

Love, Ken

Kenneth Millar to Eudora Welty, May 16, 1977

Dear Eudora:

You were very much in my thoughts this past week. Dick Moore and his excellent little movie crew were here for six days and not only was there much talk of you but they brought along the movie they'd made of you. I thought its colors were true, didn't you? I took great pleasure in seeing it and now remembering it, a foretaste of your visit next month. You looked exceedingly well.

Margaret is improving every week, and taking pleasure in life— biking, swimming, writing—but last week was not one of her best. For some reason unknown at the time, she suddenly suffered an almost total loss of hearing in her left ear. We were alarmed by the idea that the defunct cancer was spreading after all. But it turned out not to be so. Margaret's doctor reasoned or guessed that the hearing loss was connected to an arterial spasm like that which causes M's migraine attacks, and he prescribed an anti-spasm drug. A few days ago it began to work! and Margaret has now recovered most of her hearing; it improves every day!

But the week with Dick Moore didn't end as happily for him and his wife as it did for us. The second-last evening, Friday, the evening he showed me your film, Dick's wife Ruth whispered to me that she was very eager to talk to Margaret (who doesn't go out nights) and gave me her reason: "I have the same thing Margaret had, and Dick doesn't know." I passed this on to Margaret and the following day she arranged to spend some time with Ruth, and I think was able to encourage her. We hope to hear from them.

Margaret is writing, as I said, getting along towards the middle of Aragon # 2; but I'm still in the plotting stage and probably won't attempt regular writing until life is back to normal. I've written enough words not to feel too guilty, and been worried enough to look forward to a further lifting.

It will be so good to see you.

Love,
Ken

Eudora Welty to Kenneth Millar, May 17, 1977

Dear Ken,

It's been good knowing that everything was going so very well there, and also knowing I'd soon be there too & seeing for myself. Now it's only a month away tomorrow that I light out for Santa Barbara. (I just made my flight reservations while I was home between a couple of other trips.)

It's been such a crowded time, doing lectures, going to Council on the Arts meeting, etc., that I haven't had the time or strength to write a letter. (I live on nervous energy, and if it acts like all the energy that's giving us so much trouble, I better watch it!) It's been nice though, everywhere—I had a lovely time in Cornell, a part of the country I love—the Finger Lakes, hills, mountains, old glacier country—7 waterfalls I saw riding around Ithaca!—And a professor, James McConkey, who is a wonderful person—he's the one who took a chance on me, asking me to do a talk on Chekhov[7]—He himself has written a book on E. M. Forster, and some short stories that the New Yorker published.—Nona B. asked about you in N.Y. and so did Joan Kahn & Walter Clemons—

But I can tell you my news when I see you. And of course I want to know how the interview went with Dick Moore & Phil—I loved being with them—they do such an expert job, a pleasure watching them work—I found them sensitive to all that was new to them, too. Phil I felt this in in particular. I got the message you sent me through Dick when he called up, and was so glad for the latest added news of you & Margaret, that you were finding it easy to fit in the interview. So I knew days were back on their normal flow. I'm so glad for you.

I'll drop you a later line when I get back from St. Louis—Kent State & Harvard—No, I go to Harvard just before I come to S.B., but coming home first, to get my slacks & walking shoes[8]—Give Margaret my best. I'll hope to see you both soon now—Love, Eudora

Eudora Welty to Kenneth Millar, June 4, 1977

Dear Ken,

Thank you for your letter—which I believe crossed mine to you. I look forward so much to seeing you soon.

I hope that was the last scare that ever will arise out of that experience, and that Margaret is fine now and hearing well as ever. I was so sorry to hear of what it must have put you both through—The fact that it was the week you were making your film wouldn't have made it any easier. Did you finish it, by the way, or will you help later on?

I'll be anxious to see it myself, but of course all their work needs a lot of time—And I do hope Ruth Moore isn't in a bad way—It was good of Margaret to try to help her—

The film they made here I'm pleased you liked. As you could see, they are people you can respond to—a big help. I made mine the spring before I came the first time to Santa Barbara, so it seems a long while ago now. (I was interrupted here)

No wonder you have not got far yet with the actual writing of another book. I hope all is propitious now, though. I won't be coming at the wrong time, I trust. You will let me know.

This time I can't reach there the first day, as I have to go up to Harvard first. They're giving me an honorary degree, but don't tell this, they say. I'll come straight back here & switch suitcases, and expect to arrive at Santa Barbara on the Saturday, on United from L.A., about 4:30 PM—It would be lovely to have an early glimpse of you & Margaret. I notice they put us to work on the same day.

This is going to be my reward and restoration after a hard month's work—I've truly enjoyed the college visits—have met some fine people, students and faculty—but I'm spent, for the moment—One person I just have to tell you about *now*—the chairman of the English Department at Kent State is the *first* son of a family that for 9 generations has *not* been the Court Magician of the royal Court of the Netherlands! Hereditary since the 16th century. Isn't that absolutely wonderful? His name is Dr. Robert Bamberg—and he has a Magician's smile.

With love—and looking forward to the 18th,—I hope all is really fine—

Eudora

Kenneth Millar to Eudora Welty, June 9, 1977

Dear Eudora:

It was good to have your letter with its assurance that you can make the Santa Barbara trip. Nothing at this end should give you pause. Margaret is quite strong again and looking forward to seeing you, as we all are. I can feel a holiday mood (unearned) descending on me already, with a noise resembling the sound of the 4:30 plane from L.A. Which I'm looking forward to meeting on the eighteenth.

The weather is fine here, not too hot, with a kind of misty rain in the last twenty-four hours. In spite of the mounting water shortage, this place has never looked better. A good deal of water has passed under the bridge since I've seen you, and we have a lot to talk about. Come safe and soon.

Love,

Ken

P.S.—Jim comes for the summer the same day!

Kenneth Millar to Eudora Welty, June 27, 1977

Dear Eudora:

This will reach you when you'll have had, I know, a good visit with Mary Louise and, I hope, an easier trip home than you had coming. It was generous of you to come. As the chief beneficiary of your visit I thank you on behalf of all the others. Though you may have felt outnumbered by the kinds of writer you would hate to be, *you* outnumbered them. And you are the one that the student writers will remember, as I do, sitting forever at your feet.

I was bowled over by the excellence of your "Chekhov," which I return herewith reluctantly. It was wonderful to be shown his moral landscape in the light of your mind and to see expressed once and for all the moral purity and knowledge at the center of his art. Your writing in this piece is as clear as a freshly washed window, as clear as his and as uncompromising. It should stand as a definition of his work.

Margaret is feeling somewhat better and is back at work, as I am. I haven't determined what story to tell but it's fun getting ready to make a choice. Jim just came in from his first day in the Junior Lifeguard training program, and seems enthusiastic. Altogether the auspices are good.

See you,
Love,
Ken

Eudora Welty to Kenneth Millar, July 3, 1977

Dear Ken,

I was so glad we got that visit in—How good it was to see you first thing waving to me when I stepped out of the plane. And I was glad of all the times—you were generous and thoughtful all that while, and I cherish the rides and the sight again of the lovely mountains and the sea and the winding roads. Margaret's gaining strength, and her pleasure in going back to the new book she's writing,—and how well she looks— all augur so well for the good—It was warming to think that the bad painful days are getting left further and further behind with every good new day. Thank you and Margaret for having me out those lovely times for lunch, with the Pacific to go with it.

I hope you're easing into your own new book, one that will give you all kinds of good challenges and dares. I suppose you may have seen the note on "The Blue Hammer" in the latest Times list, but here it is.

I'm so glad you thought as you did about my Chekhov piece—You were more than generous but I was glad, for it was generosity on the lines I cared most to make my response to him felt. I know there could of course be nothing new I could say about the stories, it was a matter of trying to set down a response as exactly as I could. I did mean for you to keep the copy (my name & address were on the envelope because I was scared I'd leave it somewhere travelling so far) but you can have the printed one. This was the last piece to finish to go in my new book, the non-fiction collection. Ken, I wonder if I may dedicate the book to you? It would please me so deeply. It hasn't any title yet, but it's a collection—selection of *all* my pieces on writing and writers, & reviews ("The Underground Man" is here of course), plus a few personal pieces. I guess it goes back to 1947, it's really everything I've ever done in non-fiction that I've finally decided was worth keeping—Of course I wish it could be better, but I worked hard—these pieces were often harder for me than stories to write. All because I was asked to. (I never was asked to write stories!) And I may never have another book of stories, though I hope to. I'll send you a list of the pieces in it. I hope you'll let me give you my book as you gave me yours. (It would be another circle.)

Santa Fe was fine—Only Mary Lou, splendid and vivacious and full of people & plans as ever, isn't really very well. She'd had two heart attacks. They happened earlier in May while I thought she was travelling in Europe—She hadn't gone after all, owing to this—though she didn't get sent to the hospital, just cautioned to stay home—She hadn't told me, she said, for fear I wouldn't come. I wouldn't have. But she is taking care, as well as a person of her nature can—she was given a swimming tank by her friends there—one of those things on top of the ground—& swims around a little every day when the water's warmed up a little—you know Santa Fe's 9000 feet up in the mountains! She has so many friends looking after her, and her family—*especially* the son who ran away and found himself again, now living in Atlanta—are all coming out frequently. She enjoys life just as ever—She's 75—She asked about you of course. I left her your *Laidlaw* which I'd liked so much, & she seized it.⁹ Another friend of mine now living in Santa Fe, who had just come back from France where she & her husband had been over selling their house, said she'd been reading Margaret's books in French to her pleasure. Her name is Mary Mian, a good writer too.

One day on a picnic away up high in a State Park we saw 2 pairs of eagles! I was told they were very likely golden eagles. I was delighted to believe it. They were entirely majestic.

I must get to work—It was lovely being back there—seeing you, and seeing your good friends that I like to think of being there near. And seeing the mountains & the sea that are always near too—

Love,

Eudora

Of course you were right about the smoking mountain I saw from the westbound plane. It was the Los Alamos fire—In Santa Fe the smoke was still discernable, and they said the horses had been very much disturbed—[10]

Kenneth Millar to Eudora Welty, July 10, 1977

Dear Eudora:

The gift you propose to offer me is the kind of thing that might happen once in a lifetime if a man is lucky—like being knighted by a queen, not with a sword though, with a human hand—and cause him, every time he thinks of it, to laugh with pleasure. Love and friendship are surely the best things in life and may, it seems to me now, persist beyond life, as we want them to, like the light from a star so immeasurably distant that it can't be dated and questions of past and future are irrelevant. The source of the starlight might as well be thought to be inside us, and we take credit for the forces that sustain us, as being loved makes us feel loveable. If I may compound my image, staying within the elastic bounds of astronomy, or astrology, it's as if you had stopped time and handed me a glass which admits the future to our present vision, and the past too, joining present and future times, as if we had lived beyond life, as indeed we are going to do now to some extent, together. You make me very happy. You often have. And I await your book with gratitude and anticipation. I expect I'll never have awaited a book so intensely as I will this one.

It's very good to have news of Mary Lou. The news is not all good but the message is. I love to think of her swimming around in her high swimming pool, and also to learn that her errant son comes to visit her as he should (just as perhaps he should first have gone away.) And I'm glad you gave her *Laidlaw*, her recompense for including *The Black Monk* in her psychological anthology, and widening my knowledge of Chekhov. There is nobody like him, is there, or ever will be. But sometimes you come close. I wish you further stories, dear Eudora, nor need you sit pinned down by the excellence of what you have already done. You can write as you live out of a persistent joy which everyone recognizes in you. We can learn that from Chekhov, too, as you know better than I do.

Thank you so much for coming here this summer. Here or elsewhere we'll meet again before too long. Meanwhile, dear, take care, and don't be concerned for me. I've never despaired, least of all in these late good years.

Love,

K

Eudora Welty to Kenneth Millar, July 17, 1977

Dear Ken,

Thank you for your letter—so full of the generosity and tenderness of your understanding—I'm so glad you feel happy about this book. And now so do I—After the long task of searching out all the pieces for it and choosing & putting them together, now the whole is something, something more, because your letter is like a blessing to it. It *is* a blessing to it. Your letter is so like you, because you understand dedications—you who are such a giver—and you know the boundlessness of wishes. I wish this book, which is really modest and needs to be, were at the same time some way able to be all you would like it to be—every bit of it—without a shadow. Dear Ken, I'm sending you the list of the pieces in it, so you will know what my effort came to. And of course the contents themselves as soon as they are pages & Random sends them. The name of the book is to be "The Eye of the Story"—That's the title of the essay on Katherine Anne Porter—do you think much of it as a title?[11] I guess there's a page or two of introduction still to write.

I hope everything is moving along there as it should—in work, and in days, in all as it comes. It's nice to know Jim is there, too, & enjoying his Life Guard classes—I'm thinking right along that *yes*, things will and must go well—

With love,
Eudora

Kenneth Millar to Eudora Welty, July 26, 1977

Dear Eudora:

It feels like the hottest day of the year, though not by Mississippi standards. Still it feels as if it had rained, I don't know where—in Jackson maybe—but there is a sound of water in the courses. I think its central spring is the table of contents you sent me, which measured out explicitly, though that was not your intention, the dimensions of your gift, to me and everyone. You have given me a gentle powerful thrust, the more powerful by being undeserved. Perhaps good fortune always is. You should know, you've given it to so many people.

"The Eye of the Story" is a perfect title: it says so much in a few words about the kind of fiction you are concerned with, both its humanity and its art, its deadly reach and its gentle vulnerability, the telescope and the microscope in one. How extraordinary that you should make me the gift of such a book. I can't get over it, I never will.

I hadn't read "The Duel" after all—I must have got it confused with another story—but I have now and am so glad you mentioned it. I doubt I've ever gone through in such short compass such a powerfully realized and controlled imaginative experience. Nor is it the kind of excellence that silences another writer even when it puts him in the shade. It's a powerful giving, like your own steady giving in both life and art.

All well here. Margaret gets stronger and Jimmy more grown-up every day. There are stirrings in me, too, dear Eudora, perhaps climacterial in both its senses.

Love,
Ken

P.S.—I enclose a letter which surprised me from a man I don't know but perhaps will. K.

Eudora Welty to Kenneth Millar, [July 28, 1977]

Dear Ken,

Are you all right—all of you and the house? And Jim safely with you? I hate it for you so—I know Hope Ranch is at the other end of the city—isn't it? and the map reassures me of that much—But those lovely mountains—Sycamore Canyon—I feel that they all belong to you too—

At 7 AM I almost didn't turn on the TV for the Today Show news as usual because I had a book review deadline to meet, and then I had to ("Turn that on") and saw Montecito burning at 4 AM, what you must have been seeing, if, I was sorry to think, your household had been waked up—

Take care—I've thought about it all day of course—I pray they can contain it soon—I would like to telephone you but I feel it might disturb you—you'd be trying to get some rest if you had both been up all night.

Now they say the fire is under control—This is next morning. I'm glad of this much. I so hope everything is safe there with you.

I grieve for what happened to places dear to you but I hope you are all right.

Love,
Eudora

Eudora Welty to Kenneth Millar, Saturday [August 6, 1977]

Dear Ken,

I was so glad to hear you say you were all right there and your house not endangered. Thank you for calling me—it was very thoughtful of you, because even if I thought you must have been safe in Hope Ranch, how can anybody at a distance really be sure about a *fire*? It must have been an emotional experience to see the other house gone, and no sign of those huge oaks, the pepper tree, and the lovely unspoiled slope down to the creek where you've kept your lot. It's so hard to imagine something being *gone*—it would seem less difficult to imagine it *back*. Is it a true fact that fire in the end does promote nature to restore itself?[12]

I should have asked you, but didn't think in time when we were talking, if the houses of your friends in Santa Barbara were all right—I'd been thinking of course of the Freemans and the Eastons and the young Sippers—Ralph's bookstore—The downtown was not touched, was it? And the Botanical Gardens—?

I'm happy to know you're writing something new. All my best wishes to it & what it will be.

The last letter you wrote me I think must've been the night just before the fire—you said how hot it was. It was a beautiful letter, and I would have written to thank you before now, but I have been shocked and saddened by the death of an old friend here. One of that inner circle of closest friends. You never met him—Frank Lyell—he taught English at the University of Texas and was here only for Christmas and summer vacations. We went to Columbia Graduate School in the same year which was 1930–31. I typed his thesis for him. (On John Galt—do you know that Scottish writer?)[13] Our little group that's still friends here went through the Depression together here—you know that's binding—I guess I was his closest friend here. He came home from a European trip and something got the matter with his heart on the flight home. But he made it home.

I know I'm at an age when the loss of friends is not considered surprising, and I have lost my three dearest in Jackson (I was counting Diarmuid, though he wasn't exactly of Jackson.) But I am not going to learn to *accept* it for being not surprising, I'm going to hate it & protest it straight ahead—I'm indignant for their sakes—up to my last breath—I testify to their absence—

I've been warmed to have your recent letters by me—I'm so glad you're well and safe and working. And I'm happy that you like the title of the book—

What you said about Chekhov never silencing another writer by his own works being so far beyond in excellence I believe too, and I also believe Chekhov would have never dreamed of being less than an encourager, do you? Isn't "The Duel" a marvelous story—I had a feeling you'd think that—The storm scene!

Here it's hot with thundershowers every afternoon. I wish I could send you the rain you need. Love—Eudora

Kenneth Millar to Eudora Welty, August 9, 1977

Dear Eudora:

I think the phrase "the sympathetic imagination" must have been invented in expectation of you. You feel for others better than we can feel for ourselves. But I'm happy to be able to report that the general mood of this city is better than you could expect, considering the damage that was meted out. The saving grace of the situation is that there were no deaths and, I believe, no terribly serious injuries.

Here are the latest figures: 280 dwellings involved in the fire—216 levelled and 64 damaged. 141 of those completely destroyed were in the city limits. 77 percent. of all the houses touched by the fire burned to the ground. The overall cost, including the cost of firefighting, was about 30 million.

You'll be glad to know that Ralph Sipper's house was not damaged, though it was closely threatened by the fire. He sent his family away and stayed behind with his house, watering down the roof etc. That physical experience, with the warm, indeed hot, feelings of his neighbors, has changed his life to a visible extent. I suggested when he was here the other night that he was no longer a transplanted New Yorker and he agreed. His eyes have lost their defensive look—strange outcome for a fire to have. But I suppose it's such events that mold a community into a historic place, anyway *home.*

The others you ask about, the Freemans and the Eastons, were not troubled by the fire though it came close to Bob's place, just over the hill from it. His house was much more closely threatened by the last big blaze. But Bob and Jane won't move.

I'm sorry to hear of the death of your old friend Frank Lyell whose thesis you typed. John Galt is not unknown to me, though I haven't read much of him. But would you believe that my S.B. colleague Bill Gault is a member of the same family? And the city of Galt, near Kitchener in Ontario, is named after John who was a colonizer as well as a moralist. According to Bill, there were other writers in the family, too.

I share your feelings for both vertical and horizontal men. The loved dead soar forever like birds or the shadows of birds in a world of memory which keeps them alive in thought, sometimes more clearly visible than when they were alive; and not really lost. We can spend afternoons in their presence.

Which reminds me that tomorrow Margaret is going to take her first sailing lesson. You can judge of her morale by that. We are both working. Love, Ken

Kenneth Millar to Eudora Welty, August 31, 1977

Dear Eudora:

That was a powerful statement you wrote about the Sacco-Vanzetti case and your dear friend's part in it.[14] Your paragraph excoriating bias freezes the attention and burns the conscience; it stands up off the page like something in the Inferno, and in its way says everything that needs to be said. Only the pure in heart can write like that, but you have to be a darn good writer too!

Speaking of writers, we're both at work, me slowly, Margaret swiftly, but she took five years off! It's six months since her operation now, and her X-ray last week showed no lesions in the lungs at all. We're deeply relieved and much encouraged. Our summer has been enlivened by grandson Jim who's been developing into a fair sailor and just this week came into possession of his own boat, a light, fast fiberglass sailboat called the Laser. One more week and then we lose him back to school, but that's as it should be.

Whether you are writing like Dante or not, I often think of you in association with places we passed through or by together. I hope you are well and happy. Love, Ken

P.S.—This is hush-hush, but a *new* baby condor was sighted this week on the far side of the mountains. K.

Eudora Welty to Kenneth Millar, [September 1977]

Dear Ken,

I'm so glad to know the reassuring news from Margaret's check-up. That's wonderful—and it's bound to do a lot for her morale, and give a lift to everything. Life—and the two books underway—and all. The good report's a nice present for Jim too, as he leaves to go back to school. As his new sailboat is too. What a fair sight it must be to see him go by with his sails filled.

Thank you for your generous words for what I wrote on KAP. (That's the review I was doing on the day of the Santa Barbara fire.) The book she'd brought out at 87 had moved me not only for itself, for herself, but for the reason that its ever being a book had hung in the balance—KAP has had several strokes, and she feels different ways about people at different times—you know. She'd had a secretary, a very intelligent and kind—devoted—young man named Bill Wilkins (I don't know him, but he's been kind enough to let me have word now and then) and as her right arm is paralyzed & she can't write for herself, he has managed to physically take and make the book out of KAP's old notes and old versions, etc., showing her the results & talking it over as they went—She was happy to have this done, and put his name on the dedication page, and then, the way these things are, she turned against him. And then was so ill that he wrote me she might not be aware when the book came out. But she was! You can imagine my feelings when I received a letter from her. She was aware—"This was a day for me." She was pleased by my piece which she said "simply breaks my heart with love and remembrances." She said "I have been sick a long time in a bad place." It nearly broke my heart too. It was written on an unused Christmas card that I could imagine coming out of a box of stuff she kept by her in bed—and dictated of course, but I recognized the hand of this same Bill Wilkins. So she has taken him back too—

Since you felt for what the review said of her, I wanted to tell you what life has been doing to her but how she keeps coming back and coming back. She is valiant.

And I felt another valiant coming back in your letter—the new baby condor. Now after the fire from over the mountain.

I've been a long time writing—it's just work mostly, and an Arts Council meeting in Washington—I never catch up, and find myself too tired to make sense just when I've looked forward to it. (To making sense, yes—to writing a line at the end of a day.) You do know you are not out of my mind. I wanted to write your friends in Santa Barbara who were so nice to me, you will be ashamed for me, I'm so ashamed for myself, I have yet to thank them—Ralph and Carol, not only to thank them but to express my relief on your news that their house *didn't* burn—And I could imagine what saving it meant, from your having done the same thing that other time—that other house. Ralph let me have the rare copy of Henry Green's "Blindness" at a low cost, before I left town—I'm so elated to have it, to have read it, a remarkable book—you know H. G. wrote it while he was still at Eton!—If you find you have the time & the wish to read it, I'll let it go back to Santa Barbara.

Reynolds has been here—he acted as a judge with me & 1 other of an ETV contest—You know what good company he is—We spoke of you a good deal. Reynolds eats a lot! But this time I said aha, because he's always accused me of feeding him nothing but ham, and this time I fed him a salmon mousse. (Served 8. Says Reynolds, "That means me and one other.")

This reminds me of that letter you let me see that Mr. Robert Densmore wrote you which I'll enclose. I can understand exactly his wanting to give you his recipe for tamale pie, seeing it as a gift of thanks—(though I can't as easily imagine you as cooking it up. Doesn't it take a full day?) But what a genuine, grateful letter it is—a recipe is a nice language. Maybe you have since seen him and talked.

It's been hot and stormy—we always get funnels overhead after hurricanes on the Gulf Coast, and trees blew down, etc., nobody was injured. I had a book review to fail to arrive (in NY) because of the weather and they had me give it to them over the phone—which was also being affected by the weather—I think it took an hour and a half! I had to spell nearly everything—It was poor E. B. White being treated that way. (His essays.) That's a good sign to me to stop reviewing for a while now. It's hard for me even in nice weather—E. B. White is lovely though.[15]

I've been reading "Brideshead Revisited," which I'd never read—wonderful, the part on shipboard during the long storm at sea which isolated the lovers, do you remember it? And I plunge sometimes into Borges—the stories that I have the feeling you remember—I'll write better next time. I'm so glad, dear Ken, your news is good—It's the greatest cheer—

Love,
Eudora

Kenneth Millar to Eudora Welty, September 13, 1977

Dear Eudora:

I was so glad to hear from you today. When I haven't for a certain stretch of time I begin to feel a tug on my nerves, of course for no good reason, and to wonder if all is well. But of course all is well, you're simply navigating the depths and shoals and channels of your life. You're in such profound and constant touch with your life's meaning (I don't mean to make this your responsibility, but you *do* without having to intend to) holding the whole thing together with your mind and hands. And life keeps responding to your care for it. You bring good luck to your friends. I can imagine the pleasure you took in being able to respond to Miss Porter again and at such a depth in her life, and in such a central way, speaking at the same time for the past and to the future, above all simply to her, on behalf of all of us. She's such a fine stylist that she became a novelist in spite of herself, or am I wrong?

In no dutiful spirit but simply because I wanted to see them again, I've been rereading some of your early stories. Perhaps you have been educating me, I don't mean by intention but by your steady presence in my mind, because I read them so much better than I used to. They're willing to tell me more, and as they grow older the stories lend me their wisdom. "The Hitch-Hikers," for example, which reached out of its own time into the here and now, and then beyond.

We've had a most pleasant summer watching Jim and his friends taking a long step towards growing up, and perhaps doing some growing up ourselves. It was the kind of summer that makes you think there can never be another summer like it. But there was. A few years ago when I was visiting Kitchener, Ontario, a boyhood friend of mine showed me a camp picture of a boy who resembled Jim. Then I realized that it was a picture of me. Jim is far ahead of that me in many ways, both physical and moral. He treats the world kindly, and it responds. I don't know who he'll become but then it doesn't matter—he'll become what he wishes, and is well on his way.

Margaret continues to grow stronger and cheerfuller. I'm in good shape as usual. A small group of us are putting together an environmental program based on the willing labors of about twenty young university people, scientists and lawyers, here in Santa Barbara. So we fight fire with fire.

In spite of what I said at the beginning, please don't feel obliged to answer this or any particular letter. I know how much writing of all sorts you must do, and you are a woman who gives until she drops. Remember I can always read your stories.

And do, with love,

Ken

Eudora Welty to Kenneth Millar, September 16, [1977]

Dear Ken,

I feel like thanking you for another of your lovely rides—It was a dream, and when I woke up I felt refreshed and restored just the way it was there—I'd been tired out, but now it still seems that something so wide-ranging and beautiful and free was just a moment ago to be seen on all sides—

There's been a change in the air here—This is first thing in the morning, and it's cooler, with a dew, like fall—The sun has hit the sweet-olive—so I can smell that fall scent—The birds are singing fall songs again, the way they start over again at summer's end—but there've been migratory birds, warblers, flitting through the oak tree's leaves for some weeks now—I hope Santa Barbara's baby condor is making himself visible now & then straight along and that he thrives up there—

This isn't a real letter, just to tell you about the good dream—it still seems not very far away.

With love,
Eudora

Eudora Welty to Kenneth Millar, September 19, [1977]

Dear Ken,

Your letter came right after I'd mailed that little note to you—I'm sorry to have caused you any uneasiness—If you'd missed hearing, I'd equally missed writing. But you know you are in my thoughts, closer than what's going on here to keep me ever from writing. There *have* been a lot of things like that lately—my own fault, of course. If I were in trouble of some kind, I would tell you. So don't be uneasy—

You are altogether understanding of my need to write as I did about Katherine Anne, and I'm glad you felt I was speaking for all of us. Someone should have (spoken for us all) indeed, and I more than most should have been the one to do my best—She did much for me, when I was beginning, and often. She wrote me a letter when my early stories appeared and said she liked them—This stunned me—When the voice from the outside world is Katherine

Anne Porter's, it's more than encouragement, it's a sort of charge to do right—do right by our craft—She became a personal friend, of course, after that, and was always one to me. She was tempestuous in her relationships a lot of the time, and broke with many who loved her or whom she'd loved, and was a difficult person, enchanting and demanding and vain as a child, but absolutely, unyieldingly pure as an artist, never sparing herself. With depths of feeling she didn't as an artist hesitate to plumb—I mean depths as dark as night. She took them on. I don't know if you're right or not in saying she became a novelist in spite of herself. That is, I was not able to like her novel. I thought she was sort of betrayed by her own creation—but I know I am wholly partial to her short stories. "Noon Wine" is her real novel, to me. Do you find that as powerful, & chilling, as I do? Should I go back and read "Ship of Fools"? I thought a monster had hold of her sometimes in that. Still, she did it, she finished it. About 30 years it was weighing her down—

It's good to learn of the environmentalist program you've started putting together—I know you've always worked toward such ends, you and Margaret. This time, with those young scientists & lawyers stirred up too, & the fire still so present in the Santa Barbara mind, the impetus is powerful enough for great results, I hope.

And the books go well at home, I hope. It's so good too that the summer has come out rewardingly all around. It *needed* to—

Your saying you were reading some of my early stories again made me go back and read them too. (Except the few I read aloud to earn my living, I never do.) I think you are meeting me in them pretty much as I was, as a young girl—though I'd had little idea they were so revealing. There are many flaws. The feelings do come through, though, in "The Hitch-Hikers"—don't they, & others? The little one called "The Winds" is a fairly accurate portrait of my father, mother, brother Edward, & me in our house in Jackson where I was born—and of a summer in our childhood and a tornado, and the ardency (is this a word?) of beginning to be alive. Anyway, I'm so glad they are able to speak to you from over the years—and they should, really, because when we know & care for people it is their whole lives that are in the present of knowing. If only it (this unity) could be told in stories—Maybe this is what *is*.

Take care—Thank you for your letter, bringing me understanding and happiness as your letters always do. I hope everything goes well in every way with all of you. This is every day.

Love,

Eudora

Kenneth Millar to Eudora Welty, October 5, 1977

Dear Eudora:

I am slow in responding to your wonderful letters. There has been a small but significant change in my life. When our daughter Linda and indeed our whole family were in trouble I regularly saw a Santa Barbara psychiatrist named Richard Lambert. Dick had already been a friend, and has never ceased to be. A few weeks ago I started seeing him regularly again, with the idea of clearing my poor memory, and while my memory hasn't improved much yet—I don't expect sudden miracles—my spirits have. It seems that I have been isolating myself in a quiet unconscious way, for reasons that aren't entirely clear to me. But just to name the problem is a step towards solving it, and you mustn't and needn't worry on my account.

Right now, at noon on a warm overcast day in an empty house, I'm waiting for Herb Harker to come by with an important manuscript for me to read. It's a statement of hope and intent by a Mormon writer (Herb) which he's going to deliver at a conference in Salt Lake City. I think it will make him a leader in the church's rather narrow intellectual branch, if he isn't already. You can share my pride in Herb's growth, which you had an important part in developing, though perhaps neither you nor I had intended to influence the intellectual life of the Mormon Church!

All is well here. Jim is keen about high school, including Latin, which pleases my classical wife, also me. Love, Ken

P.S.—Herb read his speech, and I think it's eloquent. I hope he'll send it to you. Even of Mormonism he makes poetic sense.

K.

Kenneth Millar to Eudora Welty, October 12, 1977

Dear Eudora:

It has rather slowly occurred to me that my note of the other day might have given you a shock, which wasn't my intention. I wanted you to know that the memory problems of which I'd spoken to you were being worked on, and by a doctor who is at the same time a dear old friend. Dick Lambert was Linda's doctor when she first had trouble, and he was kind and compassionate then and remains so. Also bright. We've had several sessions now, relating my loss of memory to other circumstances of my life into which I won't go. Some day we may wish to talk about it, or forget it, as we like. But all is basically well, and will improve, already has.

Remember "Zack," Fred Zackel, the San Francisco taxi driver who blossomed into a writer at the last-but-one Santa Barbara Writers' Conference? Zack has written a hundred-thousand-word mystery novel and sent it on to me. I think it's good, though it needs some cutting and some further attention to style. One of the most impressive hardboiled novels I've seen in a decade. I hope I'm right. Fred is broke and living on a houseboat without electricity. The book is at Knopf now. I hope it has a double happy ending.[16] Why am I telling you? Because your wish may be more effective than mine.

Love, Ken

The "other circumstances of my life," which had come to the fore in Ken's sessions with Dick Lambert, and through the dream-notebook the analyst

prompted him to keep, included Ken's oft-fraught relationship with Maggie. It seemed more and more to him that his wife's idea of a successful marriage was for her to control his actions. He recorded a horrific dream in which he was frightened of Margaret, and in which she threw insects at his eyes.[17]

Eudora Welty, Bryn Mawr, PA, to Kenneth Millar, October 14, 1977

Dear Ken,

I'm leaving here today after a short trip up to Yale (work) and NYC (work & play) and here (play). It was possible while in New Haven to see the Paul Mellon Collection of English Art of the 18th Century—in spite of a strike which had closed the museum—and all those Constables! In somebody's office (besides all the ones in the show) a whole wall above the desk was hung with small framed cloud studies in watercolor. In NY I had an hour (not enough) at the big crowded Cezanne show at the Museum of Mod. Art. Nona and Joan Kahn each send you warm greetings—I spent a day & night at Rosie Russell's in the country and she too spoke so happily of their having met you in Jackson. She is well & busy & cheerful.

The leaves turned, it seemed, overnight while I was in Conn. and now it's got sharply cold—Beautiful old beeches & maples & sycamores on this campus all burning color. Last night it was so cold & still & clear, the sky had a pink flush all over the North, and a friend with me said it looked very promising for an Aurora Borealis. Have you often seen this, in your Northern years? I never have, and it didn't happen last night to my knowledge, though I kept getting up to look from the windows, in case.

I hope all's going fine with you and Margaret and the two books underway—with everything. How is the Environmental Committee getting along with the plans you've been working on?

Love to you,
Eudora

Eudora Welty to Kenneth Millar, Monday [October 17, 1977]

Dear Ken,

I'm so glad your spirits are lifted, and by now I hope are lifted *much*—Your understanding doctor who is the friend of years—and your own wisdom—give you something good to trust—I am sorry you have been troubled this way. By now I've known you, and read you, long enough to know what a really extraordinary memory is *there* (and to know how important it is)—This makes me trust it (I mean all the more) to come back, or be summoned back, in its power and fullness of strength—when I was last there, I could tell, I thought, how much better it was than the summer before—So I hope things will be easier and better all along now—

Your earlier letter I didn't get till I returned from my trip, which came in Saturday's accumulated mail, and your other one came just now while I was writing to you—I'm glad you did write again, not because I'd had any feeling of shock from what you'd written me (forget such a thing), but because I could see from the two letters together that things had grown better for you between times—I always want to know how you are—

Sure, I remember Zeke [Zack]—What an amazing amount of words. I do wish him well, but he already has the best thing going for him that he could possibly have, your word that it's good. I hope the book will come to a good end and that he will come into some warmth & comfort—I visited some kids living on a houseboat in the Seine, 2 [actually 3] years ago in Paris, and how cold a life that is, nothing alight but candles, no matter how gay (& romantic it might have been once). He isn't eligible for one of the NEA grants, do you think? He might write to Leonard Randolph, Chairman, Literature Division, Nat'l Endowment for the Arts, Washington, D.C. 20506, for an application. (I'm not on the application-reading end of it, myself, and it would do him harm to write direct to me, but maybe I could alert somebody who does judge the applications.) But personally I bet on the *book*.

Herb Harker's statement he wrote to deliver to the Conference of Mormons in Salt Lake City I *should* like to see, especially in the light of what you say about it. I like him and like his work, indeed, but you know how much all you have done for him, and been, have caused the best things to happen for him—I'm glad—not only for him. More next time—-My love, hopes, & wishes for all to go well there—As ever—

Eudora

Kenneth Millar to Eudora Welty, October 19, 1977

Dear Eudora:

Your beautiful cheering letter led me trippingly through a number of northern milieus, then out under a possible aurora borealis. I do remember those softly bright shimmering skies. Still I was and remain willing to trade them for a sea that I can swim in most of the winter. One of the keenest pleasures I know is walking into cold water (which suggests that my tastes were set in Canada after all). An almost equally keen pleasure, though, is climbing out of it.

I envy you those Constables and Cézannes but I envy you even more the people you have been seeing, Nona and Joan for instance. Speaking of Joan reminds me of Fred Zackel whom you may remember as the San Francisco taxi driver who year before last brought part of a detective novel to the Santa Barbara Writers' Conference. The *part* of his novel has now grown into a whole. I think it's good, though it's rough even by my standards. It's powerful and frightening, remarkable for such a young man. I'm trying to help Fred to get it placed and he may send it to Joan if Knopf don't take it. May already have.

This seems to be my month for receiving manuscripts from far places. This second example came heralded in a peculiar way. About ten days ago I found myself, for some reason, getting interested in the Antipodes. By the end of a week my interest had narrowed down to Tasmania, so I looked it up on the map. The following morning I received a letter from Tasmania sent by a friend I hadn't heard from since he set sail from Santa Barbara for New Zealand some years ago. His name is

Norman Sanders, and of course he's writing a novel and the dear man wants me to read it. Of course I will—he's not only a friend but he writes well—but I did suggest that sending it to me is a rather round-about approach. The fact is, though, that I like to see unpublished work and help it along when I can. *Fred* is the one who needs help, and deserves it, most. There is blood and sweat on his pages, and he is a born writer who will settle for nothing less. My main concern for people like Fred has to do with sheer survival.

Speaking of survivors, I am doing all right in spite of some mild depression. This treatment, an hour's talking once a week, is conducted by Dick Lambert who has been a good friend for over twenty years, ever since our family first ran into trouble. Let me assure you that the trouble we have now is not deep and is being alleviated. I mention it mainly because you would in any case have noticed a change in my letter. Thank you for yours—Eudora's Tour of the East. Much love, Ken

P.S.—I've asked Otto Penzler to send you a copy of *Lew Archer, Private Investigator.*[18] Not that it amounts to much—all the stories are old—but I'd like you to have them.

K.

Kenneth Millar to Eudora Welty, November 1, 1977

Dear Eudora:

You know that feeling of impossibility changing into possibility, you know it so well it seems to dwell at the center of your books and stories. It's the consciousness of life itself rising in the mind like the sun in the morning—the master passion that fathers all the others. Well, the depression that lay on my mind like a low cloud cover is lifting, and I can look over my shoulder and see most of the shapes of the remembered past. (About proper news, in the present, I'm still uncertain, but, when I think of it, I nearly always was.)

My friend and doctor Dick Lambert has got me writing about my thoughts and dreams, and that in time has awakened an autobiographical urge which may outlast this emergency. I'm wondering if it would be possible to do an autobiographical story embodying or at least using the themes of one's fiction. It would be fun to try a story moving in and out of the mind, through fiction and dreams and back into solid reality; which is not solid, which is not reality. Reality is in the relationship between the tenses. You know so well what I mean, you are a master of those who find meaning everywhere, which is one among several reasons why I am so grateful for your letters.

Margaret is well. All is well. I really welcome change, though I don't accomplish it easily. My love, as always, Ken

Eudora Welty to Kenneth Millar, [November 8, 1977]

Dear Ken,

I came home from a trip and found a letter from you—I was so glad to hear. I'd been hoping you would say that that low cloud of the depression that had lain on your mind was lifting more & more, and this was good to know. Your doctor's understanding and your own understanding must work together productively and well—that's a comfort and a good sign, isn't it? And as you write about your thoughts and dreams, who knows what might come out of it in the way of a story or novel, as you were wondering. It's where all our stories and novels come from—that relationship between what is our eyes' evidence and what is our mind's image—that reality you spoke of as the relationship between the tenses—My feeling is that the image in the mind which experience produces for us could be also in the form of a plot, a novel's plot—it (whether abstract or literal image) couldn't be any more complicated than the experience itself, heaven knows—I may not be writing this clearly enough. All I was trying to say was how much I agree with you that it would be fun to try a story moving in & out of the mind, through fiction and dreams and back to—what they arose from—The pattern wouldn't be exactly a new one for your special gifts of approach or for all your instincts and well proven strengths and your passion for getting at the spring, the truth—and it would at the same

time tax them well and use them, maybe in ways you never imagined—
not so far. The story of a search that is itself a search. Forgive me if I
put it all badly—I'm almost too tired to make sense, maybe—just home
from Vanderbilt & U. of Alabama in Huntsville—flew home through
amazing wild towering clouds & sunset lights, like illustrations for "The
Ancient Mariner" by A. Dore. It wasn't a bad flight though. Tonight
Reynolds is flying here & we are driving up to Oxford, Miss., to some
kind of symposium—I'll report on the event when we get back.[19]

In the respect of image & work, or reality and fiction, and all, I
wonder if you'd find anything of the same sort in a small exhibition of
my stuff a museum thought up here & put on, to which I'll send you the
catalogue—It's not something I myself would have ever thought of—
had not really known of such matching elements in pictures I snapped
& in stories I wrote—They both came to or from me, and it seems they
went back & forth between each other, too. I was about to send you the
catalogue anyway—but now with your remarks also in mind.[20]

And I'll be so glad to get the book. I did very much like the piece
you wrote that they used in the *Times*[21]—I started a letter about it
to you and it is still somewhere in my suitcase, I imagine—I can see
you reading as that little boy—you know reading as a child always had
something about it of stolen happiness, didn't it?

Thank you for writing. My love, as ever, and I know Reynolds
would add his if he were here yet—which reminds me to get back to
the kitchen!

Take good care—

Yours,
Eudora

Kenneth Millar to Eudora Welty, November 12, 1977

Dear Eudora:

I had word of you from New York—Joan Kahn reported that
you were "flourishing"—and now I'm glad to hear from you
that you are safely home, however briefly. It was good of you to write

me in your short time then, and I am grateful for your thoughts, the more so that they seem to chime with mine. I mean our joint idea that I might use my kind of structure to mix approaches to reality—approaches ranging from external through psychological realism into the more dreaming part of our experience, and out again. Certainly the best thing for a writer to do with a trouble of any kind is to find a personal narrative or artistic use for it. I'd been making a few more notes along these lines, and your letter parallels and strengthens them. I won't attempt to write about them now; the point is that a door has opened, or opened wider. The meaningful juxtaposition of different orders of reality is one of the things you've been doing all your life, so I hardly need to explain it to you! I'm eager to see the account of your museum exhibitions in the light of what you've written.

(Which reminds me that I haven't sent you my book of stories yet. I have no great opinion of it, and neither will you have, but I hope it will amuse you. Otto Penzler gave it a handsome binding, I think, and that is about the best I can say for it. Glad you liked the introduction, though.)

I think we all aim at telling the truth about our own lives, or at least our own experiences; aiming at leaving a kind of thumb print-mark on the material. But what about a mind-print?—Speaking of my mind, as I almost too often do these days, I can report that it continues to improve and I'm back in the normal range, I should think. My spirits are better, too, though they never sank out of sight. I'm fortunate in having Dick Lambert to reach out to when I needed him, and in the fact that psychiatry has improved remarkably since I saw Dick last, more than twenty years ago, and so has he. I look forward to our sessions, and always learn something relevant to my need, so that my life is improving. What I have learned—really re-learned—is that if we fail to change voluntarily we'll change involuntarily.

But enough of that. It's just a step or two on the way to the book I hope to write, which will come close to the bone. It would be interesting to write an autobiography as a commentary on the fiction, at least going into the fiction at crucial points; and to write of it as a commentary on the life. A biography illustrated with the pictures of imaginary people.—At any rate it's fun to translate a problem into a game, and learn its rules if I can.

All my love, as ever,

Ken

Eudora Welty to Kenneth Millar, Thanksgiving Day [November 24, 1977]

Dear Ken,

It was good to have your letter—I'm so glad you let me know that things are growing brighter and that a door has opened, or opened wider. I think along with you and out of my own life that the best thing for a writer to do with a trouble is to translate it into his work, find and make a use for it through the expression of that work. You have never been in better command of your gift—This would be a challenge you have never set it, before—Whatever happens, you will have truly gained, will have found what the work itself has brought you. I myself hope and believe that when you do make the narrative and arrive at the structure, the whole that you surmise, it will not only be a fine and original thing in itself but will act as a blessing to you—

This is a warm, cloudy day—still many leaves on the trees, still brighter after a rain—I hear the white-throated sparrow singing—you have him too. I go out to Mittie's, my sister-in-law's, for Thanksgiving dinner with the young—I hope your day is a good one—

Thank you for the book of early Archer stories and for what you wrote in it—I am so glad to have it. I've read them anew, remembering some of them well from Ellery Queen—and of course what interested me most were the flashes of what was to come later, like distant lightning. "Past his narrow cormorant skull I could see the sky and the sea, wide and candid, flecked with the white purity of sails. I spent too much of my time trying to question liars in rented rooms." What a good looking book they made—And I have a second copy, for the editor Mr. Penzler sent me one too. Is there anybody you would specially like me to give it to? The Introduction is the good, brilliant, best thing about it. I'm glad you wrote it and framed the stories in it.

I am resolving that when my commitments for lectures & campus visits are over (sometime in spring) I'll never do any more. It is interesting work, and I like young people and I like travelling, but this has taken quite a lot out of me—and while I've succeeded in earning some money to buy more time to write in, if I'm too tired to be any good, it was the wrong way to do it—In December I have my last go this year, up to our friend Joe Blotner at your old university at Ann Arbor—I wonder if you would tell Herb Harker for me that I much appreciate his sending me his paper that he read at Salt Lake City—isn't it a powerful and moving piece of work? I do mean to write and thank him properly, and for his book as well, which he sent me & which I warmly (he knows it) admire—I am hopelessly behind in the letters I want to write—And to Ralph Sipper—I'm ashamed. It's not that I have forgotten them. I'm going to dinner now—I was thankful for your letter—My love to you and good hopes, dear Ken—

Eudora

Ken was concerned enough about Eudora's financial needs, and the way she'd found to alleviate them, to write his friend Ping Ferry, who often raised funds for worthy causes, and ask if something might be done to assist Welty, "who at seventy or so is having a rather tight time making a living. For the past several months she's been going from campus to campus, teaching and lecturing and reading, all of which she does superbly well.

"She doesn't complain or if she does, her only real complaint is the interference with the work she finds she should be doing.

"It occurs to me that you [. . .] may be willing and able to help her [. . .] to get some clear uninterrupted writing time. [. . .] I think if Eudora could stay at home in her house in Jackson through next year we might all be further enriched."

After hearing again from Eudora, Ken told Ferry, "she has recovered from the sadness and is getting over the weariness, indeed she sounds downright happy. [. . .] I over-react sometimes[. . .]."[22] *But he wanted to make sure he himself was not adding to Welty's emotional burdens by sharing with her his own travails.*

Kenneth Millar to Eudora Welty, November 28, 1977

Dear Eudora:

I was glad to hear from you as of Thanksgiving Day, with the wonderfully kind concern for the problems I've been having. Dear Eudora, cross me off your Worry List, I'm coming back to life, memory and all, and really beginning to enjoy life again. And I intend and expect to make something out of this experience, this reversal of contact with the inner self. Which strangely, not so strangely, is preserved by contact with other people.—I think you and I suffer from opposite excesses, one of us from a world that is too much with her, and the other of us (me) from not enough. Your excess is better than mine, of course, as speech is better than silence, but I dearly hope that you will be able to get back to your own most private work next year, and stay with it as you wish to, and deserve. I have, by the way, passed on your greetings to Herb and also Ralph Sipper, who was most happy to hear from you and perfectly understood that your schedule has been pressing.

I was struck by your statement that these last weeks have "taken quite a lot out of you"; it certainly does suggest that you should spend some time pleasing yourself alone. That is what I wish for you. And I think your concern for me has been a drain on you. I'm sorry—I wish to be a source of strength to you. Certainly you can stop being concerned about me. Don't stop thinking about me, though, I live in the consciousness of your thought as all your blessed friends do. But my spirit is breathing again under its own power, and the life-support facilities can be removed. Partly on account of you, I never saw any reason to be afraid and was not. I only hope I didn't use too much of your strength.

Ever, with love and gratitude,

Ken

"Ever, with love and gratitude," Ken's late 1977 expression of love for Eudora, was but one of many in 1977. Threatened by the loss of his memory, he took

comfort in the constancy of Eudora's commitment to him and of his own for her. He had begun the year by telling her, "I can't tell you what a joy it was to feel that I live in your world, as you live constantly in mine." In July, after Eudora had asked to dedicate a book to him, he had told her that their connection was as powerful "as if we had lived beyond life, as indeed we are going to do now to some extent, together. You make me very happy. You often have." And now he finished the year by saying, "I live in the consciousness of your thought." Eudora responded in kind.

Eudora Welty to Kenneth Millar, [December 7, 1977]

Dear Ken,

I was so glad to get your letter and know both from what you said and how it sounded that you are feeling so much better—Your spirits sounded good again—From now on I hope spirits, work, play, everything will keep right on lifting—the book you think of will bring a good thing out of it—I wish it all you hope it will be—

I do want to tell you, you mustn't think the tiredness I was feeling (better now) has anything to do with my concern for you—Thinking of you adds to my capabilities instead of taking them away—Of course I ached to help somehow—But what I believe is that as we are needed to understand more we do understand more, in our friends, or we try and hope and *continue.*

And you *are* a source of strength to me—

A longer letter soon—I'm fine, and send you my love, and I felt such good heart in your letter—

Yours as always,
Eudora

Kenneth Millar to Eudora Welty, December 14, 1977

Dear Eudora:

I wonder if you saw on television this evening the excellent film covering the extreme northwestern shoreline of Vancouver Island, and the following one about Southern Alberta. I realized more strongly than I ever had before—I suppose this circular motion is one of the narrowing completions of age—and I felt for the moment as if I were happily rounding out my life and going home. Home to the island where my father threw his strength away on the sea, as I suppose, then home again to Alberta where, having been born seven miles apart in Ontario, my parents finally met, and fifty years later or so I went to high school. My cousin Mary Carr who taught school all her life in Medicine Hat (Alberta) has bought a car and opened her house to an Indian student (from India). Her father's beetle collection is in the University of Alberta (where Herb Harker's son teaches) collection in Edmonton, and two of the beetles are named after him: "Carri." These are some of the things my mind has been dwelling on tonight. With the subsidence of depression I find myself getting interested in a number of things, particularly the peculiarities of my own history, which had more space than it needed to move around in. But I must say I'm grateful to be alive, and for your letter, and for your good health. Love, Ken

Eudora Welty to Kenneth Millar, December 18, 1977

Dear Ken,

I'm hoping every day is going more surely better—Will Jim be coming for Christmas now? I hope pleasure comes with him and with everything.

Ann Arbor, where I've just come back from, is as you can imagine all under snow, but the extreme cold they'd been having had yielded a little, for which I was glad. My job was to give a reading and see some students in connection with the Avery Hopwood Awards—Joe Blotner and his family took me under their wing, and we had two good evenings in their house, around the fire—where I stayed was in the Inglis House—does that mean anything to you? Formerly the home of a big industrialist & benefactor of that name, now used by the University for entertaining etc. I loved the house—high up on one of those Ann Arbor hills, with gardens all around it somewhere under the snow—Inside it was early 1900's Gothic—oak paneling, spacious, solid—casement windows opening on the distant view—It made me think of the kind of house some Scott Fitzgerald girl might have had behind her—I lay in bed and waited for them to fix me my breakfast—It was really a restful trip—and my last work trip this year.

Now I'm reading galley pages in the non-fiction book, which will probably take me through Christmas week—I don't mind. The book will come out about February, I believe. I hope they send some sort of bound copy beforehand, so I can send it to you.

I think of you and send my love, you know that. And I hope the New Year will be really new, and all good—with the work and joy you want and in full measure—I hope this has already started! Take good care, and in Christmas be happy, dear Ken. With love, Eudora

P.S. Monday

I just got your letter—I wish I had seen the films of Vancouver Island and of Alberta—where you went to high school. But that was the night I was at the University of Michigan, where you went later. How glad I am that you have got the depression behind you and are finding interest again in things that can well prove fruitful—Thank you for writing. I am thankful to know things are better, dear.

Kenneth Millar to Eudora Welty, December 22, 1977

Dear Eudora:

I was so happy to get your warm letter, which came on a cold day—literally not figuratively cold. I tell how cold the season is by taking the temperature of my pool, which today went down to 53°. I stop swimming in it when it's fifty. I think I enjoy cold water, as I certainly do, in memory of the north; also because it feels so good when you come out.

Speaking of extremes of temperature, I believe I passed a couple of nights in the same guest house as you on the Michigan campus. It was terribly overheated, as you might expect, for my taste, and I couldn't figure any way to turn the heat off. Trapped in hospitality. You wouldn't have run that risk with the Blotners, though, whom I remember as gentle and considerate people.

I may go north in the summer, having been invited by Nolan Miller to sit in at Antioch on a week-long session about mystery fiction. But first I have to write some. I'm now in the latter stages of revision on the *Instant Enemy* movie treatment, which I agreed to do reluctantly, but find myself enjoying. It's really fun to be working again, and the fact that the work is rather simple, difficult though, suits the state of my mind. Something to wrestle with and make sense out of. We have to change position from time to time in order to realize how warmly the sun shines on our various surfaces. And you have to take a novel apart at least once in order to realize the complexity of its inner parts.

These are pleasant weeks, with Jim in and around the house during the long Christmas holiday, Margaret happily working on a sequel to her last book, and Santa Claus crying his wares less stridently than usual.

Christmas greetings and love from Margaret and Jim and,

As always,

Ken

Joy to the world, Eudora, and happiness in the work!

CHAPTER EIGHT

"Our friendship blesses my life and I wish life could be longer for it."

———— ❧ ————

1978

DURING 1978, Ken's failing memory was more and more evident to his friends, but he found himself, one might say heroically, unable to acquiesce in this decline or to abandon his futile efforts to turn his novel The Instant Enemy *into a viable screenplay. Eudora's memory was as sound as ever, but her ability to write languished. She continued as a speaker on the academic circuit, making at least eight such trips in 1978, though the need to supplement her income was less pressing and though speaking engagements prevented her from "getting back to blessed stories." Still, these patterns of avoidance not withstanding, Ken and Eudora more and more openly expressed what had been implicit from the start of their correspondence: the importance each held for the other.*

Kenneth Millar to Eudora Welty, January 8, 1978

Dear Eudora:

I had a deliriously happy phone call from a young man whom you will remember from our writers' conference, Fred Zackel. Fred phoned to tell me that he was in a position to move ashore from his houseboat, turn in his cabdriver's badge, and become a full-time novelist at last.

His novel *Cocaine and Blue Eyes* had sold to Coward-McCann via Dorothy Olding. Fred has been writing for about a decade and this is his first sale. I think the book will make a name for him.

I've been busy for the last couple of months, as you know, trying to rebuild the structure of my *Instant Enemy* screenplay. I gradually got interested, and I hope learned enough to justify my agreeing to write the final screenplay. This doesn't mean I've gone Hollywood; I'm working at home as usual, and see my producer once a week or so. Under these circumstances it's rather fun, a fairly easy warmup for more demanding work.

All seems to be well with us, especially since the great spell of rain we've had in the last week—five or six inches, which is close to half of a normal year's rainfall. Our grass and other plantings are already greening, and the air is fresh again. This may be interpreted symbolically too—I feel fine. LOVE, Ken

Eudora Welty to Kenneth Millar, [January 16, 1978]

Dear Ken,

You lifted my heart when you wrote those words "I feel fine."—And you sounded fine—What happy news from Zack, and how happy he must have been to tell you. (I meant after all that you'd given him.)—Not only your guidance but your understanding of what he was working toward & trying so desperately for, and when his life must have been so lacking in that—understanding. I wish him the very best of success on the book's appearance—and a much easier and safer life.

How is "Instant Enemy" going? The technical things you're finding out might have some interesting results, perhaps in oblique ways, in some piece of fiction some day, do you suppose? (I've always had a feeling of the kinship—or affinity—between the forms of film and fiction, have you? Both of them can escape from the confinements of chronological time & immovable place, for one thing, go fast or slow when they need to. And dreams can be entered into the account, and

memories revived & honored, and predictions proved or justified—&
Truth has a force—) I hope your going treatment serves its present
purpose, the very best way, that is, giving you pleasure in the doing. And
what a second pleasure the public would have, aside from all that, to be
presented with one of your novels done right by in a film version—
Here's our best chance! I've been infuriated by what others have done
to you, the TV things, and I really thought the reason was that the film
writers couldn't *read*—

Barnaby Conrad called. I told him I couldn't work at the
Conference this June—you and I felt the same when we talked, and
I held to that. I told Barney simply that I was very tired from a year
of that, which is true, but more than that my reason is that I sensed
as you did that they'd gotten into a way of using people, and of not
treating the young writers seriously. I'm not going to believe that this
will prevent me from seeing you, because surely we are going to meet,
some better way.

(more later)

Later—

That's interesting that you may be going to Antioch in the summer?
I go to Oberlin College, in Ohio too, but I think in April—

The traveling last year & work attached were a little too much for
me, I guess, but I at least have learned that I don't get over difficult
things as well as I used to—Still a good many dates to keep before
the end of the college year this summer—All the same, I live in the
hope of getting back to blessed stories—In fact I am determined, &
swear I am.

I've been reading *old* mysteries—"The Mystery of the Yellow Room"
which I'd never got hold of till Dover reprinted—Isn't it insouciant?
And *Armadale* by Wilkie Collins, which you doubtless have read—in
which there's not just *one* busy character named Alan Armadale—[1]

I'm glad you got your rain (after that *wind*?) We got some snow
and I'm not so glad—but I'm snug, feeding the birds—Work has been
keeping me busy—proofreading on the essay book, getting a new essay
underway—This one's on E. P. O'Donnell's *The Great Big Doorstep*,

a novel of the '40's I'd loved and asked Ralph Sipper to find for me again—When Matthew Bruccoli asked me to suggest a title for his "Lost American Fiction" I suggested it and he's taking it and asked me to do the afterword. (Everybody in that little story is a friend of yours—except O'Donnell, who died young, & before any of us knew him, but after you read *The Great Big Doorstep* I believe you will claim him.) It's about the Cajuns—you know, the Arcadians from Nova Scotia who found a place to go in Louisiana after the British threw them out—Evangeline and those—But this is a modern & comic novel, and I don't know any other like it.

I am sorry for the poor letter—The real main thing I wrote for was to say I'm happy in thinking of you being fine again—Love as always—
Eudora

P.S. I've just had a phone call from Reynolds—He thinks of coming down here in February, weekend of the 24th—Wouldn't it be nice if you could come too? Maybe if you've finished "Instant Enemy" the change would do you good. We'd probably laugh a lot, play records—I could ride you around in my old Ford—Reynolds will have to tape a short interview with me for the NYTBR for when my essay book comes out, but that won't take long—(Anyway you should be here as its dedicatee.) We could all stop work for a few days and take it easy—

Kenneth Millar to Eudora Welty, [January 19, 1978]

Dear Eudora:

Barnaby Conrad told me at the writers' lunch today that you were definitely not coming to Santa Barbara this summer. Although we are going to miss you, I can understand and indeed share your desire to stay home and work at something entirely your own. For similar reasons, plus the fact of Margaret's vulnerability, I've just regretfully decided to turn down an invitation for this summer at Antioch College from an old friend, Nolan Miller, whom you may know. He and I first met close to thirty years ago at the Midwestern Writers Congress in Chicago.

Well, so much for writers' conferences. I always seem to have more than enough manuscripts to read as it is. This film work I'm doing (on *Instant Enemy*) is turning out to be more fun than I'd dared hope, and I think I'm beginning to understand the rudiments. One of which is that, at least in my kind of movie, the language has to be the popular language of the mass culture. The fun is seeing how much you can say in it, in language that anyone can understand. Well, I was halfway over to that in my fiction already.

It's just started to rain again tonight, and in spite of all the rain we've had in the last couple of weeks—almost a foot, literally, at our house, and fifteen or sixteen inches in the hills, I'm still refreshed by that pitter-patter. Some recent days, it came down so hard it sounded like the flood re-enacting itself. And our little hill creeks turned into torrents which ran together as they neared the sea, in swift brown little Mississippis inundating finally the sea itself. The sheer wetness of everything and everybody is a delight, over and above the fact that our drought is over for a year, anyway. In no more than a week we got a whole year's rainfall. And every morning, "when I awoke, it rained."

Coleridge and the Ancient Mariner, which I recently reread after a long lapse, seems more than ever relevant, and at the very source of modern poetry, where everything visible is furred at its edge, or lit from within by a symbolic flame and/or the eye of the beholder. All my love, ever, Ken

Eudora Welty to Kenneth Millar, Thursday [January 26, 1978]

Dear Ken,

Your good full welcome rain was coming down when you wrote your letter—I read it in the rain here, so I might have been listening to both of them—Just to stay with it, I set down & read "The Ancient Mariner" again too—

Our letters may have crossed—I'd written to tell you about my conversation with Barny about the Writer's Conference—I think we feel the same way about that. But I hope we are going to be able to see each other in some easy & undisrupting way for you. It is hard to think of not. But when you wrote that you weren't going to Antioch after all I realized that I must have sounded so *light-headed* coming out with that wish that you and Reynolds and I could all just come together at my house—Well—Ken, I am going to trust in our good star—It's a strong one—Life is full of hard work here too—or maybe the final script you're doing isn't hard by now. It's good that it's giving you pleasure and some interesting sidelights. It is going to be published, I hope,—your script as you write it. That good series, the one that has "The Third Man" & "Brief Encounter" etc—the classic examples.

My piece on E. P. O'Donnell is still not done for Mr. Bruccoli and I must get back to the typewriter. It's cold here—We had it snow twice—There is a towhee in my backyard that at the sound of my kitchen window going up, for me to put seed on the windowsill, gives a whistle exactly like a boy's with two fingers in his mouth—

My love to you. I think we stay close—I feel that we are, every day. I hope everything goes well there, getting greener all the time—

Yours,
Eudora

Kenneth Millar to Eudora Welty, January 28, 1978

Dear Eudora:

I have been slow in answering your wonderful letter and invitation. Margaret's one-year examination—one year after her operation—was scheduled for this week, and I have been awaiting the results. The results are as good as could be expected: Margaret is physically well, with no signs of recurrence. In spite of that, I hesitate to leave her alone for a while yet. She is still sitting in the shadow of the big scare, and I suppose I am, too. Clearly it would cause her pain for me to be gone for even a few days. So I will stay here instead, and hope that your invitation will be a re-open-able one. You know how I'd love to come, and celebrate with you and Reynolds the publication of a book which is so important in my life, and will be in the lives of many people. No one has ever given me such a marvel. I wish I could take it from your hand. But I believe you will understand why I cannot.

Please give my love, which you always have, to Reynolds. I hope to see you both before *too* long.

Ever,

Ken

Kenneth Millar to Eudora Welty, [January 28, 1978]

Dear Eudora:

I have sad news. Our dear friend Don Freeman died suddenly of a heart attack in New York, where he was seeing his latest book through the presses. Don had a severe heart attack several years ago but refused to let it slow him down. He made himself available to his friends and confreres, and was constantly appearing at schools and other gatherings for the benefit of children. It seems impossible that he should have gone, he was so warm and lively. He's left behind him an incredible oeuvre, thousands upon thousands of drawings and paintings, and almost that many friends all over the country and the world. I'm glad you got to know him here, for both your sakes.

When I picked up the paper tonight I'd just written you a short letter explaining what made it difficult for me to leave home these months, even for a few days. It's simply that Margaret can't bear to be left alone, at least for a while yet. Which makes it impossible for me to travel for the present. But I trust that this will change.

Of course I thoroughly understand your feelings about the decline of our writers' conference. You were more than patient to stay with it as long as you did. But I'll do my little stint for them if they wish, I hope in the same spirit that R. M. Lovett used to attend the criminal trials in Chicago, in the hope of influencing the courts into a carriage of justice.

We're both working, M. at her nearly finished comic mystery novel, and I at the more or less final version of the screenplay. Please don't look for anything remarkable about the latter. This is my first screenplay, and I took on a complete script from another writer—a script which I've been methodically tearing apart. I find I'm rather enjoying the work of demolition, but I don't intend to stay with it beyond this single piece. It's comparatively light work and should make a fair transition back to the books I have waiting for me. My mental energy seems to be improving day by day, and I'm enjoying every day.

But I am disappointed not to be able to come and see you this spring, and to miss Reynolds as well. We had a great rain over the past several weeks—as much as an average year's rainfall—and the brown hills have turned green, and once again our water supply problem has been solved at the last minute. We have had huge tides, too, so rough that I haven't been in the ocean for over a week, and our beaches are denuded and stony. But the sand will sift back and the water will calm down a bit and we'll have a green soft spring.

I feel as you do that you and I are close, and count it one of the great blessings of my life. If our understanding flickered for a moment that's only in the nature of human affairs, and no loss. You know what pleasure and pride your friendship brings me, and what understanding, and what absolute pure thought in which I dwell content.

All my love, Ken

Eudora Welty to Kenneth Millar, February 12, 1978

Dear Ken,

Thank you for two letters—one with the warming news of the doctor's good report on Margaret—I'm so glad. And a lift to have it come just as she's ready to wind up her new book, too. I'm glad for you as well. With the days getting longer and spring getting surer, good signs and good hopes.

The news about Don saddens me, and for you and everybody that knew him. I sent Lydia a little line, hoping she'd let me say how much I value the times we'd all been together there. It was one of those lovely things that came to me through you, getting to know them a little. All that vitality and the joy he took in being a part of this world—in his big wide orbit, friends, countries, books, music—children—always joy in the doing—His name always seemed so right to me—I'm glad and grateful for the chance I had to know him. Do you remember that nice snapshot that was taken at the Club Casino the first time I came, with you & Don & myself all with smiles, around the table? I prize that— there were good times ahead of us all.

The piece I was writing for Matthew Bruccoli got finished and mailed in—He says he likes it and adds, "Let me know if I can ever do anything for you. There is a special link between us: Ken Millar has dedicated a novel to each of us." (I knew that!) When this book comes out, *The Great Big Doorstep* by E. P. O'Donnell (which another friend is another link in, Ralph Sipper, who located the book for me, which I submitted to Mr. Bruccoli for his Lost Fiction Series) I'll send you a copy. I believe you'll find it entertaining, and also of interest to you in your belief in the North American Language. (It's Cajun.)

Your work goes to please you, I hope. It sounds such an enjoyable, as well as useful, thing to take on for this time in between, and before you get back to the books you want to write. My own interlude of giving lectures has filled its purpose, too—I needed to catch up on money so as to buy time for the writing I hope to do next—but it has made me tireder than I thought it would, and I still have more to go. I'm OK, though. Spring will be good, won't it? I hope your heavy rains aren't proving *too* heavy there—(I keep up on the National Weather News.)

Of course I want you to come any time you might wish and see a chance to. I do understand how it is. I wouldn't want pain to come from my invitation either. It was the thought you were going to Ohio later that made Jackson for a moment seem not impossible. It will be just as lovely another time.

I'd better get back to work—It's a soft day—gray and somehow springlike. It's been cold—I'll go out & mail this & get a breath of spring air—My love always—

Eudora

Eudora Welty to Kenneth Millar, February 28, 1978

Dear Ken,

I hope things go well with you—Are you nearing the finish of the screenplay?

The other day Dick Moore called up and mentioned that the "Writer in America" series we both did a stint for is about to start showing on PBS, which maybe you'd already heard and he said yours was to be April 20 (as on WNET in NY) and that you'd written a wonderful letter to him after you'd seen it—that you like it very much. I look forward to my chance to see it—Mine is due May 11 (NY). It's good that finally all the work Dick & Phil did on that series will get its showing—They are so fine, didn't you think? (He didn't mention [Ruth]—)

This little item (no, it's coming separately) is just a curiosity of a kind—a magazine in France, at the University of Montpelier, for some reason of their own (the students' own) is devoted entirely to Southern writers in the U.S.A.—it's named *Delta*. My turn came up, and they asked for this little story by name, which an English editor had at some time seen in the local Archives (!)—written in my earliest beginnings & never accepted in the rounds I sent it on. Now, about 40 years later, it appears, surrounded by a cloud of French criticism of my work which I am not able to read. I saw a copy of the magazine but have not been sent one, but they sent me a handful of offprints of the story. I wanted you to have it anyway—[2]

Reynolds came, and we had a nice visit—The weather, which had been severe (16°) for here, and cold for weeks on end for the most part, brightened and warmed—it seemed almost Californian. I gave Reynolds the second copy I had of *Lew Archer, Private Investigator*, which he was delighted to get. (I had just got it back from a young man from here who's been working with film in L.A.—he knew your other work already, and was anxious to borrow this, so I risked it. He wrote how much he admired the stories, which didn't surprise me of course, but I was surprised that he really did return it. He said the Introduction helped him in his own ideas.)

I'm still working as well as I can in between trips. Next is North Dakota—I dread that a bit—recently, the weatherman on some news program mentioned that Grand Forks had something below zero with a chill factor of 69° below! I need a muff.

There's a later date I have (in April) in Lubbock, Texas, and that looks on the map to be not too far from Santa Barbara—(More than halfway.) Do you think if I were able to come on to Santa Barbara and it were easy for you we could have a day to meet and catch up on everything? Closer to the time we could see.

How is Lydia Freeman? I was happy to see in the gallery listings in the *New Yorker* that a memorial exhibition of Don's work would be held all next month—I wish I could be there to pay homage and take pleasure in all I saw—

My love to you always

Eudora

Kenneth Millar to Eudora Welty, March 8, 1978

Dear Eudora:

I loved your story about the acrobats and can't understand why a story of such originality and imaginative purity (which is your hallmark) should have had to wait so long for first publication, in France yet. Not that France is a bad place for it to be published: the original home of that kind of art, which I won't try to name. A greater event awaits me, though, which I'm looking forward to with intense pleasure: the publication of your collected criticism with my name on the flyleaf—wholly undeservedly but there. No one has ever made me such a gift as that, and that *you* should have is the best gift of all. Archer may fall by the wayside but Eudora will take me down the centuries and future scholars will be asking each other: who he?[3]

I would dearly love to see you but hate to think of you taking the long trip out here for just a day or two. I have to go to the International Mystery Congress in New York—my publishers made quite a point of it—and I realize when I look at the calendar that that will be quite soon now. I'll be in New York Wednesday, Thursday and Friday—April [actually March] 15–17—coming Tuesday evening, leaving Saturday morning—and I mention this not in the expectation but simply the remote possibility that you might be coming that way. Please excuse this hurried letter: suddenly it was later than I'd thought.

With love, ever,

Ken

Eudora Welty to Kenneth Millar, [March 23, 1978]

Dear Ken,

It's delighted me to think of you in NY—I want to hear all about it—So many of your old friends must have been on hand there, all gathered in one place. How could they have had the meeting without you? I read you quoted in *Newsweek* and the day Tom Brokaw interviewed 3 of the crime writers on *Today* I was disappointed he couldn't have you but your name was in fact spoken more times on the program than that of anybody there. And Brokaw said that John Chancellor was always alert for the publication of a new Ross Macdonald. So vicariously you were on *Today*. I wish I could have been in NY too. I was preparing for a long flight myself, to North Dakota—from which I am just back—

You might be interested to hear I was working there with Ring Lardner, Jr. I kept having the feeling you might know him, though I don't know what led me to think so. Anyway, if you don't know him, he is one of the best, nicest people to meet you can imagine—exactly like the idea you get of all the Lardners as a family.[4] Reserved, strongly intelligent, patient with other people—He read a paper on his experience as one of the Hollywood Ten, a plain, lucid, un-self-pitying, un-self-defensive, straightforward account that is classic & should remain classic of its kind—He said the Op. Ed page in the *Times* recently ran a brief excerpt, but the whole ought to be in the public print. He shows in his face signs of the sufferings his family has gone through. I felt so much goodness in him, and wasn't a bit surprised, considering who he is & who he is the son of—

He also swims every day. And there was a *swimming pool* in the *lobby* of our motel—With real potted palm trees around it—an oasis in the snow.

North Dakota, which I admit I'd been dreading, because of the time of the year, was a pleasant surprise—Ice & snow piled everywhere, of course, but the temp. had warmed up—20°s at night & 30°s by day, so my non-fur clothes were warm enough and the air was delicious to breathe. Once more I was disappointed in not having the luck to see the Northern Lights. But the flight was beautiful—Strange as a desert, empty and hill-less, white, grey, black—black dirt in sparse patterns & squares before we left it behind for all white—Endless visibility, a clarity that looked very northern—very far up on the map—and the Red River flowing north—Nice young people attending the university, mostly from farms in N.D. & Canada. But late yesterday afternoon, flying back down, it was lovely to see the land below take on tints of pale green & pink and brown, & the Mississippi *un*frozen winding down under us, & then to get off in Jackson with the trees in earliest leaf and the daffodils in people's yards (mine included) and hear the birds at it without a stop—It's balm! I'm out on my porch writing this—

You'll get the first copy of my book when they send it to me—some day soon, I guess. I hope you will like it when you read it. That life had the possibility in it that we could write books and dedicate them to each other like this seems to me such a felicitous thing—

Have more trips to go, and tired just at the moment, but with spring here I'll catch up on energy—Will write when I know more about what I have to do in Lubbock, Tex.—I hope I might get to say hello to you before too long. I hope you found all well at home and the good spring time ocean ready for you—And Spring.

My love,
Eudora

The Second International Congress of Crime Writers brought nearly three hundred authors from various countries to New York City at the end of March.

Ross Macdonald, as a, or the, star of the occasion, was interviewed by many media outlets, from Newsweek *to* BBC-TV. *At a Ross Macdonald Luncheon sponsored by his publishers, though, Millar seemed to old friends to be uncharacteristically vague.*

Kenneth Millar to Eudora Welty, April 2, 1978

Dear Eudora:

I am slow in answering your letter, though it made me happy to get it, as your letters always do. Got home from New York only to plunge into a long-deferred bout with income tax (which for me seems to mean getting the year's accounting attended to at one fell swoop.) I don't really enjoy that part of our work but I don't feel like complaining about it, either—the whole enterprise becomes so less interesting as we go along. And I enjoyed meeting with the writers in New York, though not quite as much as I'd have enjoyed being with you (and Lardner) in North Dakota. Your account of the weather there reminded me of my school days in Winnipeg which isn't so far from where you were, as the crow flies. You got there long past the real winter which can descend to forty below zero.

I in my turn ran into a confusion of weather in New York, some of it good, though I rather enjoyed a fall of heavy wet Dickensian snowflakes one day. Fortunately, the Crime Congress coincided with what was for me a more important event, the memorial service for Don Freeman in the Church for the United Nations. Lydia was there, and half-a-dozen of us spoke, notably the gallery owner who spoke at length of his art. I spoke of his secondary art, the trumpet which he blew in a kind of secular worship, and would go on blowing until Lydia told him to stop. It was a privilege to say goodbye to Don in that place, in driving rain by the river.

This note is a poor response to your letters but I won't apologize. Our friendship rests by now on deeper-driven pilings even than letters, or even than our dedications which mean so much to both of us. Your spirit lives in my mind, and watches my life, as I watch yours.

Love,
Ken

Kenneth Millar to Eudora Welty, April 13, 1978

Dear Eudora:

It's been a long winter, not in any physical sense, though we have had such roaring tides and denuded beaches, cut away to the underlying rock, as I can't remember seeing here before. But that's all exhilarating. And when I face the matter honestly, head on, I have to recognize that the quiet internal wars against shadowy fears, for oneself or for someone else, also have their slow triumphs, and continual life is the fundamental blessing. You in person and you in your stories and your letters have taught me to perceive and value the things they touch, and put them together in a single rhyming scheme, in which I can hear the slightly hesitant rhythms of your voice. My favorite of all your rhythms and rhymes, and mine, is the one in which we were able to dedicate books to each other, as you say a fortunate chance, in a fortunate season. The more so because our interests flourished and crossed in these books, your lifelong dedication to the written truth, my feeling that it could all be lost but will not be. Nothing of yours will be lost, dear Eudora.

Love,
Ken

"That life had the possibility in it that we could write books and dedicate them to each other seems to me such a felicitous thing."

Eudora Welty to Kenneth Millar, April 13, [1978]

Dear Ken,

It made me so deeply happy to read what you said at the close of your letter about our friendship—you were speaking, as you knew you were, for both of us—You live in my mind in the same way as I do in yours.

What a good thing that you went to New York—It sounds rewarding in a number of ways and I was glad you told me about the memorial service for Don Freeman—A service like that one must have meant a great deal to Lydia, to all of you—and what you contributed, about the wonderful wild free dedicated way he played his trumpet was something none of the others—except Lydia herself—could very likely have told about—not as you could. I felt glad once more that I'd been given the chance to be one of his company & to hear him play that horn into the Santa Barbara night. He was a lovely man—I got to know him long enough to know that—and to have it to remember.

It's high spring around here now—dogwood, iris, azaleas—A sweet-smelling bush, really a tree by now, magnolia fuscata, with thimble sized banana-like flowers, blooming under my window. My niece Mary Alice had a baby, too—her third child, first girl—to whom she's given the family names of Elizabeth Eudora—All has gone well in the way of spring—

I've been to Tenn., Ala., and Ohio lecturing since I got back from N. Dakota, and still have two more to go—I'd hoped to pluck out a few days on the way to West Texas to come by and see you if the time was okay there, but it won't work out this time—the Harvard U. Press has just sent me a bundle to read & judge—their short novel publishing project, which I'm strongly for and had agreed to work for—and by Texas time I might even be too tired to make sense, to you. When I did this lecture thing before, 13 years ago, I didn't get as tired, and besides the trips I was nursing my mother and seeing to things at home, between times. What I hadn't taken into account was the 13 years—But I know we will meet somewhere, before too long—Like letters, it isn't what our friendship depends on, but meetings really are blessings, added on—and your letters are very close to my heart.

Love,
Eudora

April 13 (my birthday)

Kenneth Millar to Eudora Welty, April 23, 1978

Dear Eudora:

Congratulations on the birth of your niece who will carry on, I trust, with the complex and gleeful heritage of her middle name. Gleeful is a word that also connects itself with that free and lovely picture in the *New Republic* the other day.[5] I'm so glad to witness the response that your new book is arousing, and to have a small but special share in it, myself. It's a lovely book. How could I be so lucky?

Over against the death of Don Freeman, who leaves a permanent gap in our midst, is the story of Willard Temple, another long-time member of our group. He'd been suffering from heart trouble for years, forced into a sedentary life which he thought might end any day. Just a few weeks ago he went to Stanford Hospital to have a heart valve of his replaced by that of a pig. Last week he played eighteen holes of golf. This week he's coming downtown to lunch. And so am I.

I haven't finished my first and last screenplay yet but am getting closer, a week or two from the end of the draft, then must decide if I should do the final. I'm tempted to. Whatever comes of this script, it seems to have been a good idea for me. It brought the movie project back to life, and gave me a change of pace which has been refreshing. I like the idea of being back down in the world with the long slope of the next book ahead of me, *not* downhill. I've been reading Matt Bruccoli's *Scott and Ernest*, a book so rough in parts that you may not wish to read it, but with some truth in it; and it made me feel grateful to have been spared the sweats and bleedings of the main literary marketplaces. I never came across a writer I wanted to compete with—wouldn't know how. Well, it's been a good winter and spring (with Margaret getting stronger week by week) and will be a better summer.

I loved your last letter, about Don Freeman—what a pleasure to have lived in the same world with Don, close by, near enough to be touched by his goodness, a manlier odor than the odor of sanctity. Don gave me his pencil sketch of you, though it didn't quite do you justice, either of you. LOVE,

Ken

Eudora Welty, Santa Rosa Island, FL, to Kenneth Millar, May 1, 1978

Dear Ken,

You probably saw this about Don's books, but here it is anyhow— It's a nice piece, isn't it?[6]

Here I am in Florida, on a beach-house-party—4 other Jackson ladies plus Reynolds, a friend to all![7] It's on the strip of Florida nearest to Miss., the northern part—an island called Santa Rosa—quiet & unspoiled, right on the Gulf pounding in—Along here the water often takes on a turquoise color—lots of white caps this morning. We have 3 kites up, one like a long silver eel-like fish, flashing & turning, up there, just like a swimmer—

We drove down yesterday—Reynolds flew—and I was taken by surprise by the sunset—I looked for it to happen over the *Gulf*, as if the sun were going down over the Pacific, and it was not setting over the water at all—the sun was west, the water was south—I was thinking so strongly of Santa Barbara—Well, they're all part of Ocean, the Oceans of the old maps, that lapped all around the perimeter of the known world—

Last night we ate fine fresh fish—and while we were sitting around the driftwood fire in our house the most astonishing wind came up— very loud & strong without a break, tremendous, & yet the sky was perfectly clear overhead, brilliant with stars—The wind went on all night—I thought of that ghost story, do you know it—by M. R. James—"O Whistle and I'll Come to You, My Love"—the ancient Saxon ring that when turned on the finger (I think) called up the wind.[8]

Reynolds is fresh from NY where his play "Early Dark" has been enjoying a nice run with an Off-Broadway production he is crazy about—The reviews are good, the limited run has been extended for another week, and he has hopes of a movie or TV production—He's very much excited of course, so we're all sitting around the dinner table listening—He goes back at the end of next week for the last performance—

I'm glad to have news of your movie script—If you go ahead with the final—and it might be hard to part with it at this point, turn it over to another—it will prove that much more interesting to you, I hope, & I can imagine. Let me know what happens.

I'm so glad that Margaret gets stronger all the time—Is her new novel at finishing point too? It all makes the summer sound good ahead.

My last lecture visit (till October, which will be the positive last) is May 9–11 in Virginia. Then I'll be able to go to NY 16th-24th. It's been a long time since I was there except to pass through—I wish we might have coincided. It will keep on seeming possible since the first time—

I'm glad you are seeing what the reviews (of my book) are like with me. Wasn't that a fine one Ralph Sipper did for the *Chronicle*?[9] He sent me a copy. Since I was trying a kind of book new for me I've been more anxious than I have about any other—My real concern & care is for the opinion of the few dear friends I write for—you & a few. I do want it to give all the pleasure it can to you, which doesn't need saying—

Thank you for your letter—and for the one just before, written the same day I wrote to you, companion letters. I'll write when I get home—This is a restoring little interlude—I feel peaceful & the air is sweet & fresh—Reynolds sends love, & I send all mine—

Yours,

Eudora

I love the sandpipers.
We have some binoculars for sea birds, and (they promise me) dolphins to come

Reviews of the book dedicated to Ken had indeed been good, and on May 7, the New York Times Book Review *added Victoria Glendinning's voice to the chorus of praise:* The Eye of the Story, *she declared, "should be prescribed reading for all literary critics."*[10]

Eudora Welty to Kenneth Millar, May 29, 1978

Dear Ken,

After three weeks of moving around in Virginia and the N.E. I'm back in Mississippi, got in yesterday evening. It was part work, but the work wound up almost a year of it, so I was glad. The New York part was refreshing for being long missed—the sight of old friends, and the sight of the Monet show at the Metropolitan, & a few theatre evenings, and just the whizz of life to move around in—The countryside was all in spring flower, too—

I saw some of our mutual friends in the City, Joan Kahn, Nona, Walter Clemons—All thriving—Nona has a new book out, *Critical Encounters*—She may have sent you a copy—if not, I will. People were giving parties for her and it, and she sweetly included me among her guests—She was feeling very happy about it. It's such a good book, a collection of articles, and essays she's published in periodicals over the years—She has a big, loving Armenian family, nearly all of them scholars, old & young, and they all were beaming on her—

Walter took me to *Ain't Misbehavin'*, the musical about Fats Waller's music—a wonderful show—a new young company of black entertainers who'd come to Fats's music as whole-heartedly and rapturously as if they'd grown up with it. Some of the numbers were too heavy-handed, maybe—"Your Feet's Too Big" was too heavy-handed—It should have been fastidious in the wonderful Waller style—but mostly it (the above) was quite wonderful—I could go right back & see it again tonight. It had just opened, so you couldn't have seen it, but I wonder if you happened to see "Death Trap" [11] and if you did did you like it? I thought Act I was entertaining, but the play might have been better if it had ended there—Act II got progressively weaker and cuter—But I won't say more, in case you still might see it for the first time.

Is your film script going to please you, or is it perhaps even finished? I hope it was fun to see what came of the work—I never feel that any sort of new or different work is lost, do you—it shows you things—but

I hope *Instant Enemy* was a fine triumph and lucky excursion to have set out on—I'd be glad for *Instant Enemy's* sake if it gets made the way its own author intended it to be—

Tomorrow I'll be delivered 3 weeks of mail and if there's news from you I hope it's all good. My best wishes for Margaret too, and Jim— It's deep summer here and it's nice to be back in my own climate and about to go quietly back to writing again.

Much love,
Eudora

Kenneth Millar to Eudora Welty, [May or June 1978]

Dear Eudora:

That was a gleeful letter I had from you in Florida. You'd disburdened yourself of your cares and responsibilities and were simply enjoying the hours as they came. Florida sounds spectacular, a fitting climax to your recent trends. And I'm particularly grateful for the clipping from NYTBR about Don Freeman, which for some reason I'd missed. I never took more pleasure in the contemplation of another man's life, I don't mean just as it ended but in the lucky thirty years that I knew him, a large man in every way, who handled himself gracefully without affectation. He was capable of anger in good causes; the rest of the time he was sunny; he loved his work, friends, children, animals, and hated fraud. I'm glad you came to know him.

Margaret and I have decided to do a little traveling next month, and show Jim a little bit of Canada, the country around Toronto in Southern Ontario. Apart from his seven-month's sojourn in Japan, beyond the verge of memory, Jim has never been out of California. Toronto the Good, which is comparatively crimeless, should interest him; and of course we'll spend some time in Kitchener the Industrial City, where M. grew up and where I once taught high school. We still have friends there, though their numbers are dwindling. And I want to show Jim the farm where I worked for a winter and several summers—Oxbow Farm, in a deep bend of the Grand River which I used to have to wade when

I came home late at night. Oxbow Farm was bought and preserved by the Ontario government as a permanent wild life reserve—last time I visited Canada a pileated woodpecker had been seen there in the maple sugar bush. It was a difficult life then in the depression, without enough hope but there was love and goodness in the people and I was reading philosophy at night. I wonder if any of this can be conveyed to a California boy. But of course it can. The people speak in their actions and their forebearance. I'm thinking of the Mennonites in particular, but this applies to Canadians in general. Their great virtue is patience. They can wait. Which reminds me that my oldest and dearest friend Robert Ford is retiring this year as Canadian ambassador to Moscow, and may take a post in Washington, which is more visitable. I'd hoped to get to Moscow while he was there, but shan't make it. Well, I haven't been to Washington, either. And Ford has never been to California and says he intends to visit here.

Margaret is feeling stronger as you'll have guessed from our Canadian plans. She hopes to have finished her book, and I my screenplay, before we leave. And Jim his first year of high school, where he is the fastest man on the swimming team—faster, literally, than Johnny Weissmuller in his slower day. Slower than who? Slower than you, I think.

EUDORA WELTY PLAYED HIDE AND SEEK
AND NOWHERE DID ABIDE
SOFTLY SHE WENT UP THE CREEK
AND REYNOLDS PRICE BESIDE

LOVE,
Ken

Eudora Welty to Kenneth Millar, [June 18, 1978]

Dear Ken,

Are you North, or South? I've been imagining you & Margaret & Jim in Canada, though my imagination very likely didn't get any of it right—for one thing, I've only crossed that border once, at Niagara Falls. But I think of what you've told me about your early life there—

Jim must have had a pretty wonderful new experience? It's good to know that before taking off the work was to all be got behind you—Margaret's novel and your screenplay. What a good summer!

I'm slow to write, having come home tired, and right after I sent you a line last time, an onslaught of mail fell on me and a review's deadline was pushed up—instead of 3 weeks I had 3 days. I *did* the review but not the review I'd wanted to do—on one of my heroes of the short story, V. S. Pritchett—Do you admire him a lot too? His compactness & concentration in telling his story, the intensification of meaning in quick, brief sequences, & his feeling for people in their predicaments I suspect might appeal to you too—[12]

By the way (I've been going back now & re-reading his early books) Pritchett uses the phrase "the goodbye look" himself—in a wonderful, strange, early comic story called "It May Never Happen"—It fitted his story & purpose too.[13]

Anyway, in the onslaught of mail there was a fine, welcome letter from you—thank you for it—and when you get out from under your onslaught on returning from Canada I'd love a new line on everything. I still haven't answered the mail, part of which was from people telling me they were coming here, & they came—Strangers, mostly, but nice—I feel I may never catch up. Can you throw this feeling off? I just have to catch up, or I never get rid of the guilt. (Writing to friends is a different thing altogether—as you know)

Did you see any of Dick Moore's & Phil's programs? I didn't get to, being somewhere else, or travelling, and I hated missing yours. A lot of people told me they thought the series was fine—From the Janet Flanner one and the one on myself that they showed me back in Sausalito, I believe it. They are professional and sensitive people and stick to the point of showing what matters & pertains to a writer's work—

I've just been to a young nephew's 3rd birthday party and took him Don Freeman's *Corduroy*—He already has *Dandelion*, or his older brother has—my whole flock of small kin love his books—I know the whole Conference will miss him this month.

And I miss being there—being *there*—

Have you seen the new character in "Peanuts" named Eudora? I'm crazy about her—and pretend she's my namesake—Here are some examples if you've missed them.[14]

Next time I may make more sense, but I'm sending this without worrying about a poor letter, but with much love as always,

Eudora

Kenneth Millar to Eudora Welty, [June 21, 1978]

Dear Eudora:

My day was filled with memories of you. It was my annual day to go to the S.B. Writers' Conference and answer questions. If I can judge by the questions and the voices in which they were posed, the students were a cut above previous years, as a whole, but there was the usual lack of focused seriousness, without which teaching time is mostly wasted. And I must say that there was something missing, a lift and rectitude, like a bird's joyousness in flight, which you always brought to our meetings. Like the moon rising. Now our moon has set. But you were right to turn away from a scene that could only deteriorate, and interfere with the loving action of your thought.

I can confess that the past month has been difficult for us, now that it is ending. Margaret came down with a case of the shingles and was in great pain for several weeks—gradually ameliorated by some nerve-block treatments with needles in her back, somewhat like acupuncture. It, or something, worked; and M. announced two days ago that she was over it. Not that she'd let it interfere with what she was doing. She finished a book in the middle of the attack, a wild tragi-farce which is also a mystery novel that solves itself in the last sentence, indeed I think in the last or second-last word of the last sentence. I can hardly wait to send you a copy, to know what you think of it, but that won't be for a while.

I'm continuing work on my movie script and gradually getting it into shape. It seems to be more a technical than an artistic piece of work but it has its laws and as I get to know them I can obey them. One thing, I have learned, it isn't easy work, since the words and directions that we put down are so remote from the finished product. The writing part is technical rather than creative or even imitative art. Still the thing seems to be inspiring as I hammer at it, or try other ways to outwit it. My conditions of work are unusually pleasant (for movie work!)—my young producer drives up from Los Angeles once a week or so, and I give him what I've done and we discuss what's next to be done. Then he has a swim and disappears for another week. So I have the benefit of both his presence and his absence. His name is Burt Weissbourd, he just celebrated his twenty-ninth birthday, his father is the great Chicago builder (and liberal) and his wife just finished her doctoral thesis on the James family. All of which prevents this from seeming like an ordinary sort of job, and makes it more fun.

Speaking of jobs, Jimmy, having passed the age of fifteen, went out and got himself a full-time job cleaning buildings—I think as a kind of declaration of manhood. (I started working, in a grocery store and then on a farm, when I was fifteen.) (Writing long before that, about ten or eleven. When did you start writing? I'd love to know.)

Love, as ever,

Ken

P.S. I saw Nona in New York but she failed, modestly, to mention her book. I'd like *very much* to see it. K.

PPS—Saw Charles Schultz who confessed borrowing your name.[15] K

Eudora Welty to Kenneth Millar, [July 8, 1978]

Dear Ken,

It was good to have your letter—though I was sorry to hear what a bad time this last month has given you there—instead of a good time in Canada—I hope everything is fully all right now though—all health good, all work victorious—including Jim's very first venture as a young man—

I can sympathize with Margaret in her siege of the shingles, since I have been through it too, and can applaud her with feeling for having finished her novel in the middle of it. What you say of that makes me want to read it "soonest"—that word people want to hear back from you at (I doubt if I could ever fix that sentence.). Congratulations to her—

You've surmounted your own project in the middle of it too— It does sound as if it has its pleasant and instructive aspects, the technical problems—I'm sure you licked them, which would make the pleasure—And your young producer sounds nice to work with interesting and intelligent, and intermittent—But I know you must be looking forward to getting back to what's all your own. Some time when I see you, I would love to be allowed to read your film play through. You are always able to make something of value out of the given thing.

I've been working here, without a stop—it's at a good point now—it's a long story, and it's where everything begins to fit together, the edges of the different parts, and you can almost hear it clicking into shape—But I'd better not say more. It's been hard but it makes you feel tired a good way—[16]

It's hot and we are about to have our afternoon thunder & lightning—it just won't rain for us!

I've been thinking of you and sending love, and do now—

Yours ever—don't say "our moon has set"! You were so good to go back and give your work & thought and time to the Conference again—I remember how you felt about that—All the same, if one young person writing gets any good out of what we can do, it's all right then—Some sent me letters that touched me—

I've been saving the essay by Donald Davie for you if you hadn't seen it—remembering your friendship—I liked it, and his mind—Love, Eudora

Kenneth Millar to Eudora Welty, July 22, 1978

Dear Eudora:

A beautiful moon tonight, riding clear of a bank of fog above the sea—one of those beautiful night summer skies. I just came in wet from the pool. These warm summer nights remind me of Canada when I was a boy and fill me not exactly with nostalgia but with a willingness to have been that boy which I didn't quite feel at the time. Which reminds me of V.S. Pritchett and of your asking me if I admire him. Very much. I used to teach some of his stories thirty-odd years ago, and it was gradually borne in upon my slow mind that our lives had certain things in common, notably Christian Science. For such a hopeful (it would seem) religion it leaves remarkably long trails of melancholy and uncertainty, which Pritchett grappled with all his life, successfully. But the struggle made him more matter-of-fact in his fiction than he need have been, I think. Possibly I am talking about myself. Most writers usually seem to be. But I wonder whether this is true of you?

A few days ago Margaret got a happily relieving letter from her editor at Random House. It suggested no changes in her new book but rather wistfully indicated that a few more conventional touches might have been gladly received. For my part I think M's book could hardly be improved on—and certainly not by conventionalizing the plot. Much of it is comedy which is a bit reminiscent of Evelyn Waugh in that writer's lighter moods, and I think it's one of M's best books. My own work is proceeding at a slower pace than I'd like, but the screenplay is getting written and I think it's coming into its closing stages. I'm eager now to get back to fiction, which was after all the outcome I sought. It seems to be a time of change for us, one of those finishing periods when one looks around and up. Not a little of the change has been induced by Jim, who decided in this his fifteenth summer to put away childish things and, in fact, got a man's job. He's working as a shipping clerk in a vacuum cleaner business and evidently enjoying it. I think *he's* thinking about getting a car, which he can do next year, and when that happens he can make his way to the ski slopes without having to persuade an adult to take him there. But I'm really very glad that he's a self-starter. (His job is just a summer job, of course.)

We've been entertaining our friends and ourselves (e.g. Herb Harker who is a great horseman as you might expect) by going to the horse show this week. One of the events I love has nothing to do with horses—a competitive herding of sheep by border collies—is that something that you can see in Mississippi?—Mississippi is never out of reach of my mind, dear Eudora. I can reach out and touch it, literally, in the book you inscribed to me. What pleasure that has given me in all ways, more than I deserve, but I'm just lucky, I guess. With all my love, Ken

Eudora Welty to Kenneth Millar, [July 26, 1978]

Dear Ken,

Is everything all right there? I'm trusting so, only when the mail comes without a letter in your hand after what seems rather a long time I want to make sure all is well—But I expect you are hard at work on the movie script. Margaret is fully recovered from the shingles and feeling good about her newly completed novel I hope—and those difficult times over with.

Here I've been working steadily, on a story that I'm enjoying the problems of but trying not to let it get out of the shape of a story—it threatens to. I work most of the day but do most of the typing while it's early and not so hot—I can't seem to concentrate in the same room with an air conditioner—It's distracting enough to pit myself against the electric typewriter, which *waits* on you—as if drumming its fingers while you think. But it's a help in not being (manually) such heavy work. In the afternoon I come down to the air conditioned guest room and go on with my pen. You asked me when did I start writing, and I've been trying to think—I think as early as I *could* write, that is, write words, I made little books, to give my mother, paper cut to make double pages, and a shirt cardboard cover, with holes punched in & threaded & tied—the book came first, then I filled it up with a story about a rabbit or something, and crayon illustrations (rabbit on the telephone).

Then I wrote the usual "clever" things in school but I assure you they weren't the least interesting, full of the cautious conventional—it was years (after college, even) before I broke through my shyness—when I first began sending stories out to magazines, and it was a far-away editor who would read them. Then I stopped being clever to be whatever I was without its protection.

But I still love a book for itself—I would like to be able to make it from the beginning still, & illustrate it & sew it as well as write it. It would have taken me a while longer with "The Eye of the Story" (there aren't many rabbit-characters.) You used to draw too, didn't you?

I'm getting you Nona's book but everything takes such a time[17]— She writes from London—did you get a postcard too?—that she's having a fine time. So do the Kahn sisters—they've been in London too—Mary Lou too!

A young mocking-bird is living here this summer of extraordinary beauty—he has paler grey coloring in the head & breast than usual and very wide, very white stripes on wings and tail—when he stands on the roof of the feeder and bathes in the afternoon rainshower—like now—you never saw such flashes—He's a dazzler—And the other day he was walking about in the grass of the front yard and he put back his head and looked up the length of our oak tree, that I guess is about 75 years old, and I tell you he *contemplated* it—Then decided to go back to the grass. He sings, too—

My love to you. When you get a chance, write me—don't feel pressed—I just want all to be well—

Yours ever, Eudora

Eudora Welty to Kenneth Millar, [August 15, 1978]

Dear Ken,

All of you are still all right, I hope—and didn't get bumped and spun around too hard—*how are you*? I hope the house is safe & sound, & the dogs are—The cabana—And the court house tower still standing, and Ralph's books OK—and the Botanical Gardens—and all.

That big fig tree still rooted down—There's not much news to be had on the national news, just "the most severe in 30 years"—which sounds terrible—and "nobody was killed," which sounds good—I will seek more—

Thank you for your lovely letter—I was glad to know all of that—I will write again soon. Have been reading & judging books & films for people, had to stop my story for a few days—My love to you—Take care & retroactively to cover that earthquake—

Yours ever as you know,
Eudora

Kenneth Millar to Eudora Welty, August 22, 1978

Dear Eudora:

I'm sorry to have given you reason for concern and yet I did so knowingly because it is in the nature of our loving friendship to record the dark as well as the sunny hours. Not that my life is dark now, or ever was. But there are a few clouds across the sun, gradually lifting and dispersing as I go. The worst of them, an almost literal cloud, was the shadow on my memory and therefore on my mind. But it was never dark enough to cut me off from hope or even from pleasure in the use of my mind. The only limitation, really, was in the kind of work I could do, and its extent. Fortunately I've been able to be gainfully, and I might even say creatively employed in my movie venture which is drawing to a close soon, I hope successfully. At worst I'll have supported our household and acquired (if I have) a new skill—not a high one as I practise it but a skill, and one worth knowing. A skill is not as helpful as an art but still its employment can be deeply enjoyed while leading us back to the other. The ant legions of the mind climb slowly over the mountain pass and discover that it's only a furrow. But the furrow is there, and the ants will remember its shape when it turns into print. I hope this tentative report conveys to you that I love the subjective life in all its forms, even when they are limited. Consciousness itself is the miracle, along with its twin sun love which I suppose is the source of everything we know.

All well here. Margaret fully strong again. Ken not weakening. Jim growing as we would wish. Love, K.

(How are you? Blossoming, I think.)

P.S. I kept this letter with the thought of rewriting it but then I decided not to. It records or at least touches on some mildly troubled experiences which seem to be dropping behind me. Or I am pushing ahead of them. Your letters are always lifting. K.

Ken's letter distressed Eudora, who was worried about the demands Margaret's bouts with poor health had placed upon him. Eudora had faithfully tended her mother through eye surgery, blindness, and a series of strokes. When at last her mother had to go to a nursing home, Eudora chose the best one she could find. Though that facility was fifty miles from Jackson, Eudora drove there daily when she was not away on working trips. During a decade of such difficulties, she had been able to write only two short stories. She well knew how debilitating the role of caretaker could be.

Eudora Welty to Kenneth Millar, August 29, 1978

Dear Ken, thank you for writing, for it's true I had been concerned—I'm glad to know that you are feeling ahead of what's troubled you and I hope all shadows are lightening—You have done so much—From time to time I can't help think that strong as you are and being such a source of strength to all those you care for (all that "strength" implies) you must some time need a little time or a way to restore some for your own—Forgive me if I need forgiving for saying that, and poorly as I put it in words too. I guess I felt I could say it because you've been a source of strength to me. And because I had to learn for myself about that kind of tiredness—

It'll be good when the movie script is a completed thing. I should think writing one would be an invaluable way to learn new things about the writing of stories we'd be the better for knowing—perhaps oblique ways, but I always put a value on that—I am a lover of all ways of learning to *make*—Making a film script would be a whole new, and I can well believe hard, discipline—But where maybe you couldn't use a great deal of what you'd learned in writing novels in writing the film, I wonder if what you learned in writing the film mightn't give new glimpses to the imagination of use in writing novels? Oblique, that is. Actually, I think movies and short stories have a sympathetic relationship that's fairly strong, do you?

I want to write you something more about Pritchett, and some other things I had to tell you—Oh, one remark in our paper you might appreciate for the same reason I do—When a tornado hit at Crystal Springs, south of Jackson, a man on the scene said, "It didn't sound like a freight train to *me*, or a jet either, like they always say. It just sounded to me like a bunch of wind and it looked like a sheet of water. I says to my son, 'Hoss, we're in the middle of a tornado.'"

(This didn't hit in Jackson, just went over "aloft" as they say, but the season changed, I think—Today it's cooler, clear, and it smells of a lot of fallen pine straw, clean & shining. How the mockingbird sang! I'll enclose one of his feathers he dropped in my backyard. (in lieu of the song)

Is Santa Barbara mending all right?

I think of you and send love and wishes for good days in a long line ahead, the best days of all—

Love,
Eudora

I wish this were a better letter but I am sending it all the same.

Kenneth Millar to Eudora Welty, September 18, 1978

Dear Eudora:

I shouldn't have written you when I was feeling depressed but I did so anyway, perhaps in the thought that I would sooner be known truly than favorably; but I'm afraid with the effect of depressing you. I'm feeling much better, for reasons that seem as obscure as the causes of depression. You did spell out one danger in my life, I hope not in yours, that one can be used up in the service of pain and trouble not one's own. Well, I'm not used up. I hope I was able to lean on your strength without abating it, and on your knowledge of trouble and its meanings without deepening your own troubles. The best thing that can happen to a man is to be known, and by a woman of your great kindness and light and depth. I think you read the situation and showed me a step towards change.

The world itself, not only its poor denizen, seems more hopeful than it has for a while. It seems to me that the three men at the Summit have stepped back from the edge rather finally, and that the President's good will and understanding have again justified Reynolds' opinion of him. It seemed to me that all three men showed great skill and good will.[18]

Sliding from the large to the lesser, I'm in an interesting situation. A month or so ago the Russian weekly OGONEK began to serialize my old book *The Far Side of the Dollar* under the title (in Russian) "Path to El Rancho"! My old school friend Bob Ford (Canadian ambassador to Russia) wrote to ask me if I'd authorized the edition. The answer was no. I don't seriously object but I think it's time Russia learned to go through the motions. But of course, in Russia or anywhere else, I'd rather be read unpaid than not at all. This is Ford's last year in Russia, by the way. He speaks and writes Russian, and has become a rather central figure in contemporary Russian letters. You may remember my mentioning him when you were here. And he promises when he retires next year to go home to his flat in Paris by way of California. I hope he does. He was my dearest friend in college and though (or because) we seldom meet, nothing has really changed in our relationship, though it may change quite rapidly when we do, not necessarily for the worse.

I'm getting along towards the end of my "Instant Enemy" screenplay, but have no way to judge it yet. It's something that keeps changing until it finally freezes and gives off a reassuring chill, which I emit. I have spent about six months with it and kept finding things to do, without quite knowing why—a new and rather refreshing relationship with work. Margaret has sent in her new book to Random House and got a good response, as she should. It's a wild comedy controlled by a good plot which unwinds itself finally in the last words of the last sentence.

I think you'll enjoy it, and will send you a copy when it's made, nine months or so in the future.

Well, I seem to be looking forward rather happily to the future, and perhaps I shall learn to keep still when I stumble and bump myself.

Love,
Ken

Before she received this letter, Eudora had already written to Ken.

Eudora Welty to Kenneth Millar, September 19, 1978

Dear Ken,

There's a feel of the changing season in the air with us, even though it's still hot—and I hope it's a season of coming good with you—Good work & good plans ahead. Most of all, good spirits again—

I've not much news to report—I've been writing some and cooking some and on Sunday will be helping (I hope) our little New Stage which has bought a new theatre (you were inside our old one once, that used to be a Seventh Day Adventist Church, but finally nothing was going to keep it any longer from falling in on us) by giving a program of readings at a benefit for it. Everybody else has been working quite hard asking people for money for New Stage, and *I can't do this,* so the benefit is my rather daring substitute—It's daring because I'm doing it in front of my home town—it's different with an audience of strangers or students, such as I've been working with all year—And daring because they've made it the first thing to happen on our new stage. Suppose nobody comes—

This work year has been something to physically recover from, and I think I am at last slowly making it. But I was exhausted all this summer just when I had gained the time and some money in the bank so I could carry out my hope of uninterrupted writing. I've done a good deal of writing, true—that rests me, in the best sense—but is it good?—I don't know, and the lecture year wasn't worth it if I find I need to do the writing & thinking over. (It's a good *hard* piece of work, which I like.) Well, I press on—

Talked to Reynolds not long ago, who says he's all right. He'd had a burglar in his house, though—someone had entered while he'd gone out to eat lunch, and had gone all over things, probably looking for money, but had only carried off the stereo system—Reynolds has all kinds of other things like TV, electric typewriter, camera etc. that he might have stolen. But he pawed through everything—contents of desk, dresser drawers—This wasn't the first time Reynolds has had a thief, his house is in the country, on a road with few neighbors—So he put in an alarm system. He feels better for it, and I hope these events will stop. (I'd go a little wild to be closed in & wired up with those alarms, which I've heard go off by mistake in other people's houses, but maybe it does come down to a choice. Anyway, *he* feels a whole lot better.) *You* have your dogs!

Mary Lou tells me her son Duncan is writing a book for Harper & Row called *Disappearances*—you remember disappearing is what *he* did, for the good part of a year. Putting aside all he'd been endowed with, education, training (he was a PhD, teacher of English, with a brilliant record) also, disdaining all his worldly goods which his mother had wanted him to have *young*, not wait till she was gone, and of course his family & friends, he emerged with a new name, new life, in a new part of the country—Atlanta—lived in the poorest community with a black homosexual friend, & I think started from scratch with some unskilled form of job, and has got back in touch with the world of thought and ideas and creative work again gradually, and now he is writing about it, in some aspect evidently. Mary Lou, always supportive, at all these stages, is thrilled for him now. I felt you would be glad to know of it, having known its beginning—I wonder if many such disappearances find a way back, or not, or resolve themselves in a comparable way—Of course you'll have surmised there are many other conflicting factors in Duncan's story—I hope he is coming into his own, his real own, now—A gentle, sweet, apprehensive young man—not really so young now—sensitive to all the injustices of the world, the last time I saw him (10 years ago)—

I hope the film script is getting wound up and maybe out of your way now. Good news about this and about the other things too, I hope and trust.

My love to you—

Eudora

Eudora Welty to Kenneth Millar, September 23, 1978

Dear Ken,

We do want to be known truly, and I want to know truly. I'm glad that you feel you can lean on me—it is part of trusting—you mustn't worry or imagine that anything but good could happen to me from our knowing each other—truly—the dark times as well as the bright—for you know as I do there is nothing destructive in it, only everything that moves the other way—Depressed or happy and serene, our spirits have traveled very near to each other and I believe sustained each other—This will go on, dear Ken—Our friendship blesses my life and I wish life could be longer for it—Much love and I'm so glad you're feeling better—

Yours,
Eudora

Eudora Welty to Kenneth Millar, October 18, 1978

Dear Ken,

Nona's book trickled in from the publisher at long last—now it's trickling its way to you—

It's cool and sparkling here this morning—a lot of birds. I've been hard at work trying to get some typing done and other chores, but it feels so lovely outside I had to come out where I sit now on the steps.

Ahead of me:

Sunday the next college date comes up—Connecticut College—then the University of Southern Maine—which is celebrating its

Centennial by holding a festival (or something of *southern* Southern writers—a whole bunch of us, getting our woolies together to go up! In between the 2 weekends I'll have a few days in New York. There aren't many more college dates in the year—I'll be glad when they're done. Last weekend was New Orleans, and for the first time I arrived there by air and saw a wonderful sight—white ibises going about like chickens in the grassy reaches along between the runways, unaffected by the big planes that ran along beside their own flocks, taking off and landing—This must surely have been where their own marshes were once? They could have been preserved by the ingenuity of their own innocence—but that sounds odd? One of those things you think of in the night.—But they were beautiful and strange—no words necessary for ibises.

I'll write you from the other ocean—Love to you, Eudora
I'm hoping all goes well with you.

But all did not go well: Margaret was having eye trouble, though it seemed treatable. It was new cause for worry, however, and made less time for anything else. More and more it seemed Ken's letters to and from Eudora were perhaps the strongest saving grace in his life.

Kenneth Millar to Eudora Welty, [October 30, 1978]

Dear Eudora:

I was much taken with your account of the ibises whose takeoffs and landings run parallel to human activity and were apparently helped by it. Why shouldn't the same prevailing winds help different sorts of fliers? It's a lovely image, and I'm grateful to have it to dwell on.

Our news is good. The damaged retina of Margaret's right eye which seemed for a while to threaten its sight (but not the left eye) has had two laser treatments and begun to respond to them, so well that the treatment for which she flew up to the Peninsula this week didn't have to be given, but will be in another two weeks. Dr. Guy who gives the treatments is the junior partner of the man who invented the use of laser (now deceased) and is number one in the world. So we're much cheered by his hopeful opinion.—Cheered not only by doctors. Our new pup, our fourth and final dog at least for the present is turning out to be a lovely fellow. He's a wholly black Newfoundland who gains twelve ounces a day week in and week out and eats accordingly. He's extraordinarily intelligent, already expert in the strategies of place and precedence but, like a child genius, as innocent as your ibises in his ingenuity. He simply knows geometry in his bones. I've never even met such a smart-natured dog, let alone lived with one. And the other three dogs enjoy him, wonderingly, as human beings do geniuses.

Dear Eudora, come home safely from all your journeys. Your letters gave me wings. All my love, as always, Ken

Eudora Welty to Kenneth Millar, [November 25, 1978]

Dear Ken,

It was nice to come home and find a letter with good news in it from you—that Margaret's eye is responding well to the treatment from the fine—the best—doctor, Dr. Guy. I trust things go well right along now. It sounded as if the trouble must be a torn retina—I can comprehend the scare it must have been and the relief when something could be done to mend it—and laser must be really *something*.

I've been on three college trips in a row and am still exhausted, but want to send you a line however poor. It's Thanksgiving, and I hope you had a very good one. I did, here, with my family of nieces and their husbands and five little ones. The youngest among us, by name Elizabeth Eudora, is 8 months old and can stand alone, but she still hasn't got any teeth—it seems strangely unsafe.

Your new young genius pup sounds a joyful presence. I love their broad foreheads—Labradors—your Labrador's forehead must be extra broad. Or tall, to hold that mathematical brain. You know, I think a letter you wrote me before this one must have been lost—I could tell you thought I knew about Margaret's eye, and about the puppy. I hate to miss a letter. Anyway, I'm glad the one I got had this good news.

I wish you might have had your trip to Maine, because I thought the place was wonderful. A bunch of us (the program, of the Southern Conference invited to the University of Southeastern Maine) met in Boston and drove up, so we could see some of it. I saw the sea! Most of the time, once the work started, was wholly inside the walls of the Holliday Inn, morning till midnight. But one day we (the program again) played hookey from lunch and drove up to Freeport to L. L. Bean's wonderful store, and ate some chowder too. And then one night very late I looked out my window on the 16th floor over the harbour and saw a celestial looking white ship, all lights, slowly put forth and out to sea. I found out she was going to Halifax. Some day I would like to be sailing with her—it was nice to be given at least a view of the sea, and the night sky, and the early northern mornings. Altogether different light from home. But this is very likely the light you grew up with in Canada? The roads in Maine have wonderful road-signs. "CHOICE: Left, Route 96. Right, Route 101," (or some number). They put it to you: if you go wrong, the choice was yours. Paralyzing Yankee sternness.

I mailed you a bound galley of a novel coming out by James McConkey, from Dutton [*The Tree House Confessions*]—which I had a special feeling for. It seemed to me you might like it. Love to you, and good luck. I go to NY next Wednesday for about a week—Let me hear how things go.

Love—
Eudora

Kenneth Millar to Eudora Welty, December 3, 1978

Dear Eudora:

It was so good to have your letter on your return from your journeys, and to know that you were met on your return by Elizabeth Eudora—a doubly queenly name. And I'm glad to be able to report that things seem to be going better here. Margaret is learning to handle quite well the knowledge that her right eye has recovered as much of its sight as it will. She is far from blind, and has been able to read proof on her book. Our life is pulling over the hump and moving into less frightening channels. And I think her book is a good one.

We were amused by something that happened yesterday. A couple of Monets worth a million or so had been stolen from the local museum and were returned under mysterious circumstances which are still not understood. But the secretary of the museum director turned up at my house inquiring for a copy of one of my stories ("The Bearded Lady" in *The Name Is Archer*)—she had somehow formed the theory that the actual theft was planned in imitation of my story. I don't know why that made me happy. Perhaps art is not content unless life imitates it. But the actual theft remains something of a mystery. The Monets have been returned, slightly damaged, but nobody has been publicly accused of the theft. This is a very modern mystery, don't you think? I'll have to solve it again, perhaps.

The central Canadian light is not the same as the Maritime light, which draws on the surprisingly nearby Arctic. When I took the northern route out of Montreal and across the ocean by way of Newfoundland and (nearly) Iceland, the sun went down late in the evening and came up again almost right away. And once, under that same sun, I counted fifteen icebergs in view at once. They give a special sheen to the light. And I should take my giant pup and go back there for a renewal of the light. As you have been doing so happily this year, but of course in my own fashion. I got off the ship at Liverpool, paid a visit to the art museum which seemed to me to specialize in pre-Raphaelites, then walked across the city before night fell and spent the night sleeping in a field with a bull which I didn't see until morning. He didn't attack. I was twenty.

Well, that is not a solution but memory can lead the way to one, lead one into gratitude for life, and into more interesting responses; including another step on the long road to maturity, perhaps reaching it finally just as it fades out into something else, which perhaps I should be seeking.

I'll be 63 shortly, but somehow for good or ill seem to have held onto my adolescence, waiting for the midnight sun to tan me. I'll keep you posted on S.B.'s criminal and literary life.

Love,

Ken

P.S. Saw Lydia the other evening, and she looked well.

K.

Kenneth Millar to Eudora Welty, December 16, 1978

Dear Eudora:

No solution on the stolen Monet case, but I gather it had to do with the faking and substitution of the painting hanging in the gallery. Everything will come out at the trial, no doubt. The close-mouthed gallery sent me my story back without comment. That's a trial I won't miss: a courtroom really is a place of truth where everything tends to come out. I've sat through several dozen trials, and learned my trade in the courtroom, I suppose. The most remarkable statement I ever heard in a courtroom was offered some thirty years ago by a young attorney who is now the senior Superior judge here, and a good friend of ours: indeed, he helped M. with the legal background of her new book. But thirty years ago in his candid youth he made the monumental goof of saying, about his client, a defendant in a murder case: "I'm sorry, your honor, I can't remember my client's name." He is now perhaps the best courtroom judge in California. His client, to finish the account, spent a year in San Quentin and was then released for error and then given a second trial, which set him free. He went to L.A. and became a private detective. Eventually he retired here at home in the manse in which his reverend father raised him. But I can't write his story, if I really wanted to, as long as he is alive. He might murder me! Seriously.

I believe it was you who brought my thoughts back to murder, when I reread your review of "Sleeping Beauty" in *The Eye of the Story*.[19] It had the effect of making me reread the book *in toto*, the first time I can remember doing that with any book of mine, and I must say I was surprised by its intricacy and force. But somehow those two qualities don't quite mesh, the images at times imperfectly fuse. But that use of imagery was worth trying, even if in the end it didn't quite jell.

As has happened before, your letter reached me in the midst of this letter to you. I was so glad to have it in the midst of the coming together, the often painful coming together that this season can bring—to have assurance that not all the meteors have fallen into the sea, sizzling. I had two other letters in the same mail that lifted my spirits. One was from my cousin Mary Carr, a retired school teacher who had lived close all her life to her school-inspector father, a cold man. But Mary was never cold, or ceased to be before I knew her. She treated me well during the year (age 13–14) I spent with her parents in Medicine Hat. And even now she is keeping in her father's house on the edge of the prairie a boy named Sedenthe, from India, and educating him. The other letter I mentioned came from Jeff Ring who has been writing me since he was a boy in New England. He is now a man in the Philippines, son of an army officer who seems devoted to the attention of his father's world-view. The family Jeff lives with have ten children and, Jeff wrote, "they are all so sweet." So is the world to have such people in it, and you.

Love,

Ken

Merry Xmas! And thank you for good wishes

from our friends in the east.

K.

CHAPTER NINE

"What we need is one another."

❧

1979

IN 1979, Ken Millar had more trouble writing than ever. In the absence of a new Macdonald novel, his publishers scheduled for release another omnibus volume of three earlier books, Archer in Jeopardy. *Millar labored hard on its brief introduction, and on the preface for a small-press collection of some of his book reviews. Even the physical act of writing was difficult: his hand didn't seem to move in the right ways.*

Margaret's eye troubles worsened in 1979, and she much needed his care.

Through it all, Ken kept in touch with Eudora—not as often, perhaps, but with just as much feeling. And she responded in kind.

Whether as a result of worry or not, Eudora continued to turn away from sustained work and embrace sustained travel. In 1979, she made trips to Santa Fe, Boston, Montreal, Champaign-Urbana, Princeton, Florida, Kentucky, Ohio, and England, in addition to visiting New York City three times. When Eudora did seize scattered opportunities to revise "The Shadow Club," a story begun years earlier, she may well have added material that drew upon her relationship with Ken. The backstory of Justine and Henry certainly seems to do so and to date from this time. The affinities that Ken and Eudora shared, the separate lives they maintained, and the regret attendant on separation are to some extent reflected in these characters: "Justine had told him her whole life. [. . .] He had kissed her for letting him hear all she wanted to tell him. [. . .] Yes, they had loved each other, and they loved each other now." This is love at a distance, however, because of Justine's (or Carrie's, as she is also called) caution. "My chance to get away from myself is gone. My chance to move into arms that reached for me I gave back to the giver. I ran away home."[1] In these lines, a fictional schoolteacher, caught up in circumstances quite distinct from those Ken and Eudora faced, may have provided the sort of cri de coeur *each had longed to give voice.*

Eudora Welty to Kenneth Millar, January 2, [1979]

Dear Ken,

As the New Year was coming in—not undramatically, as the tornado warning siren was blowing right along with the whistles and fireworks—I was wishing your year would be a happy and good and productive one—as different from the last as today is from the night the siren blew (The tornado didn't touch down but went over "aloft")—It's bright & clear & cold with a warm sun—this is the 2nd, after a dark rainy 1st—beautiful, & sparkling—I've been out to the airport to welcome Mary Lou, who's coming from Atlanta (her son's home) to stay a few days—Then I'm flying home with her, to spend a few days in Santa Fe—Then back after this refreshment to the joy of getting back to my typewriter—A long year of hard work in another pasture done with—

I'm hoping you too will be finding yourself at the start of a new book—& I wish so much to read it! I'm sending best wishes for books— health—dear peace of mind—to you both—Long lasting wishes, not just little whistles—

Mary Lou will want me to send her love too—And I'm sending a snapshot that Reynolds would want his best wishes to come with as well as mine—for a Happy New Year—Still another friend of us both took the picture, Dick Moore—I will write you more soon.

My love to you,
Eudora

Kenneth Millar to Eudora Welty, January 26, 1979

Dear Eudora:

As often happens in our correspondence, the *answer* to your question about the Monet case arrived today at just about the same time as your question. The *Santa Barbara News-Press* reported that the young Museum guard (aged 26) who took the Monets pleaded guilty to the crime and was given a one-year jail sentence, to be served here, with a four-year state prison term *suspended*. The young man, [M_____], may be put on a work furlough program which will mean that he can spend his working days, if not his nights and weekends, outside. There may have been a feeling in the court that he did what he did as a kind of game—replacing pictures with copies (made by himself, or his father!) in the frames. The frames he destroyed, for some reason, and he must pay for. Strange.[2]

I was sorry, very sorry, to hear of your flu attack after years of unbroken health. Eleven thousand people, and that chilling wind! I trust it has blown over quickly and that you can continue to feel your usual unconcern about the weather, both inner and outer. I think you are an intrepid woman, testing yourself against the chilly east, as I do against the western ocean, most days. We're having a better winter than we expected. Once a month we go to Palo Alto to visit the Retinal Clinic and on our last visit, a couple of weeks ago, Margaret was told for the first time that *this* time the retina of her left eye showed some slight improvement instead of the expected deterioration. We took a cab to San Francisco and celebrated over food and beer until our plane took off, and have been sort of celebrating ever since. I feel as if the tide is turning now, in our favor. I never doubt that it does and will for you. Take care, dear Eudora.

With all my love, Ken

Eudora's response to Ken is missing. In it, as Ken's next letter makes clear, Eudora reported on her plans to travel with a Millsaps College group to Oxford University in the summer of 1979.

Kenneth Millar to Eudora Welty, March 20, 1979

Dear Eudora:

I was thinking of you off and on throughout the day, and when your letter appeared in the mailbox it seemed to chime in concord with my thoughts, though of course it had been written some days before. Not all of my thoughts had been cheerful but there was a steady movement in me now towards the light. I don't know what caused my depression, or why it lasted, or why it lifted, but I am content to have rejoined the movements of the tide, its going out, its hesitations, its coming in. If I tried to escape those movements, I didn't succeed, thank heaven. I am back in a welter of papers among friends, wondering why I turned my face to the wall. Clearly I'm not through with that question, but I've been given a shove, a small shift in my balance which changes my entire posture.

Besides your letter, the mailman brought the first copy Margaret had seen of her book—*The Murder of Miranda*—and Random House had done a nice job with it, given it what I would think special care. For these and other reasons, it's been a special day. I was so glad to hear of your trip to Oxford coming up. There's still a clarity of light in England, in spite of all her troubles, a brightness that falls from the air like the thoughts of great men, and I wish you joy of it.

Thank you for your love during my silence.

As always, Ken

Eudora Welty, New York City, to Kenneth Millar, [April 9, 1979]

Dear Ken,

I'm so glad of your message—Thank you for the thoughtful and swift way you relieved my mind. The operator's note says your call was at 2:10 and at that time I was standing right there at the elevator, waiting to come up—It would have been nice to have heard your voice, but I am awfully glad anyway to know what you said.

The reason I'm up here is a meeting I was asked to come to, out at the Institute of Arts & Letters, not really a convenient time for me as I was at last getting back to work—Of course I'm enjoying seeing my old N.Y. friends—Nona by the way sends her regards to you—It's cold, with gale-force winds—In the Park the forsythia & the willow trees are the only signs of spring—Next Tuesday I'll be flying back to my azaleas—

It's good news that Margaret's new book is out, and I hope she's pleased with it—Just before I left home, I was pleased to receive a copy myself, and have it to look forward to on my return—It's good to see the attractive job Random did on it and also the nice ads in The New Yorker & the Times. I'm watching out for Mr. Broyard's review column, remembering his fine review of her last novel.

Tonight Walter Clemons is taking me to see the murder musical, I guess it could be called, *Sweeney Todd*—Stephen Sondheim's music—and the book by the man (forget his real name) whose pseudonyms are Q. Patrick & Patrick Quentin—I never did—did you—care too much about his mysteries, but will see how he turns out to write one for music—[3]

I'm happier for thinking things are all right with you tonight, and thank you for letting me know—My love to you—it's always with you,

Eudora

On Eudora's April 13, 1979, birthday, the Pearl River flooded Jackson, Mississippi. Eudora's house was not hit by the flood waters, despite Ken's assumption otherwise, and at the end of the month she felt free to join friends for a second trip to Santa Rosa Island, off the west coast of Florida.

Kenneth Millar to Eudora Welty, April 26, 1979

Dear Eudora:

I was greatly relieved to learn that you had left the flood zone. It must have been difficult for you to be forced out of your home under such circumstances. But you have friends everywhere and I know you'll have been well looked after. For a woman who speaks softly and doesn't deliberately seek adventure, you do have your share of experiences.

I hope and trust your home won't have been badly damaged. But I know this must have happened to the homes of many of your friends, and how long it will take to restore the damaged ones.

You may welcome a change of subject. Yesterday I sat in on a local murder trial in which a youngish woman is alleged to have murdered her husband by firing into his body eight shots from two guns, in self defense, according to her story. And she may just possibly make it stick, so dramatic and convincing was the step-by-step account of her thoughts and movements (and her husband's movements) provided by her defense counsel.

My fellow crime-writer on the other side of the wall, through which I can hear the television talking, received happy news today. Her first review arrived in the mail (NYTBR) and it was a dream review, the key word being "masterly."

Take care of yourself, dear Eudora, and treat yourself with kindness.

Love,

Ken

Eudora Welty, Urbana, IL, and New York City, to Kenneth Millar [May 23 and 24, 1979]

Dear Ken,

It was so good to be able to talk to each other and the timing was just right too, for me, as the next morning I was going off on this trip. I'm cheered to know things are moving along in a good direction with you, and I hope strongly for that day to announce itself to you *soon* as the day a new book begins. Its coming is as sure as time, that's how I feel about things, and your long experience must tell you the same. And *wanting* to tells you too. I'm speaking to myself as well as to you, because it's been a time when I couldn't, & still can't, work—But one of these days.

Thank you for your concern about our flood. It was almost unbelievable—it trespassed on all likelihood—a lake appearing in front of you on your neighboring street where no water had ever been seen before—not a rampaging flood, a quiet creeping up—And in the calm clear Easter moonlight, no sound in the city, except trucks carrying dirt & sand for the levees & helicopters flying over to spot what was happening. The rebuilding is going on now. I must say people everywhere behaved well—They helped each other with might & main, and nobody looted. It was scarey about the snakes. Of course they were displaced too—People getting back in their houses found them high & low. The YMCA, when it was able to be entered, had 5 cotton-mouthed moccasins in the gym, one wound around the clock.

I'm in Urbana on a 3 night stay [May 18–20]. The University Press is getting out a little book of a

Before she completed this letter, Eudora left Urbana and headed to New York City, where she would attend the annual ceremonial of the American Academy and Institute of Arts and Letters.

(cont'd on Thursday [and from New York City]) short piece I wrote, which the university magazine *Accent* published in 1942—they were good to me in my beginnings, & the editor & I have kept in touch over the years: Charles Shattuck—he was in my house when you were, that time, should you possibly remember among so many. Anyway, you have the article itself, "Ida M'Toy," in Eye of the Story. I signed the edition & when it's out I'll send you one.[4] Charles is retiring this graduation & they gave me an hon. Degree—So it's been a pleasant time with him & his family. Green, green in Illinois now—And the corn coming up this big [illustration].

As you see, I've moved on to here—a few days only—Pouring rain but it's rather nice to sit still in my little cubicle [Algonquin Hotel room] & hear the rain falling all around me—In a while I'll go out to join more old friends, William & Emmy Maxwell.

I feel we are bound to meet too—some right time—I hold it in my mind. But we're never out of touch. If not one way, then another.

Did you happen to see the movie "Manhattan," Woody Allen's? I saw it in Jackson just before I came away, and it was a marvelous essence—Funny & packed with things you will recognize—What an ear he has, and how he can use it. In some respects it was more Manhattan than Manhattan itself—Very expert, & visually a beauty—

I wrote Margaret a line to tell her how much I enjoyed her book and will send when I can find it—It's somewhere in this big brown envelope of unanswered mail I carry around in my suitcase—As you see I am writing to you instead, just this little scrap, but will do better when the last college trip gets done—Brandeis on Sunday—My love and wishes—Eudora

Kenneth Millar to Eudora Welty, June 1, 1979

Dear Eudora:

It was such a pleasure to have your letter, your letters, from far and near, and to know that you sailed unperturbed across the flood. I think it must be your letter bag that keeps you calm and at-home with all these changes going on around you, but with you at the still center. I was afraid you might have been upset by something striking so near, but even to the snakes your heart went out—"of course they were displaced too"—what a dear woman you are. Your letters always bring me back smiling into the real world and remind me what a good place it really is.

Yes, I did see *Manhattan* and intend to see it again. Woody Allen is a great comic and becoming something more, a great artist, perhaps when he feels the urge to slip out of the center of the movie and let it go on without him.

—Speaking of movies, the phone just rang (this minute!) and my Canadian friend Jerry Simon of Toronto, a philosophy teacher who just made his first movie, based on my old *Three Roads*—Jerry just called from Toronto after the first showing of the movie, and reports that it is a hit. Somewhat carried away by this success at forty, Jerry now wants to make two others, one by Margaret, one by me. Pleasant news, but after my recent experience making a movie, I'm not exactly carried away by the thought—preferring to stand by at a distance and let other people make the movies. Perhaps I'd feel differently if I were younger, but I doubt it. It's the word that I love, more than the picture, as I think perhaps you do, too.

The books by M. that Jerry favors are *Rose's Last Summer* and *An Air That Kills.* Of mine he's interested in *Find a Victim*, *Zebra Striped Hearse*, *Black Money*, among the newer books. I have to take a look at them before he calls again.

Much love, as always,

Ken

Eudora Welty to Kenneth Millar, June 26, 1979

Dear Ken,

I was so glad to get your last letter, and I'm sorry to be so late writing back. Some unlikely events have got in the way of things I want to do—or maybe you'd call the events mismatched. Anyway, first thing on getting home from my trip on June 1 (the date of your letter) I found the foundation of my house was going its own way under me, after all these years, and I have to have a lot of work done to get it back where it belongs—yes, under the house. So they've been digging holes in the yard 35 feet deep and filling them with concrete, to make pilings. A lot of bricks had to be pulled out and put back, etc. Knocking and pounding and once hammering with a big mallet thing that looked like what clowns hit the other clowns over the head with—it went all through me. I could feel the presence of my father, who thought the house was built here to STAY, telling me with tight lips "Get those people out of here." The worst of it's about over now. It was rather wonderful to learn what blue clay looks like—it's the solid stuff that doesn't move around (in Mississippi) (different from the way it moves around in California) like the clay on top—and it has small, whole *seashells* all through it. I knew the Gulf had once covered us here, or more than once, and that whales swam in it—their bones have been unearthed—but these were just lovely little undisturbed seashells—I've been sleeping over them 35 feet down under me all these years. Well, the second thing, I'd agreed to sign books for the Franklin Library for a limited edition of Optimist's Daughter and write a preface for it—so here arrived 6,000 pages for me to go to work on. (Both these figures are right, 35 feet and 6,000 pages, it's not just my bad typewriting.) The lucky part is, the Franklin Library will just about pay me for the foundation—so I'm not really just writing my name, I'm making bricks. All is supposed to be over on June 30, the deadline, and next Tuesday is the day I go over to start my work at Oxford. It's been a sort of comical meeting of events, don't you think?

Of course I've thought of you same as always and hope things are moving along as they should. Have you decided on the movie proposal, you and Margaret? I was delighted to know what a hit your "Three Roads" was making in Toronto. —I feel very much as you do about what I write being rightly on the page, in words—the only way it can be all your own work. And it makes me feel silently amused when after some dramatization of some story of mine in a college production, I'm asked, "Well, how does it feel to see your characters brought to life?" *I* thought they were brought to life already, in words—or where did the actors find or understand them? All of which is not to say that the short story and the film don't have a great deal in common—in method, and ease of movement through time and space, etc etc. I am sure you know *all* that the film and the novel have in common and all that they do not and can't be made to have, from the work you put in on your script recently. I'd like very much to know how this all turns out.

I've been wondering if the Writer's Conference might be going on in Santa Barbara—it gives me a pang to think others can see you and I can't. Well, anyway I've got seashells somewhere near me. I thought of your mountains lately when I read in the Smithsonian Magazine—do you subscribe? I expect you do—about the migrations of pigeons and how it may well be that pigeons can hear the infrasound that is generated by mountains. A wonderful article, though piteously illustrated by poor pigeons in this or that apparatus being tested for knowing where they are—sober, ludicrous illustrations, but the facts and theories in the article are wonderful, the kind of things you love to keep thinking about.

If you can, please let me hear from you in England—I'll write to you anyway, it ought to be a good place. So far, I don't really know what I'll be doing there, or what my duties are, or how free I'll be but I should find out soon. The only address I know is

c/o British Studies at Oxford
University College
Oxford University
England

I fly over (from Atlanta to Gatwick) July 3, arriving early in the British morning of the Fourth of July—

My love to you always
Eudora

Kenneth Millar to Eudora Welty, Oxford, England, July 1, [1979]

Dear Eudora:

How good to have your letter, and in time, I hope, to answer it trans-Atlantically. Recently you've seemed to be in almost constant flight, not *from* but towards, bringing the halves of the western world together. It must be exciting and satisfying. Even from the sidelines here on the other side of the continent, the continent*s*, the thought of your movements and your mind hovering over them is catching at my throat—your flight out and your flight home.

Your sense of timing is right as usual. The writers' conference is just over and from my point of view, turned out to be the most successful ever. Definite improvement in the quality of the students, and on the whole of the teachers, too. The fact is, the conference is still going on, to judge by the mss. left on my desk still. I tried a little more personal approach in talking to the students this time, pushing them in the direction of autobiography, and it seems to have reached some of their minds, I hope permanently.

We are well here, humans and dogs. Don't overdo beyond the point of enjoyment, and take care. I think of you as always with love.

Ken

Eudora Welty, Oxford, England, to Kenneth Millar, August 5, 1979

Dear Ken,

I loved your letter sent to me here, and not only because it was from you, but because it was my *only* letter—The delay in mails from home has left most of us bereft for weeks—but your letter came like an arrow. You were so sweet to write me, and from the farthest away it proves (again) something about distance defeated. I've thought of you at many different times here of course—The first ride into the country, from London—into the Cotswolds—was through high meadows where they were haying—those golden summer fields—with the stacks arrayed against the sky, and the poppies still blooming at the edges in the stubble—everything sweet smelling—& I thought of the night when you came here young and slept in the fields, that you told me about, and were waked up by larks. I've been in the country visiting on several weekends—once in the home of English friends I've known since my first visit here, a dear man and his wife, who gave me a welcome back that really cheered my heart. I've had a difficult time in one respect— my closest friends of the 50's visit here, Elizabeth Bowen most of all, are now gone, and I miss them so sharply—London didn't seem the same place at all. I realize that now I'm not as able to cope with such—not as much energy or as much resilience in going on anyway as I had when I was younger. But of course the days are filled with things to do, places to see, all to me extraordinary and I supposed now or never. The young people I meet with are top-notch, the pick of their colleges, and sweet & attractive as well as smart—I enjoy the Oxford lectures—some greatly more than others (what do you think of Mr. Rouse?) and I'm delighted with my luck in being here in the summer they're all on the Renaissance in England—so instead of Beowulf and that ilk, which was last summer, we have Marlowe, Shakespeare, Donne, Sir Christopher Wren, & co. A feast. I'm not attempting side trips on my own (too expensive) so I won't get to Scotland or Ireland or even Wales close by,—but maybe after all I *will* get back. I hope you can and will.

One fine thing in store before I fly home is a meeting with Mr. Pritchett. He had written to me in the spring asking me to let him know if I ever came to London, so I sent him a note and he has asked me to lunch with him and his wife as soon as I get back to London. You know how I love his work—and I never heard of anybody who knew him that didn't love him. I'll tell you about it afterwards. My plane flies me home (by Atlanta) on the 18th—

Ken, I hope all goes well with you, & with Margaret, & Jim—and the dogs—Deeply I hope with your work as well—It was so good to hear from you—My love always—Eudora

Kenneth Millar to Eudora Welty, August 16, 1979

Dear Eudora:

I'm so glad to know that you are on your way home, or there by now. I think the British Isles were not as generous to you as they should have been. Perhaps they feel that they have given enough to all of us in times past. But then that still puts *you* ahead of them. *You've* given us all so much, and with such grace.

The news from here is not altogether good. Our grandson Jim dropped out of school, aged 16, for reasons that aren't very clear to me but seem to have to do with the pleasures of freedom. But I'm sure that Margaret and I, with our scholastic backgrounds, must be a part of the problem. I have no doubt that Jim will come back in but he is making things difficult for himself. It will test his mettle; I must say I love him no less. What would you do?—just tell me the first idea that occurs to your mind.

It's difficult for all of us these days, knowing what to do. *Nobody* seems to know. We seem to be waiting, each man to the man beside him, waiting for signals from outer, or *inner* space. It scares me a little, quite a bit in fact, but not so much as if everything stayed bland. Our fictions, written and unwritten, are coming true.

Love, and safe journey, Ken

This was literal truth for Ken and Margaret. Each had written books and stories over the years—of hit-and-run accidents, mental breakdowns, disappearing daughters—whose events had later been eerily paralleled in their real lives. Now maybe Ken recalled various tales of Margaret's that had dealt with blindness—as well as that more recent book of hers, involving a husband losing his memory.

Again Ken and Eudora spoke by telephone.

Eudora Welty to Kenneth Millar, [September 8, 1979]

Dear Ken,

I am so glad we talked—and that voices brought us so near. Since reaching home & reading your letter I'd been so concerned to know about Jim and his leaving school, to think of its troubling effect on you & Margaret—as well as its meaning for Jim of course—I think of how you are the best understander of the young I know of, and their champion, but also their protector from threats of harm which you understand better than they do, and this is not just the young, but Jim. Yet, Ken, *he* knows this too and knows you and Margaret are *there*. He's got that trust, and going with him it is its own kind of protection, don't you think? A boy that bright and adept is bright & adept at going forth very young maybe—did you feel the same? But I hope it's soon he realizes his other potential—that he comes back to learning in school and doing exceedingly well again at his studies—I'm afraid everything I put down must read like a platitude—You know that however ignorant I am about this, I feel for the way I know it has made you feel. Going with Jim besides trust, there's mutual admiration and respect, and there's love. Nothing can change that companionship for a venture, if you're a child or if you're long-travelled in experience—I feel less & less that our years tell us all that much, just by rolling over us—what we need is one another.

These are long, hot days here, but it's good to be back—I'm working, like you, on some side issues—Some promised book reviews coming up, and a little autobiographical thing about my first published story. I'll send that along for you to read if it turns out (it isn't now) to be any good. Meantime I tend to spend too much time on chores I'm asked to do by nice civic groups I'd like to assist, only—there goes another day. The summer in Oxford was wonderfully interesting but too much for me in numbers of people always, a little class on Tues. & Thurs. afternoons, and so alluring to see & hear and go back to, the whole world of the University—and yet all that medieval got me down in a way—Every morning, before the ringing of the bell and breakfast in Hall, I'd walk out the gate and see the whizzing buses & bicycles & taxis go by in the High Street—present life! Then to a lecture by some Oxford eminence—I went to 2 a day mostly & never came out of the Renaissance till time for a beer in the garden before lunch—the heavenly gardens—I walked a lot, of course, so much to see and go back to see again—My own part would come late in the afternoon, well, it was called "Tea with Miss Welty," when I'd talk back & forth with students, 20 at a blow. I liked the students. They made me one of them, which I guess may be the reason I'm so tired! On weekends I went to the country several times, to visit friends of the last time I was in England, about 20 years ago, who were so dear as to remember me and give me a wonderful welcome. And in London I met Mr. Pritchett, as I told you. He had written to me several notes & letters over the years, which I saw to be like him—he spontaneously enjoys getting in touch with other writers, especially the short story lovers—and had asked me to let him know if I were ever in England, so I did—how could I have forgiven myself if I'd been too shy to? He and his wife Dorothy asked me to lunch at their house and had just ourselves so we could talk, and we sat talking away the whole afternoon—They're both the liveliest, kindest, most open-hearted, open-minded people—you know from his writing just what he is, he's so generous there too—I loved every minute, shall never forget this. He *rejoiced* me. He is the brightest-eyed 79-year-old you could ever hope to see. After lunch he walked me through his neighborhood to where I could catch a bus—I elected to ride home that way so as to see more—and stood and waved me out of sight. That was the best of my summer, my year.

I'm glad you enjoyed the Labrador retriever in the audience at "Lady Windermere's Fan." I thought of you such a number of times—On top of the tower in Bristol where you look into the Camera Obscura—have you ever seen it, or any camera obscura? I hadn't. But away up there— you climb & climb—they put you in the dark & then gradually, on a large, slowly spinning plate-like reflector you look down on, you see everything in the surrounding landscape appear. The Avon Gorge, the Suspension bridge, the traffic in the roads, the river bank, pedestrians, picnickers, lovers, solitary bird-watchers, playing children—the whole 365 degrees (it *is* 365?). As the man in charge said to my friend & me, "It's like a *good* oil painting: with movement." Isn't that wonderful? You see the whole world but it doesn't see you—you might witness anything!

I'm writing this at my window where there's a nice early-morning breeze, though me and my world are mutually visible—& where you can easily imagine me,—and sending you my love and my good hopes—

Yours as always,

Eudora

Eudora Welty to Kenneth Millar, September 20, 1979

Dear Ken,

I'm hoping you've had reason by this time to feel easier about young Jim—and that things are going better in every way—There's a change in the air, here—seasonal, I mean—Its skies a higher, deeper color, with many birds on the move—a coolness at night, and the smell of fresh-fallen pinestraw. I've been working hard at 2 foolishly promised simultaneous deadlines, with papers all around me, and just plain wanted to write to you instead, though there isn't much news.

One thing, Knopf still hasn't sent along your big-3 book—you said to let you know if it didn't come—I do want to have it—I'd like very much to read your introduction.

On Oct. 8, too, I have to fly to N.Y. (to a meeting at the Acad. of Arts & Letters) and will be there till the 12th—If there is any message or errand I could carry out for you, let me know. I'll be seeing Joan Kahn, & Nona, I feel sure—

By the way I had a dream in your handwriting. (My dreams sometimes come in words.) It was a little less than a page long, written in very dark ink or with a soft black pencil, on lined paper—you wrote down my dream!—Or I dreamed you wrote my dream. Where do these things come from, then? If only I could remember after waking what it said—But you see it's left traces.

Much love, take care—
Eudora

Ken struggled to write not dreams but fiction. He would not abandon hope. "[W]hile I can't certainly predict the future," he told his Knopf editor with poignant optimism, "it will surely allow me further writing."[5]

Eudora Welty to Kenneth Millar, Friday [October 5, 1979]

Dear Ken,

Here's a piece I just finished doing for the Georgia Review, that they asked for in connection with republishing my first story—I don't really know why.[6] I xeroxed it for you, poor typing and all, feeling you would read it congenially sometime—and also I keep meaning to send you a copy of this bird man's bulletin that I've been getting all year—I find it very amusing. He's a man in his 60s with family and a tree business, a businessman, who just took it into his head to see more birds than anybody else within a given time. Expense as you can see is no object, miles don't matter, and it's all so innocent, and he gets these bulletins out in the friendly expectation that the whole world's going to share it with him—I share it. He saw your condor but from far away.

It's lovely, sunny and cool here. Monday I must fly to NY, but will be back again by Friday. I think of you and send my love,

Eudora

Kenneth Millar to Eudora Welty, October 7, 1979

Dear Eudora:

Your wonderful letter with the Constable watercolor in it matching your prose has waited unconscionably long for an answer, and even now I can't write you a proper one. Fine though I feel in general, I've come down with another of life's minor but temporarily disabling tribulations—an abdominal hernia which had to be repaired and now has been. I got up the first day and now can do almost anything I normally do except swim. This was followed by a speed trip to San Francisco where Margaret was due for an eye examination, and there the results were the best she has had yet: for the first time since the inception of her eye trouble, Margaret's bad eye *improved* instead of deteriorating. You can imagine the relief we felt, and the gratitude.

In general all goes well now, but one gets set for emergencies and finds it hard to climb down from that reactive level. The wind is blowing hard tonight, and it may storm before morning. I hope you're safe and well, dear Eudora, and that you will forgive me for my sporadic notes with not much in them, except that all is well. But I think of you often and lean on the thought.

With all my love,

Ken

P.S.—I still have only one copy of *Archer in Jeopardy* but will see that you get a copy from Ash Green. K.

Eudora Welty to Kenneth Millar, Sunday [October 21, 1979]

Dear Ken,

I was very thankful to know how things are with you, and more than thankful for the good news your letter brought about your own good & speedy recovery from the operation you'd had, and about Margaret's wonderful *regaining* of what she had been losing in the vision of her eye. It's so good to know, and I hope the tide for the good keeps rolling in—I believe it will. But I'm awfully sorry you had to go through with a time in a hospital—Now that it's behind you, having gone so well, I like to imagine you'll soon be swimming again.

When you were having your high wind and stormy night, New York received something too—high wind, fog, cold, rain, a waterspout in the harbor, and a snow fall. Also we had Castro, and the dissatisfied author who came to town in a plane & buzzed Harcourt Brace Jovanovich for 3 or 4 hours.[7] I went out when I had to but it was right nice to stay in my Algonquin cubbyhole and read. I read *The Far Side of the Dollar* again, which I'd brought from home. What a beauty it is, every reading—I read it and watch it (the writing and the way it charges the novel).

Since coming back I had a few deadlines to meet and met them, and on next Wednesday I go for *almost* the last work-trip this year—to U. of Kentucky at Lexington and Denison U. in Ohio—with friends in both places so they can rescue me from merciless academics. But of course I have only myself to blame for foolishly agreeing to too many things just because they were all far off, then. Kentucky ought to be beautiful *just* now—I love the Bluegrass. I'll send you a postcard—the chances are about 99 to 1 it will be one of Man-O'-War. They always take you to his grave.

I'm writing by the window in my upstairs room where the oak tree just outside is filled with kinglets & some kind of olive-green tiny birds (warblers?) all busy feeding. It's a long dry spell here, I've been moving the sprinkler about all day trying to keep the camellias & azaleas going, they're all in bud. The other day I went with an old friend [John Robinson] now living in Italy to where we used to go on picnics—down by an area of the river, where the flood had come in so high—It was lovely—(we took another picnic)—the sweet-gums were starting to turn scarlet, the oak leaves were falling & covered the ground where the Pearl River had clawed and peeled it clean, and the water itself was just *full* of fish!—leaping up & popping up & splashing all over—Birds singing—the flood had obviously been enjoyed by all that called the place home.

Dear Ken, thank you again for writing—when some times are not as easy as others to write, though, you know as I do what is the same as ever, that we think of each other and that you are close to me. Don't worry about not writing—Just when it's a good time for you. My wishes and my love always,

Eudora

Eudora Welty, Lexington/Versailles, KY, and in a plane, to Kenneth Millar, [Late October 1979]. Written on picture postcards of Man O' War statue, two Kentucky thoroughbreds, and portrait of Daniel Boone.

Dear Ken,

Things continue to go well there, I hope. Just before I took off from Jackson, your big book came—I'm so glad to have it—wanted to take it right along but knew this work trip would leave me no free time to enjoy it. But it'll be waiting when I get back. Thank you very much— it's a handsome volume, too—and I saw it again here in Lexington turned full-face front on the bookstore shelf—[8]

Fall leaves at glorious height in this pretty town. Once the work sessions (3 days) are over, I get to go to the house of a friend who lives in a little country town, Versailles (pro. Ver-sales) where I've never been (I knew her when she taught at Vassar.) There 3 old friends will re-unite & see the countryside—

Versailles is pure peace—calm pure windless bright days—riding to a curve of the Kentucky River around high rocky banks with old forest trees—horse farms. We went into a big country barn & through hay fields. At night, around a woodfire with some Jack Daniels and a bowl of shelled walnuts (I should hope shelled, did you ever try to crack them?) and grand ham for dinner. All the tiredness of the work at the college has gone away, and it's good sleeping in a big high bed under old soft quilts, with nothing outside but trees—and the whistle of a train comes sometimes. I like being in a place where the seasons are so distinct—It makes you want to hold onto their beauty more than ever. I wish now I'd brought your book, to read it in Versailles—you have 2 other admirers in this house.

———

I've now finished the other half of this work trip—5 days at Denison Univ. in Granville, Ohio—hardest & longest, or I guess just the most incessant of the year. I try to remember how it drains everything out of you, regardless of how much you like & respect the students, so I don't do it too much again. Just one more trip, overnight to Princeton then blessed work. This isn't a complaint, just how I feel. I'll be writing a real letter next.

Thank you again for the book, & Ralph S. for sending it—My love to you, as everywhere. (Now in the air over Knoxville).

Yours, Eudora

Eudora Welty to Kenneth Millar, November 8, 1979

Dear Ken,

Your beautiful Collection of Reviews was here waiting for me when I got home tonight—I brought it upstairs & began reading the Foreword, and then on without stopping to the last page—How very much I cherish it.[9] It was good to be in your company past and present—and in the present seeing back into the past, as in the Foreword—the most touching of autobiographical writing I've seen of yours. And there was the pleasure of receiving all those flashes your reading brought forth from your mind, so many books and writers I've never had the chance before to know your thinking or feeling about. I want to go back now and read these again. I was glad to see the one I'd read before in the N.Y.T. Book Review when you let Jacques Barzun know just where (and in what antique time) he belonged. As it happened, I've just been in a spot on earth that at some time or other was the home of many of these authors you write of, or mention—Princeton—Mann & Eliot (I saw the shop where he used to buy his long red union suits) and of course Fitzgerald—weren't there more?

The book itself is so *beautiful*. And how giving you are to have each of them come with the printed line of ownership in that friend's own name—I treasure mine and love all that is in it—I like to think how you must have written them for the best of reasons—because you wanted to—

I'll write you more later, —but I was interested in what you wrote about Stephen Leacock, whose name I hadn't heard since I was young and his books were in our house and much read and admired by my father—And I wasn't in tune with them then, but I'm going to hunt them up—He used to give them to my mother for presents.[10]

I loved the connection that you tell of, running from Conrad to Alfred Knopf—But I'll be writing you more—I wanted to thank you right away, for all.

I hope things are going as they should—I hope you're swimming again—

With my love as always,

Yours, Eudora

I'm home now to stay.

Kenneth Millar to Eudora Welty, November 19, 1979

Dear Eudora:

I'm so glad you liked my reviews. When the little project was first suggested to me, I couldn't see much merit in it. But after I got into it, and especially now that you have written out your feelings about it, it gave me nothing but pleasure. Much of which came from the knowledge that I could pass it on to you. And now I have your beautiful response.

Our life is improving again, in spite of some further illness in the family. Margaret, who has suffered so much in these last few difficult years, has learned over the last several weeks that her sight is threatened by damage to her retinas which is apparently irreversible. But there is a kind of miracle in this. Margaret has been able to look at blindness and face it down. She is busy getting ready for whatever may come, and she has been able to accept my help in this, and future help, so that we are closer than we were. And there is quite a bit of music in the house.

Well, our lives change unexpectedly, irreversibly as I said, but not necessarily towards the darkness.

Love,

Ken

Eudora Welty to Kenneth Millar, Thanksgiving [November 22, 1979]

Dear Ken,

It's wonderful that the new news of Margaret's eye is robbed of its worst because you have brought a kind of victory out of it between you. I was so glad to read comfort in your letter—to know there's been an easing in your life—and music in the house—I so hope the vision holds its own. But whatever comes there are two magnificent determinations ready to meet it together.

I've been to Thanksgiving dinner with my sister-in-law & nieces and their families—5 little children now. It's raining, so they were supercharged, racing through the house,—one appearance in hats they'd pulled out of a trunk. The baby, a little girl not 2 yet, had on a broad planter's straw, bigger around than she is, swinging her arms in mighty circles—living up to the hat.

I treasure your book. And I'm so glad you found the doing brought pleasure as you want. It's no wonder, I think—I believe writing wakes its pleasure up whatever the hour. That's never lost, do you believe? I must thank you for *two* copies of *Archer in Jeopardy*—from West and East: The extra from Knopf I'm pleased to have on hand for others to read.[11] Last night I finished *The Zebra-Striped Hearse* again and all my admiration for it was reinforced, but more than that—There were moments—the hawk, rising—the baby sleeping—many observing, revealing moments, when without having forgotten them I felt their surprise and beauty as sharply as new. Everywhere, all through a novel, very particularly, you take the way that puts human insight into the strong terms of urgency—which *belong* to it. Delicate insight—bold terms. The mastery of dialogue, structure, movement, timing, of the encounters that reveal, & the connecting that is brought to bear, and to come true—from its starting up to its conclusion, it's what urgency turns into—and a crucial part of its drama is moral, of course—Archer being in absolute focus is everything—He *is* the focus, but we see him & see with him because he's a feeling man, as you've made him. Of course I've felt these things before but this time in a special way which may have come from reading *Zebra* right after *The Doomsters*—it took on the import of its sequence. *The Doomsters* was to me remarkable for its last couple of pages where before a reader's eye the world of your fiction seems to be going through a change—like the first prescience on its far horizon of a ship soon to be in sight, just under the curve. It was, too—it was *The Galton Case*, the book next to come. *Zebra* is another of the tall ships in the whole remarkable fleet that's kept coming ever since. It's strange, isn't it, that novels have a power to move our imaginations in the same way that ships on the water do? But not really strange, either. They're impelled by human dreams, and come from the hand of hopeful human beings, and reach destinations we pray will be human, like us.

With deepest love

Eudora

Once more Ken turned his thoughts and will toward new fiction. He had managed this year to write some promising story fragments that drew on his youthful stay in Winnipeg, circa 1929. Millar, betting on his own unspent potential, this December did what he'd never done before in his writing career: signed a contract for a book not yet finished. Knopf agreed to pay Ross Macdonald an advance of forty thousand dollars for an untitled mystery novel due December 1, 1981.

Kenneth Millar to Eudora Welty, December 9, 1979

Dear Eudora:

I believe your wonderful letter is coming true. I hesitate to spell out what that may mean, but I think I can say with truth that Margaret can accept whatever comes. What *has* come is not as bad as she had feared it might be. One of her eyes is virtually useless, but the other has somewhat improved in this past week. And her morale is steady, and if you asked her she would tell you, truly, that she is enjoying her life and looking forward to Christmas, and Jimmie's visit.

We had a couple of most enjoyable visitors the past week in Santa Barbara. As no doubt all the world knows by now, Kurt Vonnegut and his bride[12] came to Santa Barbara to get married, and I had a chance to get to know him—a really gentle man, perhaps matching Jill in *her* watchful gentleness. They helped us through what might have been a difficult week, and made us feel like lucky people, which we are.

Now I hope I can write a novel worthy of your expectations but if I can't I'll rest content with *your* vision of my ships. I was a sailor, you know, and so was my dad.

All my love, as ever,

Ken

Eudora Welty to Kenneth Millar, December 31, 1979

(a white throated sparrow is singing)

Dear Ken,

So many wishes to you for a Happy New Year—My feeling is strong that it's already begun for you. I was so glad to get your last letter.

Christmas was good I feel sure with Jim there to make it full measure. I was thinking of you,—my Christmas was good too, with 5 little children all over the place—I'm glad though when this time of year has been left behind and we can think of what's to do ahead. I'm glad when that longest night of the year has passed—(Do you know what I was doing, I was reading "The Woman in White" again.) What I hope is that new books come out of us all in this year—at least that they start. That healths get better and better for sure—

Your friend Mr. Yellin, who brought out your beautiful book, wrote & asked me for something if I had anything that would do—I wondered if he might be interested in that early story of mine somebody found in the Archives, "Acrobats in a Park"—I remember you liked it all right—it was in a French mag. & a South Carolina one, no book—I sent it to him to see—Thank you for putting him in touch—[13] And the Mystery Writers of America asked me to their New York dinner, in the spring!

Dear Ken, Happy New Year to you both, and I send you my thoughts and hopes and love all through the days of it—Yours as always, Eudora

CHAPTER TEN

"*Every day of my life I think of you with love.*"

———— ❧ ————

1980–1982

DESPITE his hopes at the end of 1979, by the spring of 1980 Ken Millar would be almost unable to write at all. The man who lived by and for words would no longer have words to share. He was diagnosed with Alzheimer's disease. But before silence might overtake him, he sought to tell Eudora of the change that was approaching and to assure her of their ongoing love.

Kenneth Millar to Eudora Welty, January 9, 1980

Dear Eudora:

It's generous of you to keep me in touch as you have been, even at times when I haven't written you. There seem to be times when one doesn't want to talk much, simply rest in the quiet security of love and friendship. This may sound ominous, but it really isn't meant that way. Our days are happier, Margaret is holding her own and is very much her old self and so, may I say, am I.

Glad to hear, too, about your projected book for Mr. Jellin. I'm looking forward to seeing it again, and having a chance to see it in a new physical setting.[1] I'm only now beginning to grasp the importance of these matters. I hope, with so much still to learn, that I can go on learning.

My love, as ever,

Ken

P.S.—I enclose a letter from a Chicago teacher which I enjoyed.

Ken.

[enclosed letter from Douglas D. Martin]

Eudora Welty, New York City, to Kenneth Millar, [Late January 1980]

Dear Ken,

I'm sitting in LaGuardia Airport on a bright cold afternoon, looking out on water, long stretches of skyline, planes & birds—soon to take off for Jackson—I just ran up for 3 days, for a meeting. And was glad I came,—an interruption to work was the way I first saw it, but it turned out a refreshment—The best form of rest, isn't it? I'm glad about your own.

Just before this trip came up, there was another day's interruption that was a fine occasion—Mississippi inaugurated a new governor who is a good, first-rate, vigorously thoughtful and firmly spoken man. I wouldn't be surprised if he didn't prove himself to be one of the best governors in the nation. His third try—This time he beat the disgraceful redneck scoundrel who beat him before, & who has outraged everybody so, that our man won this time by a landslide. He used the inaugural occasion to invite leaders in various fields of science, economics, history, arts & letters (this was me) who are of or from Miss., to a symposium called "Mississippi and the Nation, 1980."—connecting us with the rest of the world is his strong intention. At the Inauguration, Leontyne Price (from Laurel, Miss.) flew here from Toronto to sing. As you know, I don't often feel personally enthusiastic about political figures, to the point of working for them—I believe the last was Adlai Stevenson—but I am proud & excited that we have William Winter for Governor for the next 4 years. I thought you'd be glad we had that much sense at last, our record is so sorry in politics. While we are not bad at all in other things.[2]

Saw Joan & Olivia Kahn, eating supper with them—Went to dinner & a show with Walter Clemons. (Read the forthcoming *Newsweek* with his report on a plaigerized novel.) (Can that be misspelled? I have a bad writing these days, as it is, from arthritis in my working-hand.)—It lightens my life for yours to be lighter. With love,

Eudora

Kenneth Millar to Eudora Welty, February 7, 1980

Dear Eudora:

Your recent letters made me happy, the more so because I can answer them in confidence and good faith. For a while I was left among possibilities with nothing quite certain to say. But the possibilities have become more certain, at least for the present, and for several weeks there has been some remission in M's eye trouble. She's been drawing long breaths of relief, and talking a good deal between them. This isn't merely a psychological change, though it's certainly important in that way, but an actual improvement in the condition of her retinas—an unexpected but actual physical change, in the right direction. We made the most of the situation by getting M. a new television set for her sixty-fifth birthday, just passed. I haven't reached that age just yet, and won't until next year, but it appears to be not a bad time of life, when we turn our backs at last on the lost hopes of the past, and find new reasons for hope.

And though I am not touched by it as deeply as I'd like to be—as you are—I feel that I'm living in the same world, one I'd lost and may soon recover. At least I can't and won't turn away,

Love,
Ken

P.S.—Every now and then I get out OLD SARUM and take a look.

This was the last letter Eudora would receive from Ken. She continued to set a busy pace, lecturing, traveling to see friends, and trying to write fiction, but there was now a huge gap in her life. Still she sent letters to Ken.

Eudora Welty, Chicago, to Kenneth Millar, April 14, 1980

Dear Ken,

I'm in Chicago for this week, working at the University—the last of my springtime visits. I'm always hoping all is going well there—better all the time.

Yesterday in Charleston, South Carolina, all was coming into bloom almost under your eyes & azaleas & dogwood full & bright—and it was 80°—I woke up this morning and Chicago was white with snow—I really *am* a Southerner—At home, though we had a very slow, mixed-up spring—the blooms kept being slapped back by untimely cold spells, and some flowering trees just skipped flowers & resigned themselves to just go ahead and leaf out. It was as if confusion was all over the world.

In Charleston I was reading for The Citadel, a very old military college—never dreamed I'd be inside The Citadel. This was built, all in white, all with battlements, all inside big iron gates with real swords worked into the grillwork, around a large green quadrangle (no connection with the Quadrangle Club where I'm writing from!), lined with ancient live oaks—I coincided with the annual parade of the troops before some general, & viewed it from the seat behind him (where the English Dept. was put). We first faced this wide flat (seacoast flat) empty green, the white buildings across from us seen full front & 2-dimensional, strangely like papier-mâché in the waiting silence, then from behind us, through one arch after another, poured the cadets, streaming to the drums as the band struck up—onto the huge field, and surrounded it. The general rose, was driven all around the field and then a dreadful thing, the cannons were fired in a 19-gun salute. I'd never been close to any fire-arms. Not only deafening but the earth under your feet seemed to rock, and the shock went right up you. Terrible. Then there was a lot of marching and wonderful music, and bagpipes & Scots in their plaids—we got up time after time (like in the Episcopal church) & laid our hands over our hearts at the playing of various tunes, as they marched, ending of course with *Dixie*, which whenever I hear it makes the tears jump out of my eyes—They say Gen. Mark Clark (who lives there) started the Scots troops & the bagpipes, & usually comes but didn't this time. Prince Charles, they say, loved coming, I'm not sure if he didn't take part.[3]

While I'm on the Confederacy, I wonder if you read the long historical essay by Robert Penn Warren on Jefferson Davis in *The New Yorker* recently—it's really a wonderful piece—So many of the historical facts in it I never knew before—such as that Davis after the surrender was kept for a time in chains—& given no light—and that they had hoped to get Robert E. Lee to testify against him by offering him a pardon! The essay is beautifully controlled & plain & eloquent out of both mind and heart.[4] Love, Eudora

On May 4, 1980, Ken made what seems to be his last attempt to contact Eudora via letter. Evidently, this letter was never mailed, but it survived as part of his estate and is now in the private archival collection of Lucius M. Lampton.

Kenneth Millar to Eudora Welty, May 4, 1980

Dear Eudora:

It's a barbarously long time since I've written but I have been in a long non-writing state. I think you may understand better than most, perhaps better than anyone, how hard it can become to speak after a lapse into silence. But I couldn't stay quiet long in the midst of your good news and the pleasure it must have brought you, the expressions of good will from all over the world which I hope I may join.

With all my love, dear Eudora, as ever,
Ken

The "good news" that Ken mentions seems likely to have been the selection of Eudora as a recipient of the Presidential Medal of Freedom to be presented on June 10, 1980, by President Jimmy Carter to her, Robert Penn Warren,

Tennessee Williams, ornithologist Roger Tory Peterson, and nine others. Perhaps sensing Ken's keen interest in this high honor, she wrote to him as if in direct response.

Eudora Welty to Kenneth Millar, July 11, 1980

Dear Ken,

I hope that rest and serenity and abundance of work and play have attended your house all summer, and that all news is good—particularly in respect to Margaret's eyes.

It's hot here, as in the rest of the South and Southwest—I don't mind—since I can hole in with an air conditioner and live on tomato sandwiches, and work in the insulation that such heat really is. At night the lightning bugs fly very low & slow—and above the trees the heat (I guess) makes a constant sheet-lightning—Even the telephone book is blood-heat to the touch.

I saw Reynolds recently and his news is that he's within 4 or 5 pages of the end of his new novel. He sent me a snapshot taken of him when he went to Rome at Easter and I thought you might like to have it.

Reynolds came to Washington when Pres. Carter gave me one of his Medals for Freedom. This was a gracious, hard-to-believe occasion, which stirred me as you can imagine—One of the others who received the Medal was Roger Tory Peterson, I thought it might interest you to know. (A totally humorless man he appeared to be.) (But humor may not be necessary around birds.) I came home to the page-proofs of my Collected Stories, coming out in October. It was a strange experience, reading them all at one blow and most of them read again for the first time since I wrote them. All in 6 days time passing before my eyes— They're not in any literal way autobiographical, but they showed me my life—I guess they are my life.

I hope it was all bright, the whole summer for you & keeping on—

Love,

Eudora

In the fall of 1980, Eudora was interviewed by novelist Anne Tyler in conjunction with the imminent publication of her Collected Stories. *She traveled to New York to help publicize the new book. Then, after returning home, she flew to Baltimore. Old friend Katherine Anne Porter had died, and Eudora went for the memorial service. Back home again, she at last received word from Ken, though indirectly. Santa Barbara book dealer Ralph Sipper, as an act of concern, friendship, and admiration during a difficult time for Ken, proposed to publish a collection of his autobiographical pieces with an introduction by Eudora. Sipper had made the request at Ken's suggestion, and Eudora responded first to Ken. He could not write to her, but she needed to write to him.*

Eudora Welty to Kenneth Millar, October 20, 1980

Dear Ken,

Today a letter came from Ralph Sipper about a proposed book of yours, but before I answer it I wanted to write and say I was glad of it as a sort of communication from you to me, that you thought his idea of my doing a bit at the beginning was a good one. I know you said the last time you wrote that sometimes things go better without letters, and I wanted to follow your wish with this but it has been such a long time. My understanding I would keep questioning, but I did not want to risk what might break in in any way or what was so necessary to you then—respecting that wish for just being quiet and serene without needing words. I need words so much myself that it measured for me what this meant for you. But the truth is it's been so long without knowing how you are that I *am* writing, as you see, on the basis (excuse) of Ralph's letter. And I would love to do the little piece for anything of yours, or do anything ever that I could, as you know. The book is a fine good idea. It would help me to be allowed a chance to say a word in it.

I hope it was not a bad time to write. It's always seemed to me nothing but a good time when we are in touch. My love and wishes as always,

Eudora

I pray things go well with you. I know how serious they are.

At the end of October, Eudora went to New York for the publication of her Collected Stories *by Harcourt. There she was feted royally at a publication day reception and also managed to see many old friends. Before she left New York, the reviewers of her life's work as a story writer were waxing ecstatic. Mary Lee Settle in the* Saturday Review *and Maureen Howard in the* New York Times Book Review *compared her to Chekhov, the writer Eudora herself considered the master of the short story. Their paeans were echoed by many others, including Anne Tyler and Reynolds Price. And Hortense Calisher, concluded her* Washington Post *review with a fervent wish: "May readers swarm." They did.*[5]

But news was not all good. On October 28, Ralph Sipper sent sad tidings: "[Ken] has not, to the best of my knowledge, written much if at all within the last year. Not only has he been distracted as I wrote to you, but he seems not able to remember or focus on those little mundane details necessary for communication with friends and acquaintances. Perhaps he's just going through a bad period. I fervently hope so."[6] *So did Eudora, but that hope seemed increasingly faint. All the more reason, she must have felt, to write to Ken.*

Eudora Welty to Kenneth Millar, December 13, 1980. Christmas card.

Dear Ken,

I wonder what the day is like there. You wrote once that you call it winter when it rains a bit. But I hope you get your sun and your swim. It's cold here, but some camellias bloom. White-throated sparrows are all over the yard today.

It's been a hard working year, but luck came too. I wish both for you—and keep my wish going.

I hope you do take care of yourself as well as other people, and that new work & good health are yours. You're dear in every way to me and I think of you in such concern and love.

Yours as always,
Eudora

On St. Patrick's Day 1981, Herb Yellin, who had published limited editions of her work and Ken's, wrote to tell Eudora of his recent meeting with Ken and

Maggie. He described Margaret publicly "berating Ken and literally screaming at him," Ken's acknowledging his inability to write a letter, and Ken's desire that Eudora be made to understand his plight. The man once so like his character Lew Archer, Yellin reported, was "literally holding my hand at one point, and asked us to stay." "It must be like living in a lunatic asylum," Yellin then declared.[7]

There seemed to be no way for Eudora to protect Ken, but when she made an April trip to New York City and the Algonquin Hotel, where she had first met him, Eudora wrote to offer her support, whether moral or otherwise.

Eudora Welty, New York City, to Kenneth Millar, [April 13, 1981]

Dear Ken,

This is my birthday, and I wanted to send you my love on it, and from here [Algonquin Hotel]. Of course I send it on the other days and from wherever I am. A work-job, short one, up the Hudson at Vassar brought me to N.Y. Flowering trees are out. I went up & spent a night with Rosie Russell, and I've seen other friends of yours & mine too. Joan Kahn being one—

Ken, if at any point you needed me or if I could just come a day to see you, you could say so to Ralph Sipper and he would give me the message, I know. In the deepest sense we could never be out of touch. In the daily, enduring way, I think of this too. It does me good. Please dear take care of yourself.

Love always,
Eudora

In May, Ralph Sipper sent word that Ken had gone into the hospital for a surgical procedure to remove excess fluid from his brain, a procedure doctors hoped would improve his memory. Three weeks later, though, Sipper reported that Ken was much as before, if not worse, and that the Millars found it more and more necessary for Ralph to handle Ken's business and personal correspondence. "I am truly sorry to hurt you with [. . .] sad information," he added, "but I know that you want to and must know what is happening to Ken. We have talked about you and it is clear that you are very dear to him. It occurs to me that you might want to think about visiting him."[8] *Indeed she did, as she had for some months.*

Eudora Welty to Kenneth Millar, c/o Ralph Sipper, June 15, 1981

Dear Ken—

I've been feeling for some time that I'd give anything to see you— Now some time has opened up for me—I'd be free to come out, if you found it a good time for you too. Would the last week in June be too near—I could come later, in July or August, if that's easier. Just to walk or sit or ride by the sea and talk again. I would dearly love to see you.

Ralph has been so kind about letting me know how you've been getting along—It's so rotten, the time they've been giving you—I hate it for you—I pray for it to change.

Ralph will give this to you, so whatever you think about our chance to see each other, you might just convey to him and he'll pass the word along—If the time just doesn't seem right at all, of course tell me—I think of you every day, wherever we are, you know that.

My hopes and love,

Eudora

Eudora Welty to Kenneth Millar, October 30, 1981

Dear Ken,

I was so happy to lay eyes on your book [*Self-Portrait: Ceaselessly Into the Past*]. What a good thing you've given us. I hold it dear. It will be valued by a great many people all around. And I want to thank you once again for the pleasure it gave me to write the little note in front—I wish I could have said more and more—and to tell you once again how lastingly I cherish the piece you did about me on my coming to Santa Barbara.

It was a splendid idea that Ralph made happen. His interview being there, and his own piece, make the publication event very special.

Lately I was riding through Ontario on a train and thinking so often of you. That sky you grew up under looked as big as all North America. They had been cutting the hay. Once, because of a derailment up ahead, we all got off the train and rode across country for two hours and saw it up even closer, and we saw deer, shadowy deer. We went from Swift Current to Medicine Hat on the Moose Mountain bus. I got off in Banff and stayed awhile. They'd told me I might see bears walking about the streets, and I pictured them upright. But all I saw was Japanese tourists walking around. It was beautiful there but I felt closer to the gentle mountains of Santa Barbara than I did to the Rockies, all hardness and ice. The magpies in Banff were the first I'd ever seen, feeding as big as chickens on the front yard of the post office.

Then in New York, I had the pleasure of meeting your friends Julian and Kathleen Symons. We of course spoke of you—they said they hoped to see you when they got to the West Coast, and promised to give you my love.

I'm always sending it to you myself. You are in my thoughts every day and dear to my heart.

As always, Eudora

"I need words," Eudora had written to Ken a year earlier. Now she had more of Ken's words in book form to give her comfort. And she sought to find her own words to describe his situation. She shifted from a long story she had called "The Shadow Club," keeping parts of it for use in "Henry," a new story with a title character whose life is blighted by Alzheimer's disease.

Eudora Welty to Kenneth Millar, December 25, 1981. Christmas card.

Dear Ken,

I've been reading your pieces in "Self Portrait" over again all afternoon and I have the finest feeling of having had a long visit and talk with you. They say so much! My love to you as always. Many strong wishes for the New Year to you and Margaret and all good hopes,

Yours,
Eudora

As 1982 began, Margaret Millar's twenty-third novel was published. The Los
Angeles Times *sent Assistant Arts Editor Wayne Warga to interview her and
Ken, and during the course of the interview Maggie made Ken's battle with
Alzheimer's a matter of public record: "He knows what is happening to him
some of the time, but he doesn't really feel things. It's something I think about,
nightmarelike, all the time. I needed the help first and then everything changed
and all the responsibility came to me. [. . .] I've faced my own problem pretty
well. I haven't faced his well, at least not as well as I think I should." Later in
the interview, Maggie told Warga, "Mostly we have these long, silent nights now.
I never leave him."*

*But not always silent. "I lose my temper," she conceded, "and then I go on
guilt trips. The trips aren't as big as they used to be, but the temper remains the
same."⁹*

*Ralph Sipper and Dorothy Olding both sent Eudora copies of the article.
Sipper also sent somewhat comforting words, given the situation: "Ken does
seem cheerful, is cheerful. He couldn't fake that in my opinion."¹⁰ Eudora would
seek through letters to abet that good cheer.*

Eudora Welty to Kenneth Millar, c/o Ralph Sipper, March 16, 1982

Dear Ken,

I think of you every time I see the wonderful "Life on Earth"
program on public television—Tonight we heard the singing of the
whales, deep down in the sea. All the whales sing the same song, and the
song is a new song every year. There are so many wonders.

Dear Ken, I have all your letters to keep me company. Every day of
my life I think of you with love. Yours always, Eudora

Eudora Welty to Kenneth Millar, June 1, 1982

Dear Ken,

I've been sending you love from one place after another—travelling
around. In Knoxville, Tennessee, Reynolds and I had a meeting to be
on the Today Show and discuss Southern Literature, for 2 ½ minutes—

lucky we agreed as there wouldn't have been time to argue. Then we had all day to wander around the World's Fair, and be on our own, and we were talking about our good meetings with you and how we think of you so much and we found we were both reading all your novels again. Then I was in New York, where I did some readings, and Columbia gave me an honorary degree. I thought of you on the platform, how you would be amused to know that my citation was written by the member of the Columbia faculty who writes mysteries under the name of Amanda Cross.[11] Then I went to visit my editor [John Ferrone] on his farm in rural Pennsylvania, where over the weekend everything was bursting out in spring. A cardinal nest by the porch popped up with baby birds, a mother Mallard duck was just *about* to give birth, sitting all day on her nest with that very intelligent bright eye on us, only she never did—the father Mallard came to pay half-hour visits in the vicinity, which he spent standing on the deck into the pond, and once he just fell down! Have you ever seen a duck just fall down? His mate just watched imperturbably. In an old apple tree you could hear, standing close to the trunk, a flicker's nest deep inside, and a steady whirr, whirr, whirr sounding from within. I guess those babies *had* come. There were a lot of Mennonites and Amish living around there—we saw their peaceful farms, and saw their buggies. I thought of our ancestors, yours and mine both.

I have been reading the novels of Robertson Davies—full of mystery and humor and of Ontario as he knew it growing up.[12] He's probably your old familiar.

My love to you as always, dear Ken

Eudora

Nona Balakian sent you greetings too.

Even as Eudora was writing to Ken, Ralph Sipper was sending her "Good news!" "When I telephoned the Millars this morning," Sipper reported, "Ken sounded particularly alert. I remarked on this to Maggie after she came on the phone and she told me that Ken had had a very good two weeks, the best she could remember in recent months. She conjectured that perhaps Ken did not have Alzheimer's after all (you will remember that the disease is diagnosed by a process of elimination) and that the doctors could be wrong."[13] Eudora had long cherished that very hope, and it was reinforced when on August 26 Ken and Margaret phoned her. Such hope would soon be chastened.

Eudora Welty to Kenneth Millar, August 26, 1982

Dear Ken—

I was so grateful for the call—Thank you and Margaret—I hold those moments dear when we were hearing each other's voices—It was like a wonderful and unexpected present, one I would rather have had than any other I can think of—

It came on a hot afternoon—the cicadas singing from the tree in the yard in long choruses—when it starts getting dark, hundreds of lightning-bugs will begin signaling, high & low—Dear Ken, I think of you every day, but today was when I heard your voice on the telephone—

With dearest love,
Eudora

Margaret Millar to Eudora Welty, September 5, 1982

Dear Eudora,

It was very good of you to write so quickly and fondly. Ken appreciates it very much. By an odd coincidence, and a happy one, the following day while going through some of my papers I came across this wonderful picture of you and Don Freeman and Ken. I've forgotten whether I sent you one at the time or not. I have not exactly reached the forgetful stage, but I have so many details to remember now that Ken is totally unable to help with any.

Last night was kind of a low point in his condition which fluctuates so much that I am continually off balance. He decided to take a walk with the two dogs. We had just come in from dinner and when he went down the hall I assumed he was simply going to rest. The police found him almost all the way down to the beach, walking in traffic, on the wrong side, walking very rapidly, they reported. This was quite a switch, as his usual gait is very slow though he's physically in good shape. Anyway, one of the dogs had sense enough to come home by himself: the smaller one stuck with Ken. He asked me if I had a room for him, he didn't know who I was or my name. He had never done such a thing before, and of course has no memory of it. I wish I could forget as easily.

A long cold summer. Some of the locals are blaming Reagan which is meteorologically unsound but psychologically tempting.

Much love & admiration,
Margaret

Eudora Welty to Margaret Millar, [September 1982]

Dear Margaret,

Thank you for writing to me, and under such difficulties. I appreciated it very much, for I think and wonder and hope every day about the way things go. And I realize how every day is its own story.

What I would like to do is come. I have been hoping for a long time that it would be all right, would not give any kind of worry or inconvenience, if I came out briefly to see Ken—just whatever would seem to him natural and easy. I could get a room at the Hotel Miramar and take my chances on its being a time there that [would] be all right on the day. If there would prove to be some way I could be useful to you—I would try my best. It seems possible to me soon, if there is nothing at that end to keep me from it. I think Ralph would help in any way, though I haven't mentioned it to him lately.

Thank you so much for sending me the Coral Casino photograph of that happy time. I cherish having it.

Thank you again for writing to me and for that phone call—I'll write again and I'll be writing to Ken, though without mentioning coming to Santa Barbara. I would like to know how this seems to you.

I send my love today and every day. It isn't the same thing as help, but it wants to be.

With love and hope,
Eudora

P.S. I'm sending a note to Ken today—plus a picture—if he'd like to see it—

"What I would like to do is come," Eudora had written to Margaret, and in October Margaret sent word that she might. As Eudora told Reynolds Price, "Ralph Sipper called up, saying Margaret asked him to do so for her. It would be OK there 'if I was up to it' she said, I 'didn't need to get permission from her,' and that the sooner the better because of the weather, which will be the rainy season before long. She also said she had a car if I wanted to use it. (But I can't drive in S.B.—the Freeway!) Ralph is going to be out of town at the beginning of November for about a week, and what I think is that I'll go out on Nov. 11 and stay till the 20th—I very much would like any element of rush or strain to be out of it so Ken would feel it was an easy time, & we could meet without anything pressing. If Ralph is in town (I pray I'm right on his dates—I'll check to be sure) he will help make things easy."[14] Eudora knew that Reynolds could accompany her once his faculty responsibilities for the fall semester ended, but she felt the situation was too urgent for delay. So she wrote separately to Margaret and to Ken, confirming her solo arrangements.

Eudora Welty to Margaret Millar, November 9, 1982

Dear Margaret,

Ralph gave me your message that it will be all right at that end for me to come—I want very much to come. I'll be flying out on the 15th, and will telephone the next morning—we can see then when's a good time for me to come out, or whatever. It turns out that Ralph and I are to be coming in on the same plane, both taking it at Denver, and Carol will meet us both. I made a reservation at the Miramar, where I feel at home, and brought work along too—so it will be easy for me just to be there and to see Ken when it's a good, relaxed time for him and no burden on you. I look forward very much to the time, and our meeting. And I'm so happy the time coincides with the L.A. Times Award to Ken—which I hope to see you accept, I'll be there too.[15]

Love,
Eudora

Eudora Welty to Kenneth Millar, November 9, 1982

Dear Ken,

My news is that I'm flying out to Santa Barbara to see you—something I've wished to do for a long time. I'll telephone you and Margaret next Tuesday (November 16), my first morning after I get in. I hope to be in town for several days—it will be so good to spend a little time together whenever it's good and easy there. It will make me so happy to see you. Till then,

My love to you,
Eudora

In Santa Barbara Eudora was for the first time in five years able to see Ken face to face. He was still handsome, still with the build of an athlete, but there was a bitter irony in that fact. As Eudora told Ken's biographer, "He remembered how to swim, and he had someone to go swimming with him every day [. . .] he just looked wonderful, right at the last. All of that, it did him no good."[16]

Eudora felt his situation was made even more dire by Margaret. Eudora could overlook thoughtless, or perhaps barbed, comments that came her way—Margaret reported that Ken, when asked if he remembered Eudora, had replied, "Sure, he's a fellow I used to do business with." But she was distressed by remarks that wounded Ken himself. She told Ken's biographer of a particularly hurtful pronouncement that came out of the blue during a lunchtime conversation.

Margaret said, "Well, of course I had to poison the dogs. [. . .] I didn't have any time left to attend to those dogs [. . .]." She tells this to Ken.

You know: the loves of his heart. [. . .] It doesn't matter whether it was
true or not, it was just [. . .] Punishing him all the time. She loved
those dogs too. It was terribly difficult, the whole situation, of course,
just terrible. No telling what she did go through. She was probably at
her wit's end about everything and just flew out with that, I don't know
why. I couldn't see into her mind, at all. [17]

Eudora's time alone with Ken proved a blessing to them both, though a poignant one for Eudora. Ralph Sipper believed Eudora "could reach" Ken as others could not. And Eudora, as she confided to Mary Lou, felt that connection: "He did know me, smiled that same big smile, and put his arms around me and kissed me, as indeed he did every time he saw me. We spoke back and forth in perfectly clear conversation, only there was a lot of silence too, but it was Ken. At one point somebody said it was nice I'd come so far to see him, and when I said that he'd come just that far to see me, he looked delighted and recognizing of that [. . .] He was as always gentle and courteous and sweet. The loss of abstract thought and all the wonderful workings of his mind was terrible, but even the non sequitur of his thinking didn't keep his character from its firmness and kindheartedness."[18]

The point during Eudora's visit when Ken seemed best able to overcome the "non sequitur of his thinking" and to have access to once-cherished memories came when Eudora told him of her travels on the trans-Canadian railroad: "I remembered as much as I could, because everything I could tell him was something that rang a bell. It was amazing. But I was thrilled, because it turned out that we could really talk [. . .] You know it both broke your heart, and—you realized how much would go through his mind, even fleetingly, and clue him in on something, and he knew it. And I know so much of his boyhood was with him all the time, and he could call on it if he needed to."[19]

Heartsick at leaving Ken, Eudora eventually settled down to work on a series of three lectures for Harvard University—the William E. Massey Sr. Lectures in the History of American Civilization—to be delivered in April 1983. Harvard professor and old friend Daniel Aaron had invited her to discuss how she became a writer. Eudora, having observed Ken's memory loss, set about this project, which required that she exercise her own memory, and the project itself ultimately became one that extolled the importance of remembering. In the published version of her lectures, Eudora declared that memory was "the treasure most dearly regarded by me, in my life and in my work as a writer. Here time, also, is subject to confluence. The memory is a living thing—it too is in transit. But during its moment, all that is remembered joins, and lives—the old and the young, the past and the present, the living and the dead."[20]

As January 1983 drew to a close, Ralph Sipper wrote that Ken could no longer remain at home. Sustained periods of total memory loss kept him from tending to daily tasks of dressing and grooming, and his Alzheimer's had also led to falls. At a doctor's recommendation, Ken was now living, serenely according to Sipper, in the city's best convalescent facility.[21]

Eudora was far from serene. A fictionalized account she wrote for a story about Ken seems to describe her response to Sipper's letter:

This was Meadowbrook, but surely [I] was driving on it in the wrong direction. Now [I] was moving along North State, supposedly, but it looked unfamiliar and the intersections empty of life and movement. [. . .] A letter that morning from a mutual acquaintance told [me], "He is no longer able to sign his name."

This was the town where I was born, but [. . .] the years had, it seemed, without warning, changed it. He could no longer read, or write a word, even his own name. Driving over the streets of my home town where he had never been, finding myself nowhere that looked familiar, finding wherever I turned, and then reversed myself and turned again, that I was lost, I thought now that I had been very close to him. It had brought [us] together when [I] needed it most, this aimless and timeless ride through the gray rain of a city which had proved itself thus easily slipped from memory, as if we had clasped each other one last time. I felt a surging comfort of not knowing where I lived, the loss of any certainty—almost blindness itself—this was all nearness to him. As if it were a confidence or a promise, I treasured that hour and forty minutes just given to [me]. Anything, anything can affirm love. And I am seizing it.[22]

Ultimately, Eudora moved beyond her imaginative identification with Ken and coped by visiting friends, by continuing to work on her lectures, and by seeing the effect those lectures had on overflow audiences at Harvard, but more bad news lay immediately ahead. In mid-June Ken suffered a "cerebrovascular accident" and was hospitalized. Then his condition deteriorated, and on July 11, he died.

Eudora's response was intense and complex but expressed to only a few close friends. To Mary Lou, she described the wrongs she felt Ken had endured in life and death: "I'm glad it is over for him, and what I've come to feel is that he is FREE. In particular of Margaret Millar, whose screaming abuse of him (it was in public) never did cease, when all he could do was stand there and take it. After he was dead, when she was talking to her agent Dorothy Olding (also Ken's agent) in New York, when Dorothy asked if Ken had yet been cremated, she said, 'Well, I really don't know—he may have been. At some point a charter plane scatters the ashes over the Santa Barbara Channel, it's a service—I have nothing to do with it, and I'm working.' She was home working the night Ken died, and I don't know whether or not anybody was with him."[23]

Six weeks later, in a letter to Bill and Sonja Smith, Eudora wrote less of anger and more of the love she and Ken shared and of the sense of loss that was now hers. "I've been grieving," she told the Smiths, "about Ken Millar who died of Alzheimer's Disease, or so it was diagnosed. I went out to see him [. . .] and we had a good visit—talked together and got to be together every day for a while for about a week—As you know, we loved each other, and what happened to him was so abominable—He hadn't been able to write for two years but a mutual friend in Santa Barbara had kept me in touch. He remained himself—gentle and enduring."[24]

To Eudora, Ken's "gentle and enduring" spirit seemed powerfully present as months passed and the first anniversary of his death drew near. "I feel that Ken has knowledge of what you've been going through and is sending love and encouragement," she told Reynolds Price, who had recently undergone surgery for a tumor "intricately braided" within his spinal cord. Then she added, "I've never ceased to feel close to him in matters close to me. I can say this just to you." Perhaps it was this mystical sense of connection that gave Eudora the courage, after she had finished revising her Harvard lectures and seen them published as One Writer's Beginnings, *to confront again the horror of Ken's final years.*

She believed, as had Ken, that "the best thing for a writer to do with a trouble is to translate it into his work." Indeed, she had found during occasions of personal crisis that relying upon the disguise of fiction both protected privacy and enhanced understanding. That was certainly the case in the late sixties when writing The Optimist's Daughter *helped her cope with the loss of her mother and brothers. In the spring of 1984, she returned to this strategy, drawing upon accounts of Ken's suffering and memories of their relationship as she once more labored over the story about a character named Henry. But this time her strategy failed. So painful was the story to write that it remained in a most fragmented state, almost an enactment of Alzheimer's itself, with some scenes written by hand on envelopes or bank-deposit slips, with bits of dialogue or description on partial pages of paper. Eudora could not and would not complete it.[25]*

"Henry": An Unfinished Story

———— ❧ ————

"We all write on the verge of silence"

—Kenneth Millar to Eudora Welty

EARLY in the 1970s both Eudora and Ken published fine novels and received critical acclaim for them, but in the wake of their accomplishments both struggled with writer's block. Ken's ongoing memory loss seriously hampered his work and left him depressed. For her part, Eudora's difficulty writing became tied to Ken's memory problems. She wanted to write about his plight as a way of coming to terms with it and of honoring him. In a letter encouraging Ken to write about his father, she had asserted, "We somehow do learn to write our stories out of us, however disguised and given other players who can move and act where possibly we can't—and all, but in the end, if the hurt still stays, that's wrong." [1]

She had been working on an incipient novel called "The Shadow Club," one drawing upon Jackson's recent and distant past, when she first learned of Ken's efforts to retain his memory. Ken's deepening troubles prompted Eudora to change the course of this piece so that it included references to the relationship she and Ken shared. Then by the fall of 1981, she abandoned "The Shadow Club" for a different story called "Henry," one focused upon Ken's present situation but also incorporating long-ago incidents from their separate lives. As she wrote, Eudora even attributed her own memories to the character Henry, metaphorically declaring the confluence of their lives.

As hard as she worked to translate Ken's experience into fiction, Eudora remained dissatisfied with her efforts. At some point, she began to develop a second version of the Henry story, which seems to have been titled "The City of Light." This new version included elements rather overtly based upon Ken, Maggie, and herself; the tensions in the Millars' marriage; and the love she and Ken shared. Then in 1985, as a letter from Eudora to William and Emily Maxwell indicates, she destroyed nearly one hundred manuscript pages of this text, leaving a number of fragments, but without order or sequence supplied. "Henry" she did not destroy, at least not on this scale, perhaps because its "players" were more deeply disguised. Unfinished, disjointed, but extensive, the surviving narrative evocatively makes use of Ken's battle with Alzheimer's disease and Eudora's response to that battle even as its characters exist at a greater remove from actuality than those in "The City of Light."

We are proud to include "Henry," abridged for readability, in the following pages.[2]

HENRY
by
Eudora Welty

———— ❦ ————

Part 1

IN the text labeled "Part 1 Affinities," there is no sustained narrative, but these eighty, randomly filed bits and pieces do establish the beginnings of a story line. At times Eudora has lined out passages in the eight fragments included here; we have, when they seemed crucial, kept these passages in the text with strike-throughs indicated. Editorial ellipses within brackets indicate omitted passages, which are either illegible or too cryptic to be understood. Omitted or errant punctuation marks that seem clearly to be typographical errors have been silently corrected.

Eudora called the following fragment her "opening scene."

"Mrs. Paulding? I'm Rachel Guest. I was in Dr. Paulding's class in Linguistics 14-A."

"You're who? In what?"

"I'm an English teacher from Columbus, Alabama. I was here in summer school summer before last."

"What have you come for? Dr. Paulding is not teaching any longer."

"I was in New Orleans for the day—I called at Dr. Paulding's office at the University. Dr. Fields thought it would be all right if I called to see

Dr. Paulding—I have something to give him." I let her see my package, the unmistakable book. "Dr. Fields thought it would be all right if I called here."

"He ought to have his head examined."

~~"I'm a teacher, too."~~

~~"You didn't need to tell me. It's written all over you." Her look added, "So is old maid."~~

I'm sure it's true; and that is what I am. But what blazed in front of my eyes was her belligerence. She challenged me as to who did I think I was in <u>coming here</u>. Could it be that she thought Henry and I had been lovers? She would not have been able to understand at all what H. & I had been to each other—I found it hard to believe, looking at her now . . . that she would understand the meaning of the word for it, the word Henry had used almost at the beginning.[3]

In various fragments that were to follow this opening scene, Mrs. Paulding or Donna, who will later be called both Connie and Beverly, describes the Alzheimer's disease that has stricken her husband Henry.

"He used to get so upset. In the beginning," said Donna. "He didn't know what things there in front of him were <u>for</u>. He didn't understand, oh, the return-address labels he found on his desk. He just sat at his desk looking at them. <u>My husband didn't understand what those little stickers were for with his name and address on them</u>. That was the first time he blacked out. Down on the floor breaking his glasses. I just threw the labels away. All I could do when Henry was upset was put things out of his sight. He sits in here content, like you see him now. I don't think he'd even ask if he saw them today what the labels said. He's more contented now than he ever was in his life." She looked at me. "You understand he's lost his memory."

"Now he doesn't worry any longer that he's lost something he knows he once had without knowing what it is. He doesn't try to understand what's happening to his mind. Well, that's a good thing."[4]

"His book," I said. "When he sees all he's written, and hasn't finished."

"Oh, that's gone," she said. "When he came home from the hospital I had everything cleared out of his room, his desk moved out, and he's never spoken a word about it to this minute."[5]

Donna cooking the egg, while Henry waits seated at the kitchen table.

"He knows what's the matter with him," Donna said. "We talked it over right at the beginning, right here in the kitchen. He was capable of understanding at the time. This thing is irreversible, just keeps on." The egg sizzled. "But Henry doesn't feel things. Henry's content with things now, whatever way they are." With a furious jab of the spatula, she turned the egg over. "It's _me!_" she screamed. "What am I going to do? What am I going to do with _him_?"

She carried Henry's breakfast plate to him where he sat at the table.

"Won't one of you join me?" He looked up and asked. ~~He couldn't help his courtesy. But I felt I couldn't bear it~~ that he was making no distinction between us.[6]

She carried his tray into the kitchen and I followed her. "Donna, is there nothing anybody can do?"

"It's Somebody's Disease—not a name anybody could ever remember . . . Or they said they <u>thought</u> it was that. They would assume it was what Henry had. No, there's nothing they can do. It just has to get worse. [. . .] Oh, God." She was standing in the door looking out at Henry sitting in his chair. "He goes <u>somewhere</u>, I don't know where."[7]

"He doesn't take any medicine! There's no medicine he can take. There's nothing can be done for him. Or for me either!" she cried in her sudden dramatic way. "He's not the only one in this house!" At whatever she saw in my face she replied, "He doesn't feel much, not any longer."

I said to Henry, rising & going toward him with the book, "I came to give this back to you—it's something that belonged to you a long time ago and still does.—I found it right here in New Orleans—" [. . .]

As if he were deeply willing for what could still hurt him to be cut out of him. But what had hurt him, I thought, was deprivation of everything else—everything else but the pain. As if the way to heal deprivation was to cut out the pain it had left.[8]

Donna then tells Rachel about a troubling incident.

"He left home to meet his class & walked into Lake Ponchartrain at three o'clock in the afternoon with his good clothes on. Of course he could quite easily have drowned. But they saw him drifting, floating face down, and pulled him in. He never remembered a thing about it. They said he had a mild seizure, whatever that is, out there in the water."

"Where was Cuchulain?" I asked.[9]

"Who?"

"Henry's dog?"[10]

Part 2

PART 2, which Eudora labels a flashback, is the only place in the group of man-uscript pages about Henry where there is a sustained narrative. The names of the characters, however, are not sustained. Dr. Paulding is often called Dr. Duling, and Rachel is Caroline, May, Nell, or Justine, or is simply unnamed. Though Eudora intended to change the story from a third-person to a first-person nar-rative, she did not do so consistently. Nor did she manage to prepare a fair copy. The pages are heavily revised and can be difficult to decipher, with handwritten insertions and deletions and with typed insertions pinned-on over the original text. In addition, a lined out title "The Shadow Club" indicates that she had used parts of an earlier story, never completed, in this flashback to a time before Henry's catastrophic memory loss.[1]

"Linguistics is the study of the human language," he said in a voice of uncommon politeness and uncommon deliberation. Directly seated in front of him in my molded plastic chair, alone on the front row, I wrote this down and so started my notebook.

Linguistics e-409 was scheduled from two to three o'clock every afternoon, Monday through Friday. The classroom on the second floor was windowless and lit by fluorescent bars tracked across the ceiling but the light of day could be seen through a door onto an iron fire escape. Cold air was nozzled down through gratings high in the walls. The city of New Orleans, for all that it could not be seen or heard or smelled, was out there just the same.

I knew on sight that the other members of the class were high school teachers too. And she, like them, must be washed with lavender by the fluorescence, her outline flickering with it from time to time like theirs. But when the teacher walked in and stood before them, he seemed to face and to ~~withstand~~ its fluctuations. This was Mr. Duling, sandy-haired and middle-aged, who looked out at a point just over the heads of his class [and] hardly moved his body, his hands, or even his head, as he talked.

On the second Monday, Professor Duling placed a china dish on his desk, ~~and opened class by saying, distinctly and~~ formally What was he about to say? [. . .] "I hope that Linguistics e-409 will not object seriously if my young dog attends for a few days while my wife is away from home." He walked out again into the hallway and a young Collie walked in alone, like a leading actor making his first entrance onstage, and stood looking at the class down his slender white nose. Waving a plume-like tail, he investigated what proved to be listening cubicles and shelves of cassettes. The teacher, who was taking up "General Features of Language," touched him quietly on the ear, and he settled down beside the desk, lowering his head onto damp sandy paws.

One of the class, perhaps inspired by the ~~interruption~~ of the dog, waved her hand and asked why they couldn't make it all come alive by letting members of the class join hands and act out the parts of speech to make a living sentence. Prof. Duling didn't appear to have heard what she said, and after she sat down he rose, picked up the china dish and went out into the hallway to fill it from the drinking fountain. He brought it back carefully. It was a rather pretty small tureen, with a faded floral pattern and only one handle.

Everybody waited, watching his dog splash up the water. His noisy tongue looked purple under fluorescent light. Had Prof. Duling forgotten the class waited on him?

With pencil lifted over her notebook, Justine was anxious for him to go on as before. Without really following him yet, but ready to find the clue, yet almost following him, ~~she~~ felt in the very evenness and the very reserve of Prof. Duling's voice something pressing, a quality of suspense, like an undertone she was growing able to detect.

As the days of class followed on one another, she wrote down "Cognitive Structures," "Symbol Systems," "Verbal Behavior," and so on to the sober monotone of the teacher and the occasional and erratic, violent thumping of the dog's tail coming from the floor, at his feet. Listening to his unvarying voice, listening for she didn't know what, May felt more and more in a state of odd suspense. Once when the dog woke up [and] barked she found herself exchanging glances with the teacher.

She was shocked all the more to get back her first test paper with a low mark on it. Indeed it was a failing mark—the first she'd ever received in her life. After all, <u>she</u> was a teacher. An English teacher at that. She hadn't even suspected how little she had learned about linguistics. Had she alone failed? Prof. Duling, who had not until now singled a student out by name, requested that Miss Downing wait after class in his office.

"Would you come into my office?"

Behind his chair, many books were crammed onto the shelves behind glass doors. All those in front of me on his desk were Linguistics books, with paper markers hanging out of them like tongues.

At a desk across the room sat another professor, smoking a pipe and going over papers, paying no attention to our low conversation. (This is Dr. *Morrow*.)

He asked her in plain words why she was in this class. "Is it through some mistake in your assignment? Your test shows that you hardly came prepared for Linguistics e-409. I feel bound to ask you," he said, "would you like to change your course? Would you like me to try to change it for you? Before we go any farther? It isn't too late."

"It isn't what I thought it would be." She added without premeditation, hearing all her Presbyterian upbringing in her words, "I want to learn it <u>because</u> it's hard for me."

He did not laugh. He bent his long, subdued, scholarly face—she saw it was patchy with sunburn—under the untidy hair. "Then I think we understand each other," he said, and as if it followed, "Would you like an hour of fresh air?" The Collie had already begun barking as he reached for a leash in his pocket.

Nell, with her book and notebook, sat among the books in the passenger seat. Mr. Paulding, on the sidewalk, lifted the dog in his arms. "All right Cuchulain."

"Cuchulain!"

"I'd like you to hold him," he said, "if you would."

He had to lift the dog bodily to get him inside the old unwashed Plymouth. Justine held him on the seat between them, to calm his strenuous trembling and struggling. If the car slowed down or stopped for a traffic light, he whimpered like a puppy.

"Miss ~~Downing~~ won't throw you out," Prof. Duling said.

"Cuchulain's himself once he gets loose on the beach," Mr. Paulding said. "He just doesn't like riding in cars."

Lake Ponchartrain opened wide as a gulf, where Mr. Paulding drove directly to a spot on the featureless beach, and had hardly stopped the car when Cuchulain discharged himself from her lap and raced off over the sand, at large. Mr. Paulding, whose name she knew was Henry, led Justine to a strip of shadow inside the seawall, where she sat down. He himself shed his jacket, his shoes and socks, and then folded his spectacles and put them away in his jacket pocket. Then man and dog raced off along the beach. Cuchulain ran tossing his head back, giving arrogant challenging, youthful barks. Mr. Paulding, whose legs were long, could almost keep even. The Lake, too bright to be blue, brimmed at their heels. Out a little way, the water was churning beneath the surface, intensely bright, as though the sun were about to bring it to the boil. And the sky overhead was as brilliant with disorderly summer clouds. [. . .] I hadn't sat on a beach very often. The sand seemed to me too hot for the bare skin to touch. I watched the teacher, with his scholarly face and his running body, and his dog with the Irish hero's name reeling and spinning before him and behind.

Cuchulain loose on the beach was another dog. Away from the fluorescent light of the classroom, his coat was almost red, his ruff salt white. The streak of white marked his nose with an arrow.

~~"Both of you like to run," Caroline ventured, when Henry came and sat down to watch too.~~

~~He looked at her; his kind, far-sighted eyes were dark-brown.~~

"Yes, you can't leave an animal this high-strung alone all day in an empty apartment. He'd be sure you were never coming back."

Cuchulain came up before the Professor and waited, his eyes large and shapely as a human child's.

Henry sat cross-legged, throwing his shoe for his dog. He did not speak the language of small-talk at all. Even on the beach, where ~~they~~ we sat within the sound of other people laughing and splashing, he was a still, contained man. Above his high, lined brow, his fair hair stood up, forked by the rising Lake breeze, measuring the time he'd forgotten to have it trimmed. Some gray hairs were starting through it.

I thought how unlike home in Inverness, Alabama, this was. Life had brought me close enough to this man to know that the fine lines in his face almost surely had not come there from laughing, and yet know nothing about him, or about anyone a single step away from him. It was outside my experience to know somebody by himself, in no other way but as he was alone, and to be offered such undemanding silence, to know him in. I thought, if he came from anywhere in the South he would have seized advantage of this time off to talk about himself and his life and his whole family's life, and I would most likely have discovered some parts of it [I] could take [my] clue from, have found a familiar name along the line somewhere, a possible connection. It would have emerged that some cousin of his had been best man in a wedding in Andalusia where my father is the pastor of the Presbyterian Church. Or even that his absent wife would turn out to be kin to me. Somehow I felt that the <u>wife</u> must be a Southerner. And if he'd been a Southerner, my name would have meant something to him, most likely the story everybody heard about my parents. But I knew from the start that what drew [me] to this self-contained man was that he was <u>not</u>

connected. Here together on the beach not knowing each other. Both were mysteries.

"You are smiling at my dog," Henry said.

"He's tireless."

"He's tired by the time he gets home," said Henry. His kind, far-sighted eyes were dark brown. "So am I."

~~Reticent people need reticent people, she thought. Those who tell you you need the other kind have been wrong all the time.~~ This hot, nearly untouchable beach by Ponchartrain, where we sat, though constantly tracked along by strangers [...], already seemed to me a place of not only privacy but safety; Henry Duling and I [our]selves might have silently assigned [our] mutual safety to it. The way it is now, [I] thought, is perfect.

Pleased she rose and walked with them along the water's edge. Her long hair was whipping across her eyes, completely out of its pins. They were caught in a dazzle as forceful as a downpour of rain. Cuchulain flashed his young teeth and his tongue as blatant as a flag, throwing back his head and barking in constant proposal to their faces. He streaked into the water and bounded back again, shaking his drops over their legs, sparkling. He ran close alongside Henry, setting his teeth in Henry's wrist and holding onto it seriously, as if taking his pulse.

The beach ahead was shadowed by a cloud as peremptory as a curtain drawn across a window. The thunder that followed had a household sound no further away than the slamming of a bureau drawer upstairs. Then the tops of their heads received heavy drops that felt too warm to be rain. Henry caught Cuchulain and forcibly got him back inside the car.

Henry drove Justine back to her boarding house with her clasping the wet, struggling Cuchulain, while Cuchulain licked at the sweat that was running down Henry's cheek. They got through the steaming rush hour to the door of her boarding house just ahead of the downpour.

"Thank you for your company," said Henry.

As the summer intensified, as her notebook filled, they went every weekday afternoon to Pontchartrain. It was always the same hour, scheduled in between linguistics and the rain, which from now on was punctual too, and always the same point on the beach.

Only the library books in the car seat changed. Justine rode holding some of them, as well as Cuchulain at times, in her lap. The books were all on linguistics. One day she found herself making a place in her lap for a book on "Transformational Grammar," exactly the subject of Henry's lecture just over with. She was struck with surprise followed by anxiety for him that for all his conscientiousness he was apparently just keeping his own head above the water.

One day on the beach, he said, "Linguistics isn't exactly my field— it isn't the course I would normally be giving. I hope you aren't sorry you stayed with the course. But this summer linguistics happened to come my way when I needed it. I'm grateful for it." [. . .]

Every evening, Justine sat at her study table in the boarding house bedroom and applied herself to her work.

This was a boarding house where some of the other teachers in the class were living too. They, at night, would often go out sampling the Quarter. One night, late, she heard the teacher next door, the one who had wanted to act out the parts of speech, throwing up in the bathroom. She was aware that she was considered stand-offish when she didn't join the gang. Her friendship with Henry was outside their knowledge; she heard them laughing at his wife's having run out on him, and said he tried to teach his dog linguistics. Yet they seemed to be getting linguistics. They had taken to it. As Cuchulain took to Lake Ponchartrain.

Her lecture notes daunted her in the evenings when she couldn't hear Henry's voice making quiet logically ordered statements. There was of course the textbook. If something was down in a book, she could master it. That was what Henry was doing. She would pass his course. But she didn't know her way in the subject, really. Just as, while she now recognized the names of a number of streets in New Orleans, she remained lost in the city. The old streets followed the curve of the river—it was hard to straighten out their north and south. She seldom knew exactly where she was, was never sure of her bearings.

Without Henry to drive her in his car, she would not have trusted herself to find her way from the campus to the Lake and back to this boarding-house.

It came to her, waking in the night after she'd gone tired to bed, that linguistics wasn't the subject that had grown large in her mind. Linguistics was only its distraction, perfectly devised.

On the afternoon of the last class, Henry did not bring Cuchulain. Then had his wife at last returned? He had not mentioned her since the day he had told the class of her temporary absence from home. He gave an extra-long lecture, reviewing the course. He reminded them that the examination was scheduled for the next morning at eight.

After dismissing his class for the last time, Henry shook hands with all of them as they filed out and waited at the door for Justine.

"It occurred to me that you might prefer a walk down Royal Street to the Lake—if you're not busy this evening?" he said.

"It's my last night," she said. "I'd like that."

That last afternoon, the one when they didn't go to the beach, two young people running along it were struck down and killed by a bolt of lightning. Justine read about it in the (Picayune) as she watched for Henry's car. But when she greeted him with the news, he didn't ~~seem to be listening.~~ His face had the concentrated look it wore in the lecture room, as if he must keep his mind on the evening ahead of them.

Henry parked his car on a sidestreet so they could go into the Quarter on foot.

The only sound they made between them came from the click of her high heels on the uneven stones of the sidewalk—a small-town sound.

The night itself was flying with city sounds turned loose, the clanging bells and sirens and blares and hoots, the shriek of a streetcar, and now and then the clap of running feet that overtook May and Henry and passed them fast.

Then like the stroking of velvet, notes from an old slide trombone playing "Mood Indigo" reached out through an open door just off the sidewalk somewhere in the vicinity of the Cathedral. "Listen," May said. ~~As she spoke the word, he touched her elbow and~~ guided her through a doorway inside. The rigidity and the peace of their summer's routine was left behind them.

La Lune first appeared to be in total darkness. There was a square hole, about the size of a kitchen table top, in the roof, its lid raised to the night and propped open on a step-ladder. It was as simple-looking as a mousetrap. The moon, the real moon, was supposedly to shine down through that hole onto the dancers.

The table they were guided to was so close to the source of the music that they could never hope to hear each other's voices. The bandstand could be made out—scarcely larger than the podium where Henry had lectured on linguistics. The spotlight beam took in the sleeve and caressing movements of the trombonist and the lady's purse and paper grocery bag on top of the upright piano. And for an instant the pianist's uncompromising face as she let them have the words over her shoulder, like handfuls of scraps she threw over the fence to her yard full of chickens.

> ~~"Good man! . . .~~   (Get better song)
> ~~Hard to find! . . .~~
> ~~Always get! . . .~~
> ~~Other kind! . . .~~

He stood and bent down to her, though at first she couldn't believe Henry was asking her to dance. He led her onto the floor into the thick of the crowd. He danced his own way—moving to the music belatedly, as though it were coming to him from a great way off. And she followed him easily. All the alarms of the street accident might have waited until now to catch up with her, ~~turning with him she was part-ner in his immunity.~~ They had little by little turned the complete circle on the floor, stepping off the dimensions of an island to which he had invited and taken her, bounded it all the way around.

As we broke, I looked into his face.

"My wife taught me to dance," he said.

And when he was guiding her back to the table, she saw under the spotlight that he was wearing an old pair of leather easy slippers: he had never really left home. Yet while they'd been moving so restrainedly on the floor she'd once been reminded of riding in the car with her arm laid along the youthful back of Cuchulain at any minute capable of springing into the air.

As the music started again now he tried to look at his watch. Then he made his voice heard, "Cuchulain's hungry. Would you like to run by home and let me see what I can find for his supper?"

"Of course," she nodded, readily realiz[ing] that he didn't remember that it was they who hadn't had supper yet. Actually, he hadn't noticed when the drinks had arrived on the obligatory order when they had gained their table, and were now left behind untasted.

As they came out the door of La Lune, in front of pulsing blue and red lights, whistles, running feet, approaching sirens, loud arguing voices—a crowd had converged at a street intersection. She saw Henry give it his distant glance, before he took her arm and they pressed unhurriedly through the crowd, walking the other way.

He was driving through the city in concentrated silence; she didn't know in what direction.

It was a while before he came to a stop.

"One of our class said that the reason you can't see the Mississippi River anywhere is because it's behind the wall of the levee and running above our heads," she said. "Is that true?"

"How could you have escaped the river? I can show it to you any number of places. And you can hear it from our house." He cut off the engine. "Listen."

A distant hooting reached them.

"The ferry to Algiers. All night long," said Henry.

They had reached a shell-paved street that seemed to end just ahead of them in a scattering of palm trees. Some two-story white frame houses stood visible under the streetlight, not far back from the sidewalk, most of them dark-windowed by now. Henry led her through an ornamental wire gate and over squares of paving stone set in monkey grass, around to the side of the last house. There was an outside staircase leading to the second floor.

"We live upstairs."

We came up the staircase [. . .]. He opened the door, and Cuchulain was throwing himself against Henry's chest.

Light came from a doorway at the back. Now Henry turned on some lamps in here and they were standing in a living room. When had there been a wife here? When Henry took Cuchulain out, after he'd seated her, she thought she'd never been in a room so wifeless. There was pleasant enough furniture—a rather grand highboy against a wall; and beyond it a table, with a book lying on it—she saw there was a dining room beyond, with a bare round table in its center. Perhaps it was the lampshade that made her feel how bereft it was with [its] silk that had turned to tobacco brown long ago. Or was it the fine sifting of sand over the floor. She felt grains of it in her chair, through her thin dress.

They were back, Cuchulain skidding and sliding down the cross-hall and Henry followed. It was missing a kitchen smell, but she heard a spoon against a pan back there, beneath Cuchulain's clamor, a clattering of the dish.

"The first time I saw him," Henry said, returning and taking the armchair facing hers, "he was wandering the streets. Starving. I saw him standing on the streetcar track in the middle of St. Charles, with the streetcar coming. So weak that when I got him home I had to carry him bodily up the steps. Even now, he suffers if he's left by himself."

"I think he'd been thrown out of a moving car," said Henry. He had not yet eased back in his chair.

Cuchulain, showing off, paraded in with a sock of Henry's and then a ball. Henry threw the ball for him.

"You wouldn't care to smoke?" he asked. "Though I'm afraid we—But may I offer you an after-dinner drink?" I quickly said yes, or he might suddenly realize that we had not had dinner. All the floorboards sang underfoot as Henry walked across the room toward the open door of a room that was in darkness; the uneven floor met it with a little step up. Over the doorframe had been taped, not recently, a small cardboard square on which was written in a large, childish backhand, "DUCK." And as he stepped up he did as the sign teased him to do and ducked his tall forehead. He didn't turn on a light in the room, but the streetlight shone through the window and dustily lighted it; the palm tree just outside, lighted as well, looked like a piece of furniture on the other side of a bed. Henry was opening the door of what appeared to be a large armoire. He came out bringing a bottle, while Cuchulain followed behind him carrying, this time, a slipper.

Henry went through to the kitchen, and on his return he brought two unmatching wine glasses, filled to the top, trembling somewhat in his fingers.

We set our glasses down carefully and at the same time, both untasted, on the arms of our chairs. I don't remember how the drink tasted; I don't know what it was. Henry barely sipped it.

"Donna, my wife, is away for an indefinite period," he said at last. "She has decided to spend some time on the Mississippi Gulf Coast. It's not all that far away, is it?"

He waited not on me to reply but on himself to speak. "I believe she's developing an interest in a pottery class," he said. "There's a flourishing folk art community on the Mississippi Gulf Coast, perhaps you've heard something about it? . . . I believe she's beginning now to find herself," he said presently.

Cuchulain sidled up to him with the slipper. Henry stroked his head and then threw the slipper, which Cuchulain raced for.

"You can't do these things overnight. Not when you're making a relatively late start." Henry raised his eyes to mine. "And it's very important to her that she find herself before it's too late."

Here was Cuchulain back with the slipper, a small-sized pink-tinted one.

"She wanted a respite from being a faculty wife," Henry said. With a grimace of deliberation he threw the slipper again. "And I'm sure she deserved it."

"And when she comes back it'll be of her own free will. I honor her wish. She knows that."

Now Cuchulain was ready to let me take my turn. He pranced up with the slipper held in his jaws by the heel. It was a rather worn pink satin mule.

"I'm afraid I don't know one pottery bowl from another," Henry was saying humbly.

"No, Cuchulain. No, take it away." I was not going to touch the slipper. How could any woman have done that to him?

Henry put out his arm and in a firm hand took the shoe from Cuchulain. "But the important thing about it is she's surviving the crisis," he said. "I know that much. I tell myself that's the beauty of a major credit card. I know Donna is alive. Better than from postcards of the Biloxi lighthouse." And he threw the pink slipper with great force, almost as far as the dining room table in the next room, without ever seeming to notice what object it was he threw, or the little glass he'd knocked off the arm of his chair, spilling the wine and breaking it. "She's found Ray, now—a puppet maker friend, who's given her another sort of respite. He's homosexual." Cuchulain brought him the slipper and he held it rigidly before his eyes—the little thread of pink ostrich waving from the toe, the inside sole stained with the print of a small bare foot. "I <u>was</u> slow to respond fairly when it came to Ray. But my wife used to tell me I never saw the joke in things. It isn't a joke to hold yourself in. I want to go find where she is, bring her back. But that would be the stupidest thing I could do. In that Connie is not much like other women." "She'll come back of her own accord, don't you think?" he suddenly asked me. "Wouldn't you?"

Justine said, "I wonder how it was you happened to know her?"

"It was the most natural way in the world," he answered at once my first personal question to him. "I taught her. The Romantic Novel." He continued to look at me. Presently he said, [. . .] "It wasn't until last night, when I had to prepare my exams, that I realized you would actually be going away. That very probably I should not see you again. It finally dawned on me—I realized how selfish I'd been allowing myself to become. You'd missed what the people who flock here to study in summer expect. . . I meant to make it up to you in some small way tonight, wondering if we mightn't have dinner in a nice restaurant, take one walk through the Quarter—I hadn't really thought ahead as far as the dancing, and only when we reached the door I remembered—my wife always took Mississippi visitors to La Lune. This was before she was interested in ceramics."

"Henry, thank you! It was a great kindness. I liked coming along all those afternoons to the beach too. I'm glad I stayed with your course."

"I've counted on you being here," he said. "I wanted you to know—I wanted you to <u>know</u>, Rachel. That's why I planned this evening, different from the other times—what I feel toward you is <u>gratitude</u>." [. . .]

He set his jaw and was still. And I knew now that his whole present life, starting with the pedantry, the monotony of his linguistics lectures—for that was what they'd been really like—was one untiring effort at self-control, one long concentration simply on getting through the days and nights, on staying alive. Linguistics was his discipline. Just as waiting itself was his achievement. And so every day needed to be the same. I was afraid and ashamed now that his evening with me had given him a hard time by causing him to break this discipline for the sake of courtesy, that he'd hated the Quarter and La Lune, maybe even the dancing. I had let him forsake, for my last night, what was to him an unstopping necessity.

Now Cuchulain came offering Henry a book.

Henry patted his head. "Why, you've brought me 'The Tower,'" he said, taking carefully a narrow book of bleached green with gilt bars on it.[2] He showed it to me and then as if in a sudden resolve he got to his feet. "You might as well see the rest," he said, leading the way, I bringing the book. We passed a china closet with <u>four</u> flowered tureens—the set Cuchulain's water dish had come from—and the round dining room table of plain oak, with an open book lying on it where the chair was drawn up.

They entered the room at the back where the light had been left on. Cuchulain pressed in ahead and, suddenly exhausted with the joy of tonight's reunion, spun around and stretched full length on the floor at the foot of a cot and at once lay asleep.

Under the light of a student lamp the small room was in disarray. On the desk were piles of papers, and papers that had escaped from piles, jammed pigeonholes above. There were open books, open notebooks—everything was opened. Bulging manila folders were crowded into the bookshelves in and among the books, and had piled up on the floor under the dictionary stand. Books were lying open on the wrinkled-over, re-covered couch, where a bed pillow was punched in against the wall at the head. There was an alarm clock sticking partway out from beneath the pillow. On the strip of carpet lay a well-gnawed bone, one of a pair of Henry's good shoes beside it, and with his chin on the other shoe, Cuchulain sleeping.

Henry stood looking down at his desk, at some written-over notes as if he were not really seeing them, only remembering them. No alarm showed in his face, no surprise at the whole row of books with the bleached green spines lying fallen over like dominoes across the back of the desk. They'd toppled a stack of bluebooks.

[. . .] "I'm hoping to get a little ahead now that Linguistics is coming to an end—a fresh look at the Red Branch with "The Shadowy Waters," Henry said.[3] Now he gathered the books and slowly, methodically stood them in a row again, as if performing that act for the hundredth time. "Some of my most treasured copies <u>have</u> got away from me, over the years," he said. I set "The Tower" in its place for him at the end of the row. As I slowly performed this little act, his hand slowly came down and firmly covered mine.

I saw it, as if the shock of contact had made [me] psychic, beneath its summer tan, all marked over with the worn calluses and the scars and burns and still unclosed wounds of a terrible, long-enduring, almost killing life, which I had not even yet dreamed he led, until this moment. His hand, by not moving, by not leaving [mine], conducted such long and patient desperation that my own hand, in receiving it, could not have moved either, had I even wished to move it or tried to take it away. Both unmatching human hands stayed still, as if time had stopped.

There was a sudden high-pitched sound of startling eagerness, almost human. It was Cuchulain. All four feet in running position, he was having some dream.

I remembered that I must study tonight. "Last chance."

"I think we might walk," he said. [. . .] The tossed pink slipper, the untasted cherry bounce were left behind. As we descended the outside stairway, I could see where the house stood was really the end of the street, too; it stopped in a scattering of palm trees.

The streets through which Henry and I walked were dark and deserted. The houses stood dimly back, all windows were dark. Giant oaks made their presence known as if they breathed, they lined the way. Their limbs arched over Henry's head and mine like a succession of gateways.

"Hocking County, Ohio, is a section of the country that lies very open," Henry began in the dark. "You can get into it from any side, without any trouble. You can see where you're going. You know where you are. All the roads are clearly and plainly marked. That's where I come from. The country lies open, though the people living there may not by nature be so open to the stranger. It's farming country, orderly country, very plain. Peaceful. It grows and yields well. It isn't a wasteful country. It's bountiful. And looks it. It looks peaceful." Like Henry with his eyes closed, she thought in the dark now effortlessly in step.

There was for a while the sound of their walking.

"They were Amish, a long time back, my family. The Pauldings still cling to the land. My brother and his wife and family still own our old farm. It was my family's dining room table that you touched as you went by in my apartment. They were quiet, plain people, people of peace. My father never used to talk much to me until after I had begun living away from home and would travel home for a visit, and then not until just the night I was leaving. And then his confidences would pour out. As I think back it makes me smile a little. Nothing with any reason for keeping back at all, nothing to be ashamed of, just the bare unvarnished facts. I used to wonder if he didn't regret my knowing those later. But I think he was fond of me. And I was breaking away from the farm. I was looking for something farther away and harder to get, you understand. I was determined upon a good education."

He told her that he'd put himself through the University of Wisconsin. "I happened to discover Yeats, reading through some of the stacks in the Library. I read the early and then the later poems all through the same one afternoon, standing up, by the window. I read—" His voice was so different from his lecturing voice that she was almost prepared to hear him recite the poem itself—"I read 'Sailing to Byzantium,' standing up in the stacks, by the light of falling snow. It seemed to me that if I could stir, if I could take the next step, I could go out into the poem the way I could go out into that snow. That it would be falling on my shoulders. That it would pelt me on its way down—that I could move in it, live in it—that I could die in it, maybe. So after that I had to <u>learn</u> it," he said. "And I told myself that I would. That I accepted the poem, the invitation." [4]

In the dark, she was uncertain if the indrawn breath she heard was his laugh. "And I didn't know or dream that 'Sailing to Byzantium,' that changed my life, was a poem about old age—<u>I</u> was youth! Then, I saw other things—about the spirit and the flesh—about heart's desire, and the hope of finding it, and not finding it—that it was about making something at last out of what you'd found. And now I think maybe youth and old age themselves are about those things. Growing old is 'about' 'Sailing to Byzantium.'" He went silent. At a distance the ferry boat hooted. "The poem's not so much 'about' growing old—growing old is 'about' the poem."

"The poem's simply what isn't going to die," he said, "And we are."

~~"And don't you know," he cried, "I'd give it up, give Yeats up even, if she would come back again and ask me to?"~~

The air was stirring a little as if they'd come to an opening space. There was a faint light of shells in front of our feet. A turfed embankment showed itself; there was paleness in the sky. Henry kept on in his straight line, past bushes that touched my waist, scraped my legs, up the slope. We came to a stop in the open. The place we, though it seemed almost without knowing it, stood on was broad and high. Gradually we made out the river, brimming not far below, full of night, running past us. He'd brought [me] here after all, as he'd promised. We stood at a point on its great emerging curve. At a distance unknown, faint, countless lights pulsed starlike in its outreaches of the city. A little jewel box of lights traveled across the space of profoundest darkness, as slowly, it seemed, as a planet through the sky. She knew without his telling her that it was the ferry to Algiers. We were somewhere on the stark cleanswept levee.

"In the meantime—in the meantime! Why shouldn't people be merciful to one another?" At the sound of his voice rising so sharply, birds close by moved from thicket to thicket, as if following some rule of safety. It was a valedictory voice as if now they were leaving something behind them, as if it were the end of a story he had come to the end of now.

"Because it's a thing we can <u>learn,</u> come to <u>learn,</u>" he said, while the air stirred now, coming over the water into our faces. "Don't you believe? It's not too much to try for, is it?" His voice through the stillness was once more lifted, almost like that of a young man. "It's never too late, do you believe?" At the force of his voice, the birds rose and flew out over the water. It became an impossible blue. We could see one another.

In his exclamatory face there had come something I had not seen there before. He was looking down at my own face as if he saw something to love there.

"You have been reminding me of Beverly," he said. "That must explain it—"

"Not to me," she said, as desperately as he.

He was putting his arms around me. I had no power to keep me from holding just as tightly to him. I was embracing him too.

"It was your voice," he said. "I only realized it when you spoke to me in the dark. It was like a miracle how you brought her back to me as she was in the beginning when we were just starting out together."

"I can't let you think that," I said. "I <u>couldn't</u> be like her," I flashed out. "I couldn't have done what she did!"

"She had a great deal of innocence about her—yes, and expectation, hope. It was what I could hear in your voice. We might be at our beginnings this very morning. Don't you feel it too? Only stay close to me. You have restored me. You are so beautiful. I never knew this would [come] to me as long as Donna wishes to remain my wife. But I'm so happy! I'm so happy." ~~Henry protested to the (place) around him.~~

~~"Stay with me."~~

I heard in his words and his voice what I had seen almost psychically in his hand—the desperation. Of course I loved him with a desperation of my own! I did not know what to do. What solved it, and I think it was the last thing I expected, was the sun coming up.

The mysteriousness of the dark and the dawn dissolved. So did every bit of the shadowiness that had wrapped us. [. . .]

The broad light of the sun ran us down, more brazen every minute, eye-hurting. Without speaking again we embraced each other so closely that the light could not get in, we were shields for each other and closing our tender eyes against the hard light.

The sound of some distant iron bell, ringing the hour from deep in the city, was laid on our middle-aged shoulders. Under the great spillage of heat and light, we left the river and walked on down the levee again, and soon into a paved street as if answering to the bell which continued to ring. By the time we reached a paved street, a cruising taxi was coming into sight, its headlights brownly burning. It reached us and, without being signalled, stopped, as though it were morning routine to round up strangers in the city of New Orleans who had lost their way in the night just ended. The driver reached back and opened the door, and Henry helped me inside. I flew home to the parsonage that evening.

In the margin is Eudora's note to "cut most" of the paragraph above.

There are several partial pages with extra material for the flashback. Three follow below.

FLASHBACK

"What will it be like when you go back tomorrow, Rachel? Are you still living in the house where you grew up?"

"Yes, the parsonage. It's quiet between one Sunday and the next. Do you know that my mother and father live there side by side and they haven't spoken to each other for twenty years? They can't change anything, because Father is the Presbyterian minister."

Under a streetlight I saw that he only nodded as though I had told him nothing to astonish him.

Presently he said,

OHIO[5]

"Once in a second hand shop I came across that poem in a beautiful little book to itself. Yeats had dedicated it to a woman artist, and she had painted pictures for it. I like to think of partnerships in imagination. They must share many clues and secrets between them. Like a good marriage. I had it for a while, that book—it was lost in one of my moves. I can't call up for myself what the pictures were like any longer. The poem has absorbed them for me, as it's absorbed so much."[6]

Henry in being so preeminently a married man was that much the dearer to me, for of course I knew it was this that made him need me. What you could call my bringing-up can't be blamed for what I did— the parsonage was part of what had left me. I think that I was simply afraid of great joy. It had never come so close to me before. I didn't know what to do. Any more than Donna, with Henry disappearing in front of her eyes, knew what to do now. Does anyone know how to love? I stumbled into some bushes when I turned; my eyes weren't seeing ahead of me. Henry brought me to my feet and then with his arm around me guided me down, from that bright levee top behind us.

"Poor Rachel," he said.[7]

The flashback ends at this point, and in a partial draft labeled "Spring '84 Pulled out to be of use in Henry story," the narrative returns to the present. Stella, a.k.a. Rachel, finds her visit with Henry and memories of their relationship called to a halt when Donna reappears.

Daylight struck the room. The front door had opened. Donna stood there, as if she'd come in by a flash . . ..The front door, left open behind her, was drifting farther ajar. Still more daylight was escaping into the room, running over the carpet like an overflow of water. Donna came a step further and then stopped trying. She sank to the floor, and sat with her back to the wall and her legs out in front of her.

"Baby's home," she said.[8]

Part 3

Among the thirty pieces of "Spring '84" text, there is one scene focused on Stella's return trip to her home.

I left my seat and walked off the plane during the twenty-five-minute stop in Birmingham. I had not yet telephoned Dr. Fields; I must do it here; not at home. It was a quarter past three on Saturday afternoon in the Birmingham airport.

The concourse was empty. I found myself the single walker on the long silent expanse of carpet; at every gate, it was the same, the chairs in their rows empty; no one attended the check-in counters; the bulletin boards had not a flight or arrival posted. Le Snac was shuttered down. The newspaper vending stands stood emptied.

I ~~paced along, and then the thought~~ reached me as if a stone in flight had struck at my forehead: here is the picture of what has happened to Henry's mind. It has been deserted. In the corridor I saw no face: for him there was no expectation of a face to know. No place, no destination, no time is posted where he no longer reads. In his mind, no one is coming, and everyone has gone. I was not there either. Where

I'm walking, everyone is gone and there is no one meeting me. I am seeing everywhere around me his mind that I love emptied of all it held, all that packed it, pressed it, lighted it up—memory.[1]

What seems to be a closing scene is grouped in "Part 1 Affinities," along with the story's opening scene. In this passage, Eudora had not yet decided upon a name for the narrator's hometown; at one point it is called Inverness and at another Cedar Springs.

This is not a story about me, unless except inasmuch as the story of Henry has now become mine as well. All I record here is that I managed to lose myself in my own home town of Inverness while driving home from the tiny airport.

It was as if, on my painful journey away from Henry, I was everywhere being conducted through Henry's mind, but nowhere did this come closer to me than when I disembarked in my home town. I found myself lost. I was born in Cedar Springs, in the house I live in now (the Presbyterian Rectory) but I could not get there.

For a moment, there at the wheel of my car, I was terrified. But I saw that there was nothing—that there never would be anything— to be terrified about. In trying to enter Henry's mind where I could still be with him, I'd found that it was everywhere I went. It was all around me when I walked through the deserted airport, and now, as I was lost for the moment, in my home town. I was remaining close to Henry, as if I still had my arm around him.

Then I made my way safely home, into the Rectory. And I felt very close to Henry. When I could have let myself drop to the floor in the airport, I felt a kinship with Donna too.[2]

ACKNOWLEDGMENTS

———❦———

THIS volume might never have been compiled had not Tom Nolan greeted me at the 2006 Virginia Festival of the Book with the suggestion that we collaborate on just this project. I embraced Tom's suggestion as did my book club in Jackson, Mississippi. Eventually, Tom and I managed to clear the decks and begin.

Mary Alice Welty White, Eudora Welty LLC and the Margaret Millar Charitable Remainder Unitrust u/a 4/12/82 granted us permission to transcribe and reproduce all the letters collected here. The Mississippi Department of Archives and History has been a good home to the letters and steward of their use. To these individuals, corporations, trusts, and institutions, we are deeply in debt.

We are honored that Mary Alice Welty White, Eudora Welty LLC, and the Mississippi Department of Archives and History consented to the transcription and publication of Welty's unfinished story "Henry."

No one more ardently desired for *Meanwhile There Are Letters* to be published than did Bettye Jolly, Martha Blount, Lynn Evans, Susan Shands Jones, Linda Lane, Judy Parker, Sister Simmons, Julianne Summerford, Katherine Wiener, and Rebecca Youngblood. This group read and discussed Ross Macdonald novels, listened to me read passages from *Meanwhile* in manuscript form, and encouraged me every step of the way. Katie Bowen and Lee Anne Bryan, two of my star students from years past, along with my supportive friend Paula Kemp, took time away from their own careers and families to help proof the text and revise my own stylistic infelicities. Betty Uzman, Alanna Patrick, and Forrest Galey of the Mississippi Department of Archives and History provided essential and cheerful research assistance as did Jennifer Ford (another star student from the past) at the University of Mississippi Library. Ralph Sipper and Luke Lampton generously shared their private collections of Welty and Miller correspondence, and Sipper granted us permission to quote from his own letters. William Price permitted us to cite his brother Reynolds's letters to Welty, the David M. Rubenstein Rare Book & Manuscript Library at Duke University did the same for materials in the Reynolds Price Papers, and the Washington University Libraries provided access to material in the William Jay Smith Collection.

Special thanks to Kent Wolf, Rob McQuilkin, Craig Tenney, and Loretta Weingel-Fidel, the agents who facilitated this project, to Cal Barksdale and his colleague Max Brown for their wise editorial counsel, and to Millsaps College and the Eudora Welty Foundation for their sustained support of my work.

Longstanding and ongoing appreciation and love go to my husband, Rowan Taylor, whose wisdom and encouragement, patience and ability to call time, have been unwavering for lo these many years.

Eudora Welty was my close friend for almost twenty years, and she graciously allowed me to write her biography. That undertaking has proved crucial to the compilation and editing of the Welty/Millar letters. As always, Eudora, one of America's finest writers, has my deep gratitude not only for her fiction and correspondence but also for her friendship and greatness of spirit.

Suzanne Marrs

* * *

Eudora Welty first told me in 1990 of the existence of her correspondence with Kenneth Millar, and Reynolds Price urged me to pursue her almost sotto voce offer to let me read it; but Miss Welty's fragile health and other factors intervened. Years passed before the collaborative partnership of Suzanne Marrs (whom I cannot imagine ever committing "stylistic infelicities"), the caring efforts of four agents, the yeoman work of Max Brown in preparing the manuscript, and the enthusiastic commitment of editor Cal Barksdale enabled the halves of the Welty-Macdonald correspondence to be rejoined and shared.

Thanks to the University of California, Irvine, Special Collections and Archives for access to the Millar papers, to the Harry Ransom Center, the University of Texas at Austin, and Julian Symons for providing access to letters by and to Kenneth Millar, and to Scribner for the use of my interviews with William Campbell Gault, Brad Darrach, Reynolds Price, Ralph Sipper, and Eudora Welty. A special thank you to Nicholas Latimer, at Knopf.

The formidable research done for my Ross Macdonald biography has been essential to this work. I am forever indebted to the creative commitment of the estimable Mary Rousson.

New projects are nourished by old friendships. Among those whose good wishes I treasure are Diana Cary, Larry Dietz, Billy James, Hank Jones, Rae Lewis, Dick Lochte, Bill Ruehlmann, David Strick, Joan Long Sweeney, Dan Wakefield, and Mary Alice Wollam.

My wife Mary makes writing possible and life worth living.

Eternal gratitude to Margaret Millar and Eudora Welty for their generosity and trust.

Tom Nolan

* * *

PERMISSIONS ACKNOWLEDGMENTS

Millar Kenneth, excerpt from a letter to Jill Krementz, reprinted by permission of the University of California, Irvine, Special Collections and Archives and of the Margaret Millar Charitable Remainder Unitrust u/a 4/12/82, copyright © Margaret Millar Charitable Remainder Unitrust u/a 4/12/82, 1974.

Millar, Kenneth, excerpt from a letter to Julian Symons, reprinted by permission of the Margaret Millar Charitable Remainder Unitrust u/a 4/12/82, copyright © Margaret Millar Charitable Remainder Unitrust u/a 4/12/82, 1973.

Millar, Kenneth and Margaret, letters to Eudora Welty, reprinted by permission of the Eudora Welty Collection–Mississippi Department of Archives and History and of the Margaret Millar Charitable Remainder Unitrust u/a 4/12/82, copyright © Margaret Millar Charitable Remainder Unitrust u/a 4/12/82, 1970–80.

Nolan, Tom, excerpts from interviews with William Campbell Gault, Brad Darrach, Reynolds Price, Ralph Sipper, and Eudora Welty reprinted with the permission of Scribner, a Division of Simon & Schuster, Inc., from *Ross Macdonald: A Biography* by Tom Nolan. Copyright © 1999 by Tom Nolan. All rights reserved.

Price, Reynolds, excerpt from a letter to Eudora Welty, reprinted by permission of the Eudora Welty Collection–Mississippi Department of Archives and History and of William S. Price Jr. literary executor for Reynolds Price, copyright © Reynolds Price, 1973.

Sipper, Ralph, excerpts from letters to Eudora Welty, reprinted by permission of the Eudora Welty Collection–Mississippi Department of Archives and History, and of Ralph Sipper, copyright © Ralph Sipper, 1980–1982.

Welty, Eudora, excerpts from letters to Mary Louise Aswell, reprinted by permission of the Eudora Welty Collection–Mississippi Department of Archives and History and of Eudora Welty LLC, copyright © 1971, 1977, 1983.

Welty, Eudora, excerpts from letters to Reynolds Price, reprinted by permission of the David M. Rubenstein Rare Book & Manuscript Library, Duke University, and of Eudora Welty LLC, copyright © Eudora Welty LLC, 1982, 1984.

Welty, Eudora, excerpt from a letter to William Jay and Sonja Smith, reprinted by permission of the Washington University Libraries' Department of Special Collections and of Eudora Welty LLC, copyright © Eudora Welty LLC, 1983.

Welty, Eudora, "Henry," reprinted by permission of the Eudora Welty Collection–Mississippi Department of Archives and History and of Eudora Welty LLC, copyright © Eudora Welty LLC, 1981–1984.

Welty, Eudora, letters to Kenneth and Margaret Millar, reprinted by permission of the Eudora Welty Collection–Mississippi Department of Archives and History and of Eudora Welty LLC, copyright © Eudora Welty LLC, 1970–1982.

NOTES

———— ❦ ————

Introduction

1   Kenneth Millar to Jill Krementz, typed copy of autograph letter, University of California, Irvine, Special Collections and Archives.

2   Eudora Welty responded to Kenneth Millar's letter on April 23, 1971.

3   We include all but fourteen of these letters. The fourteen letters are dated: February 10, 1971; February 16, 1971; February 21, 1971; January 17, 1972; June 11, 1972; December 18, 1972; [September 1973]; May 20, 1974; July 30, 1974; October 24, 1974; May 28, 1975; October 22, 1975; March 11, 1977; and November 14, 1977. These letters reiterate information included elsewhere in the book. They are available for research in the Eudora Welty Collection at the Mississippi Department of Archives and History in Jackson, MS.

4   Cleanth Brooks, *Eudora Welty: A Tribute 13 April 1984* ([Winston-Salem]: Printed for Stuart Wright, 1984), n. page; Ann Patchett, "The Best American Short Stories 2006," in *This Is the Story of a Happy Marriage* (New York: Harper, 2013), 209.

5   John Leonard, "Ross Macdonald, His Lew Archer and Other Selves," *New York Times Book Review*, June 1, 1969, 2; Michael Kreyling, *The Novels of Ross Macdonald* (Columbia, S.C.: University of South Carolina Press, 2005), 164–65. In 2012, critic Malcolm Forbes wrote that Macdonald "subverted" genre; Macdonald himself maintained that transcendent detective novels fulfilled the genre: Malcolm Forbes, "True Grit: Ross Macdonald Gets His Due," *The Daily Beast*, http://www.thedailybeast.com.

6   Kenneth Millar to Eudora Welty, January 2, 1977.

7 Welty to Millar, September 25, 1973; Millar to Welty, October 10, 1974.

8 Millar to Welty, September 18, 1972.

9 Eudora Welty, "No Place for You, My Love," *The Bride of the Innisfallen and Other Stories* (New York: Harcourt, Brace and Company, 1955), 3–4, 22. A somewhat different version of this paragraph appeared in Suzanne Marrs, *One Writer's Imagination: The Fiction of Eudora Welty* (Baton Rouge: Louisiana State University Press, 2002), 158.

10 Millar to Welty, April 2, 1978; Welty to Millar, September 23, 1978.

11 Writing to Millar on August 1, 1971, Welty worried that the use of letters in Nancy Milford's biography of Zelda Fitzgerald had been misleading, and she told Ken "it makes you want to warn people everywhere to burn their letters." Eudora herself had evidently at some point burned most of the letters sent to her by John Robinson, but she came to believe in the importance of preserving letters as she so eloquently indicated in her introduction to *The Norton Book of Friendship* (1991).

Chapter One

1 Walter Clemons, "Meeting Miss Welty," *New York Times Book Review*, April 12, 1970, 2. "Icky" was a term of opprobrium from the Swing Era, a period Welty experienced at its height during 1930s visits to New York City, when she patronized Harlem clubs and may have attended Benny Goodman's 1938 Carnegie Hall jazz concert. "Icky" meant saccharine, non-swinging, corny.

2 This is the first of twenty Welty letters included here that were part of a collection owned by Ralph Sipper and that have become part of the Mississippi Department of Archives and History collection. The other letters are those of January 24, 1971; June 3, 1971; June 16, 1971; July 1, 1971; April 30, 1972; October 15, 1972; October 24, 1973; June 22, 1975; January 12, 1976; February 23, 1976; July 2, 1976; August 18, [1976]; [September 2, 1976]; December 29, 1976; July 3, 1977; [September 1977]; September 19, [1977]; [November 22, 1979]; and October 30, 1981.

3 Kenneth Millar to Alfred A. Knopf, June 23, 1970, Harry Ransom Center, the University of Texas at Austin, Austin, TX.

4 Kenneth Millar to Ash Green, November 1, 1970, University of California, Irvine, Special Collections and Archives. Ashbel Green (1928–2012) was Ken's longtime editor at Alfred A. Knopf.

5 Eudora's poem "A Flock of Guinea Hens Seen from a Car" had been published in the April 20, 1957, *New Yorker*; it received separate publication by Albondocani Press in 1970.

6 Eudora Welty, "The Stuff That Nightmares Are Made Of," rev. of *The Underground Man* by Ross Macdonald, *New York Times Book Review*, February 14, 1971, 29–30. The review began on the front page, but the lines cited here are from inside pages.

7 Welty to Millar, February 21, 1971, Eudora Welty Collection, Mississippi Department of Archives and History.

8 John Barkham, "Where Writing Is No Mystery," *New York Post*, August 21, 1971.

9 Walter Clemons's February 19 *Times* review of *The Underground Man* was as positive and perhaps as influential as Welty's: "Mr. Macdonald's career is one of the most honorable I know. His later books are better than his early ones, but I haven't read one that I'd advise against. [...] You can find most of [them] in paperback. Get busy!"

10 Ford Madox Ford (1873–1939), an English novelist, poet, critic, and editor, founded the *English Review* and received critical acclaim for his novels *The Good Soldier* and *Parade's End* (a series of four books). Ford's biographer Arthur Mizener had previously written a biography of F. Scott Fitzgerald. Welty well remembered Mizener's disparaging remarks about E. M. Forster, remarks made when they both attended the 1954 American Studies Conference at Cambridge University. Those comments had infuriated Welty at the time just as Mizener's view of Ford now angered her. Her review of Mizener's *The Saddest Story: A Biography of Ford Madox Ford* appeared in the *New York Times Book Review* on May 2, 1971. This critique would eventually become part of *The Eye of the Story* (New York: Random House, 1978), a collection of her nonfiction.

11 The artist and writer Don Freeman (1908–1978) first gained notice as a chronicler of New York City street and theater life in the 1930s and '40s, then as the author (alone, and in collaboration with his artist wife Lydia, [1906-1998]) of a number of popular children's books. The Freemans moved to Santa Barbara in the 1950s.

12 Perhaps Frank MacShane, who had written an earlier biography of Ford, and Ford himself, who was known to friends as "Fordie."

13 Welty had evidently purchased or been given a photograph of Ford Madox Ford, which she in turn gave to Millar and he to Ford's daughter.

14 "Henry Green: A Novelist of the Imagination," *Texas Quarterly*, 4 (Autumn 1961): 246–56. This essay was later collected in *The Eye of the Story*.

15 This letter is not part of the Eudora Welty Collection at the Mississippi Department of Archives and History but is owned by Dr. Lucius Lampton, a publisher of the literary journal *China Grove*. An image of the letter was printed in 2013 in the first issue of the journal as was an image of the inscribed cover of a Doubleday, Doran pamphlet featuring "The Key."

16 Eudora had known Albert Erskine (1911–1993) from his days at the *Southern Review*. Erskine became an editor at Random House in 1947 and by 1959 was a vice president and editorial director there.

17 May Sarton (1912–1995) was an American poet, memoirist, and novelist.

18 Millar to Alfred and Helen Knopf, May 28, 1971, Harry Ransom Center, the University of Texas at Austin; Eudora Welty, interview with Tom Nolan, *Ross Macdonald: A Biography* (New York: Scribner, 1999), 311.

19 Richard Lingeman, "The Underground Bye-Bye," *New York Times Book Review*, June 6, 1971, 6.

20 Poet and critic Allen Tate (1899–1979) was one of the original Nashville Agrarians and served as Poet Laureate Consultant in Poetry to the Library of Congress from 1943 to 1944. He was a longtime friend of Eudora's. Previously married to writers Caroline Gordon and Isabella Gardner, Tate was now married to Helen Heinz, the mother of his two sons.

21 The book was *The Composition of Tender Is the Night: A Study of the Manuscripts* (Pittsburgh: University of Pittsburgh Press, 1963).

22 Matthew Bruccoli's *Kenneth Millar/Ross Macdonald. A Checklist* with an introduction by Kenneth Millar was published by Gale Research Company in 1971.

23 Ring Lardner (1885–1933) was an American satirist who wrote sports columns, short stories, and plays. *What of It?* was published by Charles Scribner's Sons in 1925.

24 A biography of F. Scott Fitzgerald's wife by Nancy Milford was titled *Zelda: A Biography* (New York: Harper & Row, 1970).

25 American poet, novelist, and critic Robert Penn Warren (1905–1989) and Eudora had long been friends; in the 1930s, even before they met, Warren as editor of the *Southern Review* had accepted a number of Eudora's stories on behalf of the magazine.

26 Duncan Aswell, the son of Eudora's close friend Mary Lou Aswell, had abandoned his position as a professor at Haverford College and then disappeared. His mother was frantic with worry, but eventually he sent word via a friend that he was all right and would be in touch. Eudora had earlier told Mary Lou about meeting Ken and had reported: "I had the strangest feeling that it ought to be possible to ask him personally to find D. and that he could do it—but even so I felt it was a sign" (Eudora Welty to Mary Lou Aswell, [June 11, 1971], Eudora Welty Collection, Mississippi Department of Archives and History).

27 The ambassador R. A. D. Ford (1915–1998), with whom Ken attended the University of Western Ontario in 1937–38, was also a distinguished poet, winner of the Governor General's Award in 1956. He was made a Companion of the Order of Canada in 1971.

28 The Apollo 14 mission during which Alan Shepard and Edgar Mitchell walked on the moon.

29 Andrei Andreyevich Voznesensky (1933–2010) was a Soviet and Russian poet of international renown. He would eventually tell Bob Ford of his great enjoyment in reading the fiction of Ross Macdonald, both in English and in Russian translation.

30 William Jay Smith (1918–) is an American poet, who from 1968–1970 served as the nineteenth Poet Laureate Consultant in Poetry to the Library of Congress. Smith and his first wife, the poet Barbara Howes, were living in Florence in 1950 when Eudora spent some time there. A common friend, John Robinson, introduced them.

31 In her biography of Zelda, Nancy Milford quoted a line Zelda had written to her psychiatrist and added a note: "I believed I was a Salamander [Zelda may have been referring to the mythical salamander, which was able to live in fire and endure it without harm.—N.M.] and it seems that I am nothing but

an impediment" (176). Eudora felt that Milford was oblivious to a common southern practice of looking for the salamander in a fire. And Eudora further suggests that Zelda's statement is hauntingly prophetic of her eventual death in a fire at Highland Hospital in Asheville, North Carolina.

32 Donald Duart Maclean (1913–1983) was an English diplomat, one of the so-called "Cambridge Five" who became spies for the Soviet Union; he was stationed in Washington from 1944 to 1948 and defected to Moscow in 1951. Kim Philby (1912–1988), another of the Cambridge Five, fled to the USSR in 1963.

33 Novelist and critic Wilfrid Sheed (1930–2011) attacked the detective story genre in an essay "The Good Word: It All Depends on Your Genre" (*New York Times Book Review*, September 5, 1971, 2). He began his piece by writing: "In movies, they're called genre writers; in real life they're called hacks. [. . .] Occasionally some ingenious rogue tries to smuggle a genre-hack into literature. In recent months, P. G. Wodehouse, Ross Macdonald, James Cain and others have all turned up on the front page of the *Book Review* with prodigious references. [. . .] Each of these writers has, in fact, some interesting claims: yet they have it in common that when they are approached as major writers they lose all their strength, and don't even seem as good as they are."

34 Alexei Kosygin (1904-1980) was premier of the Soviet Union from 1964-1980.

35 Dick Diver, a psychiatrist character in F. Scott Fitzgerald's novel *Tender Is the Night*, attains psychological and professional maturity (in Ken's interpretation) only toward the end of the book, when he leaves Europe and moves back to his native America.

36 Margaret's book described Ken standing on the roof during a forest fire and watering down their house with a garden hose.

37 This statement may be translated as saying: "One sees what, in this history of crime passed on through many generations, can seduce a southern novelist like Eudora Welty. *The Underground Man* has in effect seen itself accorded the privilege, without precedent for a detective novel, of an article on the first page of the *New York Times Book Review*, signed by Miss Welty, whose public interventions are, however, extremely rare."

38 *Permanent Errors*, a collection of stories by Reynolds Price, was published in 1970 and is dedicated to Eudora Welty.

Chapter Two

1 Paul Theroux, "The Details of Death," *Washington Post Book World*, May 14, 1972, 35; Howard Moss, "Eudora Welty's New Novel about Death and Class," *New York Times Book Review*, May 21, 1972, 1.

2 Dame Ngaio Marsh (1895–1982), a native and resident of New Zealand, was a mystery writer whose novels featured Detective Roderick Alleyn and were primarily set in England. In 1966, she was named a Dame Commander of the Order of the British Empire.

3 Brendan Gill's review of *One Time, One Place* appeared in the December 25, 1971, issue of the *New Yorker*.

4 Eudora's friends were Mary Lou Aswell (1902–1984) and the painter Agnes Sims (1910–1990).

5 The distinguished American writer Katherine Anne Porter (1890–1980) championed Eudora Welty's fiction and wrote the introduction for Eudora's first book of stories.

6 *The Iron Gates* (1945), Margaret Millar's sixth novel, and her third for Random House, was a critical and commercial hit and was bought for filming by Warner Bros. (though no movie was made). Its success enabled her to buy the Millars' first house in Santa Barbara.

7 Clifford Irving's purported interviews with Howard Hughes were revealed to be fakes, and *The Memoirs of Chief Red Fox* were discovered to contain plagiarized materials. McGraw Hill was and was to be the publisher of each book.

8 In 1971 the *Compact Oxford English Dictionary* was first published in two volumes. Because of reduced print size, it included every word from the thirteen-volume set. The two-volume edition came with its own magnifying glass.

9 This never-published story may be one that exists in draft form under the titles "Nicotiana" and "The Last of the Figs." It is part of the Eudora Welty Collection at the Mississippi Department of Archives and History.

10 Eudora Welty, *The Optimist's Daughter* (New York: Random House, 1972), 159–160. See Eudora's letter of May 11, 1971, and Ken's of July 2, 1971.

11 Jon Carroll, "Ross Macdonald in Raw California," *Esquire*, June 1972, 148–149, 188.

12 Walter Clemons reviewed *The Optimist's Daughter* in the May 22, 1972, issue of *Newsweek*. Howard Moss, poetry editor of the *New Yorker* and a poet himself, reviewed the book for the *New York Times Book Review* (May 21, 1972). And James Boatwright, editor of the literary review *Shenandoah*, reviewed *The Optimist's Daughter* in the June 10, 1972, issue of *The New Republic*.

13 Alan Pryce-Jones reviewed *The Optimist's Daughter* in the July 14, 1972, *Times Literary Supplement*.

14 British biologist Julian Huxley (1887–1975) was the author of a Middle East travelogue titled *From an Antique Land* first published in 1954.

15 Stephen Fay, Lewis Chester, and Magnus Linklater, *HOAX: The Inside Story of the Howard Hughes–Clifford Irving Affair* (New York: Viking, 1972; Bantam, 1972).

16 Henry Mitchell's interview with Eudora appeared in the August 13, 1972, *Washington Post* and is reprinted in Peggy Prenshaw's *Conversations with Eudora Welty* (Jackson: University Press of Mississippi, 1984).

17 *The Santa Claus Bank Robbery* (New York: Alfred A. Knopf, 1972) by A. C. Greene was based on an actual 1927 robbery in Cisco, Texas.

18 Mystery writer H. C. Branson (1904–1981) published *The Leaden Bubble* in 1949 (Simon and Schuster).

19 James Meriwether, "An Introduction to *The Sound and the Fury*," *Southern Review* 8 (Autumn 1972): 705–10.

20 Eudora refers to Ken's novel *The Zebra-Striped Hearse* (1962).

21 Charles Bunting's interview with Eudora appeared in the *Southern Review*, 8 (October 1972) and is reprinted in Prenshaw's *Conversations with Eudora Welty.*

22 On December 12, 1972, Eudora Welty and Walker Percy were interviewed in Jackson, Mississippi, by William F. Buckley Jr. for his public television program *Firing Line*. The taped interview aired on PBS on December 24, 1972. A transcript appears in Prenshaw, *Conversations with Eudora Welty.*

Chapter Three

1 The Christmas Bird Count, sponsored by the Audubon Society, is an annual census of birds in the Western Hemisphere, undertaken by volunteers. In any given area, the census may occur on a day from December 14 to January 5.

2 Evidently, in a missing letter or a phone call, Ken told Eudora of seeing the program, which in his last letter of 1972 he reported having missed.

3 David L. Chappell, *Inside Agitators: White Southerners in the Civil Rights Movement* (Baltimore: Johns Hopkins University Press, 1994), xxv.

4 Hugh Kenner describes the lessons in narrative given him by Ken Millar in the essay "Learning," written for the anthology *Inward Journey,* edited by Ralph B. Sipper in 1984.

5 Ken was mistaken. His 1965 *Show* piece, "The Writer as Detective Hero," became the lead essay of a 1973 Capra Press "chapbook" (*On Crime Writing*) Millar later this year sent Welty, and would still later be included in *Self-Portrait: Ceaselessly Into the Past* (1981), edited by Ralph B. Sipper (with a foreword by Eudora Welty). Ken's 1953 Ann Arbor lecture, "The Scene of the Crime," would be printed in the anthology *Inward Journey.*

6 Ken refers to the three essays that Smith College published in 1962 under the title *Three Papers on Fiction*. Included were Eudora's essays "Place in Fiction," "Words into Fiction," and "The Short Story."

7 Producer-director Craig Gilbert told the *Los Angeles Times* (January 11, 1973): "The American culture is fashioned on California. [. . .] I read Ross Macdonald's 'The Underground Man' and he described with absolute accuracy the kind of family I was looking for. I found he lived in Santa Barbara and called him up. He invited me out. He had a lot of newspaper people over from the *Santa Barbara News-Press* and we talked [. . .] [S]omeone [. . .] from the staff of the paper [. . .] told me about the Louds," eventual subjects of *An American Family.*

8 This production did not materialize.

9 Eudora did indeed catch up with this essay; it had been published in the *Virginia Quarterly Review* in the spring of 1955. The editor was Charlotte Kohler.

10 This British film from Ealing Studios was first screened in 1945.

11 Eudora was named to the National Council on the Arts by President Nixon and served on the Council from 1972 to 1978.

12 On February 21, 1973, Southern California experienced an earthquake centered in Point Mugu. This quake came two years to the month after the 1971 Sylmar temblor, which caused the water in the Millars' Santa Barbara swimming pool, 90 miles to the north, to overflow.

13 Æ was the pseudonym of the writer George William Russell (1867–1935), an Irish nationalist, poet, mystic, and theosophist.

14 John Buchan (1875–1940), a Scot and the first Baron Tweedsmuir, served as the Governor General of Canada from 1935 till his death. He was also a novelist; his spy thriller *The Thirty-Nine Steps* is perhaps his most well-known book. Millar heard him give a high school commencement address in 1938, and this would prove a spark to his career.

15 Eudora first met Anglo-Irish novelist Elizabeth Bowen (1899–1973) in 1950 when she was invited to Bowen's Court, Bowen's home in Ireland; the two writers became fast friends, who visited each other in the United States and the British Isles.

16 The formal name of this Natchez, Mississippi, house is Longwood.

17 Henri "Hank" Coulette, who lived and taught in Los Angeles, became friends with Millar in 1965 and used a line from Ross Macdonald's *The Ferguson Affair* in his poem "The Blue-Eyed Precinct Worker." Ken later took Hank's poetic phrase describing the pulse-beat for the title of his final novel, *The Blue Hammer*.

18 Jean Gabin (1904–1976) was a French film star and the winner of the Legion d'Honneur.

19 British writer Jean Overton Fuller's book *Double Webs*, published by Putnam and Co. in 1958, details her investigation into the betrayal of British secret agent Noor Inayat Khan, an Indian woman who was the first female radio operator sent into occupied France during World War II.

20 This seems to be the second time Ken has sent the *TLS* review; "Eudora Welty, The Art of Fiction No. 47," *Paris Review* 55 (Fall 1972): 72–97—Linda Kuehl conducted the interview in May 1970 in New York.

21 The dedication page of *Sleeping Beauty* reads simply "To Eudora Welty," but in Eudora's copy Ken has written under these words, "my good angel/with gratitude and love/Ken."

22 Herb Caen (1916–1997) was a columnist for the *San Francisco Chronicle*. In 1996 he received a special Pulitzer Prize.

23 Anthony Boucher was the pseudonym of William Anthony Parker White. Boucher (1911–1968) was a science fiction editor, author of mystery novels, and reviewer of mystery fiction. He highly admired Ross Macdonald. The photographer was Hal Boucher, who was the house photographer for the Biltmore Hotel in Santa Barbara.

24 To interviewer Sam Weller, Bradbury would later say he was especially struck by Welty's "remarkable ability to give you atmosphere, character, and motion in a single line." "Ray Bradbury, The Art of Fiction No. 203," *Paris Review* 192 (Spring 2010), http://www.theparisreview.org/interviews/6012/the-art-of-fiction-no-203-ray-bradbury.

25 Millar to Green, May 7, 1973, University of California, Irvine, Special Collections and Archives.

26 Nona Balakian (1919–1991) was a reviewer and editor for the *New York Times Book Review*. She and Eudora first met in 1944 when Eudora worked at the *Book Review* for several months. Balakian came to Jackson for Eudora Welty Day, and her article about the festivities, titled "A Day of One's Own: The Last Word," was published on page 23 in the May 27, 1973, *New York Times Book Review*. Kenneth Millar to Julian Symons, May 7, 1973, courtesy of Julian Symons.

27 Eudora Welty, *Losing Battles* (New York: Random House, 1970), 362.

28 Millar to Symons, May 7, 1973; Welty, interview with Nolan, 340.

29 Mary Lou Aswell had been a fiction editor for *Harper's Bazaar*, but had since moved to Santa Fe, New Mexico. Eudora had earlier discussed the disappearance of Mary Lou's son, Duncan, with Ken without mentioning their names. See note 26, Chapter One.

30 Crawford Woods, "The [*sic*] Sleeping Beauty, Another Case for Lew Archer," *New York Times Book Review*, May 20, 1973, 55; Anatole Broyard, "The Case of the Quick Read," *New York Times*, May 21, 1973; the *New Republic* review appeared on page 29 of the June 2, 1973, issue.

31 Reynolds Price to Eudora Welty, June 4, 1973, Eudora Welty Collection, Mississippi Department of Archives and History.

32 *The Portable Irish Reader*, edited by Diarmuid Russell, was published by Viking in 1946.

33 Eudora had received an honorary degree from Queens College (now Queens University of Charlotte).

34 Peter S. Prescott (1935–2004) was the senior book reviewer at *Newsweek*.

35 Ken himself had been one of the protestors so chased.

36 John Prince and his wife Catherine were good friends of Eudora's. Prince dealt in real estate in Washington, DC, and had been introduced to Eudora by his distant cousin, the writer Caroline Gordon. Martha Mitchell was the hard-drinking, flamboyant, press-phoning wife of former attorney general and 1972 Nixon campaign director John Mitchell, who would eventually be convicted for his part in the Watergate scandal.

37 Eudora did accept and preserve her correspondence with Diarmuid, ultimately giving it to the Mississippi Department of Archives and History. The letters are the subject of Michael Kreyling's book *Author and Agent* (New York: Farrar, Straus and Giroux, 1991).

38 Among the bestsellers jousting with Macdonald's this season were Kurt Vonnegut's *Breakfast of Champions*, Frederick Forsyth's *The Day of the Jackal*, Jacqueline Susann's *Once Is Not Enough*, and Richard Bach's *Jonathan Livingston Seagull*.

39 Art Buchwald (1925–2007) was a political satirist for the *Washington Post* and the winner of two Pulitzer Prizes. During the Watergate hearings in a column critical of President Nixon, he parodied the popular television series based on John Galsworthy's *The Forsyte Saga*.

40 Ken sent Eudora his book *On Crime Writing* (Santa Barbara, CA: Capra Press, 1973). The friend he mentions is Noel Young (1922–2002), who founded Capra Press.

41 Ken's letter appeared in the August 5, 1973, *New York Times Book Review*.

42 Patrick O'Brian (1914–2000) is best known for writing the Aubrey/Maturin novels set on British ships during the Napoleonic Wars.

43 Eudora Welty, "Writing and Analyzing a Story," in *The Eye of the Story*, 114.

44 *The Wildflowers of the United States* by Harold William Rickett, in six volumes with fourteen parts, was published between 1966 and 1973 and was completed before Russell's death.

45 All were friends of Eudora, and all had attended Eudora Welty Day in Jackson. Joan Kahn edited mystery novels, primarily at Harper & Row; Joan's sister Olivia was an artist.

46 *Great Stories of Suspense*, selected by Ross Macdonald, was published by Knopf in 1974.

47 The xantu murrelet is one of the rarest seabirds in the world.

48 Ken here alludes to Eudora's short story "Petrified Man," which was collected in her first book of stories, *A Curtain of Green* (1941).

49 "Some Notes on Time in Fiction" was published in *Mississippi Quarterly*, 26 (Fall 1973); Eudora later collected it in the book Ken was urging her to prepare, *The Eye of the Story*.

50 The distinguished scholar Leon Edel (1907–1997), who received a National Book Award and a Pulitzer Prize for his work on Henry James, also wrote a biography of Willa Cather.

51 Marsh's protagonist Roderick Alleyn meets his future wife, Agatha Troy, a painter, in *Artists in Crime* (1938).

52 Donald Alexander White Jr. was the first child born to Eudora's niece Mary Alice and her husband Donny White.

53 The Willa Cather Centennial Festival was held at the University of Nebraska in Lincoln, Nebraska.

54 Professional and administrative workers at the museum had begun this strike in October 1973, asking that the minimum starting wage be raised, that rights for union membership be expanded, and that workers have a voice in setting museum policy. The strike ended on November 29.

55 Helen Eustis's *The Horizontal Man* and Kenneth Fearing's *The Big Clock* were both published in 1946. Fearing published several other novels; perhaps the disappointing novel to which Eudora refers is *Loneliest Girl in the World*, published in 1951.

56 Symons's *The Plot Against Roger Rider* was published in 1973.

57 Richard Ader, the lawyer who handled Eudora's investments, and his wife Tessa had attended Eudora Welty Day.

58 No story by Patrick White appeared in the anthology.

59 O'Brian's *H.M.S. Surprise*, the third novel in the Aubrey/Maturin series, was briefly reviewed in the December 9, 1973, *New York Times Book Review.*

60 Eudora Welty, *One Writer's Beginnings* (Cambridge, MA: Harvard University Press, 1984), 104.

61 Reynolds Price, interview with Nolan, 340, and with Suzanne Marrs, *Eudora Welty, A Biography* (New York: Harcourt, 2005), 387.

Chapter Four

1 Frank MacShane (1927–1999), a member of the Columbia University faculty, was a literary scholar who took detective fiction quite seriously, refusing to ghettoize it. His biography *The Life of Raymond Chandler* was published to critical acclaim in 1976.

2 Eudora seems to have sent Ken a recording of Sweet Emma and the Preservation Hall Jazz Band in concert at the Guthrie Theatre in Minneapolis (1964). Sweet Emma Barrett (1897–1983) was a jazz pianist who ultimately played with the Preservation Hall ensemble; Alcide "Slow Drag" Pavageau was a jazz guitarist and bass player who ended his career playing at Preservation Hall. Brothers Willie Humphrey (clarinet) and Percy Humphrey (trumpet) were also mainstays at the same venue. Tommy Sancton is the son of journalist/novelist Tom Sancton and his wife Seta, who was Eudora's lifelong friend from Jackson. Tom Scranton Jr. was the Paris Bureau chief for *Time* magazine from 1992–2001. His book *Songs for My Fathers* details his early experiences among the jazz greats of New Orleans.

3 Eudora's remarks at the Willa Cather Centennial were reprinted in part in the *New York Times Book Review*, January 27, 1974; Eudora would include the entire essay in her collection of nonfiction, *The Eye of the Story*, under the title "The House of Willa Cather." William Koshland was the president of the Alfred A. Knopf publishing house.

4 The records were ones included in the *Smithsonian Collection of Classic Jazz* (1973).

5 At Hollins College, Eudora had been honored with a two-day "Celebration for Eudora Welty" organized by Bill Smith, who was on the faculty there. Bill, Reynolds, and a number of scholars paid tribute to Eudora's work, and Eudora responded with a reading from *Losing Battles*. None of this did she report to Ken. Her letters focused more on the personal than the professional.

6 Stanley Gordon Moyer (1887–1968), Ken's maternal uncle, was a painter and also a writer who published stories (and artwork) in Canadian magazines. Millar credited his Uncle Stanley with teaching him as a youth to see "with a painter's eye."

7 Walter Clemons reviewed Joseph Blotner's *Faulkner: A Biography* in the March 25, 1974, issue of *Newsweek*; Eudora reviewed Annie Dillard's *Pilgrim at Tinker Creek* in the March 24, 1974, *New York Times Book Review*.

8 Ken refers to Joseph Blotner (1923–2012), whose massive, two-volume biography of Faulkner (1897–1962) had been criticized as heavy on detail and lacking in analysis.

9 Barnaby Conrad (1922–2013), author of the best-selling 1952 novel *Matador* and several other works of fiction and nonfiction, had also fought bulls in Spain (where he'd been an American Vice Consul), served as secretary to Sinclair Lewis, and owned a night club in San Francisco. He met the Millars in Santa Barbara in the late 1940s. In 1973 he founded the Santa Barbara Writers Conference.

10 William Frost (1917–1988) taught in the English Department at UC Santa Barbara from 1951 until his death.

11 Millar to Welty, May 20, 1974, Eudora Welty Collection, Mississippi Department of Archives and History.

12 Novelist Kurt Vonnegut (1922–2007) was at the time still married to his first wife; he and photographer Jill Krementz (1940–) would marry in 1979. Krementz is best known for her photographs of writers. She had previously photographed Eudora and in 1972 photographed Eudora and Reynolds Price together.

13 When Millar received the inscribed photo of Welty from Krementz, he wrote the photographer of the qualities he saw reflected in it: "Pathos, gentleness, courage,

feminine fluorescence and iron discipline, the blessed light at the windows. Your picture goes to the heart, as its subject does, and I am going to have to hang it on my wall" (June 11, 1974; typed copy, University of California, Irvine, Special Collections and Archives).

14 Brad Darrach, interview with Nolan, 350–351.

15 Eudora had sent Ken an article about Charles E. Wiggins, who was a Republican congressman from California. In the summer of 1974 he led the defense of President Richard Nixon as the Watergate Hearings began. The *New York Times* called him "a silky Southern Californian who would feel at home in the pages of a Ross Macdonald detective novel" (R. W. Apple, "Wiggins, Sandman, Dennis: For Nixon, Outnumbered; Benign Explanations Three-Level Battle," *New York Times*, July 30, 1974.).

16 Eudora loved all the work by British writer V. S. Pritchett (1900–1997) and would be delighted to meet him when she visited England in 1979. They would become great friends.

17 This book about the American who became world chess champion was called *Bobby Fischer vs. the Rest of the World* (1974).

18 Darrach's interview of Ken appeared in the July 8, 1974, issue of *People*.

19 Eudora's essay "Is Phoenix Jackson's Grandson Really Dead?" appeared in *Critical Inquiry* 1 (September 1974). In this essay, she dealt with a question readers of her short story "A Worn Path" had often put to her. She would later include the essay in *The Eye of the Story*.

20 Eudora has sent Ken a short piece, which seems to be by Josephine Jacobsen (1908–2003), poet and short story writer, who served as Poetry Consultant to the Library of Congress between 1971 and 1973.

21 Eudora is referring to Margaret and to incidents related in her book *The Birds and the Beasts Were There*. "Guardian" is an interesting word choice, especially when not followed by "angel."

Chapter Five

1 Eudora's review of Bowen's *Pictures and Conversations* appeared in the January 5, 1974, *New York Times Book Review*. Her 1943 essay "A Pageant of Birds," along with photographs Eudora had taken of African American cast members at the Farish Street Baptist Church, had received separate publication by Albondocani Press in 1974. Both pieces can be found in *The Eye of the Story*.

2 Eudora is anticipating an invitation to the Santa Barbara Writers Conference from Barnaby Conrad, its director.

3 The film *Chinatown* (1974) starred Jack Nicholson, Faye Dunaway, and John Huston; it was directed by Roman Polanski. Robert Towne won an Oscar for its screenplay.

4 Eudora reviewed Patrick White's novel *The Cockatoos* in the January 19, 1975, *New York Times Book Review* and subsequently put this essay in *The Eye of the Story*. White (1912–1990) was born in England, but lived in Australia from the age of six months; he won the Nobel Prize for Literature in 1973, the first Australian to do so.

5 *The Drowning Pool* was directed by Stuart Rosenberg and starred Paul Newman and Joanne Woodward. Its lead character was called Lew Harper rather than Lew Archer. Newman had made a 1967 movie called *Harper*, which was directed by Jack Smight and based on Ken's novel *The Moving Target*.

6 The 1934 mystery by Agatha Christie (1890–1976) was a 1974 movie with an all-star cast, including Albert Finney, Sean Connery, Lauren Bacall, and Ingrid Bergman, who won an Oscar as Best Supporting Actress.

7 Ring Lardner penned this couplet as one of a series in a take-off on Cole Porter's song "Night and Day." It appeared in a 1936 *New Yorker* column.

8 The musical version of Eudora's *The Robber Bridegroom*, with book by Alfred Uhry (1936–) and music by Robert Waldman (1936–), opened in Saratoga with Kevin Kline and Patti LuPone in the starring roles.

9 The film about Eudora aired on PBS as one of an eight-part series called *The Writer in America*. Another of the episodes would be devoted to Ross Macdonald.

10 The English writer Eric Ambler (1909–1998) was one of the most significant authors of espionage fiction in the twentieth century. Among his best-known works are *A Coffin for Dimitrios*, *Journey into Fear*, and *Passage of Arms*.

11 Updike's review appeared in the April 14, 1975, *New Yorker*. Wright Morris (1910–1998) was an American novelist, photographer, and essayist. Novelist John Updike (1932–2009) was a frequent reviewer for the *New Yorker*.

12 Eudora's novellas *The Ponder Heart* and *The Robber Bridegroom* became Broadway plays, but she did not write the scripts.

13 Eudora's notes for introducing Ken are held at the University of California, Irvine. Ken's introduction of her is part of the Welty Collection at the Mississippi Department of Archives and History. A somewhat abbreviated version of his text is included in *Self Portrait: Ceaselessly into the Past*.

14 Mary Conrad, who along with her husband Barnaby directed the conference, kept a scrapbook with clippings that document the 1975 date of this presentation. Herbert Harker identifies it as 1976 ("Excavating Myself," *Dialogue* 11 [Summer 1978]: 62), but seems to be mistaken.

15 The PBS series *The Writer in America* was produced by Richard O. Moore and Phil Greene.

16 Margaret Millar to Eudora Welty, June 30, 1975, Eudora Welty Collection, Mississippi Department of Archives and History.

17 John Leonard, "I Care Who Killed Roger Ackroyd," *Esquire*, August 1975, 60–61, 120.

18 Eudora's gratitude for being able to "non-lecture," perhaps indicates that her formal presentation was short, twenty minutes or so, or perhaps that it was not newly minted. An uncropped "Words into Fiction," from which her presentation was drawn, had been first published in 1962.

19 Virginia Kidd, a professor of communications studies at California State University–Sacramento, had attended the Santa Barbara Writers Conference where she took a photo of Ken and Eudora.

20 Frederick Zackel, "Have You Ever Thought about Doing Something Serious . . . Like Detective Fiction," *January Magazine*, April 1999. http://januarymagazine.com/features/zackel.html.

21 Cliff Finch (1927–1986), whose subsequent administration would be marred by scandal, defeated William Winter (1923–), who would later be elected and become Mississippi's most progressive governor.

22 Bruccoli's *The O'Hara Concern: A Biography of John O'Hara* was published by the University of Pittsburgh Press in 1975.

23 Oakley Hall (1920–2008) was a California novelist best known for his books about the American West.

24 Evidently, a house built for Jordan Lambert (1851–1889), an inventor of Listerine mouthwash, or his son, Gerald B. Lambert (1886–1967), the president of Lambert Pharmaceutical Corporation.

25 *The Great Gatsby* was made as a feature film in 1926, 1949, 1974, and again in 2013 (starring Leonardo DiCaprio). It was also made as a movie for television in 2000.

26 Alfred Knopf published his book *Sixty Photographs* to commemorate the sixtieth anniversary of his publishing business. The included photographs were ones he had taken of notable individuals he had met.

27 Eudora's *A Fairy Tale of the Natchez Trace*, an essay dealing with her book *The Robber Bridegroom*, was given separate publication by the Mississippi Historical Society in 1975; her essay "The Corner Store" appeared in *Esquire*'s December 1975 issue. Both pieces are included in *The Eye of the Story*.

28 This 1970 film of Chekhov's play starred Laurence Olivier, Alan Bates, and Joan Plowright; it was directed by Olivier and John Sichel.

Chapter Six

1 William Campbell Gault, interview with Nolan, 365.

2 Precognitively or not, *Ask for Me Tomorrow* (Random House, 1976) involved, among other things, a wife dealing with a husband whose memory is disintegrating: "What else had he forgotten? A minute here, a week there, or great whole chunks of time? Things were moving inside his head, in directions he could no longer control. Sometimes they met and merged, or they broke off and parts disappeared."

3 *Humboldt's Gift* by Saul Bellow (1915–2005) won the Pulitzer Prize for Fiction in 1976.

4 The Coral Casino was the beach club, across from the Santa Barbara Biltmore, to which the Millars had belonged for over a quarter-century.

5 This 1860 novel is, along with *The Moonstone* (1868), one of two masterpieces by Wilkie Collins (1824–1889), a contemporary, friend of, and influence on Charles Dickens.

6 Ken has garbled the facts of Christie's biography, which was not nearly as well known in 1976 as it would become through later books and movies, including Richard Hack's *Duchess of Death* (Phoenix Books, 2009).

7 Welty to Millar, July 28, 1976.

8 Other participants in the National Book Critics Circle panel led by Nona Balakian in which Ken took part, at Columbia's Low Library, included Hortense Calisher, Wilfrid Sheed, and Anatole Broyard.

9   Eudora neglects to say that she was going to Chapel Hill to receive an honorary degree from the University of North Carolina.

10 Rosie Russell was the widow of Eudora's agent Diarmuid.

11 British mystery writer Dick Francis (1920–2010), a former jockey, depicts the world of horse racing in his novels.

12 John Franklin Bardin (1916–1981) was an American mystery writer whose reputation rested on novels published in the late 1940s.

13 Michael Woods reviewed *The Blue Hammer* in the June 13, 1976, *New York Times Book Review*. Eudora's copy had arrived in advance of the publication date.

14 Eudora Welty to Margaret Millar, [July 1976], Eudora Welty Collection, Mississippi Department of Archives and History. In this letter Eudora mentions her reading of "Where Is the Voice Coming From?"—a story first published in 1963 in the *New Yorker*.

15 Eudora Welty, interview with Nolan, 369–70.

16 *The Blue Dahlia* was an original screenplay by Raymond Chandler published in 1976. The 1946 film starred Alan Ladd and Veronica Lake.

17 The British romantic painters John Constable (1776–1837) and J. M. W. Turner (1775–1851) were contemporaries of poet Samuel Taylor Coleridge (1772–1834), about whom Ken had written his PhD dissertation.

18 The fictional painter Richard Chantry looms large in Ross Macdonald's *The Blue Hammer*.

19 In New York, Nelson took Millar to a David Forman recording session. In Santa Barbara, Paul introduced Ken to singer-songwriter Warren Zevon, a great Macdonald fan, who later dedicated his 1980 LP *Bad Luck Streak in Dancing School* to the novelist.

20 Previews of *The Robber Bridegroom* began on September 28, 1976, at the Biltmore Theatre on Broadway; the show opened on October 9 and ran until February 13, 1977.

21 Eudora's front-page review appeared on November 14, 1976, and was later collected in *The Eye of the Story*.

22 As opposed, of course, to the narrator of Eudora's famous story "Why I Live at the P.O."

23 Ken had been to Europe and back—without benefit of Maggie, who at the last moment chose to stay home and continue work on her new novel.

24 Ken refers to the Tate Gallery in London where so many Turners and Constables were part of the collection.

25 From October 1949 to June 1950, Eudora traveled about Europe, making an extended stay in Florence, where John Robinson was studying. Her friend Dolly Wells, a Jacksonian who now worked in the New York City publishing world, came for a May and June 1950 tour of Italy, and the two old friends joined William Jay Smith and his wife Barbara Howes, both poets, for a visit to Venice.

26 Eudora had been in Ohio for a speaking engagement at Denison College.

27 "The Blessed Damozel" is Dante Gabriel Rossetti's poem inspired by Edgar Allan Poe's "The Raven." The first stanza of Rossetti's poem is:
    The blessed damozel leaned out

From the gold bar of Heaven;
Her eyes were deeper than the depth
Of waters stilled at even;
She had three lilies in her hand,
And the stars in her hair were seven.

28 Ken's lecture was published as "Down These Streets a Mean Man Must Go" in the Spring/Summer 1977 issue of *Antaeus*. Daniel Halpern (1945–) is an editor, publishing executive, professor, and poet.

29 Ken has been reading Albert Borowitz's book *Innocence and Arsenic: Studies in Crime and Literature* (New York: HarperCollins, 1977) and Donald Davie's 1976 Clark Lectures at Cambridge University (*A Gathered Church: The Literature of the English Dissenting Interest, 1700–1930* [Oxford University Press, 1978]). Davie (1922–1995) was a poet and critic associated with the English Movement.

Chapter Seven

1 Welty to Aswell, [January 20, 1977], Eudora Welty Collection, Mississippi Department of Archives and History.

2 This was a startling opinion to be expressed by Ken, who had always felt marriage was a bedrock of civilization. In the 1960s, he had broken with one lifelong friend who left his wife for another woman.

3 Eudora reviewed *Selected Letters of William Faulkner*, edited by Joseph Blotner, for the February 6, 1977, *New York Times Book Review*. This review appears in *The Eye of the Story*.

4 Margaret Millar's novel *Ask for Me Tomorrow*.

5 Harker's second novel *Turn Again Home* was published in 1977.

6 Joan Fleming (1908–1980) was a British writer, who twice won the Gold Dagger Award from the Crime Writers Association.

7 James McConkey (1922–), emeritus professor at Cornell University, is a novelist and literary critic with books on Forster and Chekhov.

8 Eudora was traveling in order to receive honorary degrees from Washington University, Kent State University, and Harvard University.

9 *Laidlaw* is the first in a series of three Glasgow-based mysteries by Scottish novelist William McIlvanney (1936–).

10 The destructive La Mesa fire began on June 16, 1977, and was not contained until a week later.

11 This might as aptly serve as title for a book or essay by or about Ross Macdonald, in whose private-eye stories ocular imagery and information are omnipresent.

12 The Millars' previous home, which featured in Margaret's book *The Birds and the Beasts Were There* and which Ken successfully defended from burning embers during the 1964 Coyote fire, was destroyed during this Sycamore Canyon fire in July 1977.

13 Frank Lyell's PhD thesis was actually done at Princeton University. John Galt (1779–1839) was a Scottish novelist and the first novelist to deal with the issues of the Industrial Revolution.

14 Eudora reviewed Katherine Anne Porter's book *The Never-Ending Wrong* in the August 21, 1977, *New York Times Book Review*.

15 Eudora, who in 1952 had reviewed *Charlotte's Web*, reviewed *Essays of E. B. White* in the September 25, 1977, *New York Times Book Review*. She included the earlier review in *The Eye of the Story*.

16 Zackel's novel, *Cocaine and Blue Eyes*, represented by Ken's agent Dorothy Olding, was published in 1978. It was eventually made into a film starring O. J. Simpson.

17 Millar Papers, University of California, Irvine, Special Collections and Archives.

18 This collection had just been published in New York by the Mysterious Press. Otto Penzler, owner of The Mysterious Bookshop in New York City, had founded the press in 1975.

19 The University of Mississippi hosted a Eudora Welty Symposium that drew 800 people from thirty-two states and three foreign countries to Oxford. Cleanth Brooks, William Jay Smith, and Reynolds were on the program, as was Eudora, who read from *Losing Battles*. Ken's introduction to *Lew Archer, Private Investigator* was published as "The Private Detective" in the *New York Times Book Review*, October 23, 1977.

20 This exhibition at the old Capitol Museum in Jackson, Mississippi, was prepared by museum director and Welty friend Patti Carr Black. The catalogue for the exhibit is titled *Welty*.

21 Ken's introduction to *Lew Archer, Private Investigator* was published as "The Private Detective" in the *New York Times Book Review*, October 23, 1977.

22 Kenneth Millar to W. H. Ferry, November 28, 1977, and December 12, 1977, typed copies, University of California, Irvine, Special Collections and Archives.

Chapter Eight

1 *The Mystery of the Yellow Room* by Frenchman Gaston Leroux was published in 1908 and is one of the first locked-room mysteries. *Armadale* is an 1866 mystery by British writer Wilkie Collins.

2 Eudora's story "Acrobats in a Park" dates from 1934.

3 "Who he?" was a manuscript query famously associated with the *New Yorker*'s original editor Harold Ross.

4 Ring Lardner Jr. (1915–2000) was an American journalist and screenwriter who won the 1942 Oscar for Best Original Screenplay. Following World War II, Lardner was one of the "Hollywood Ten" investigated by the House Committee on Un-American Activities and found in contempt of Congress. He was then blacklisted in Hollywood.

5 Ken refers to a picture next to Louis D. Rubin Jr.'s review of *The Eye of the Story* in the April 22, 1978, *New Republic*. Rubin (1923–2013), who would be known as the dean of southern literary historians, had long written about Eudora's fiction.

6 Barbara Bader's article about Don Freeman appeared in the April 30, 1978, *New York Times Book Review* under the title "Child of the Theater, Artist to Children; Theater."

7 Eudora's friend Jane Reid Petty had a beach house on Santa Rosa Island; Patti Carr Black, Charlotte Capers, Ann Morrison, Reynolds, and Eudora had joined Jane for a visit there. Ken had met all of these friends when he came to Jackson in 1973.

8 M. R. James (1862–1936) was a medieval scholar, provost of Kings College, Cambridge, and later provost of Eton College. He was also the author of ghost stories. In her letter, Eudora misnamed one of those stories. Its actual title was "Oh Whistle and I'll Come to You, My Lad"; the change of "My Lad" to "My Love" seems almost symbolic.

9 Ralph Sipper's review appeared in the *San Francisco Examiner & Chronicle*, April 23, 1978.

10 Victoria Glendinning, "Eudora Welty in Type and Person," *New York Times Book Review,* May 7, 1978, 7.

11 Murray Horrowitz, one of the creators of *Ain't Misbehavin'*, saw a 'strong and beautiful' line of connection between his show and Eudora's 1941 short story "Powerhouse," a story which itself had been inspired by Waller (Horowitz to Eudora Welty, October 22, 1988, Eudora Welty Collection, Mississippi Department of Archives and History). *Deathtrap*, a play by Ira Levin, was made into a feature film in 1982.

12 Eudora reviewed V. S. Pritchett's *Selected Stories* in the *New York Times Book Review* of June 25, 1978.

13 Ken's novel *The Goodbye Look* had been published in 1969.

14 On June 13, 1978, Charles Schultz introduced the character "Eudora" into his comic strip "Peanuts" where she would remain until June 13, 1987. Her appearance was distinctive—long, straight black hair, typically topped by knitted cap.

15 Schultz, a Santa Barbara resident, no doubt encountered Eudora at the Writers Conference in which he too took part. In 1983, the year Ken Millar died, Schultz would have his character Lucy make a reference to Ross Macdonald.

16 Eudora was still at work on "The Shadow Club," which she would never complete or publish.

17 Nona Balakian's book *Critical Encounters: Literary Views and Reviews, 1953–1977* was published by Bobbs-Merrill in 1978.

18 Ken refers to the meetings between US President Jimmy Carter, Egyptian President Anwar Sadat, and Israeli Prime Minister Menachem Begin that led to the Camp David Accords.

19 Eudora never reviewed *Sleeping Beauty*, which was dedicated to her, but her review of *The Underground Man* is included in *The Eye of the Story*, which she dedicated to Kenneth Millar. This slip on Ken's part seems especially alarming.

Chapter Nine

1 Eudora Welty, "The Shadow Club" papers, Box 268, Folder 5, Piece 2 and Folder 3, Piece 4. Eudora Welty Collection, Mississippi Department of Archives and History.

2 Strange, too, that Ken doesn't make overt reference to similarities between these real-life events and the plot of his 1976 novel, which involves a painting apparently stolen by a museum guard, alleged forgeries, and an artist father.

3 Patrick Quentin and Q. Patrick were pen names used by Hugh Callingham Wheeler (1912–1987) and collaborators in writing mystery fiction. His collaborator on novels in 1933 and 1935 was Mary Lou Aswell, who would later become Eudora's good friend. Wheeler wrote the book for *Sweeney Todd*, with music by Stephen Sondheim.

4 *Ida M'Toy* was published by the University of Illinois Press in May 1979. The essay had previously appeared in 1942 in *Accent*, a periodical published by the Master of Fine Arts Creative Writing Department at the University of Illinois from 1940 to 1960.

5 Millar to Green, September 3, 1979, quoted by Green in "A Tribute," *Dictionary of Literary Biography Yearbook: 1983.*

6 Eudora's essay "Looking Back at the First Story" was published in the *Georgia Review* 33 (Winter 1979). Besides writing this essay in the fall of 1978, Eudora had attempted to review the Ecco Press reissue of Elizabeth Bowen's *Bowen's Court*, but she never completed the review. A draft of it is held by the Mississippi Department of Archives and History in its Welty Collection.

7 Fidel Castro spoke at the United Nations in October 1979; author Robert Baudin was thought to be buzzing the United Nations in a single-engine plane. In fact, however, he was buzzing Harcourt, Brace, Jovanovich, in an effort to publicize his book *Confessions of a Promiscuous Counterfeiter*. Baudin felt that the publisher had done an inadequate job of publicity.

8 On October 16, 1979, Ken had inscribed this copy of *Archer in Jeopardy*: "To Eudora with triple love and affection, as ever, Ken."

9 Herb Yellin's Lord John Press published *A Collection of Reviews* by Ross Macdonald in 1979.

10 Ross Macdonald's review of *A Catalogue of Crime*, by Jacques Barzun and Wendell H. Taylor (originally published in the *New York Times Book Review* of April 25, 1971), chided the co-authors' narrow, outdated definition and discussion of crime fiction. Canadian author Stephen Leacock (1869–1944) wrote several popular volumes of satirical short stories, essays and memoir, which influenced such writers as Robert Benchley. Kenneth Millar's review of Ralph L. Curry's *Stephen Leacock: Humorist and Humanist* was originally printed in the *San Francisco Chronicle* of January 3, 1960.

11 *Archer in Jeopary* included three novels: *The Doomsters, The Zebra-Striped Hearse*, and *The Instant Enemy*.

12 Jill Krementz.

13 Yellin's Lord John Press published *Acrobats in a Park* in October 1980.

Chapter Ten

1 The formality of Ken's reference to and the mispelling of Yellin in this handwritten letter were likely signs of the writing and memory difficulties besetting him.

2 William Winter served as governor of Mississippi from 1980–1984 and spearheaded the state's transformative Education Reform Act of 1982. Leontyne Price, the acclaimed soprano, became one of the first African Americans to sing leading roles at the Metropolitan Opera. Eudora had supported Adlai Stevenson

(1900–1965) in both his campaigns for president against Dwight D. Eisenhower; she even canvassed for him in New York during the 1950 campaign.

3 General Mark Clark (1896–1984) was the youngest American three-star general during World War II. As head of the Fifth Army, he was in charge of the invasion of Italy in which Eudora's friend John Robinson had participated.

4 Warren's essay "Jefferson Davis Gets His Citizenship Back" appeared in the February 25, 1980, issue of the *New Yorker*.

5 Mary Lee Settle, "Welty's Splendors," *Saturday Review* October 1980: 84; Maureen Howard, "A Collection of Discoveries," *New York Times Book Review* November 2, 1980, 31; Hortense Calisher, "Eudora Welty: A Life's Work," *Washington Post Book World* October 26, 1980, 2.

6 Ralph Sipper to Eudora Welty, October 28, 1980, Eudora Welty Collection, Mississippi Department of Archives and History.

7 Herb Yellin to Eudora Welty, March 17, 1981, Eudora Welty Collection, Mississippi Department of Archives and History.

8 Sipper to Welty, June 10, 1981, Eudora Welty Collection, Mississippi Department of Archives and History.

9 Wayne Warga, "The Millars: Tale of Fortitude," *Los Angeles Times*, February 11, 1982.

10 Sipper to Welty, February 25, 1982, Eudora Welty Collection, Mississippi Department of Archives and History.

11 Caroline Heilbrun (1926–2003) was a feminist scholar, whose book *Writing a Woman's Life* (1988) would be critical of Eudora's autobiography *One Writer's Beginnings* (1984).

12 Robertson Davies (1913–1995) was a Canadian novelist, dramatist, critic, and journalist, who taught at the University of Toronto. He was Ken's long-distance collaborator on a weekly Toronto magazine column Ken wrote while a graduate student at the University of Michigan in 1940 and 1941.

13 Sipper to Welty, June 1, 1982, Eudora Welty Collection, Mississippi Department of Archives and History.

14 Welty to Price, October 26, [1982], Reynolds Price Papers, David M. Rubenstein Rare Book & Manuscript Library, Duke University.

15 Ross Macdonald would be the third recipient of the Robert Kirsch Award, given annually at the *Los Angeles Times* Book Prizes. This award's previous recipients were Wallace Stegner and Wright Morris.

16 Welty, interview with Nolan, 406.

17 Welty, interview with Nolan, 406.

18 Ralph Sipper, interview with Nolan, 407; Welty to Aswell, August 4, 1983, Eudora Welty Collection, Mississippi Department of Archives and History.

19 Welty, interview with Nolan, 408.

20 Welty, *One Writer's Beginnings*, 104.

21 Sipper to Welty, January 26, 1983. A Xerox typescript of this letter is part of the Reynolds Price Papers, David M. Rubenstein Rare Book & Manuscript Library, Duke University.

22 Eudora Welty, "Henry, Part I Affinities," Box 248, Folder 4, Piece 9, Eudora Welty Collection, Mississippi Department of Archives and History.

23 Welty to Aswell, August 4, 1983, Eudora Welty Collection, Mississippi Department of Archives and History.

24 Eudora Welty to William Jay and Sonja Smith, September 19, 1983, William Jay Smith Papers, Washington University Libraries' Department of Special Collections, St. Louis, MO. This letter, with its memories of Ken, was fittingly enclosed with a Xerox of the copyedited typescript of *One Writer's Beginnings*, a book in which Eudora described memory as her "treasure most dearly regarded."

25 Welty to Price, July 9, 1984, Reynolds Price Papers, David M. Rubenstein Rare Book & Manuscript Library, Duke University; Reynolds Price, *A Whole New Life* (New York: Atheneum, 1994), 28; Welty to Millar, [November 24, 1977]. Part of this paragraph appears in a slightly different form in Marrs's *Eudora Welty, A Biography*, 490.

Appendix: "Henry": An Unfinished Story, Editors' Introduction and Part 1

1 Welty to Millar, November 29, 1976.

2 The Eudora Welty Collection at the Mississippi Department of Archives and History holds two sets of manuscripts grouped under the title "Henry." The more developed one includes a folder Welty labeled "Part 1 Affinities," a folder she called "Henry" with the added notation "Part 2 Flashback—Insert 'Affinities,'" a folder she labeled "Spring '84 Pulled out to be of use in Henry's story." (The contents of these original folders have now been divided into multiple archival folders.) A smaller number of fragments, separately filed, are part of a rather different story, perhaps titled "The City of Light," and are focused on an architect/protagonist named Henry. Eudora evidently worked concurrently on the two stories for a time, continued with the second one after abandoning the first, and eventually destroyed most of the second manuscript. See Eudora Welty to William and Emily Maxwell, June 1, 1985, in *What There Is To Say We Have Said: The Correspondence of Eudora Welty and William Maxwell* (New York: Houghton Mifflin Harcourt, 2011), 399.

The more extensive and intact version of "Henry," abridged here, does not exist as a fair copy and includes only one sustained narrative segment, the flashback scene in Part 2. We have included all of the flashback, except for occasional words or lines we could not decipher; these are indicated by bracketed ellipses. The present action of this "Henry" version exists in brief fragments (including bits of dialogue on strips of paper and paragraphs written on grocery receipts, envelopes, or pieces of incoming mail). From the randomly filed fragments of "Part 1 Affinities" and the loosely ordered ones in "Spring '84," we have chosen to include passages that, it seems to us, most clearly suggest, complement, or adhere to the plot and characterization found in the flashback. We have excluded fragments that, in our opinion, do not do so as clearly or that duplicate material in selected fragments. We hope our editorial decisions have provided a story text that, because abridged, is both authentic and coherent.

3 "Affinities," Box 248, Folder 14, Piece 43, Folder 3, Piece 8.

4 "Affinities," Box 249, Folder 1, Piece 56.

5 "Affinities," Box 249, Folder 1, Piece 58.

6 "Affinities," Box 249, Folder 1, Piece 63.

7 "Affinities," Box 249, Folder 1, Piece 60.

8 "Affinities," Box 248, Folder 13, Piece 42.

9 Cuchulain is one of the great heroes of Irish mythology. His father was the sun god Lug, and Cuchulain himself became a great warrior, who at one point single-handedly and successfully defended Ulster from an invading force. There is a reference to Cuchulain the Hound of Ulster in Ross Macdonald's 1956 Lew Archer novel *The Barbarous Coast*.

10 "Affinities," Box 249, Folder 1, Piece 64.

Part 2

1 "Part 2 Flashback" is located in Box 249, Folders 4, 5, 6, 7.

2 William Butler Yeats published a book of poems titled *The Tower* in 1928. Among the poems in this book are "The Tower" and "Sailing to Byzantium." In the spring 1984 text, Donna has taken a break from home and the stresses of caregiving, permitting Stella to sit for a number of hours with the stricken Henry. Donna's return pulls Stella away from memories of a vigorous Henry talking about "Sailing to Byzantium."

3 The Red Branch or Ulster Cycle of Irish folklore was written in old and middle Irish and featured Cuchulain. Yeats made use of tales from the Red Branch cycle in his "dramatic poem" called "The Shadowy Waters" and in his poem "The Two Kings." He made Cuchulain the major character in four plays.

4 This experience was one Welty herself had. She attempted to put it into a story early in the 1950s, but was unsatisfied with the result. Later she described the experience in her autobiography *One Writer's Beginnings*, though the Yeats poem that inspired her was "The Song of Wandering Aengus" (*One Writer's Beginnings* [Cambridge: Harvard University Press, 1984]).

5 "Flashback," Box 249, Folder 8, Piece 30.

6 "Flashback," Box 249, Folder 8, Piece 31.

7 "Flashback," Box 249, Folder 8, Piece 36.

8 "Spring '84 Pulled out to be of use in Henry story," Box 250, Folder 7, Piece 23.

Part 3

1 "Spring '84," Box 250, Folder 8, Piece 27.

2 "Affinities," Box 248, Folder 4, Piece 10. At some point Welty worked on an alternative ending for the story, in which Henry's wife dies of cirrhosis of the liver, and Henry has gone to live in a "sort of boarding house for invalids." Rachel visits him there: "He gave me his sweet smile—his smile never changed at all, never—and we often sat in the wicker chairs in the Visitor's Lounge, sometimes holding hands. We had little to say, but at our age it didn't matter so desperately that he had little or no memory of Rachel Friarson—perhaps I don't remember her all that well either. But I would never forget that Henry was dearer to me than anyone else in the world. [. . .] We were both, I believed, content that, so far, survival had itself been survived./He had continued to grow bald. The white fringe around his forehead was about all he had left." Box 249, Folder 2, Piece 76.

INDEX